Christian Light Social Studies Series

INTO ALL THE WORLD

The earth is the LORD's, and the fulness thereof (Psalm 24:1a).

A Christian text on world geography and social studies

Writer: Roger L. Berry

Editorial Committee:
    John Coblentz, Editor-in-Chief
    Fred Miller
    Paul Reed
    Ernest Witmer
    Sanford Shank, CLE Director

CHRISTIAN LIGHT PUBLICATIONS, INC.

Harrisonburg, Virginia 22802

INTO ALL THE WORLD

Christian Light Publications, Harrisonburg, Virginia 22802
© 1991 Christian Light Publications, Inc.
 Published 1991
Printed in China

Seventh Printing, 2017

1998 Revision

ISBN 978-0-87813-925-5

2821919

Introduction for Parents and Teachers

The social studies represent a particularly crucial course in the school curriculum. This is because such a study teaches young people social values which help build a philosophy of life.

If the philosophy of a social studies curriculum is God-centered, it becomes a powerful tool for molding lives into the likeness of Jesus Christ. On the other hand, if the social values are cleverly distorted, a social studies text can be a most devastating part of the total curriculum and a direct cause for children of Christian parents to be spoiled through "philosophy and vain deceit" (Colossians 2:8).

Most social studies texts of today are humanistic. This means that they are man-centered. They assume that man is innately good and that through the persistent efforts of modern science he will eventually solve all of his problems. According to this philosophy, the world is moving toward a utopia where man will have learned to coexist in uninterrupted peace. The cancer of this demonic philosophy has crept from the classroom into professing Christianity. We have seen only the beginning of the havoc to follow in the form of arrogant individualism, disrespect for Biblical authority and traditional values, and a situational approach to ethics or matters of right and wrong.

Many modern social studies texts boldly assert the concepts of humanism that were peddled only cautiously in the textbooks of yesteryear. Alarmed by these bold attacks on the roots of society and Christian faith, Christian Light Publications has been moved by God to prepare a social studies curriculum based upon the revealed value system of God's Word.

Into All the World is the fourth in a series of Bible-centered social studies texts published by Christian Light Publications. This text aims at the fourth grade level.

The writers and editors of this new social studies series have labored to build their curriculum upon the solid principles of the Bible. In contrast to many social studies texts, this series assumes the depravity of man since the Fall in the Garden of Eden. It develops a system of social values based on God's revealed Word, recognizing the New Testament as God's final revelation to men. The way of salvation through Jesus Christ is presented as the only remedy for man's present deplorable condition both individually and socially. The spread of this Gospel of salvation is presented as the responsibility of the Christian community.

The Christian Light Publications social studies series also recognizes God's hand in history as well as His sovereignty over developments on the world scene. The series highlights God's blessings upon people who obey and honor Him, even when facing persecution and death. It also recognizes that God often uses wars and other disasters to judge those who disobey Him.

In this series, the remnant of God's people is traced throughout the history of mankind. They appear as a bright ray in contrast to mankind as a whole, which is plunging deeper and deeper into spiritual blindness and depraved humanistic ambitions. The student is encouraged to follow in the train of the faithful followers of God who stand on the unchanging values of His Word in an aimlessly changing world.

Into All the World focuses on the beauty of the earth God has created and on the wide variety of natural resources God has placed here for our use and enjoyment. As they study each part of the world, students will learn about the physical blessings of God in that region. They will learn how man has used these blessings and has sometimes abused what God has given.

The second great focus of this text is on the people God has made to inhabit the earth. In humanistic social studies texts, the emphasis is on man's great accomplishments and how he is striving for utopian living conditions. **Into All the World**, however, focuses on understanding people and their needs; appreciating them, though their customs and way of life may be very different from our own; and seeing how obedience or disobedience to God affects their lives for good or ill. Emphasis is also placed on the need for God's people to reach out to others with the Gospel of Jesus Christ.

We trust that **Into All the World** will help meet the crucial need for a Bible-centered, Christ-honoring social studies program in Christian schools and homes. We pray that God will receive all the glory and that students will be drawn closer to Him as they use this text.

3

CONTENTS

MAPS IN THIS BOOK

(Maps in bold type are of the main continents and countries studied in this text.)

**The earth is the LORD'S, and the fulness thereof;
the world, and they that dwell therein.
For he hath founded it upon the seas,
and established it upon the floods.**

Psalm 24:1, 2

Introduction for Students

Dear Students:

Do you enjoy traveling to see new places and new people? The next best thing to traveling to other countries is to go there through books and pictures.

Into All the World will take you to many parts of the world through pictures, maps, and reading. The purpose of this book is to teach you more about the wonderful earth that God made for us to live on. We call this study of the earth and the things God has put here for us to use, *geography*. A second goal of this book is to help you learn more about the many peoples God has made to fill the earth. Hopefully you will learn to appreciate them, love them, and understand their needs. When we study geography along with people and their needs, we are studying *social studies*. A third aim for this textbook is to discover ways God is at work among the peoples of the world and how God can help them live better lives.

We will begin our study of the world close to home. We will study about North and South America where most of you live. Next year you will learn much more about North America.

After we study the Americas, we will go on to Europe. The ancestors of many of the people in the Americas came from Europe. Then our travel through reading and pictures will take us to Asia, Africa, Australia, and finally to Antarctica.

We will not have time to study every country as we go. Instead, we will study only a few countries on each continent. This way, we can spend more time getting to know the people. Each unit will begin with the geography of a region or part of the world. Next we will learn about some of the peoples who live in each region. Finally we will learn about a country or countries in that region.

Into All the World is divided into nine units with several chapters in each unit. **Into All the World** has 29 chapters. Throughout the book, you will find maps, charts, and photographs to help you in your study. On page 6 you will find a list of all the maps that appear in the book.

At the end of the book you will find more study helps. The *Glossary* explains many new words and ideas. As you read, you will see some words in **bold type, like this**. The meaning of these words can be found in the *Glossary*. The *Index* follows the glossary. It lists the people, places, things, and ideas found in this text. The *Index* will tell you where to find these things. Following the *Index* is the *Scripture Index* which lists the Bible passages found in this text.

Last year you learned about just a few places in the world that God made. This year you will learn about many more people and places. You are ready to begin a trip around the world through social studies.

May God bless you,

Roger L. Berry, the Writer

God's World for Us

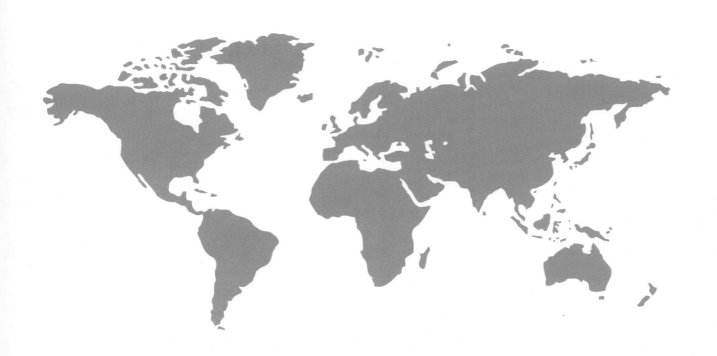

What you will learn . . . in unit one

"In the beginning God created the heaven and the earth" (Genesis 1:1).

What is your address? Is it Lancaster? Estacada? Wellesly? Your address is more than the name of the town, the street, and the route. It is more than Pennsylvania, Oregon, or Ontario. It is even more than the U.S.A. or Canada.

Whatever your mailing address, the earth is your home. God made the earth for you and me and millions of other people. The earth is full of the riches God has made for us to enjoy. He has given us food, water, and air to keep us alive. He has given us much more. "[He] giveth us richly all things to enjoy." As far as we know, the earth is the only place among the stars and planets where people can live.

I Timothy 6:17b

Our earth is shaped like a great round ball. Have you ever wondered what keeps us from falling off this big ball? You can jump as high as you want, but you come right back to the ground. A pull or force called **gravity** holds you on the earth.

The big earth seems small when you think of the millions and millions of stars and planets we call the **universe.** No one but God knows how large the universe is.

The nearest star to us is the sun. The earth and eight other planets circle around the sun. We call the sun and its planets the **solar system**. *Solar* means "of the sun." The solar system is the system of the sun.

Today you begin a study of the earth and the people God placed here to care for it. But first of all we will take a trip into space!

This is a drawing or diagram of our solar system. Each planet circles around the sun in a path called an orbit. Which four planets are much closer to the sun than the others?

1. Here Is God's Earth

A Trip Into Space

Imagine for a few minutes that you have traveled on a spaceship to the farthest part of our solar system. If you traveled in today's fastest spaceships, you would not reach the farthest planet for many years. You will need to pretend that you could travel many times faster than today's spacemen do.

From Pluto, the most distant planet, you cannot see the earth. Indeed, the sun looks like just another star in the black sky. Pluto is

cold and lifeless, and you are eager to turn around and come home to your family and friends, to the world God made for man.

As you travel homeward, you pass Neptune, Saturn, and Jupiter, and you see that they appear to be hidden under thick clouds. Each planet circles around the sun in a giant path called its **orbit**.

When you reach Mars, the earth looks like a bright star. For many years some people hoped men would find life on Mars. If you took time to

11

This picture of our earth was taken from far out in space. It shows how beautiful the earth is. You are looking at North and South America. Can you see the western part of North America near the top of the picture? Clouds cover some of the land and ocean.

land there, you would see a rocky, lifeless world that looks much like the moon.

God's Beautiful Earth. Your heart beats just a little faster as you near the earth. You can hardly describe the beauty of what you see. You are happy to be nearing home.

The earth is shaped like a giant ball. Anything shaped like a ball is called a **sphere.** Careful measurements show that the earth is not quite a perfect sphere, but almost.

Do you wonder what holds the earth in the heavens? What keeps it from crashing toward the sun or flying off toward the stars? The amazing power called gravity keeps it in an orbit around the sun. You cannot see gravity or feel it, but you know it is there by what it does. The Bible

tells us that God is at work keeping the world in place.

"He stretcheth out the north over the empty place, and hangeth the earth upon nothing."
Job 26:7

The earth is the only planet in our solar system that has the things we need to live. In all the universe, the earth may be the only place where we can live without taking things along with us. Men who go up into space must take food, water, air, and special clothing with them. We do not usually think of these things as treasures, but they are. Men have also found other treasures on the earth, buried under the ground, and in the sea. This year you will learn about many of these treasures.

On the earth God made for us we have air, water, food, and clothing. If we traveled out into space, we would need to take all these things with us.

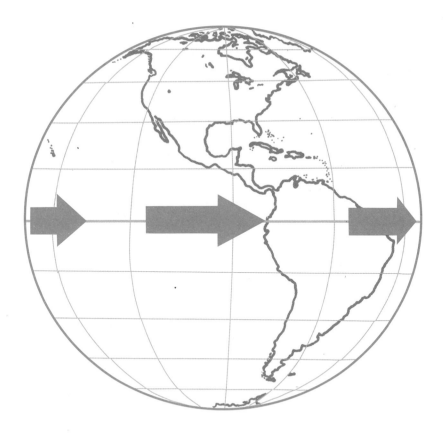

God made the earth to spin around on its axis so we would have day and night. The arrows on the globe show the direction the earth turns as it spins.

Our Moving Earth. If you could stay out in space for a long time, you could see that the earth moves. Imagine that your spaceship stayed in the same place for a year. You would watch the earth move in a giant path around the sun. This path is the earth's orbit. The earth would slowly leave you as it goes on in its orbit. A year later the earth would return to the place where you first saw it. It takes one year for the earth to circle around the sun.

If you could stay with the earth as it moves in its orbit, you would see that it moves in another way too. The earth spins around and around. It spins as if it had an imaginary rod stuck through the middle. This imaginary rod is called the earth's **axis.**

The earth moves, or orbits, around the sun once each year. The arrows show you the direction the earth moves around the sun.

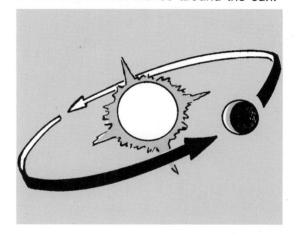

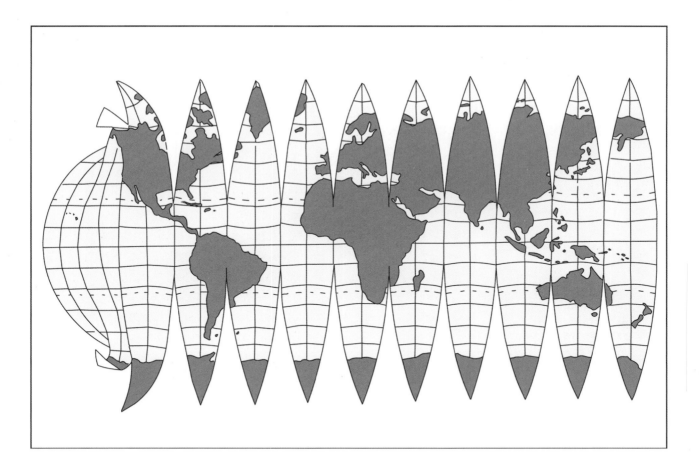

This picture shows you the shape of map pieces that are pasted on a globe to make a globe map. A globe looks much more like the earth than any flat map.

This picture of the earth from space shows how clouds can hide the land. Compare this with the picture on page 12, which shows more land. What color is the land you see in that picture?

The sun shines on the earth as it turns. While the side toward the sun has daylight, the other side has nighttime. As the earth turns on its axis, the sun shines first on one side and then on the other. The earth makes one complete turn on its axis in 24 hours, or one day.

As long as God lets the earth spin and the sun shine, we will have day and night. The Bible promises, "While the earth remaineth, seed-time and harvest, and cold and heat, and summer and winter, and day and night shall not cease."

Genesis 8:22

14

What Is a Globe?

You know that our trip to the farthest part of our solar system was only imaginary. No one has ever traveled that far away. Men have traveled to the moon and back. They have seen the beauty of the earth from space. Few, if any of us, will ever see our world from more than a few miles up.

The next best thing to looking at the earth from space is looking at **a globe.** A globe is a map that has been pasted or printed on a sphere. Because the earth is also a sphere, a globe gives us a good picture of the earth.

Do you have a globe in your classroom or at home? Look at it. You are looking at the earth much as you would see it from space. Of course, space travelers looking at the earth do not see lines and words as on a globe.

Colors, lines, and words on a globe help you find places. Blue on a globe shows areas of water. Brown, green, and other colors show areas of land.

If you could see the earth from space, you would see blue or blue-green oceans. The land would appear green where plants are growing and brown where few or no plants are growing. The white areas are covered with snow and ice. You could not see some places on the ocean and land because of clouds. It is always cloudy somewhere in the world.

Day and Night. Turn your globe so that your state or province is in front of you. Slowly turn the globe so that your country moves to the right. This is the way the earth spins on its axis.

With a globe you can show how we have day and night. You will need a flashlight or a lamp without a shade. Darken the room. Shine the light on the globe as in the picture. Slowly turn the globe to the right until your state or province turns into the light. You are now having "sunrise." Keep turning the globe

The part of the earth on which the sun shines has day. The other part of the earth is in the shadows. We call these shadows night.

HOW GREAT THOU ART

until the place you live starts to go into the darkness. It is "sunset." Now turn your area into the darkness. Other places are having "daytime." Name a place that has daytime when you are having night.

You will use your globe often as you learn more about this wonderful world God made for us.

What Do You Say?

1. a. What is the universe? b. The solar system?

2. a. Who holds the earth in space? b. How does He do it?

3. Imagine that you have just returned from a trip to the moon.

Tell what you saw as you came back to Earth.

4. Why is a globe a good map of the earth?

What Does the Bible Say?

1. Who owns the heavens? Find the answer in Psalm 89:8-11.

2. Read Psalm 19:1 and fill in the blanks: "The heavens a._____ the glory of God; and the firmament [the sky] sheweth his b._____ ."

3. Read Genesis 1:31 What is true about everything God has made?

16

Studying God's Earth

Did your parents ever let you explore an old abandoned house or a cave? If so, then you know how exciting it is to discover new things.

In this book you will explore the whole earth! It would be fun to travel around the world, but that would cost too much money. But you can travel by reading books. You will explore the earth this year through stories, pictures, and maps.

As we study, we will be asking questions and searching for answers. Here are a few of the questions we will study: How does God plan for our food, clothing, and shelter? Why did God put people on the earth? What does God want people to do on His earth?

What Is Geography? The study of the earth, its people, and its treasures is called **geography.** We will

learn much about geography this year. The word *geography* comes from two words that mean "earth writing." Long ago geography was mostly a study of drawings of the earth called maps. Geography today is the study of maps, and much more. You will learn of places too cold for you to live and of places where you

This picture shows part of the huge ice cap that covers much of Greenland. This place is too cold for people to live.

17

of the globe. Do you see more land or more water? The ocean covers much more of the world than does the land. The large mass of water on the earth is sometimes called the world ocean. Men have given names to different parts of this ocean to help us find places and to know which part of the ocean we want to talk about. The names of oceans, seas, gulfs, and bays can be found on globes and maps.

Find the Atlantic Ocean on a globe map or on your classroom globe. You can see that the Atlantic Ocean lies between the Americas, Europe, and Africa. From Africa move your finger to the right until you find the Indian Ocean. You would have to sail through this ocean to reach India by ship. Keep moving your finger to the right until you reach the Pacific Ocean.

The Pacific is the largest part of the world ocean. Turn your globe until you are looking at the middle of

would be hot all the time. You will explore riches God has given us on the earth, under the earth, and in the sea. You will learn how people live in faraway places. Most importantly, you will learn how God wants us to live on the earth He gave us. Let us begin our study of geography.

The Ocean. Look at the pictures

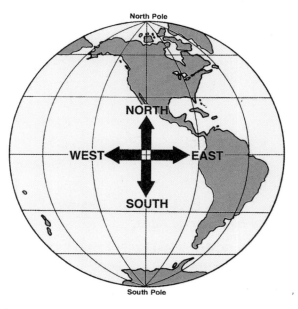

the Pacific Ocean. How much land do you see? Did you know that the Pacific Ocean covers almost half the earth?

Now look at the top of your globe. Find the North Pole. The ocean around the North Pole is called the Arctic Ocean. This ocean is covered with ice much of the time.

Find the South Pole at the other end of your globe. The South Pole is on land, in Antarctica. The Atlantic, Pacific, and Indian Oceans meet in the icy waters around Antarctica. Some people call the part of the ocean around Antarctica the Antarctic Ocean.

In this book we will talk about four main parts of the world ocean—the Atlantic, the Pacific, the Indian, and the Arctic Oceans.

How to Tell Directions on a Globe

Look at your globe again. Do you see the lines on it? They are called **direction lines.** Here is how to use them:

You remember that the earth spins on its axis, an imaginary rod through the earth. The ends of the axis are at the North Pole and the South Pole. The poles give us two directions, north and south. On globes, the direction lines that run from the North Pole to the South Pole are called north-south direction lines.

Move your finger along a north-south direction line. If you move it toward the North Pole, it is moving north. If you move it toward the South Pole, it is moving south.

God made the poles to help us know directions. Directions help us find places that we want to visit or know about.

The Bible says, "The heavens are thine, the earth also is thine . . . . The north and the south thou hast created them."

salm
9:11a, 12a

East and West. Do you see the direction lines on the globe that circle the earth the other way? These lines cross the north-south direction lines and give us the directions east and west.

Follow an east-west direction line to the right. Your finger is moving east. Follow the line to the left. Now you are moving west. The east-west line that is exactly halfway between the North Pole and the South Pole is called the **equator.**

Did you discover that the North Pole is as far north as you can go? No place is farther north. How far south can you go?

Now move your finger east along a direction line. How far east can you go? How far west can you go? You can keep on going east or west as long as you please!

The Bible tells us, "As far as the east is from the west, so far hath he [God] removed our transgressions from us." That is a long way!

Psalm
103:12

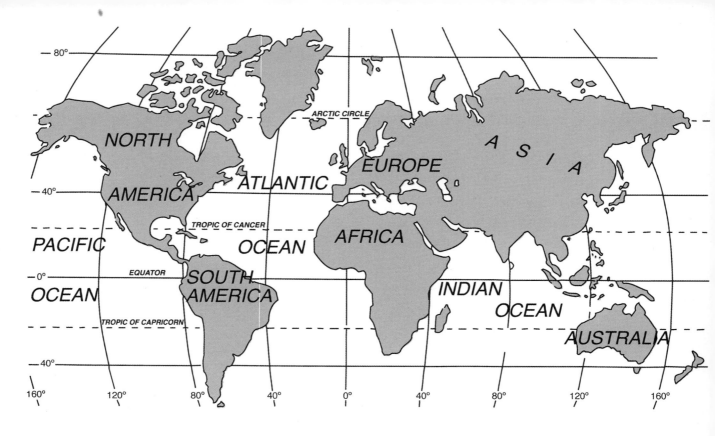

This flat map shows you where most of the continents and oceans can be found. Find the continents on this map; then find them on a globe map.

The Continents. The largest masses of land are called continents. The smaller pieces of land surrounded by water are called islands. The world ocean is so large that it surrounds all the continents. They are like huge islands.

When you read about the ocean, you saw the names of some of the continents. Let us find them on the globe one by one.

The two continents in our part of the world are North America and South America. Find them on your globe. Each of these continents is almost completely surrounded by water. They are joined together by a very narrow strip of land. A strip of land that joins two larger masses of

A strait is a narrow strip of water between two bodies of land. This is the Strait of Gibraltar between Europe and Africa.

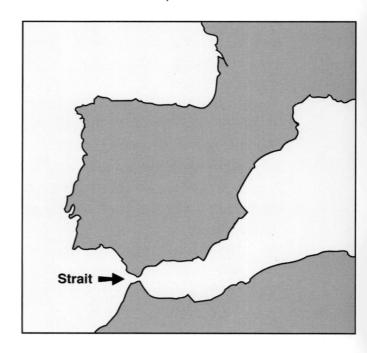

20

North
America

South
America

Europe

Asia

Africa

Australia

Antarctica

The seven continents are illustrated here, showing how they compare in size. Which one is the largest? Which one is the smallest?

land is called an **isthmus** (is´ məs). The Isthmus of Panama joins North and South America.

If you move your finger east or to the right from North America, you will come to the continent of Europe. Just east of Europe is Asia, the largest continent of all. You can see that it is hard to tell where Europe ends and Asia begins. Both continents are part of the same large mass of land. The two continents together are sometimes called Eurasia.

South of Europe you will find the continent of Africa. Africa almost joins Europe at one place. A narrow strip of water called a **strait** separates the two.

South of Asia you will find the smallest continent, Australia. Australia is so small that some people call it the **island continent.**

If you travel south from Australia, you will finally arrive at the cold, frozen continent of Antarctica. Antarctica was the last continent men discovered. Because of the cold and ice, some parts of it have not yet been explored.

What Do You Say?

1. Name three things you will learn about when you study geography.

2. Which is bigger, the ocean or the land masses of the world?

3. Name the four main parts of the world ocean.

4. a. Which way is north on a globe? b. Which way is south? c. Which way is east? d. Which way is west?

5. Name the seven continents.

What Does the Bible Say?

1. Write Proverbs 3:19.

2. Read Psalm 24:1. The earth is the _____.

3. Who did God tell to care for the earth? (Find the answer in Genesis 2:15.)

Chapter One Review

Using Globes and Maps

1. Use a globe to show the direction the earth turns on its axis.

2. Show on a globe how your state or province has day and night. Name some places that are having night when you are having day.

3. Find the following on a globe: Atlantic Ocean, Pacific Ocean, Indian Ocean, Arctic Ocean. Point out the places where the oceans meet. Where do the Atlantic and the Pacific meet? The Indian and the Atlantic? The Arctic and the Atlantic?

4. From what two places on the earth would you be facing the same direction no matter which way you turned? Hint: Find these two places on a globe and show that no matter which way you move your finger, it will be moving in the same direction.

5. From your state or province, in which direction would you need to travel to reach Europe? Which direction would you go to reach South America? Antarctica? The North Pole?

6. Look at the continents on your globe. Then answer these questions. a. Which two are completely surrounded by water without touching any other continents? b. Which are joined to another continent by an isthmus? c. Which two are part of the same land mass? d. Which continents are entirely north of the equator? e. Which are entirely south of the equator? f. Which are partly north and partly south of the equator?

New Words and Terms

Here is a list of new words and ideas you met in this chapter. Can you match the words in the left column with their meanings at the right?

_____ 1.   gravity

_____ 2.   universe

_____ 3.   solar system

_____ 4.   orbit

_____ 5.   sphere

_____ 6.   axis

_____ 7.   globe

_____ 8.   direction lines

_____ 9.   geography

_____ 10.   north

_____ 11.   south

_____ 12.   isthmus

a. The stars and planets.

b. The study of the earth, its people, and its treasures.

c. A strip of land that joins two large masses of land together.

d. A map pasted or printed on a sphere.

e. Anything shaped like a round ball.

f. The direction toward the North Pole.

g. The pull or force that holds things to the earth.

h. The direction toward the South Pole.

i. The path of a planet around the sun.

j. Thin, dark lines on a globe which show north and south or east and west.

k. An imaginary rod through the earth and around which it spins.

l. The sun and its planets.

Thinking Together

1. Why do people on the "underneath" side of the earth (in Australia and Antarctica) not fall off the earth?

2. What do you think holds the planets, including the earth, in their orbits around the sun? Check an encyclopedia article on "earth" or "planet."

3. How is looking at a globe different from looking at the earth from space? Hint: Would you see as much of the surface of the earth as you do on a globe?

4. The Bible tells of a time when the sun stood still for almost a day. Read about it in Joshua 10:12-14. We do not know for sure how God made the sun stand still, but we can guess. From what you know about the earth's movements, what may have happened to the earth to keep night from coming?

5. In this chapter we learned that the earth is only a tiny speck in a huge universe. Each of us is only a tiny speck when we think about how large the earth is. Read Psalm 8:3-9. How does God feel about man, even though man is tiny compared with the universe?

6. Try to think of at least three reasons why we study geography.

7. If someone showed you which direction is east, could you decide where west and north and south are? Hint: Remember which direction (right or left) you move your finger on a globe to go east.

For You to Do

1. Read about the planet Mars in an encyclopedia. a. Why could you not live there? b. Where could you get the things you would need for a trip to Mars?

2. In an encyclopedia article about the earth, find out exactly how long it takes the earth to go around the sun.

3. Pretend that you have just returned to the earth from the moon. Tell a friend what you saw as you came close to the earth.

4. In an encyclopedia article on the ocean, find out how much of the world's surface or crust is covered by water.

5. Blow up a ball-shaped balloon. With a felt-tipped marker make a rough outline of the continents on it. Use a globe as a model. Mark where you live. Let the air out of the balloon and cut it in half. Try to flatten the halves to make a flat map of the earth. Do you see how hard it is to make a flat map of a round world?

2. The Land God Gave Us

God Made It. "The earth is the LORD'S and the fullness thereof; the world, and they that dwell therein. For he hath founded it upon the seas, and established it upon the floods."

Psalm 24:1, 2

God shaped the earth to be just the right place for us to live. Scientists believe that the earth is made mostly of rock. They believe the earth is so hot at its center that the rocks there are melted. Nobody knows for sure how hot the heart of the earth is.

We live on the outer layer of the earth called the **crust**. At some places on the earth's crust, you can see the bare rock. At other places the crust is covered with a layer of soil. If

Many parts of the world are hilly like this farm in the state of New York. Unlike steep mountains, hilly land can be very useful for crops and grazing.

God has given us many beautiful landforms to enjoy. These beautiful mountains are found in Montana. They rise above a grassy plain.

you dig down, you will soon come to solid rock. A large part of the earth's crust is covered by the oceans.

The Bible tells us that in the beginning water covered all of the earth. Then God divided the water from the land. "Let the waters under the heaven be gathered together unto one place, and let the dry land appear: and it was so. And God called the dry land Earth; and the gathering together of the waters called he Seas."

Genesis 1:9b, 10a

The Shape of the Land. God formed the dry land into many different shapes. We enjoy the hills, moun-

Unusual rock formations add interest and beauty to the world God has created.

Other people enjoy the plains and lowlands. Imagine how tired we would get of seeing only vast plains or nothing but steep mountains.

Have you ever seen the ocean? Did you walk out to the edge of the water and let the waves lap at your feet? The place where the land meets the ocean is called the **coastline** or seashore.

When you are standing on the seashore, you are standing at **sea level**. Places on land that are as low as the sea are said to be at sea level. We measure distance above or below sea level in feet or meters. Nearly all places on land are above sea level. A few places are lower than the level of the sea. Higher land around these places keeps the ocean from covering them.

Riches in the Earth

The earth's crust is more than a big mass of rock. It is full of wonder-

Ecclesiastes 3:11a

tains, valleys, **plains,** and other shapes of the earth around us. God has made the earth beautiful for us to enjoy. "He hath made every thing beautiful in his time."

In some places God formed the earth's crust into hills. The highest hills are called mountains. Hilly and mountainous places are sometimes called **highlands.** Low places near rivers, lakes, and oceans are called **lowlands.** Flatlands are called plains.

People who live on the plains enjoy going to see the mountains.

In this photograph of Honolulu, Hawaii, you can clearly see the coastline, where land and ocean meet. Notice that the buildings of this city reach right to the coastline.

26

ful things we can use to make tools, build houses, and keep ourselves warm. The Bible says, "The earth is full of the goodness of the LORD." These supplies that God has given us to use are called **natural resources.** Plants and animals are **living resources.** Stones and other nonliving things from the earth's crust are called **mineral resources.**

Most of the earth's crust is rock. We clear rocks from our gardens and fields. Men blast them out of the way to build tunnels and roadways. You may wonder whether or not rocks are good for anything.

Ordinary rocks are an important natural resource. Long ago sturdy buildings were made almost entirely of rock or stone. The stone called granite makes an especially sturdy building. A beautiful stone called marble is used for such things as buildings, counter tops, and bookends. Your great-grandparents may have written their lessons on tablets made of a stone called slate.

Though rocks are not used as much as they once were, today tons and tons of them are still mixed in concrete for buildings and walkways. Crushed stone is very important in building highways for travel.

Metals From the Earth

Today we do not use as much stone as people did long ago. Something else has taken its place. Look around you and you will see what it is.

God has given us many natural resources to use. What natural resource is this man using for building? Is there much of this natural resource in your community?

What holds your desk and chair together? What are the doorknobs made of? What is the bus that brought you to school made of? All these things are made of metal. Metal is one of the most important mineral resources today. Many kinds of metal are found in the earth's crust. Aluminum and iron are the most plentiful. Does your mother have any aluminum skillets? Does she still use an iron skillet?

27

In this illustration are some of the useful things we use that are made of steel or partly of steel. Can you name some more things made of steel?

Copper, gold, silver, lead, tin, and zinc are a few other important metals. Steel is a strong metal made from iron.

Try to imagine what life would be like without metals. We would have no automobiles, no modern machinery, no metal screws and bolts to hold things together, and few pots and pans. Life would be difficult without metals.

Iron and Steel. We use more iron than any other metal. Iron is found in the ground mixed with other minerals. This mixture is called iron ore.

Iron ore is treated in special factories to remove the iron. The iron can be made into skillets, stoves, fences, and many other things. Iron can be treated to make steel which is much harder and more useful than iron. Most iron is made into steel.

Cars, buses, machinery, nails, and thousands of other things are made with steel. Large steel beams support huge skyscrapers. Stainless steel can be made into shiny knives, forks, and spoons for your table.

Steel parts in machinery make it possible for the machines to do hard work. In fact, steel machinery is used to crush, cut, or shape steel to make more machines and other steel products.

Farmers need steel to do their work. Steel plows, planters, cultivators, and harvesters help us farm the land. Steel milking and storage containers collect our milk to sell.

To see how important steel is to the farmer, follow milk from the cow to the grocery store. Steel is used to make the milkers and the storage tanks at the farm. The truck that carries the milk from the farm is made mostly from steel. Steel is an important part of the machine that pasteurizes the milk at the milk plant and of the refrigerators that store the milk at the grocery store.

Fuels in the Earth

Metals are not the only treasures buried in the earth. Some of the most important natural resources in the earth's crust are not metals at all.

Does your school or home have a furnace for heating? Unless it burns wood, the furnace likely burns coal, oil, or **natural gas.** Coal, oil, and natural gas are fuels that are found buried under the ground.

Coal. Coal is a black- or brown-colored fuel. It is a rock. Coal may be burned to heat houses and factories. It can also be burned to make steam that turns big generators which make electricity.

Coal was once used as fuel for trains. A coal fire was built in the engine's firebox. The heat from the coal boiled water. The hot steam from the boiling water was used to move the train. Such engines were called steam engines or steam locomotives.

Oil. Another fuel found in the earth is oil, also called **petroleum.** Oil can also be used to run generators that make electricity. It can be treated to make gasoline for cars, trucks, and

other machinery. Diesel fuel is made from oil and can be used much as gasoline is used.

Natural gas. Coal is a solid fuel. Petroleum is a liquid fuel. Natural gas is neither solid nor liquid. It is a gas like the air we breathe.

Natural gas is often found in the same places where petroleum is found. It is found in underground caves and in holes in underground rocks. Natural gas is most often used for heating, cooling, and cooking in homes, schools, hospitals, and factories. Some natural gas is used for generating electricity.

Natural gas has no color and no smell. Gas companies add something that gives the gas an odor, or smell, so that people can know about a leak.

Natural gas is one of the valuable natural resources God has given in the earth. Natural gas is an invisible, orderless gas that can be used for cooking food, heating buildings, and for many other useful purposes. People who sell natural gas add an odor to it so that we can tell if there is a leak or if a burner is left on.

Here are some of the items made from coal, oil, or natural gas. God gave us these natural resources thousands of years ago. Only in the last 100 years have people begun to learn of the many uses of these natural resources.

Other Uses of These Fuels. Did you ever take an aspirin for a fever? You were swallowing something with coal in it!

Hundreds of other useful things are made from coal, oil, and natural gas. The tires on the bus that brought you to school do not look a bit like coal or oil. The plastic bag your mother put in your lunchbox does not look like oil. Soaps, plastics, paints, and chemical fertilizers do not look like petroleum or natural gas. But all these things are made, at least partly, from fuels God put in the earth.

What Do You Say?

1. What is the earth's crust?

2. What is the shape of the land outside your classroom window? At your home?

3. How can a place on land be below sea level and not be covered with water?

4. What is a natural resource?

5. Name some ways the following resources are used in your community: metal, coal, oil, natural gas.

What Does the Bible Say?

1. Read Psalm 33:5b. What is the earth full of?

30

2. Deuteronomy 8:7-10 tells about the good things God's people found in the land of Palestine. a. What were they? b. We find many good things in our country too. Name some of these gifts God put in the earth.

Changes in the Earth

Since God made the earth, its crust has been changing slowly. The crust moves. At some places the crust cracks and moves up and down or sideways. Some scientists think the crust is floating on top of melted rock.

Volcanoes. Under its crust the earth is very hot. Sometimes hot, melted rock pushes its way through cracks and holes in the crust and pours out of the ground.

Melted rock that pours out of the ground is called **lava.** A place where lava pours out is called a **volcano.** Some volcanoes furiously explode and shoot lava, rocks, smoke, and gases high into the air. Sometimes dust from an exploding volcano travels around the world.

Volcanoes that still spew out lava or erupt are called **active volcanoes.** Volcanoes that have not erupted for hundreds of years are called **dormant volcanoes.** *Dormant* means "sleeping." Other volcanoes which have not erupted for thousands of years are said to be extinct. *Extinct* means "dead" or "no longer active."

Nobody knows when a dormant or extinct volcano will erupt again.

This volcano is Mount Saint Helens in the state of Washington. Mt. Saint Helens was dormant for over 100 years. In 1980 it erupted and covered thousands of acres (or hectares) with lava and ashes. In this picture, gases and smoke are still escaping from the volcano.

Nobody knows when a new volcano will form.

Sometimes volcanoes erupt under the ocean. Some of them pile lava higher and higher until their tops stick out of the water. The tops of these volcanoes become islands. The Hawaiian Islands are the tops of volcanoes. Some of these volcanoes are still active.

A picture taken in the 1940s while Parícutin was erupting. As you can see, the volcano was not very high. Many people were able to see and photograph the birth of this new volcano. How high did this volcano become?

A New Volcano

In 1943, while plowing his cornfield near the Mexican village of Parícutin (pə rē′ kə tēn′), a farmer noticed something like smoke coming from a small hole in the ground. He covered the hole with a rock and kept plowing. Soon he saw more smoke pouring out around the rock. He set out for the village and told what had happened. A group of men came to see the smoke. They found a large hole in the ground. Thick, black smoke poured out.

That night the first of many explosions came. They turned the field into a volcano. Smoke, ash, and large stones blew into the sky. The stones and ash fell to the ground. The people who lived nearby fled in terror.

Soon hot, melted rock called lava began pouring from the new volcano. The village of Parícutin lay buried under ash and lava. Only the roof and tower of the church could be seen.

The ash, rocks, and lava piled higher and higher, forming a mountain 1,500 feet (457 meters) high. The new mountain was named Parícutin.

Parícutin was the first new volcano in North America in over 150 years. Many scientists, photographers, and curious people came to watch.

A few years after Parícutin formed, it stopped erupting. It is now a dormant volcano. Only God knows if the mountain will ever erupt again.

Partly burned trees from a volcanic eruption. The ashes around the tree are at least a foot deep. Volcanic ash helps make the soil around a volcano very rich for future plant life.

Earthquakes. Did you ever stand beside a busy highway as a large tractor trailer rumbled by? Did you feel the ground shake? Then you have an idea how a small earthquake feels.

Earthquakes are not caused by trucks or anything people can do. Earthquakes are caused by the slipping of the earth's crust.

At places in the earth's crust there are cracks. These cracks are called **faults.** Some faults lie deep under the ground. Faults such as those in California can be seen on top of the ground.

The earth along a fault sometimes slips up or down or sideways. This slip causes an earthquake. The ground shakes at the fault and for many miles around.

Earthquakes may be felt almost anywhere, but the worst quakes are felt near faults.

An earthquake can cause far more damage than a volcano. Earthquakes may cause damage for hundreds of miles around a fault. In an earthquake the ground sometimes shakes so much that stones are thrown into the air. Large cracks may open in the earth, swallowing trees and buildings. Buildings shake and sometimes fall. Roadways may break. Broken gas lines can cause fires.

The Bible tells us that we may expect great earthquakes in many places as the end of time draws near.

"And great earthquakes shall be in divers places, and famines, and pestilences; and fearful sights and great signs shall there be from heaven."

Luke 21:11

Earthquakes can do much damage to buildings and cities. The land on one side of this street dropped eleven feet (more than three meters) in an earthquake.

What Do You Say?

1. Name some ways the earth's crust is changing.

2. Would you rather go camping near the top of an active volcano or a dormant volcano? Give a reason for your answer.

3. What happens to the earth's crust that causes an earthquake?

What Does the Bible Say?

1. Read Matthew 28:2. a. Who rolled away the stone from the grave in which Christ was buried? b. What else happened at this time?

2. Read Acts 16:25-30. How did an earthquake help God's servants?

God Gave Us Soil

You walk on it every day. You do not like to get it on your hands or your clothing. You may call it dirt or **soil**. People who do not work with soil may not think about its value. Soil and water are our most important natural resources.

We could learn to live without metals, coal, and oil. We could not live without soil.

Without soil we would have no food to eat. Plants, of course, grow in the soil. The animals we use for food depend on plants for their food. Meat, eggs, sugar, and honey all come in some way from the soil.

What Is Soil? Does this seem like a silly question? One look at a handful of soil does not tell us how wonderfully God made it.

Just one handful of soil has dozens of things in it to make plants grow. Tiny pieces of rock are a part of soil. These pieces may be so tiny that you can hardly see each one. Many tiny grains of sandstone, called sand, help make sandy soil.

Plant food that we call minerals is found in soil. Some important minerals for soil are lime, nitrogen, phosphorus, and potash.

Good soil also has many bits of dead and decayed plants and animals. Many wild plants grow on soil that people do not farm. Worms burrow into the soil and loosen it. Insects and animals live on the land. When these things die, they decay and become mixed with the soil. New plants and animals take the place of those that died. They will one day die and help make the ground richer.

Water, minerals, and other plant foods from the soil are taken into plants through their roots. We get some of the minerals from plants when we eat their fruit, leaves, stems, or roots.

Humus is formed from decayed plants and animals in the soil. Humus is rich in minerals that plants need to grow. Humus helps to keep the soil loose. It also acts as a sponge to help hold moisture close to plant roots.

Using the Soil God Gave Us. Farming the soil is one of the most important jobs in the world. About half the world's workers are farmers. Some are able to grow just enough food for one family. Others grow food for themselves and many other people. In the United States and Canada, one farmer grows enough food each year for about 50 people.

Farmers must learn how to care for the soil God gave. If they take good care of it, they can feed many people for years to come.

Soil Wears Out. Soil in woodlands and grasslands usually grows richer and richer. Wild plants and animals decay and add humus. But then people come along to farm the land. They cut down the forests or plow the grasslands. Wild plants no longer cover the land and add humus. If farmers do not continue to add humus to the soil, the land will become useless.

Farmers usually raise crops such as corn and potatoes for food. Cotton and flax are raised to make cloth. The farmer does not leave his crops on the soil to add humus.

Crops take many minerals from the soil. The farmer must find ways to put these things back into the soil or it will wear out. Each year that crops are planted on worn-out land the harvest gets smaller. If the soil could talk, it would cry, "Help!"

35

Rich soil that God gave produces these winter vegetables near Phoenix, Arizona. Water from nearby rivers keeps the crop growing.

Straw mulch in this garden helps to hold moisture in the ground. When the straw rots, it will help make the soil richer.

Helping the Soil. God does not want us to wear out the good soil He made. He gave man the work of taking care of the earth. "And the LORD God took the man, and put him into the garden of Eden to dress [work] it and to keep it."

Genesis 2:15

Many farmers have learned how to keep their soil rich year after year. They add things to the soil to keep it rich. Anything added to the soil to keep it rich is called **fertilizer.** Manure, straw, wood shavings, peanut hulls, and many other things that decay add humus to soil. Farmers in Ireland spread peat on their fields. Peat is made of decayed plants. Some farmers in Japan spread seaweed on their fields.

Many farmers add minerals to the soil. Lime is a mineral made from heated limestone. Potash is found in wood ashes. Nitrogen fertilizers may be made from coal or oil.

Did you ever hear of green manure? A good way to add fertilizer to soil is to plant some kind of grass or bean crop such as alfalfa or soybeans. While the crop is growing and green, it is plowed into the soil where it will decay and add humus. This is sometimes called green manure.

Another important kind of fertilizer is animal fertilizer. Manure is one of the most important animal fertilizers. It gives plants many important minerals. It adds humus to the soil. The bodies of animals that die can also be made into good fertilizer. Bone meal and blood meal are fertilizers made of certain parts of animals.

Much farmland has been ruined because careless farmers raised their crops but did not use any fertilizers. The crops took most of the plant food from the soil.

Poor soil can again become good farmland. Sometimes grasses and trees grow again on the land and improve the soil. After many years, the soil may become rich again. A quicker way to enrich the soil is to add large amounts of fertilizer, especially humus. However, this takes more money than many of the world's farmers have.

Disappearing Soil

Have you ever watched a creek or river after a heavy rain? The water becomes muddy. Why? The water is carrying away some of the soil from nearby fields. Did you ever stand beside a plowed field in dry weather? Did you see dust picked up by the wind? Both wind and rain can take soil away. When soil is being taken away, **erosion** is taking place.

If the land is covered with forests, thick grasses, and other plants, only a little soil will be lost by erosion. Decayed plants and animals will add as much to the soil as rain and wind take away.

This farmer is plowing a field of buckwheat. The buckwheat plants plowed into the ground will rot, or decay, and enrich the soil. Enriching the soil by plowing this crop under is an example of using green manure.

This field was once covered with rich topsoil. Many years of planting row crops, plowing the soil, and letting the rain wash it away caused this erosion. Now it is a badly eroded gully.

This rushing river carries tons of good topsoil away from the land. Where do you think this topsoil will finally go?

But when people take over the land, they often cut down many of the forests. They plow the land for their crops. Then rain can easily wash soil from a plowed field. In dry weather wind can blow away some of the good soil.

Where Does the Soil Go?

Rain carries soil from a field. Let us follow the soil to see where it goes. Imagine rain falling on a field of freshly plowed ground. As the rain falls, it washes some of the soil into little trenches or gullies in the field.

Water from the gullies in the field carries the soil to a stream.

The muddy water from the stream runs into a larger stream nearby. The larger stream then empties its muddy water into a river. A river may carry soil from hundreds of fields nearby. The more the rain falls, the faster the water in the streams and rivers will move. The faster the water moves, the more soil it can carry.

The river grows larger and larger as it flows toward the ocean. Finally the river reaches low, flat lands near the ocean. The river slows down. If the river overflows its banks, it will drop some of the soil that has come from far up the river. Such a river valley is called a **flood plain**. The soil on a flood plain is very rich because of the soil that has been left on the land when the river floods.

The muddy river travels on to

How does strip farming in hilly land keep soil from washing away?

the sea. As it flows on it travels more slowly. It drops the soil, sand, and gravel that it has carried for many miles. The materials a river drops as it slows down are known as **sediment**.

Sometimes the sediment becomes deep at the river's mouth, where the river meets the ocean. Sometimes this deep sediment forms new land at the river's mouth. Land formed at the mouth of a river is called a **delta**. The land in a delta was once good soil in thousands of fields farther up the river.

Stop Erosion! Some farmland has been used for hundreds of years and is still good land. What stopped erosion from taking the best soil?

Farmers must work hard to stop erosion. Here are some ways they have learned to save their soil:

Farmers with hilly land have learned to plow across rather than up and down their sloping fields. This is

What do you think will happen to the soil carried by this water in a flooded river valley? What will happen to the crops covered by this water?

39

How does planting a crop in sod as this farmer is doing help keep the soil from blowing or washing away?

called **contour plowing.** The plow follows the shape or contour of the land. This makes ridges or furrows across the hills. The furrows keep water from rushing down the hills. Can you guess what would happen if the furrows were made up and down on the hills?

Farmers in both flat lands and

How does this clump of trees help hold the soil on this steep hillside?

hilly lands have learned another way to stop erosion. They plant crops in strips. In some strips they plant crops such as wheat or clover. These crops cover the ground and help keep water and wind from carrying away soil. Between these strips the farmers plant crops such as corn or soybeans that do not cover the ground as well. This method of farming is called **strip farming.**

Strip farming helps to hold precious soil on hilly land. In heavy rains, soil from strips planted in corn or other crops that do not hold soil well may begin to wash away. The nearby strips of wheat or grasses below it catch most of the mud and keep it from washing farther down the hill. In flat, dry country, strip farming helps keep the wind from picking up much soil.

Some farmers plant corn and some other crops on fields covered with grasses. The grass is sprayed with weed killer so that it does not grow. Then the corn is planted in the dead grass or sod. **Sod planting** or no-till planting helps hold moisture in the ground. When heavy rains come, the sod holds the soil and very little washes away. Sod planting lets a farmer plant crops on steeper hills than once was possible.

Some land is too steep even for sod planting. The wise farmer allows trees, bushes, and grasses to grow on this land to keep it from washing away.

There are many ways to save our

This land is not hilly but almost flat. Why do you think the crops in this field are planted in strips?

soil. We call these ways **soil conservation.** Christians will want to learn all they can about taking care of the soil. God is not pleased to see people wearing out the soil or letting it wash away.

What Do You Say?

1. What is soil?

2. In what way do we get eggs from the soil?

3. Name some things we can do to keep the soil from wearing out.

4. What is erosion?

5. Suppose you owned a field on a hillside. Name three things you could do to stop erosion.

What Does the Bible Say?

1. Read Genesis 2:7. a. Of what did God make the first man? b. How are our bodies still made of the same thing?

2. Read Genesis 3:19 and fill in the blanks. "For a. _____ thou art, and unto b. _____ shalt thou return."

3. Read Psalm 115:16. a. To whom did God give the earth? Now read Genesis 2:15. b. What did God ask Adam to do with the good earth? (*Dress* here means "cultivate" or "farm.")

Chapter Two Review

Working With Maps

1. Make a map of your state or province. Use green color for lowlands, yellow for hills, brown for mountains, and blue for rivers, lakes, or ocean.

41

2. Turn to the map on page 87. How does that map show lowlands? Mountains? Water?

New Words and Terms

Fill in the blanks with words from the list on pages 42 and 43. Each word is used only once.

1. A place where land meets the ocean is a _____ .

2. Melted rock flowing out of a volcano is called _____ .

3. _____ is a liquid fuel found in the earth.

4. The earth's outer layer of rock and soil is called its _____ .

5. Soil, sand, and gravel dropped by a river form _____ .

6. Growing crops in dead grass or sod is called _____ _____ .

7. _____ is decayed bits of plants and animals in the soil.

8. Making furrows around hills instead of up and down is called _____ _____ .

9. _____ is a black or brown rock used for fuel.

10. A _____ _____ has not erupted for years.

11. An _____ _____ is one that still erupts.

12. Planting crops in strips to prevent wind and rain erosion is called _____ _____ .

13. A _____ is a crack in the earth where earthquakes often take place.

14. We call low, flat land along a river a _____ _____ .

15. Dirt which contains minerals and humus is called _____ .

16. Flatlands are also called _____ .

17. Low places in the land near rivers, lakes, and oceans are called _____ .

18. A hole in the earth from which lava, rock, and gases pour is a _____ .

19. _____ _____ is a gas taken from the earth to be used as fuel.

20. A volcano that has not erupted for thousands of years is called an _____ _____ .

21. A place is at _____ _____ if it is on land as low as the ocean.

22. Hilly and mountainous places are called _____ .

23. Earth's supplies that God has given are _____ _____ .

24. _____ takes place when soil is carried away by wind or water.

25. _____ is something that is added to the soil to keep it rich.

crust	lowlands
coastline	sea level

42

petroleum
dormant volcano
soil
flood plain
highlands
natural resources
volcano
extinct volcano
fertilizer
contour plowing
fault (in the earth)

natural gas
active volcano
humus
sediment
plains
coal
lava
sod planting
erosion
strip farming

gold. How do you think it earned that name?

6. Why should we be thankful for soil?

7. Suppose someone sold you some farmland that was worn out. What are some things you could do to make it useful again?

For You to Do

1. Bring some samples of soil to class. Can you find any rocks in your samples? Try to find decaying leaves, twigs, or other plants. Perhaps someone in your class can bring some rich soil from under the leaves in woodland. Why is this soil so rich?

2. Do an experiment on a mound of dirt in a large pan or in the schoolyard as the teacher directs. On one side of the "hill" (mound) make furrows with your hand across the slope. On the other side make some furrows up and down. Water the furrows evenly with a sprayer or sprinkling can. What happens to the soil where the furrows are made across the slope? What happens where the furrows run up and down? Why?

Thinking Together

1. Suppose God had made the earth all lowland. a. In what ways would this be good? b. In what ways would it not be good?

2. a. What is a natural resource? b. Do you think water is a natural resource? c. Why? d. Would you call air a natural resource? e. Why or why not?

3. Suppose you could take all the metals out of your classroom. What would be left?

4. A traveler long ago saw something he had never seen before. He called it "black stones that burn." What do you think he saw?

5. Petroleum has been called black

Sometimes the ocean appears to be peaceful. But at other times it crashes against the shore. This place in Maine is called Thunder Hole. Can you guess why it has that name?

3. The Ocean Around Us

Water, Water Everywhere!

Most of us live many miles from the ocean. We see much more land than water, so we do not get a true picture of what the world is like.

Hold a globe in your hand. Do you see how large the oceans are? Hold the globe so that you are looking down at the South Pole and the places south of the equator. The southern part of the world looks as though it is almost all ocean. There is more land north of the equator, but even there we see more water than land.

At the time of creation God sepa-rated the water and the land. He made the land into continents and islands. The continents are like very large islands in one large world ocean.

Can you name the four main parts of the world ocean? Can you tell where they are found? Find all the oceans on your globe and on a flat map of the world. Review all the continents too. You will need to know the oceans and continents well as we study places around the world.

Blessings From the Oceans

Have you ever visited the ocean?

44

If you have, you have seen just a little idea of how large and wonderful the ocean is. Even if you live near the ocean, much of it remains a mystery to you. You do not see much of the ocean. You cannot see most of the natural resources in the ocean. The ocean is very valuable. Man has not finished learning about all the resources God gave us in the oceans.

Resources in the Water. The most important natural resource in the ocean is the water. In Chapter 4 you will learn why we cannot do without water in the ocean. Did you ever taste water from the ocean? If you never did, you may be surprised. It tastes salty.

The water you drink is likely from the ground or from a lake or river. This is called fresh water. Even fresh water has a tiny bit of salt or other minerals in it. But you may not be able to taste them.

Seawater is very salty. One hundred pounds of seawater has about three and a half pounds of salt in it. One kilogram of seawater has about 35 grams of salt in it.

The water in the ocean is so salty that you would become sick if you drank much of it. Drinking salt water makes thirst greater. A person will soon die if he keeps on drinking salt water.

Did you know that salty ocean water will kill most plants? Most land plants need fresh water to live and to grow. Seawater cannot be

used to water plants. The salt must be taken from seawater before it can be used for people or plants.

The salt can be removed from

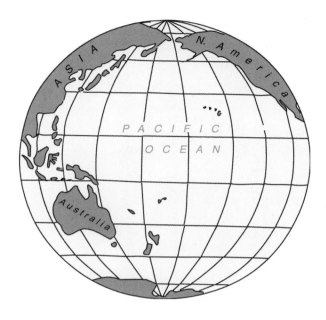

These two globe maps give you just a little idea of how much water is on the earth. The half of the world that centers on the Pacific Ocean is nearly all water. The southern half of the world that centers on the South Pole is also mostly water.

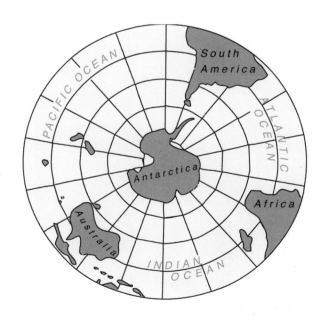

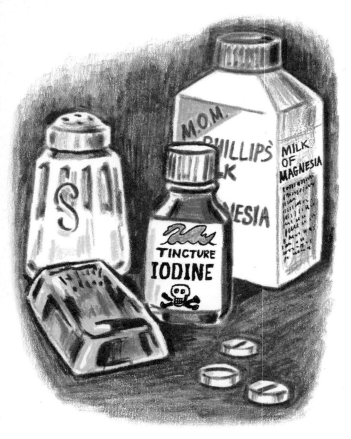

Here are some of the useful things made from minerals in seawater. The pills represent calcium. What do you think the other items represent?

Underwater workers and explorers must take air along with them. This worker carries a tank of air on his back. Hoses carry the air to his nose and mouth.

seawater, but the equipment to remove it is very expensive. Scientists are working on cheaper ways to remove the salt. If the salt could be removed, the ocean would have plenty of water for people to drink and to water millions of acres of dry farmland.

Much of the salt in the ocean is like the kind you sprinkle on your eggs. For thousands of years people have been collecting table salt from places where seawater has evaporated. The water contains other kinds of salt too.

Some of the salts and minerals in seawater are far more valuable than table salt. Plenty of aluminum, a lightweight metal, is found in seawater. No one has yet found a good way to remove it from the water. Men are already taking the mineral called magnesium (mag nē′ zē əm) from water. Magnesium is a metal used in airplanes, cars, boats, and other places where light weight is important. Did you ever take milk of magnesia when you were sick? Milk of magnesia is powdered magnesium in water. It helps settle an upset stomach.

More Wealth in the Oceans. Besides the salts and minerals in seawater, untold wealth lies on the ocean floor, the bottom of the ocean. There explorers have found little lumps of such minerals as nickel, copper, and cobalt. Cobalt is used as a coloring in paints. It is used with metals to help make them hard so they are able to withstand heat. Even

46

vitamins can be made from cobalt.

Under the ocean floor man has found yet more treasures. Vast stores of petroleum and natural gas are buried under the ocean. The supply of these fuels on land is running out. More and more, people are turning to the ocean.

Much of the wealth on the ocean floor and in the rocks under the ocean cannot be used yet. Machines for working in the ocean are expensive. Men cannot live and work underwater without special equipment and a supply of air. The cold, the darkness, and the weight of the water make work slow, hard, and expensive.

Much wealth is being taken from the shallow waters near the continents. Many important oil and gas wells are found in shallow seas. Man is only beginning to use the wonderful resources in the oceans God made. Thank God for the oceans.

"Thy way is in the sea, and thy path in the great waters, and thy footsteps are not known."

Psalm
77:19

Living Resources in the Ocean.
Millions and millions of plants and animals live in the ocean. More living things can be found in the oceans than on land.

When you think of living things in the ocean, perhaps you think first of fish and whales. But thousands of other animals also make their homes in the sea. Seaweeds and other plants grow in shallow waters because they need sunlight to live. Sunlight does not reach deeper than

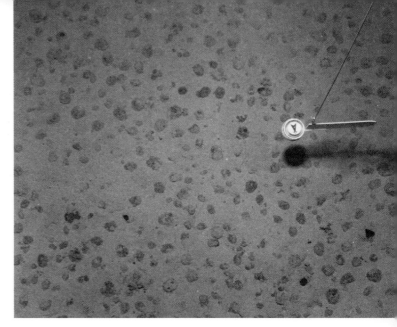

God placed these valuable pieces, or nodules, of manganese on the ocean floor. These nodules are at a depth of about 16,500 feet (5,000 meters). The man-made object in this picture is a current meter. It measures the direction and speed of water movements.

These are some useful plants and animals found in the sea. Can you name them? If not, check in an encyclopedia article about the ocean.

47

about 600 feet (180 meters).

Some plants and animals in the sea are so small that you could not see them even if you looked! Do you wonder how we know they live in the ocean if we cannot see them? People have seen them by studying seawater under microscopes. Plants and animals we can see only with the help of a microscope are called **microscopic** plants and animals.

Whales are the largest living animals on sea or land. The blue whale may grow 100 feet long (30 meters) and may weigh as much as 50 or more automobiles.

The smallest animals in the sea eat the microscopic plants. Small fish eat small animals, as well as the plants. Large fish eat the smaller fish. Whales and other large sea animals eat fish. Some sea animals eat the remains of other sea animals. Living things in the ocean depend on each other for food.

People use many living products from the sea. People eat fish, oysters, shrimp, and many other sea animals. In some places people eat certain kinds of seaweeds. Sea animals or their bones may be ground up for fertilizer. As you learned in Chapter 2, the Japanese use seaweeds to add humus to the soil.

It is low tide along the Bay of Fundy in Nova Scotia. At high tide these boats will float on top of the water. The water will reach almost to the top of these wooden posts or piles. How much higher is the water here at high tide than at low tide?

What Do You Say?

1. Name the four main parts of the world ocean.

2. An old poem tells of a man who once sailed on the ocean. He looked out over the water and said,

   "Water, water everywhere
   Nor any drop to drink."

   Why do you think he said that?

3. a. Name some mineral resources God has placed in the ocean.
   b. Name some animal resources.
   c. Name some plant resources.

4. How are the microscopic plants in the ocean very important for the large fish and the whales?

What Does the Bible Say?

1. Read Genesis 1:9, 10. a. What did God call the dry land? b. What did He call the ocean?

2. Read Psalm 104:24, 25. Fill in these blanks. In a. _____ God made all things. The earth is full of God's b. _____ . In the sea (ocean) there are c. " _____ ."

The Moving Ocean

If you live near the ocean or have visited the ocean, you have seen the ocean moving. Even on a calm day the water is never still. If you wade along the shore, you will soon see the water move back toward the ocean leaving your feet uncovered. Stand still. In a few minutes the water will return and cover your feet again.

If you had time to stand on the shore all day, you would notice the rising and lowering of the ocean. At certain times in the day, the ocean lowers and leaves much of the sandy beach uncovered. Later in the day the ocean slowly rises higher and higher. Each time the waves roll in, they come just a little closer than they did the last time. The daily rising and falling of the ocean is called the **tide**.

The water is lowest and farthest out to sea at low tide. The water is highest at high tide. At most places along the coast the high tides are several feet higher than the low tides. Some places have a high tide 50 feet (16 meters) or more higher than low tide.

What Causes the Tides? The tides are caused by the moon and the sun. The moon's gravity pulls on the earth enough to raise the water in the oceans several feet. Of course, the earth's gravity is stronger and holds the ocean in its bed. The sun also pulls on the oceans, but not so much as the moon. The sun is much farther away.

As the earth turns, the moon pulls on the part of the ocean facing it. The water bulges upward toward the moon. Places where the water bulges have high tide. At other places on the earth there is no bulge in the water. These have low tide. As the earth turns, the places that had high tide will have low tide. The places that had low tide will have high tide. The tide changes about every six hours.

The tides are like clocks for men and animals along the seashore. Birds learn to flock to the beaches at low tide to look for fish and other small sea animals left by the high tides.

People who want to fish along the seashore like to know when the tide will be high and when it will be

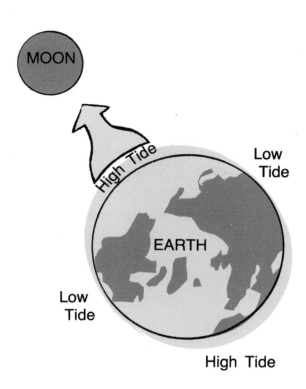

The moon's gravity pulls on the earth enough that the water in the ocean is pulled slightly toward the moon. This pull causes the tides.

low so they can know when to fish. People who want to use small boats like to know when the tides will be high or low so they can know when and where to sail their boats.

Other Movements in the Ocean. Tides come and go. The ocean is always moving in many different ways. Right now the wind is blowing over the ocean. The wind helps move the water along. At most places in the ocean the wind usually blows in the same direction day after day. In some places the wind usually blows from the west. In other places the wind usually blows

50

from the east or from some other direction.

The winds move streams or currents of water in the ocean. The turning or rotation of the earth also helps **ocean currents** move. Warm water currents flow from warm seas near the equator toward the North and South Poles. The warm water helps to warm cold oceans and the winds that blow over them.

Cold ocean currents from near the poles flow toward the equator. The cold waters help to cool seas close to the equator.

The Gulf Stream. One of the most famous ocean currents is called the **Gulf Stream.** It begins in the warm waters of the Gulf of Mexico. Find the Gulf of Mexico on the map. The Gulf Stream flows past Florida and the eastern United States, giving off warmth.

Winds that blow over the warm waters become warm too. The Gulf Stream and its warm winds keep moving north and east across the North Atlantic Ocean. The warm water spreads as it nears the coast of Europe. Near Europe the warm waters are called the North Atlantic Drift.

Find Norway on the map. It is a country in the far north. It is as close to the North Pole as much of icy Greenland. You would expect Norway to be a very cold land covered

This map shows some of the most famous ocean currents. Which one warms northern Europe? Which warms the northern Pacific Ocean and Alaska?

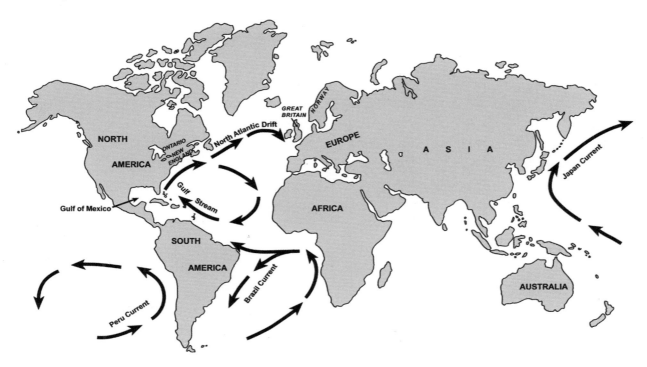

Part of the tidal electric plant on the Rance River in France. When water rises and falls through this structure, the power of the water turns generators to make electricity. How high does the water rise in this river at high tide?

with ice and snow. But warm waters wash against Norway's coast. Warm breezes blow in from the ocean. As a result, much of Norway has weather somewhat like southern Ontario or the New England states. Yet these places are much farther south than any place in Norway.

Another famous ocean current is the Japan Current in the North Pacific. This current flows north and east from warm places in the Pacific near the coast of Asia. Warm ocean breezes from the Japan Current make farming possible in many places in southern Alaska. The warm current keeps the coast of British Columbia, Washington, and Oregon warm and rainy.

Power in the Ocean. Tides, cur-

rents, and other movements in the ocean are powerful. Ocean waves pounding on the shore can slowly wear away sand, soil, and even rocks. Ocean waves stirred up by storms and earthquakes can smash the mightiest ships or crash into the land, wrecking cities and killing hundreds of people.

People have tried to think of ways to use the great power of the moving ocean. Tides rise and fall every day. Could they somehow be used to make electricity? In 1966 the first tidal electric plant opened in France. This is how it works:

Some ocean bays and rivers on the coast of France and other places have very high tides. Twice a day the tide rises about 44 feet (13 meters) on the Rance (róns) River near Saint Malo, France. Men built a large dam across the river. While the tide is rising, openings in the dam let water flow in behind the dam.

The tide falls a few hours later, leaving a deep lake behind the dam. Twenty-four big electric generators in the dam make some electricity as the tide rises. After the lake is full, water tumbles through the dam making more electricity.

There are also places along the coast of Nova Scotia (the Bay of Fundy) and Maine in North America where high tide runs as much as 50 feet above low tide. Perhaps someday the tides there can be used to make valuable electricity.

What Do You Say?

1. Suppose you visit the ocean and see small sea animals in the sand. Are you seeing the ocean at high tide or at low tide?

2. London, England, is about as far north as Calgary, Alberta. In January, London is cool and often rainy. Snow falls only once in a while. Calgary has very cold January temperatures with snow. Look at the map on page 51 and tell why London is so warm in January.

3. What causes the tides?

Using Globes and Maps

1. Study your classroom globe. Name all the oceans. Can you remember the names and locations of the oceans without looking at them on a globe or map?

2. Study the article on "ocean currents" in an encyclopedia. Show on a globe or world map where the warm ocean currents begin and to what places they travel. Where do cold ocean currents usually begin? To where do they flow?

What Does the Bible Say?

1. Read James 1:6. What causes the waves in the sea?

2. What can the waves of the ocean do to rocks? (Find an answer in Job 14:19.)

New Words and Terms

Can you tell the meaning of the following words and tell where the places are located?

1. Atlantic Ocean
2. world ocean

3. Pacific Ocean

4. Indian Ocean

5. Arctic Ocean

6. natural resources

7. magnesium

8. cobalt

9. microscopic

10. tide

11. ocean currents

12. Gulf Stream

13. North Atlantic Drift

14. Japan Current

Thinking Together

1. Why did God cover so much of the earth with water? Could we not use more land?

2. Why do we sometimes speak of a world ocean instead of many different oceans?

3. You cannot drink ocean water, and it would ruin crops. Suppose someone told you ocean water is useless. How would you answer?

4. a. Name some of the valuable things which lie at the bottom of the ocean. b. Why are they hard to take from the ocean?

5. If you took a journey in a submarine through the ocean, what are some forms of life you might expect to see? (For help, read an article on "ocean" in an encyclopedia.)

6. If the moon would suddenly disappear, what effect would its disappearance have on the ocean?

7. What great movements that we cannot see are going on in the ocean? What do these movements do for the earth? (Think about what would happen if all the warm water stayed in the part of the ocean near the equator and all the cold water stayed near the poles.)

8. Suppose someone told you that God did not make the ocean but that it all happened by chance. What have you learned that could help you answer?

For You to Do

1. In an encyclopedia read about each of the divisions of the world ocean. Make a chart of the following facts about each ocean: place, size, deepest spot, length, and width.

2. Obtain some ocean water if possible. Boil a half gallon (about two liters) until the water all evaporates. What is left? What color is the material that is left? (If you cannot obtain ocean water, use very hard water, or dissolve some salt in water. Use one ounce [30 grams] of salt in each quart [1 liter] of water. This will at least show that what looks like clear water has some salts and minerals in it.)

3. Plant several bean seeds in two different pots or cans. After the plants are several inches high, begin to water one pot with ocean water. Continue to water the other with ordinary tap water. What happens to the beans in the two pots? Why? (Note: If you cannot obtain ocean water, make salt water as in activity 2.)

4. Our Ocean of Air

You have just studied about the vast ocean that covers much of our world. Did you know that you are living at the bottom of a much larger ocean—an ocean of air? The ocean of air covers all the water and all the land on earth. We call this ocean of air the **atmosphere.**

We use air in so many ways. We breathe it to live. We blow up balloons and pump up tires with it. How many more uses of air can you think of?

Without the atmosphere you could live only a few minutes. You would be like a fish out of water. Without the atmosphere, the earth would be a lifeless planet.

You cannot see air. A bucket you call empty is not empty at all. It is full of air. You can feel the air when the wind blows. You can feel the air rush past you when you ride your bicycle. You breathe air in and out.

You know that the earth whirls around on its axis. It also speeds around the sun. Did you ever wonder what keeps the atmosphere from flying off into space? The powerful force called gravity holds you and the ocean of air on the earth.

The Moving Atmosphere

All over the world the atmosphere is always moving. We call this movement **wind.** If the movement is too slow to feel, we say the air is calm. When the air moves enough to stir leaves and tug gently on your clothes, a *breeze* is blowing. *Gale* winds may vary in force from making trees sway to breaking them. *Hurricane* winds do even more violent damage, sometimes uprooting trees.

Calm   Breeze   Gale   Hurricane

God made trees to move gracefully in the breezes. Trees can stand very strong winds. But hurricane winds can break off branches and even uproot trees.

The wind brings us heat and cold, rain and snow, and skies cloudy and clear. When the wind blows from places that have been warmed by the sunshine, the wind is warm. Cold winds blow from places that are cold.

The conditions of the atmosphere and the changes that take place in it are called **weather.** Are you having sunny weather today? Is the weather cold or is it warm? Is the weather windy or calm?

Water in the Atmosphere. Did you ever lie outdoors and watch the clouds float overhead? The clouds are on the move in our ocean of air. Wind pushes them along.

If wind blows from places where there is plenty of rainfall or moisture, it brings clouds and maybe

Winds move beautiful clouds across the sky. Without the wind the skies would not change and clouds would not bring rain. A look at the sky often tells us much about our weather. What kind of weather do you think this place is having?

Name the three forms of water shown here. Which is hottest? Coldest?

container you want. How do we know that ice is solid water? All you need to do is melt ice, and you will have liquid water.

Did you know that water comes in another form? Boil some water in a pan. In a few minutes the water boils away. You see steam rising. The steam seems to disappear into the air. The water that was in the pan is now in the atmosphere around you. The drops are so tiny that you cannot see them, but they are still there. When water "disappears" into the air, we say that it **evaporates**.

Tiny drops of water floating in the air are called water vapor. Water can be a liquid, a solid, or a vapor.

Place a shallow pan of water in a sunny place. Watch it for a few days. The warmth and sunlight slowly evaporate the water. You cannot see the drops leaving the pan. They are very small and far apart. In a few days the water all leaves the pan.

rain or snow. Winds that blow from dry places bring sunny skies and few clouds.

Clouds are made of millions and millions of tiny drops of water floating in the atmosphere. How does the water get up into the sky? Where did it come from? Where is it going? Before you can answer these questions, you need to know something about water and how God made it.

You think of water as a liquid. You can pour it from one container to another. It takes up a certain amount of space. It takes the shape of the container into which you pour it.

Water is not always a liquid. It is sometimes a solid. Ice is solid water. It is hard. You cannot pour it. You cannot make it fit into just any

Evaporation on the Ocean. What do you think happens when the sun shines on thousands of miles of water in the ocean? You are right! Water evaporates from the ocean. The salts and minerals are left behind in the ocean. The warmer the air and the brighter the sunshine, the faster the water evaporates.

The warm air filled with water vapor rises high into the air over the oceans. Winds blow the moist air across the oceans. Some of it blows over the land. Warm, moist air rises

If it is very cold outside, water will condense from the air and form drops on the inside of a window. What does this show us about the air inside the house?

high into the atmosphere especially when it moves over high land and mountains.

The moist air cools as it rises. God has caused something interesting to happen to the moisture in the air as it cools.

You can see what happens in cooled air if you fill a glass with iced water. The air next to the glass cools. Drops of moisture from the air form on the outside of the glass. When water drops form from the air, we say that the water **condenses**.

When moist air rises and cools, the moisture in it begins to condense. As more and more water condenses in the atmosphere, clouds form. Clouds are made of many tiny water droplets that are very close together. Steam from boiling water is a tiny cloud.

What are clouds like? Some appear light and fluffy, and others look dark and heavy. Clouds may look heavy, but if you could stand in one you would hardly feel anything except the dampness against your skin. Airplanes easily fly through clouds. Did you ever walk or ride through fog? You were in a cloud that touched the earth.

A thundercloud is forming. As more and more moisture rises from the ground or is blown in by the winds, the cloud becomes heavier and heavier. Do you know what causes the water drops to start falling from the cloud?

59

As more and more water condenses in clouds, the water drops become larger and heavier. Soon the heaviest drops can no longer stay in the air. They begin to fall to the earth as rain or snow. If the temperature in the cloud is above 32° F (0° C), drops of rain form. If the temperature in the cloud is below 32° F (0° C), flakes of snow form.

Water that evaporated from the ocean hundreds of miles away condenses and falls to earth as rain. In this way the ocean waters the land.

What Happens to Rain. Rain falls to the earth from clouds filled with water vapor. The rain falls on trees, houses, fields, and cities.

Most of the rain sinks into the earth, especially when it falls on fields, woodlands, and gardens.

Plants take water from the soil into their roots. Some of the water sinks on down into the soil and reaches the rocks many feet under the soil. This water is called **groundwater**.

People dig wells to reach this groundwater. Sometimes it is found on top of the bedrock. Sometimes it is found between layers of rocks. At some places, groundwater collects in streams and lakes underground. When little rain falls for a long time, the groundwater gets low. Wells may go dry. Even if there is enough rain, wells may also go dry if people use too much of the groundwater.

Some of the rain that falls runs off the land. In towns and cities much of the ground is covered with buildings, streets, and parking lots. Rain runs down into the storm sewers and then into streams and rivers.

God made the water cycle. Describe the way water from the land goes back to the sea and then returns to the land. The Bible told about this water cycle long before many people had thought of it. (See Ecclesiastes 1:7.)

Rivers carry rainwater to the ocean. Some of this water may evaporate someday and again water the land. Water makes a great circle from the ocean to the land then back to the ocean, around and around. This great circle is called the **water cycle**.

The Bible spoke about the water cycle long before modern scientists discovered it.

"All the rivers run into the sea; yet the sea is not full; unto the place from whence the rivers come, thither they return again."

Without the world's vast oceans, there would be no water cycle. If land covered most of the earth, little water would evaporate and almost no rain would fall. God knew when He planned the earth that we would need far more water than land.

What Does the Bible Say?

1. Without the wind we know that water could not be carried from the oceans to the thirsty land. What does Psalm 147:18 say is the cause of wind and flowing water?

2. What is the wind doing according to Psalm 148:8b?

3. Read Ecclesiastes 1:6, 7. a. What do these verses say about the wind? b. About water?

Chapter Four Review

What Do You Say?

1. How can we tell that the atmosphere is all around us?

2. What are the three forms of water?

3. a. What is the water cycle? b. What does the water cycle do for the earth?

Using Globes and Maps

1. Dip a balloon or a large ball in water. Do you see the thin layer of water that sticks to the ball? If the earth could be shrunk to the size of the ball, the mountains would be no deeper than the water on the ball. The atmosphere would be only about one-

esiastes

tenth of an inch deep (about one-fourth centimeter).

2. Find your state or province on a world map or a map of North America. Can you trace the rivers near you to the sea or ocean?

3. Look at a globe and see what a large part of the earth is covered with water. Hold the globe so you are looking at the middle of the Pacific Ocean. a. About how much of the world is covered by the Pacific Ocean alone? b. What do you think would happen to the water cycle if the oceans were only half as large as they are?

New Words and Terms

Pretend that you are explaining these words to someone who has never heard them before.

1. atmosphere
2. wind
3. weather
4. evaporate
5. condense
6. cloud
7. groundwater
8. water cycle

Thinking Together

1. Try to imagine what the world would be like with no atmosphere. Name some of the things that would be missing without an atmosphere.

2. If there are no clouds in the sky and the wind is calm, how can you prove to someone that there is air all around us?

3. Anything that gravity holds to the earth is said to have weight. Did you know that the air around us has weight? Check your encyclopedia under "atmosphere" and "atmospheric pressure" to find out how much the atmosphere weighs.

4. What are some things which cause weather? Check "weather" in an encyclopedia. Describe the weather in your area today.

5. Solid water (ice) weighs less than liquid water. Because of this, when ice forms it stays on the top of a lake or pond. a. What do you think would happen if ice were heavier than liquid water? b. What would this do to plant and animal life in the water?

6. a. Name the three forms of water. b. Tell how each of these forms would be used today. c. How would you see each form in your kitchen? d. Which form might never be seen in hot lands?

7. After a rain you see puddles all around on the ground and on paved streets. What happens to the puddles when the sun comes out?

8. a. What is happening when a cloud forms? b. What is happening in the cloud when rain or snow begins to fall from it? c. What is happening when clouds become smaller and seem to disappear?

9. Write a story about an imaginary raindrop that journeys from the land to the ocean and back again.

10. a. What happens to rain that soaks down into the ground instead of evaporating? b. How do we use this water?

in an encyclopedia on "air" and "atmosphere."

2. We often say that certain things are empty when they are full of air. a. What fills an automobile tire? b. What would happen to the tire if it became truly empty?

3. Set a tray or shallow dish of water in a sunny window. Set a similar tray in a dark, cool place. Leave the trays for three days. What happens in each? Why?

4. Find out what a humidifier does. (Perhaps you have one in your own home.)

5. Blow on a mirror or on a piece of cold metal. a. What happens? b. Why?

6. Draw a chart showing the journey of a raindrop in the water cycle.

For You to Do

1. In addition to breathing, in what ways do we use air? See articles

5. God Made Climate

You have already learned that weather is the condition of the atmosphere around us. Today's weather may be cloudy or clear, cold or hot, rainy or dry. Tomorrow's weather may be very different.

The weather over a long period of time is called **climate.** Perhaps you can expect warm, showery summers and cold, snowy winters in your community. If so, people who study climate would say that you are living in a continental, moist climate. If you live in a place where very little rain or snow falls, you live in a desert climate.

The climate in your community is the kind of weather conditions you can expect year after year. Weather changes from day to day, month to month, and year to year. But you can expect the climate to be about the same from one year to the next. Do you remember the last three or four winters in your area? They give you some idea of what to expect next winter. Next July will be much like last July.

The Bible does not use the word *climate,* but it does tell about the climate of Palestine and other Bible lands. In the Book of Job we learn, "Fair weather cometh out of the north." A person who lives in Palestine learns to expect sunny, cooler weather when the wind blows from the north. This is part of

Job 37:22a

the climate.

What do you expect in your community when the wind blows from the north? From the south? From the east? All this is part of your climate.

Why Is Climate Important?

Imagine that you and your family are moving to a new place in a faraway state or province. You will need to know about the climate there. Your knowledge will prepare you for work and play when you arrive.

What kind of climate do you think this place has? Is it a wet or a dry climate? Do you think the climate here is a cold climate or a warm one?

64

Climate and Clothing. If you plan to move to a place with a warm climate, such as Georgia or Arizona, you will not need many heavy coats. If you were moving to Minnesota or Alberta, you would be sorry if you did not take along plenty of warm clothing. The winters are always much colder in those northern places than in the south.

If you plan to move to Georgia, you will want to sell your ice skates before you leave. In Minnesota you may want your skates and plenty of warm clothing for outdoor work and play.

Climate and Shelter. Did you ever think about the fact that houses, barns, and other buildings might be different in different climates? Houses in cold climates must have plenty of insulation against the cold. In warm places houses may have thick walls and insulation to keep out the heat. In the south your new home may have a ceiling fan or air conditioning. In the north neither of these is necessary. In the south your father's barn may be open on one side to let in plenty of fresh air. The cows will spend much of their time outside all year. In the north barns will be built for warmth and protection from blizzards and cold.

Climate and Crops. If you move to a new community, you will need to know about the climate so you will know what crops to raise. If you move to Alberta, you will discover that the summers are too short to grow some crops, including corn. If your father is a farmer, he might want to raise wheat, barley, oats, sugar beets, or flaxseed, which are leading crops in Alberta. He would need to purchase equipment to irrigate his crops. In Alberta, a rainfall of 10 to 15 inches (25 to 38 cm) each year is normal.

In your garden in Alberta, you could grow greens, green beans, squash, strawberries, potatoes, and other vegetables that do well in cool climates with short summers.

If you moved to Georgia, however, your father could grow many crops different from those in the north. He could grow corn, soybeans, cotton, and even rice. He may not need irrigation equipment unless he plans to grow rice. Most years he can expect 40 to 50 inches (102 to 127 cm) of rainfall.

In the vegetable garden you could grow corn, sweet potatoes, melons, peanuts, and other crops that need long, warm summers.

What Causes Climate?

God planned climates and the things that help make them. Long ago God told the psalmist the main cause of climate, the sun. "The day is thine, the night also is thine: thou hast prepared the light and the sun. Thou hast set all the borders of the earth: thou hast made summer and winter." **Psalm 74:16, 17**

65

Have you ever noticed that almost always nights are colder than days? The sun warms the earth during the day. At night the earth cools. The coolest part of the day is usually just before sunrise.

When the sun rises, the air becomes warmer. As the earth turns, the sun moves more nearly overhead. The day becomes warmer because the more direct rays of the sun from high in the sky are warmer than the slanted, spread-out rays of the morning. As the sun sinks into the west, its rays become more slanted and less direct. Evening is cooler again.

From the daily path of the sun across the sky you learn that the more nearly overhead the sun is, the more direct are its rays and the warmer the weather becomes.

Direct Rays Warm the Earth. Near the equator the sun shines almost directly overhead at noon every day of the year. Places where the sun is directly overhead for at least part of the year are called the **tropics.** The climate zone map shows you where the tropics are located. The edges of the tropics are shown as two lines called the Tropic of Cancer and the Tropic of Capricorn. Which is north of the equator? Which is south?

Because of the direct rays from the sun, most places in the tropics are warm or hot all year. We say these places have tropical climates.

Slanted Rays Are Cooler. People who live or visit near the North and South Poles see the sun very low in the sky during most of the year, even at noon. The sun's rays meet the earth at a slant as they do in the early morning at your house. The rays stay slanted all day. It is always cool or cold near the poles because the slanted rays of the sun do not warm the earth much.

The Arctic and Antarctic Circles mark off what are called the **polar regions.** Every place within these two circles has at least a few days each year when the sun does not rise at all. The weather is coldest during the long winter nights. In summer the sun shines most of the day but stays very low in the sky.

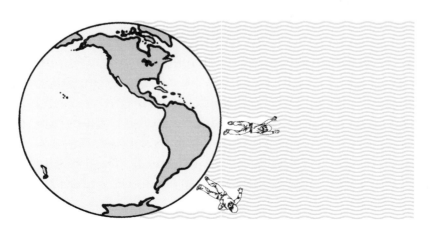

The boy standing closest to the equator has the sun shining directly on top of his head. Nearer the North and South Poles the sun is low in the sky and the rays are slanted.

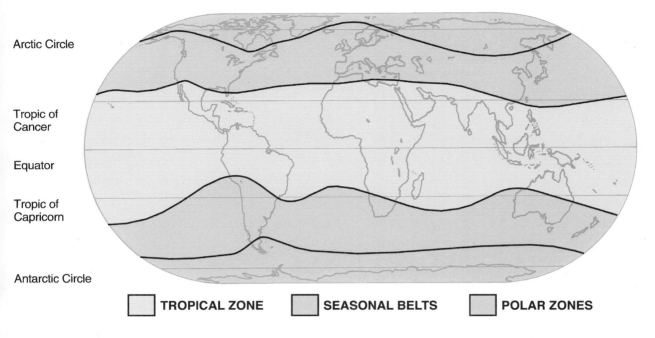

Arctic Circle

Tropic of
Cancer

Equator

Tropic of
Capricorn

Antarctic Circle

□ TROPICAL ZONE   □ SEASONAL BELTS   □ POLAR ZONES

Changing Rays. Between the polar regions and the tropical regions are places where the sun's rays change during the year. During the winter the sun is low in the sky and its rays are slanted. In summer the sun is high in the sky and its rays are more direct. These places are called the **seasonal belts** or temperate zones. The area between the Tropic of Cancer and the Arctic Circle is called the north seasonal belt. Where is the south seasonal belt?

In the seasonal belts the summers are warm or hot because of the sun's direct rays. Winters are cool or cold because of the sun's slanted rays. If you live in the United States or Canada, you likely live in the north seasonal belt. In the United States only Hawaii is in the tropics. Find North America on the map above. In what part of North America would you need to live to be in the polar zone?

Why do the Seasons Change?

Look at the picture on page 68 of the earth's path around the sun. You can see that the earth is tilted on its axis. The axis is an imaginary rod through the center of the earth connecting the North Pole and the South Pole. Some globes have rods through them and are tilted as the earth itself is tilted. As the earth travels around the sun, it remains tilted in the same direction.

Summer. During part of the earth's journey around the sun, the North Pole is tilted toward the sun. The sun shines more directly on the northern half or **hemisphere** of the earth than on the southern half. When this happens, we in the **Northern Hemisphere** have summer. The sun is high in the sky. Its rays are direct and warm.

67

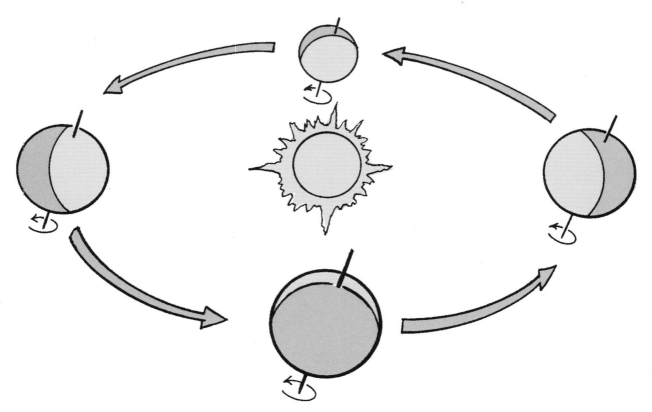

As the earth goes around the sun, the seasons change. When the North Pole is tilted toward the sun, the Northern Hemisphere has summer. See the globe on the left. The Southern Hemisphere has summer when the South Pole is tilted toward the sun, as the globe on the right shows.

As the earth turns on its axis, places near the North Pole do not turn into nighttime. The sun shines all the time day after day. These places have what is sometimes called "the midnight sun." Can you guess why?

Winter. Six months after summer in the Northern Hemisphere the earth has circled halfway around the sun. Now the Northern Hemisphere tilts away from the sun. We see the sun low in the southern sky. The air is colder. At places near the North Pole, the sun does not rise for weeks and even months. The Northern Hemisphere is having winter.

Spring and Fall. Twice during the earth's orbit the sun shines directly on the equator. Neither the North Pole nor the South Pole is tilted toward the sun. When this happens, every place on earth has days and nights of equal length. In the north and south seasonal belts, the weather is cooler than in summer.

Seasons in the Tropics. The tropics never tilt very far away from the sun. There is not much difference between the warmest and the coolest months. People in the tropics do not speak of winter and summer as we do in the north seasonal belt. Some places in the tropics have a rainy season and a dry season each year. Rainfall, not temperature, makes the seasons.

Seasons in Polar Lands. People who live in polar lands may speak of summer and winter, but these seasons are not the same as summer and winter farther south. Summer is the time of very long hours of daylight.

Which place has the warmer climate? Which is colder? Why could the trees not live close to where the seal does? Do you think the seal could live in the tropical forest?

During part of the summer the sun does not set at all. Later in the summer the sun sets for several hours, but the sky does not become completely dark. Summers are cool in polar lands. The cold winters may last for nine months.

Seasons in the Southern Hemisphere. The South Pole is always tilted in the opposite direction from the North Pole. When the North Pole is tilted toward the sun, the South Pole is tilted away from the sun. The seasons are exactly opposite. When the Northern Hemisphere has summer, the Southern Hemisphere has winter. When winter arrives in the Northern Hemisphere, the Southern Hemisphere has summer.

In the United States and Canada we think of cold weather and perhaps snow when we think about Christmas. In Australia and New Zealand young people think about the hot summertime and summer vacations.

What Do You Say?

1. What is climate?

2. Here are three pairs of sentences. Which sentence in each pair describes weather? Which describes climate?

a. Two inches of rain fell in Montreal last night.
b. The average yearly rainfall in Montreal is 37 inches (94 centimeters).

a. On a July day in Washington, D.C., you can expect the temperature to be around 88° F (31° C).
b. It was 95° in Washington, D.C., today.

a. The usual date of the last killing frost in our community is May 1.
b. This spring the last killing frost came on May 13.

3. What is the main cause of climate?

4. a. Name the world's climate regions beginning at the North Pole and going to the South Pole.
b. In which region could you find a place that has 15 hours of daylight in summer? c. A place that has sunlight 24 hours a day in July? d. A place that has days and nights about 12 hours long all year?

What Does the Bible Say?

1. a. What does Genesis 8:22 say

70

about the earth's climates?
b. What can we expect in the future?

2. According to Proverbs 25:23a, what does a north wind do to the climate of Palestine?

A Trip to the Tropics

Would you like to take a trip from your country to the Amazon River in South America? January is a good time to go, especially if you want to escape the cold in the north. Follow the journey on a map or globe. You will be traveling from the north seasonal belt to the tropics.

You will leave by plane from New York City on a Monday morning in January. As you leave, the temperature is a chilly 20° F (−7° C), not unusual for New York City in January. A six-inch blanket of snow covers the ground. The winter sun is low in the southern sky.

You will fly from New York City to Miami, Florida. From there you will take another plane to Brazil and the Amazon River. A few hours after leaving New York, you land in Miami. How warm it feels when you step out of the plane! Someone says that the temperature is 65° F (18° C). By afternoon it will be 70° F (21° C) or more, quite normal for January in Miami.

You plan to spend the afternoon sightseeing in sunny Miami. The sun

rain forest

is higher in the sky at noon in Miami than in New York City. Here you are much closer to the equator. You expect Miami to be much warmer than places far to the North. Miami is only about 150 miles (240 kilometers) north of the Tropic of Cancer.

At 7 p.m. you board the big Varig airbus, AB 300, which will take you to Brazil. *Varig* is the name of one of Brazil's most famous airlines. From Miami you will fly nonstop to Belém (bə lem′), Brazil, near the mouth of the Amazon River. Your trip will be 2,835 miles (4,573 kilometers) long and will take a little

71

This is a steamship traveling along the Amazon River in Brazil.

The Amazon River is the second longest river in the world. Only the Nile River in Egypt is longer. The Amazon contains far more water than the Nile and the Mississippi Rivers together. The Mississippi is the largest river in North America.

The Amazon River flows from the Andes Mountains in western South America across northern Brazil to the Atlantic Ocean.

The Amazon flows through the world's largest **rain forest**. Rain falls almost every day in many parts of the rain forest. The rain causes trees to grow as high as 200 feet (61 meters). Trees and vines

less than six hours.

Soon after leaving Miami, you cross the Tropic of Cancer. From there the plane flies over lands and seas that stay warm all year. Just before landing in Belém, you cross the equator. Even if it were daylight outside, you would not see a line on the water and land below. But your globes and maps tell you that you are exactly halfway between the two poles. Here is a land of unending summer.

Just before 3 a.m., Belém time, you land at this large Brazilian port city. Belém lies about 90 miles (145 kilometers) from the Atlantic Ocean on the Pará (pə rä′) River. The Pará is one of the mouths of the mighty Amazon River.

As you travel along the Amazon River, you may see little clearings like this with just a few houses. Why do you think more people do not live along the Amazon?

These are some of the animals and plants found in the Amazon rain forest in Brazil.

are so thick that only a few rays of sunshine spill through to the forest floor.

Into the Rain Forest. After sunrise you board a small steamboat at the busy harbor in Belém. A cabin and a roof over much of the boat protects you from the hot sun and the rain.

The steamboat stays close to the shore and makes frequent stops at little villages along the river. After you leave Belém and move into the main stream of the Ama-

zon, the river is so wide that you cannot see the opposite shore. You feel almost as though you are sailing along the edge of the ocean.

As you sail upstream, you pass mile after mile of thick forest which comes right to the edge of the river. Here and there you spot enough land cleared for a single hut or for a small village. Very few people live in the rain forest. Can you guess why?

People who live in the rain forest must work hard to clear the land of the thick growth of plants. If the cleared land is left to itself, the forest soon takes over again.

In most parts of the rain forest the rich soil is thin and not the best for farming. The heavy rains wash the rich nutrients away. After a few years, the soil no longer produces good crops. Farmers must clear new land. Too much rain is almost as bad for farming as too little rain.

The first afternoon of your journey you notice towering masses of clouds forming in the sky overhead. Suddenly the sky grows dark. Thunder crashes and rain very suddenly begins to pour. The downpour may last an hour and then stop as suddenly as it began. As evening comes, the sky clears.

On your second day, you pass more jungle. The next day is much the same. Day after day you sail through the jungles. The dampness or humidity makes the hot sun feel even more hot. The first few nights you have trouble sleeping because of the noise of parrots squawking and monkeys chattering in the trees. Occasionally you hear the bellow of an alligator. The rain forest is teeming with birds, insects, and larger animals.

The temperature in the daytime reaches about 80° F (27° C) and almost never higher than 90° F (32° C). The long nights may cool down to the upper 60s and low 70s (about 20° C). Almost every state and province in the United States and Canada has recorded 100° F (38° C) or above in the summer. The

weather has never been that hot in the rain forest of the Amazon. The clouds, rainfall, and twelve-hour nights throughout the year keep the temperature from reaching 100° F.

Your journey up the Amazon could go on for days and days. Boats can travel all the way to Peru, about 2,300 miles (3,700 kilometers) from the Atlantic Ocean.

A Journey to the Far North

"He giveth snow like wool: he scattereth the hoarfrost like ashes. He casteth forth his ice like morsels: who can stand before his cold?" **Psalm 147:16, 17**

A journey to the far north is very different from a journey to the hot rain forest of South America. You will need to travel in the middle of the summer. Winters are bitterly cold and dark in the lands of the far north. Even in summer you will need warm clothing.

The best way to see the far north is to travel by airplane, touching down now and then to see certain places more closely. Follow this journey on the map on page 75. On this trip let us leave from Chicago in the U.S.A. July is usually hot in Chicago. The temperature is usually in the 80s but sometimes soars into the 90s. It has reached as high as 104° F (40° C). The sun is high in the sky and shines for over 15 hours a day. Fewer clouds and less rain than in the South American rain forest make many summer days hotter in Chicago than along the Amazon! The

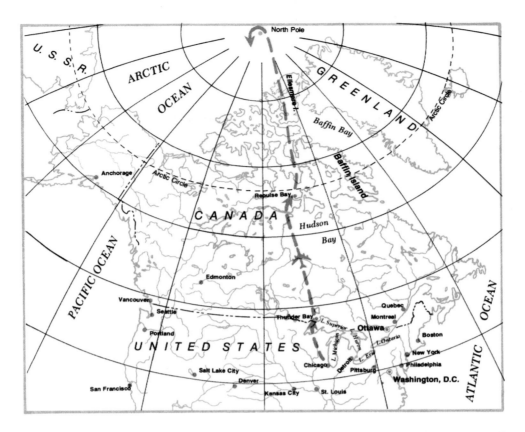

This map shows the route an airplane might take from Chicago to the North Pole. Through what countries does the plane pass?

weather may feel hotter along the Amazon because of all the moisture in the air. We say that it feels "sticky" if the air is hot and very moist.

As you fly north from Chicago, notice the patchwork of towns and farmlands to your left. Lake Michigan lies to your right. You fly over Wisconsin. As you travel farther north in Wisconsin, you see less open land and more forest. Fir trees become more and more numerous. Trees that lose their leaves become fewer, for they cannot stand long, bitterly cold winters. By the time we reach the northern peninsula of Michigan and Lake Superior, we see even more fir trees. Across the

lake in Canada we see great fir forests. Our first stop will be Thunder Bay, Ontario, along the northern shore of Lake Superior.

The summer air feels warm. We learn that here the temperature has reached as high as 97° F (36° C). The summers are warm but very short. Frost may come as late as early June and then again in early September. Winter lasts from November to April. Summer days are very long here at Thunder Bay, with more than 17 hours of sunshine. The long days explain why summers can be so warm this far north.

We board our plane to continue our journey north. We fly over hundreds of miles of forests and lakes in

75

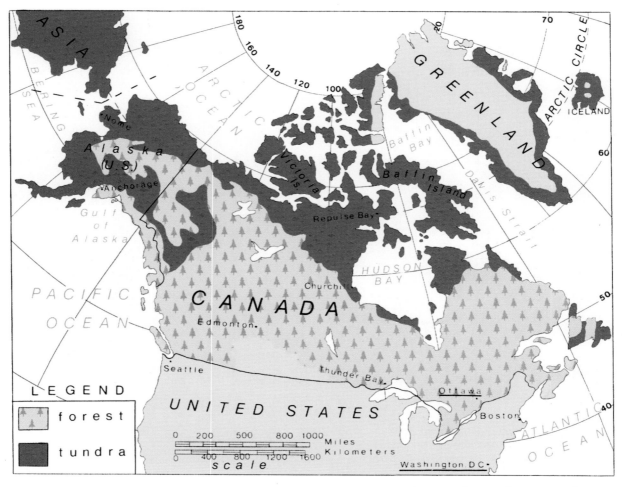

Forests cover most of Canada. North of the great forests lies the marshy tundra covered with mosses, grasses, and bushes.

This photo was taken near the tree line in northwestern Manitoba, Canada. The low places have patches of tundra covered with mosses.

northwestern Ontario. Few people have chosen to live in the great northern forest.

After several hundred miles of flying, we begin to see open spaces in the forest. The trees become smaller and fewer in number. We are leaving the great forest and are entering a land so cold that fir trees will not grow.

Ahead we see something which looks like the ocean. According to our map this must be Hudson Bay. Our plane flies over the western part of the bay for several hundred miles. Then we head inland again. Now we

76

are flying over low, flat land covered with grasses, flowers, and a few low shrubs. Snow covers the ground for about nine months each year. This land is called the Arctic **tundra**. *Tundra* is a Russian word meaning "a marshy plain."

Our plane lands on the tundra at Repulse Bay. We are at the Arctic Circle. The time is 10:30 p.m. and we discover that the sun is still shining! Nights here in midsummer are very short. The sun sets for a while, but the night does not become completely dark. On June 21 the sun shines all day and all night from the Arctic Circle to the North Pole. At the North Pole the sun shines all the time for six months.

Summers at Repulse Bay are cool. Frost can be expected during any month. The cold winter lasts from September to May. In midwinter the sun shines only briefly each day. From the Arctic Circle to the North Pole the sun does not rise at all during part of the winter.

No crops can be grown in Arctic lands. During the short, cool summer, flowers bloom and grasses grow. But deep down the ground stays frozen all year. This frozen ground is called **permafrost**.

On our plane again we fly north from Repulse Bay to Ellesmere Island, the northernmost place in Canada. Even in summer much of the island is covered with ice and snow. **The sun shines 24 hours a day, but it is so low in the sky that its rays do not warm the air much above freezing. The ocean around**

Pictured here are a winter and a summer scene in the Arctic tundra. Why are not more plants, bushes, and trees growing in the summer?

polar
bear

seal

lemming

whale

reindeer

These animals are found on the land and in the sea in North America's Arctic region.

Ellesmere Island is covered with floating pieces of ice. In the dark winter, the ocean is frozen.

North of Ellesmere Island lies the Arctic Ocean. The North Pole is in the middle of the Arctic Ocean about 500 miles (800 kilometers) from the northern tip of Ellesmere Island. We can fly over the North Pole, but we cannot land there because of thin ice.

The North Pole is not a real pole at all. No marker tells us when we arrive. Instruments on our plane tell us when we have reached the northernmost place on Earth. The cold, white, ice-covered Arctic Ocean is all we can see in every direction.

We are glad when our plane turns back toward home in warmer lands. We are glad for the climates God has given us with bright hours of summer sunshine. God "giveth us richly all things to enjoy," including climates.

1 Timothy 6:17b

What Do You Say?

1. Describe the climate in the rain forest of Brazil.

2. Why does the temperature in the rain forest never go as high as some summertime temperatures in much of the U.S.A. and Canada?

78

3. Tell about the climate in the far north.

4. Why do crops not grow in the Arctic?

What Does the Bible Say?

1. Turn to Job 37:5-13. a. Name some great things God does to the earth's weather. b. Name the three different purposes for the weather God sends.

2. Read Psalm 65:9, 10. Name the good things the Lord does for the earth. (The word *corn* used here means "grain.")

3. Read Amos 4:6-8. How did God use rain to punish the people?

Chapter Five Review

Using Globes and Maps

1. Find a globe that is tilted on its axis as the earth is. Darken the room as much as possible. Place a light on a table or desk. Walk around the table with the globe in your hand. Keep the North Pole always tilted in the same direction. When is North America having "summer"? When is it having winter? Spring? Fall?

2. On a globe point out the tropics, the north seasonal belt, the south seasonal belt, and the polar regions. In which of these belts is Illinois (U.S.A.), Venezuela (South America), Argentina (South America), Great Britain, Greenland?

3. Stand several feet from a chalkboard. Point a flashlight straight at the board. Have someone else draw a chalk line around the lighted area. Now shine the light at an angle onto the board. Circle the lighted area. The places in the world that receive the sun's rays from overhead receive more sunlight on a smaller area. The rays are stronger and warmer than slanted rays.

4. In an encyclopedia, find an article on "Tropical Rain Forest." If the article shows a map of the tropical rain forests, study the rain forest areas. Then on your classroom globe or world map point out the world's tropical rain forests.

New Words and Terms

The following statements use the new words and terms in this chapter. Are the statements true or false? If the statement is false, change it to make it true.

1. _____ Your *climate* is the weather in your community today.

2. _____ People who live in the *tropics* usually have cool weather for a few months of the year.

3. _____ The *Tropic of Cancer* is found in the Northern Hemisphere.

4. _____ The temperature is always cold or cool in the *polar regions*.

5. _____ The *seasonal belts* have daylight for about the same amount of time each day during the year.

6. _____ The earth rotates on its *axis*.

7. _____ A *hemisphere* is a half of the earth.

8. _____ Places that have *seasons* have different kinds of weather at different times of the year.

9. _____ The *midnight sun* is seen only near the equator.

10. _____ It is always warm and rainy in a *rain forest*.

11. _____ The *tundra* is too cold for trees to grow.

12. _____ Ground that thaws out for at least three months each year is called *permafrost*.

Thinking Together

1. How would you describe your climate to someone moving into your community? What would he need to know about shelter, clothing, and crops?

2. Sometimes the weather is unusual for the climate of a place. There may be a freeze in south central Florida, floods in a desert, or a heat wave in Alaska. Can you remember any unusual weather in your community? Ask your parents to tell you of unusual weather they may remember.

3. How would the climate be different in your area if the earth did not tilt on its axis so that the sun

always shone directly overhead at the equator? (Hint: Describe the weather in your community at the times of year when the sun shines overhead at the equator—spring and fall.)

4. a. What would happen to the seasons in your province or state if the North Pole always tilted toward the sun? b. What would happen if the South Pole always tilted toward the sun?

5. a. How would the temperatures in your area be different if you had much more cloudiness and fog? b. If you had desert conditions? c. If you had shorter days?

6. What do you think would happen to the earth's climates if the earth started moving closer to the sun? Farther away from the sun?

7. How has God "done all things well" as far as climate is concerned?

For You to Do

1. Keep a record of the weather conditions at noon or at recess each day for the next week. Your teacher will need to place a rain gauge away from buildings and trees and place a thermometer in a shaded location. Record temperature, rainfall (if any), and sky condition (cloudy, partly cloudy, clear). Repeat this experiment in January and again in May. How are your three records different?

2. Draw a picture of the skyline west of your house. (Include buildings, trees, hills, mountains, behind which the sun appears to set in the evenings.) On this drawing, mark the place where the sun sets in summer. Also mark the place where it sets in winter. Ask your parents to help you if you do not remember. At what place does the sun appear to set this week?

3. Suppose you have a friend who lives in the tropics. Write him a letter explaining the seasons in your community. Be sure to explain carefully the things he never sees, such as ice, frost, snow, the sun at different places in the sky, and the changes in plant life through the seasons.

4. Ask your teacher to set up an outdoor thermometer in a shaded or northerly spot. For the next week keep records of the temperatures when you arrive at school and at one o'clock or two o'clock. Which time of day was usually warmer? Why?

5. An encyclopedia normally describes the climate of each American state and Canadian province as well as of each major country. Read an article on a state or province besides your own and give a report on its climate, written or oral, as your teacher directs. Read about the climate of a foreign country and report on it.

The Lands God Gave Us— The Americas

Unit 2

What you will learn . . . in unit two

We will begin our study of the world close to home. There are several good reasons for starting at home. For one thing, home is the place we know best. We can often learn things at home that help us to understand other places better. If we learn about natural resources at home, we learn facts that will help us study natural resources in other places.

When we study about our own country or continent, we find out how much more there is to learn. There are always more interesting facts to learn about a land so vast as the Americas.

Another important reason for learning more about our own part of the world is so we can appreciate it more. We can learn to be more thankful for the natural resources and beauty of our own homeland by studying it. As you study the Americas, thank God for the lands He has given us.

Each continent and country has its own unique people. Our studies of people around the world will help us better understand them. To understand people helps us to get along with them when we meet them. Understanding people helps us know better how to show them the love of Christ and tell them of their need for salvation.

6. Our New World Neighbors

Deuteronomy 4:17b

Where can you find large deserts, hundreds of snowcapped mountains, vast frozen lands, and the largest rain forest in the world? This land also has some of the world's best farmland. This land of great beauty is found on the continents of North America and South America. It is "the good land which the LORD giveth" to us and to our neighbors.

The countries of the Americas are our closest neighbors on the earth. Two large oceans lie between the Americas and the rest of the world. Name these two oceans.

When mapmakers draw maps of the Americas, they often show the two continents in the middle of one-half of the earth. The other half of the earth is Europe, Asia, Africa, and Australia. Our half of the earth is called the **Western Hemisphere**. The other half of the earth is the **Eastern Hemisphere**. Hemisphere means "half a globe."

We will begin our trip around God's earth from the place most of us know best—North America. We will first study about North America. Then we will study about neighboring South America.

Most of us have lived in North America all our lives. Perhaps your parents and grandparents have lived here all their lives. To you our continent may seem like an old land. People have lived in the Americas for a long time. Some of the first people to come from Europe called the Americas the **New World**. The land

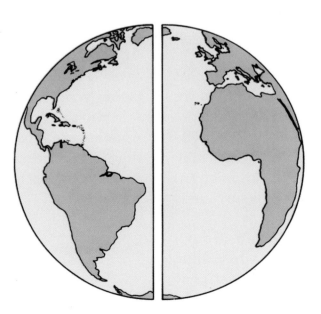

Western
Hemisphere

Eastern
Hemisphere

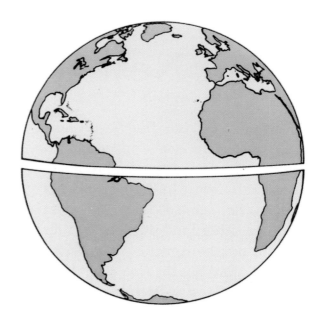

Northern Hemisphere

Southern Hemisphere

was brand new to them. But the Americas were not a new world to the American Indians who already lived here. We will begin our study of God's earth in the "New World." Then we will study the "Old World."

Looking at the Americas. Suppose you could look down on North America and South America from a spaceship. What would you see? You could not see all of both continents unless you were many thousands of miles out in space.

North America reaches almost to the North Pole. An island in Canada is only 500 miles (800 kilometers) from the North Pole. The southern tip of South America is only about 600 miles (960 kilometers) from icy Antarctica which surrounds the South Pole.

North America and South America are shaped somewhat alike. The northern part of each continent is very wide. The southern part of

each continent is very narrow.

Very high mountains lie in the western part of both continents. Some of these mountains rise to four miles or more above the ocean. They are covered with snow in summer and winter. The eastern part of both continents has mountains too. These mountains are not nearly as high as the western mountains.

Between the eastern mountains and the western mountains of both continents you will see vast flatlands. In some places these **plains** are covered with waving grasses. In other places great forests cover the land.

North America and South America are alike in some ways. But they are different in many, many ways. Are you ready to explore the Americas?

The Shape of the Land

What does the land look like near your home and school? Is it flat?

86

Perhaps it is hilly or mountainous. In North America you can find almost any shape of land possible. We call the shape of the land the *landform*. The map shows you something about the shape of the land in North America. It shows some of the largest mountain regions and the largest plain region in the United States.

If you fly from the Pacific Ocean to the Atlantic Ocean, you will see many of these regions. Imagine for a few minutes that you are flying this route.

Your plane is flying from Hawaii in the middle of the Pacific Ocean. The first thing you see as you near the coast of California is mountains. As you fly nearer, the mountains seem to rise from the ocean. Very little lowland lies along the Pacific Coast of North America. The mountains and valleys along the Pacific Ocean are called the *Pacific Mountain and Valley Region.*

As you cross the Coast Ranges of California, you cross the wide Central Valley. Then you see another chain of mountains rising from the valley floor ahead. These are the snowcapped Sierra Nevada (sē er′ ə nə vad′ ə). *Sierra Nevada* means "snowy mountain range" in Spanish. High above the earth the air is always cold. So it is always cold on top of the Sierra Nevada. Snow usually falls there instead of rain.

Beyond the Sierra Nevada you fly over rough-looking land. There are some flatlands in places. Mountains rise here and there. You see some narrow, steep-sided river val-

Here is a map of the landforms of the United States. This map shows the names of various groups of mountains and plains. On this map, can you find the landform regions named in the text?

United States—LANDFORMS

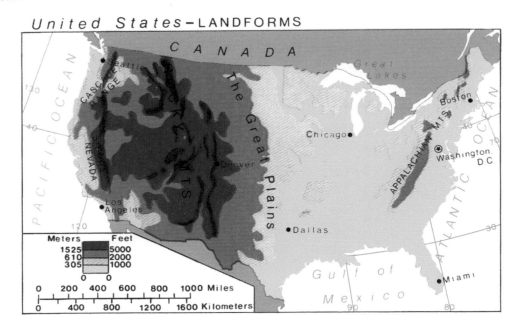

These mountains are found in the Rocky Mountains region. Notice how steep and sharp these mountain peaks are.

leys called **canyons**. This area is called the *Intermountain Region* because it lies between the Coast Ranges to the west and the Rocky Mountains to the east.

The Rocky Mountains ahead of you are snow covered the year around. They stretch all the way from New Mexico to northern Alaska. You can see how the Rocky Mountains earned their name. The tops of these mountains are rocky, with little soil. Great forests grow on the lower slopes of many of these mountains. Fewer people live in the Rocky Mountain region of the United States than in any other part of the country. Can you guess why?

After you cross the Rockies, suddenly you see flat land. Here begin the vast plains that cover much of the middle of North America. In the United States these plains are over 1,000 miles (1,600 kilometers) wide. You will need several hours to fly over them. In the middle of these plains flows the great Mississippi River.

Finally you reach the Appalachian Mountains in eastern North America. They are much lower than the Rocky Mountains. Most of them are covered with forests to the very top. They are not covered with snow except in winter.

As you cross the last of the Appalachian Mountains, you see hilly land. In a few minutes you are flying again over land that is nearly flat.

These farmlands near Aberdeen, South Dakota, are in the Central Plains region of North America. Why is this land called a "plain"?

These forest-covered mountains are found in the Appalachian region of eastern North America. How are these mountains different from those in the picture of the Rocky Mountains?

This is part of the Atlantic Coastal Plain. This plain follows the Atlantic coast of the United States to the southern tip of Florida. The widest part of the plain is in the southeastern United States.

In which of these great land regions do you live? In which is Florida? Most of Ohio? Manitoba? Utah?

What Do You Say?

1. What is the Western Hemisphere?

2. In what ways are North America and South America alike?

3. What are some landforms you see in a trip across North America?

4. What are the six main landform regions of North America from west to east?

What Does the Bible Say?

1. Read Psalm 24:1. a. What belongs to the Lord? b. Can you name anything that does not belong to Him?

2. Very few people have looked down on the earth from a spaceship. Do you know that the Bible speaks of someone looking down on the earth? Who looked down and why? (Read Psalm 14:2).

3. The people in North America and South America are our nearest neighbors on our big world. How should we feel about these neighbors? (Read Galatians 5:14).

The First Americans

Many people have wished they could go back in time to visit the people of long ago. Of course, we all know that we cannot do that. Try to imagine what life was like at that time.

The first people who lived in North America were called native Americans or **American Indians.** Columbus saw some Native Americans in 1492 when he first visited the Americas. He called the people *Indians* because he thought he had discovered some islands near India. While the people he saw were not from India, they still are often called Indians. If we are always careful to say "American Indians," we will remember that these people are not from India.

When Columbus first saw America, there may have been about 50 million American Indians in all of

This illustration shows a village of the Eastern Woodland Indians of North America. Some Indians farther west used cone-shaped dwellings called tepees.

The arrows on this map show the way scientists believe the American Indians spread through the Americas. The Bible teaches us that the first people lived in Asia. So it seems reasonable that the first people in America came from the part of Asia closest to the Americas. The arrows begin in Asia, near the top of the map.

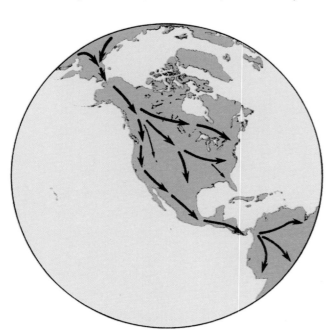

North America and South America. Indian villages could be found scattered through the vast wilderness.

Where? When? How?

How did the first American Indians arrive here? From where did they come? When did they come?

Most people who have studied Native Americans believe they came from Asia thousands of years ago. The small map shows the route they may have traveled across the Bering Strait between Russia and Alaska. Perhaps the narrow strip of water was frozen over. Some believe that lowland once covered the place where the Bering Strait is today. These first settlers in the Americas probably spread south in search of new land and warmer weather. Finally they had spread all the way to the southern tip of South America.

Are there any hints that the American Indians might have come from Asia? Many American Indians look somewhat like the brown-skinned people of eastern Asia. The Eskimos look a little like the Chinese people.

The Bible teaches that people spread from Asia to other parts of the earth. Noah and his family left the ark in the mountains of Ararat, in Asia. The tower of Babel was in Asia. It seems reasonable that people spread across Asia and then crossed the Bering Strait to Alaska.

Indian gods. Did the American Indians know about the true God? When the first white people came to the Americas, they found Indians worshiping many gods. If they ever

Another Story

Most American Indians, no doubt, came from Asia. However, some people believe that some of them may have come by boat from Europe or Africa. Some American Indians are light-skinned and look more like people from Europe than from Asia.

We know that in Bible times a people called Phoenicians built strong ships and sailed from Palestine in Asia to the Atlantic Ocean. Did they reach the Americas?

The Indians in Mexico used to tell a strange story about a man who came by boat from the east. As the story goes, he was a white-skinned, bearded man who landed on the coast of Mexico. The Indians called him Quetzalcoatl (ket säl′ kwät′ əl). Quetzalcoatl taught the people how to farm and how to use metals. He also gave them a calendar. Later the Indians worshiped him as a god.

Quetzalcoatl finally left in a boat and sailed east toward the rising of the sun. What was this ocean to the east of Mexico? Look at a map if you do not know.

Quetzalcoatl promised to return again someday. When the first white men came from Europe to Mexico almost 500 years ago, some of the Indians thought Quetzalcoatl had returned!

Archaeologists, those who study things that were made and used by people of long ago, are at work in Mexico and many other places. Will they discover that people sailed from Europe to America thousands of years ago? Perhaps they will find the remains of ancient boats from Europe or of coins used in Bible times.

The Aztec god Quetzalcoatl is shown here carved on the side of a bowl.

knew of the true God, they had forgotten about Him.

Many Indians worshiped a rain god. They hoped their corn, potatoes, and other crops would be watered. Some worshiped spirits they thought lived in mountains, trees, and rocks. Some made images of their gods from wood and stone. The Indians around what is now Mexico City worshiped the white-skinned god Quetzalcoatl about whom you read earlier. Most Indians feared evil spirits and honored or worshiped the spirits of the dead.

Some white men tried to force the Indians to accept white men's ways and beliefs. A few other white men cared for the Indians enough to tell them about Jesus Christ.

Gifts From the American Indians.
The first settlers from Europe saw the

Indians eating many foods no one in Europe had ever seen. The settlers had never seen corn, pumpkin, squash, potatoes, tomatoes, sweet potatoes, lima beans, or green beans. Indians taught the newcomers how to raise some of these delicious vegetables.

Some Indians in what is now Mexico made a drink of ground cacao (kə kā′ ō) beans. They called the drink "chocolate." They believed chocolate was a food for the gods. Only a few very important people were allowed to drink it.

The vegetables the Indians grew have spread around the world. Russia, Poland, and China each grow more

This picture shows a Mayan Indian calendar stone. The Mayas had a 365 day calendar and knew much about the movement of the sun and stars. The Mayas lived in Central America south of where the Aztecs lived.

potatoes than does any country in the Americas. Potatoes were first grown by Indians in South America.

Corn was also first grown by the Indians. Today people around the world depend on corn for much of their grain. Corn, wheat, rice, and potatoes are the four leading food crops in the world. Which two came to us through the American Indians?

Keep a record of the foods you eat today and tomorrow. How many of the vegetables were first grown by the Indians? Do you ever go a day without eating some of these "Indian" foods? A favorite dish of the Indians was succotash (sək′ ə tash′), a mixture of corn and lima beans. Ask your mother to prepare succotash sometime.

Name the different uses of corn shown in this picture. Can you think of any other uses of corn? Where did the gift of corn come from?

Wonder Grain From the Indians

In Mexico it is called *maíz* (mä ēs′). In England it is called **maize** (māz), or Indian corn. In the United States and Canada it is called *corn.* This grain is probably the most valuable food the Indians have taught us to raise.

The Indians used corn in many different ways. They roasted it, dried it, ground it into flour, and ate corn on the cob. They removed the outside hull of the grains and cooked the inside. They called this *hominy.* The Indians also raised popcorn, still a favorite treat. The dried grains of this special kind of corn explode when they are heated.

Indians in Mexico sometimes used cornstalks for the sides of their houses and for fences.

Today corn is still used in many of these ways. It is rolled or puffed to make many kinds of breakfast cereals. The oil from corn can be made into margarine. The stalks and the ears are used to feed cattle. Corn can be made into alcohol. This alcohol can be mixed with gasoline and used as fuel. Perhaps someday our machinery and cars will be made to run on alcohol alone.

What Do You Say?

1. a. Why were the first people who lived in the Americas called "Indians"? b. What other names are used for them?

2. How did the first American Indians probably reach the Americas?

3. a. Name at least six vegetables American Indians first raised. b. Which do you eat most at your house?

Rich soil is one of God's richest blessings to the Americas. If this soil is to stay rich, people will need to be careful how they take care of it.

What Does the Bible Say?

1. Read Acts 17:24-26. What is true of white and black Americans as well as of American Indians?

2. We can thank the American Indians for teaching us how to grow and use many new vegetables. Read Psalm 104:1, 14. Whom should everyone thank for these things?

God's Gifts in North America

God planned many good things in North America for those who came here to live. "Every good gift and every perfect gift is from above, and cometh down from the Father of lights." **James 1:17a**

God provided plenty of land in America. Only two continents are larger than North America. They are Asia and Africa. The North American country of Canada covers more land than any other country in the world except Russia.

God planned North America with some of the largest areas of rich farmland in the world. The good land is one of the greatest natural resources on the continent. North America has one of every six acres of

94

The deep waters that tumble over Niagara Falls come from the well-watered inland regions of the United States and Canada. God's gift of water makes possible this beautiful scene.

land in the world and only one out of ten people in the world. North America ships millions of tons of food to other parts of the world.

God Gave Soil. Some of the first white men in North America spent their time hunting for gold. They did not think about the riches at their feet—the soil. A few years later other men and women came who wanted to live and raise their families here. They learned about the rich soil.

Much of the land was once covered with forests and grasses. For thousands of years plants and animals had been dying and decaying on the ground. The soil became richer and richer with humus.

God Gave Water. "I would seek unto God . . . Who giveth rain upon the earth, and sendeth waters upon the fields."

5:8, 10

Our rich soil would do us little good without water to make plants grow. North America is well supplied with water for its people and thirsty fields. Much of the water falls as rain or snow. Most of the eastern half of North America usually receives plenty of rain. Some places along the western coast of North America receive over 100 inches (250 centimeters) of rain each year.

Not all of North America has plenty of rainfall. Some desert areas may receive only a few inches of rain in a year. If you traveled through one of our deserts, you would soon find out that not all of America has plenty of water.

But God has not forgotten the desert lands. He has provided plenty of water at places even in the driest deserts. How can that be?

At some places in the desert, water is found close to the surface of

Here is a desert oasis found in western North America. How can you tell where the oasis is located in this picture?

95

The deserts of the Americas can produce very good crops. In many places the soil is rich. All that is needed is water. This scene from Mexico shows desert land with watered land in the distance.

When drought comes to a well-watered region, rivers sometimes dry up, like this one. Wells also may go dry. Plants, animals, and people may suffer.

the ground. Plants and trees grow there. Such a place is called an **oasis** (ō ā´ sis). The plural of *oasis* is *oases* (ō ā´ sēz). Some oases are very small. Some are so large that several million people may live on them.

Rivers also bring water to some places in the desert. Their waters may be used for drinking or for irrigating nearby land. The water in these rivers comes from places that receive more rain. Some desert rivers begin on the sides of snow-covered mountains. In summer the snow melts and feeds the streams with clear, icy water.

The Colorado River in the United States and Mexico flows mostly through desert land. Hundreds of thousands of acres of land are irrigated with water from this river. Water is piped from the Colorado River to the city of San Diego, California, over 200 miles (320 kilometers) away.

On many rivers men have built dams of earth, stone, or concrete. Large lakes of water collect behind the dams. Pumps push water from the lakes and rivers to irrigate nearby fields. The dams, pumps, and irrigation systems were built by man. Some people forget that God gives the water to fill the rivers. Man's irrigation systems would fail if God did not give the water.

"Great things doeth he [God], which we cannot comprehend. For he saith to the snow, Be thou on the earth; likewise to the small rain, and

96

Job 37:5b-7 to the great rain of his strength. He sealeth up the hand of every man; that all men may know his work."

Other Riches in America. Nearly seven of every ten North Americans live in the United States and Canada. Four out of five acres of land on the continent are found in these two countries.

The people in these two countries are some of the richest in the world. Farmers in the United States alone raise more corn, citrus fruit, tomatoes, and soybeans than farmers in any other country. Also more beef cattle, chickens, and turkeys are raised in the United States than in any other country.

God has also provided many different fuels to warm our homes and run our machinery. About one-third of the world's coal supply is found in North America. This continent supplies one of every five barrels of oil taken from the earth.

Some people in these two North American nations are poor. But most are rich when compared to the poor people in many parts of the world. Many of our "poor" people have electricity, running water, and even automobiles! Millions in the world could not afford these things.

Living in Rich America

David Smith is a fourth grader who lives in southern Ontario, Canada. He lives in the city of Windsor. Nearby is Canada's richest

These pictures show three of the crops that grow well in the rich soil of North America. Corn is the most widely grown crop in North America. Soybeans are grown in many places such as in this field being cultivated by tractor. The orchard below has rows and rows of citrus trees. Citrus fruit such as oranges and grapefruit grow well in the warmer regions of the Americas.

Here is shown an automobile factory in Windsor, Canada. Can you guess what kind of work is done on cars in this plant? You will find a hint on the sign.

farming region. This part of Canada also has hundreds of factories that make almost anything the people need. Making things by machine is

This rich farmland is near Windsor, Canada. In what land region of North America would you think Windsor would be located?

called **manufacturing**. Southern Ontario is Canada's richest manufacturing area.

In Windsor manufacturing automobiles is big business. David's father works in an automobile factory. About 27 of every 100 workers in Windsor help make and sell automobiles or automobile parts.

Most people in Windsor live in fine houses or apartments. David lives in a large home with four bedrooms, two baths, a playroom, and more. His parents own two cars.

When people have plenty of money and the things it can buy, we say they are **prosperous**. David's parents are prosperous. Even the poor people in Windsor are prosperous when compared to many of the world's people who live in tiny huts.

Many people in Windsor and

throughout rich North America put money first. People who care too much for money and the things it can buy are **materialistic.** Anyone who puts "things" before Jesus Christ is materialistic.

Even though a poor person can be materialistic, prosperous people are more likely to put things before Christ.

The Bible warns people everywhere, "They that will be rich fall into temptation and a snare, and into many foolish and hurtful lusts, which drown men in destruction."

1 Timothy 6:9

Riches seem to cause people to forget about God and His Word. "The care of this world, and the deceitfulness of riches, choke the word."

Matthew 13:22b

David Smith enjoys many things some children have never had. He can walk to school. He has already learned to read and write. He will be able to go to high school when he is older. Over half the people in the

world do not read and write.

There are dozens of churches in Windsor. David's family could go to any of them. The family goes to church together at Easter and Christmas. Sometimes David's parents send him to Sunday school.

The Smiths need someone to tell them more about Jesus Christ. They need to accept Him as Lord. Millions of North Americans such as the Smiths need Christ.

In North America we have freedom of religion. We are free to go to church and to witness for Christ. We can tell our friends and neighbors about Him. Take time now to thank God for this freedom.

Large houses with two-car garages show how wealthy some North Americans are. Is it always good for people to be rich? Why not?

What Do You Say?

1. Name the two greatest natural resources God has given North America.

2. Name two ways desert regions may receive enough water for crops.

3. In what ways is North America rich?

4. a. What makes a person materialistic? b. How could a poor person be materialistic?

What Does the Bible Say?

1. From Psalm 147:7, 8 name some good things the Lord has given us.

2. Finish this verse: "Nevertheless he left not himself without witness, in that he did good, and _____" Acts 14:17.

3. Read Proverbs 11:28. What will happen to the person who trusts in riches?

The next part of North America we will study is Mexico. On this map, Mexico stands out in a darker color. Name the two countries in North America to the north of Mexico.

South to Mexico

Three large countries cover most of North America. The largest is Canada. The next largest is the United States. The third large country is Mexico. How would you like to visit this beautiful land to our south?

Though Mexico is not far away, most Canadians and Americans have never been there. Today you can easily visit Mexico by airplane or by car. A trip in a car is the best way for you to see the land and the people.

To enter Mexico you will need to drive south either to Texas, New Mexico, Arizona, or California.

On our imaginary journey we will cross the border at Laredo (lə rād′ ō), Texas. At Laredo we cross into Mexico on a bridge over a river called the Rio Grande (rē′ ō grănd). *Rio Grande* means "great river" in Spanish. Find the Rio Grande River on the map of North America on page 100. You will find it south of the United States along the northern border of Mexico.

You look down in surprise at the little river below you. You could almost wade over it in places. Dry weather along the Rio Grande causes it to be small. Farmers in the United States and Mexico use the water for irrigating thirsty fields. No wonder the Rio Grande is not so grand after all! The Mexicans call it the Rio Bravo (rē′ ō bräv′ ō), the "Bold River"!

Across the river in Mexico you are in Nuevo Laredo (nu ā′ vō

The international bridge that joins Laredo, Texas, and Nuevo Laredo, Mexico, crosses an important river. What is it? The palm trees on the left suggest the warm climate of this area.

lə rād′ ō). *Nuevo Laredo* means "New Laredo" in Spanish.

In Nuevo Laredo we study our map of Mexico. We will drive south to Monterrey (män′ tə rā′) about 140 miles (225 kilometers) from Nuevo Laredo. We will follow the highway from Monterrey over the mountains and through the highlands to Mexico City. In all, our trip will be more than 700 miles (1,100 kilometers) long.

Soon after we leave Nuevo Laredo, we climb into the hills and mountains. For much of our journey we will wind over and around the mountains. When compared to the United States and Canada, Mexico has little flatland. It is mostly covered with mountains or high plateaus. A **plateau** (pla tō′) is a highland between the mountains. It is almost flat with a few hills and low mountains.

It is hard to imagine how rough and steep the hills and mountains in Mexico are unless you see them.

101

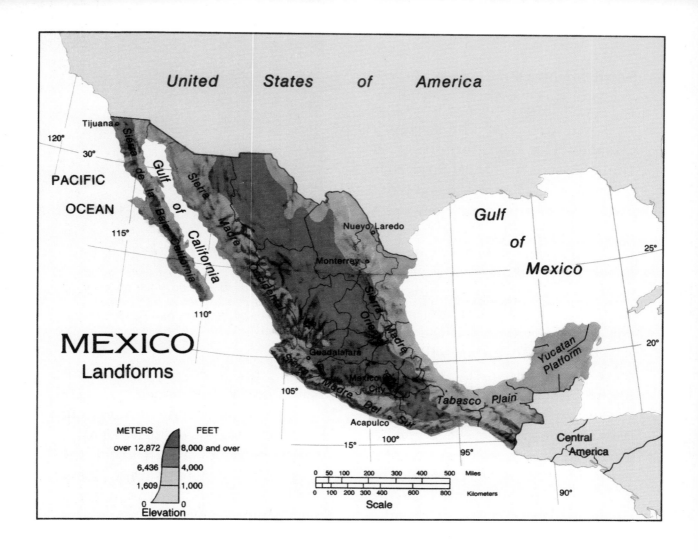

MEXICO
Landforms

METERS	FEET
over 12,872	8,000 and over
6,436	4,000
1,609	1,000
0	0

Elevation

Scale

Long ago a man traveled from Mexico to Spain. He talked to the Spanish king about Mexico. At that time Spain owned Mexico and called it New Spain.

"Tell me about our new land," said the king. "What is it like?"

The visitor could not think of words to describe the many kinds of land in Mexico. Then he took a piece of paper from a table and crumpled it in his hands. "There, your Majesty," he said, "is a map of New Spain." This was his way of saying that the country has plateaus, valleys, hills, and mountains.

Today new roads in Mexico make travel through the rough lands much more pleasant than it was years ago. Your great-grandparents would have found mostly trails and paths through the country. They could not have traveled to Mexico City by car.

Along the eastern side of Mexico is a mountain range stretching to the south. Monterrey is in the northern part of these mountains. Another mountain range along the western part of Mexico runs south and east. These two mountain ranges join each other in southern Mexico. The Mexicans call these mountains the

Sierra Madre (sē âr′ ə mä′ drā) which means "Mother Mountains."

Between the eastern and western Sierra Madre lies the great central plateau of Mexico.

The plateau is windswept and quite dry, especially in the north. Our guide through Mexico tells us that most of the people in Mexico live on the plateau.

"Why would so many people want to live on a dry plateau surrounded by high mountains?" we ask. "Even with this good road, the journey to the plateau is long and steep."

"Just wait, and you will soon find out," chuckles our guide.

Our car climbs up around curve after curve. When we left Nuevo Laredo, the weather was hot. As we climb the steep mountains, the air feels cooler. We need to put on sweaters.

The air on mountains is almost always cooler than in the lowlands

Plant life is thick in the warm, moist lowlands of Mexico. What name do the Mexicans give to the hot lowlands? (Look for the answer on the next page.)

around them. The higher the mountains, the cooler they are on top. Some mountains in Mexico are so high that they are covered with snow all year.

Finally we reach the top of the eastern Sierra Madre, then descend to the plateau. The plateau is hilly in some places and nearly flat in other places. The plateau is lower than the Sierra Madre, but it is still much higher than places near the ocean or even at Nuevo Laredo. On the plateau we stop beside the road to rest and find that the sun is bright, but the air is cool. Millions of Mexico's people find this climate much more pleasant than that of the hot lowlands. For this reason more people live in the highlands than in the lowlands.

Three Lands in One. In the United States and Canada, the farther north you travel, the cooler the weather becomes. In the south the climate is warmer.

Farmland in the great plateau of Mexico north of Mexico City. What mountains lie near this plateau?

Northern Mexico is only a little cooler than southern Mexico. In Mexico, highlands and lowlands make more difference in temperature than distances north and south. It is this way in all lands close to the equator.

In Mexico and other parts of Central America there are three kinds of climate depending on how high the land is.

The lowlands near the ocean are almost always hot. These hot lands are often wet lands. The Mexicans call the hot lowland region the *tierra caliente* (tē âr′ə kä yen′ tā). *Tierra caliente* means "hot land."

Not many people live in the *tierra caliente* because of the heat, the dampness, and the mosquitoes, which carry diseases. The people who do live in the *tierra caliente* never need to worry about cold and snow. They raise bananas, cacao or cocoa, rice, sugarcane and other crops

This picture shows the mountainous highlands between Mexico City and Vera Cruz. What is the climate like in the highlands of Mexico?

that grow well in a hot climate.

On higher ground just above the hot lands we find the *tierra templada* (tē âr′ə tem plä′ də) region. *Tierra templada* means "mild or moderate lands."

Most of the people in Mexico live in the *tierra templada*. In these lands it is never cold and almost never too hot. The weather is comfortable for work and play throughout the year.

Farmers in the *tierra templada* raise coffee, corn, oranges, and other crops. These crops would not do so well in the hot lands. They could not stand cold weather either.

The third region in Mexico is the *tierra fría* (tē âr′ə frē′ə) *Tierra fría* means "cold land."

Mexico City is in the *tierra fria*. People in Mexico City say their climate is like spring all year. Most places in the *tierra fría* have frost in winter. The mountains have snow.

People who live in the *tierra fria*

This village is in the warm lands of Mexico between the hot lowlands and the cool highlands. What is this region called?

raise corn, wheat, beans, and potatoes. These crops can be grown in the few months of summer when the weather is warmer. They can stand cool weather much better than coffee or citrus fruit can.

The highest parts of the *tierra fría* are too cold for most crops. Cold and frost can be expected at almost any time. Few people live in these parts of the *tierra fría*.

This small farming village is about 50 miles (80 kilometers) south of Nogales, Mexico. Nogales is in northwestern Mexico, south of Arizona in the United States.

What Do You Say?

1. Why is the Rio Grande not a very large river?
2. Why would a crumpled piece of paper resemble the land in Mexico?
3. Name the three climate regions of Mexico. Describe the weather in each one.

What Does the Bible Say?

1. Many people in the United States speak of Mexico as "our neighbor to the south." The United States and Mexico do not always get along well together. The two countries would have better feelings toward each other if everybody obeyed Romans 13:10. Write this verse.

Village Life in Mexico

After we cross the eastern Sierra Madre, we are on the high plateau of Mexico. The main highway is often lonely, for few people live in dry northern Mexico. The closer to Mexico City we come, the more villages and people we see.

Many Mexicans in the big cities live much as do the people in the United States. But thousands of others live in much the same way as their grandparents and great-grandparents before them.

Half of all Mexicans make a living by farming. Most of these farmers live in small villages. They farm just enough to make a living.

These buildings belong to a poor farmer on the plateau of Mexico. Although the farmer is poor, he has land to call his own. The poor in Mexico's cities live in crowded shacks and have little to call their own.

To see a Mexican farm village, we need to turn off the main road onto a winding dirt road. Soon we see an oxcart with large wooden wheels lumbering along the road. The cart is loaded with corn, potatoes, and

In many Mexican villages, the buildings are made of adobe brick. The roof nearest you is a thatch roof. The other buildings have tile roofs.

squash for market. Farther on we meet little donkeys called *burros* loaded down with things for market.

We soon notice that ours is almost the only car on the road. Only a few farmers can afford trucks for taking things to market. Most of Mexico's cars are in the cities.

Over another hill and around another bend we arrive in a small village. **Adobe** (ə dō′ bē) houses line the street. Adobe is sun-dried brick made from clay or soil. The clay is mixed with straw or grass and made into bricks. The bricks are dried in the sun for several weeks. Some roofs are made of grass. They are called **thatch** roofs. Other houses have roofs made of tile. The lower picture on this page shows both kinds of roofs.

Most of the villagers we meet have dark brown skin, black hair, rounded faces, and high cheekbones. They are American Indians. Many years ago their forefathers ruled in Mexico.

Long ago the Spanish who came to Mexico began taking Indian wives. For this reason some of the villagers are part Indian and part Spanish. Mexicans who are only part Indian are called **mestizos** (mes tē′ zōz).

You may not be able to tell an Indian from a mestizo just by looking at him. Often the Indians are the poorest people in a village. Many mestizos and whites are more well-to-do. They may dress in better clothes and own more property, maybe even a truck or a car.

106

Many men who live in villages of Mexico wear white shirts and loose white trousers. These garments help keep them cool in the hot sun. Most men wear tall hats with wide brims. They are called **sombreros** (som brär′ ōz).

Many Indian women wear long dresses with full skirts. They allow their hair to grow long and wear it in braids. In many villages the people still dress as they did many years ago. But in the cities, especially, many are wearing short dresses and other immodest clothing.

A flock of brown-eyed, black-haired Indian children gather around us as we come to a stop near the village market. You cannot understand anything they are saying. You listen to hear some of the Spanish words you have learned, but you do not hear any.

Our guide explains that these boys and girls are speaking an Indian language. At least a million Indians in Mexico do not speak Spanish. Other Indians can speak Spanish, as well as an Indian language.

The village market is something like an open-air farmers' market. Some of the fruits and vegetables to be sold are spread on the ground. Some are displayed on wooden stands. Farmers have also come from other villages nearby. They hope to sell a little extra corn, squash, or cotton which they have raised. With the money they can buy cloth for clothing or perhaps a **machete** (mə shet′ ē)

In Mexico and many other Spanish-speaking lands of southern North America, many people are becoming Christians. Above is a photo of Christians and their families from the village of Paquib in Guatemala. The picture below shows where the missionaries live who have come to teach the people about Christ.

for chopping corn, weeds, and bushes.

Some villagers will spend their money for things they should not buy. Some will buy strong drink and become drunk. Others will bet money at a cockfight or a game of dice. The families of the drunkards and gamblers will be poorer than ever.

Most of the villagers do not know Jesus Christ and do not follow the teachings of the Bible. The people are poor, and sin only helps make them poorer. From God's Word they could learn things that would help them spend money wisely.

"Wherefore do ye spend money for that which is not bread? and your labour for that which satisfieth not? hearken diligently unto me, and eat ye that which is good, and let your soul delight itself in fatness."

Isaiah 55:2

Our guide now takes us to the new school in the village. The Mexican government has been building hundreds of new schools. They send building materials to a village. The men of the village build the school.

In the year 1910 only about one

There are many beautiful buildings and roads in the heart of Mexico City. Mexico City is growing rapidly and may be the largest city in the world.

Mexican in four could read and write. Today nine out of ten can read and write.

In school the children learn to speak and read Spanish. Many Indian children learn Spanish for the first time when they go to school. Yet most Mexican parents take their children out of school after four or five years to help with the work.

All too soon we must leave the little Mexican village. We will go on to Mexico City. In this big city we will see another side of Mexican life.

On to Mexico City

The closer we get to Mexico City, the more villages we see. We also see more cars and trucks on the road.

Mexico City is one of the three largest cities in the world. Over eighteen million people live in the city and the area nearby.

Mexico City is the largest and one of the richest cities in the Americas south of the United States. The city is built on land that was once a lake. Now some of the tallest and heaviest buildings are sinking into the soft earth.

In Mexico City you see the best roads in all of Mexico. You see the tallest buildings, the most beautiful parks, the most cars, and the richest people.

In certain parts of the city you will also see some of the poorest people in Mexico. Thousands of poor Mexicans come to Mexico City to find jobs. Some do, but many do not. The jobless build little huts of cardboard and large wooden cartons—anything they can find.

The poor parts of cities are called **slums**. Several million people live in the slums of Mexico City.

Standing on a street corner in Mexico City is a good way to learn about the city. You will see rich people driving by in big American cars. They are dressed in the latest styles from the United States. You will see American businessmen who work in Mexico City. Indian women with baskets on their heads show you that Mexico is also an Indian land. Many poor people also pass by. Perhaps they are looking for jobs or begging for a handout. Oxcarts loaded with corn and other vegetables remind you of the Mexican villages. The farmers sell their goods in one of the city's many markets.

In many ways Mexico is like the countries to its south. In most of these countries the people speak Spanish. Millions of Indians in Central America and South America remind us that Indians once ruled the land. Most countries to the south have even warmer weather than that of Mexico.

Many of the people in Mexico and countries to the south are very poor. Even with all its poor, Mexico is one of the richest countries south of the United States.

Let us go on to the south to learn more about our American neighbors.

What Do You Say?

1. Name some things you might see in a Mexican village.
2. In what ways might we help poor people in Mexican villages?
3. What might you see in Mexico City that shows it to be a rich city?

What Does the Bible Say?

1. Read Luke 4:18. Here you find the most important thing Christians can do for the poor. What is it?
2. According to Proverbs 14:21, how does a person feel who has helped the poor?
3. Proverbs 20:1 tells of the danger of wine and other strong drink. Write this verse.

Bridge to a Southern Continent

You have just explored the three largest countries in North America. Canada, the United States, and Mexico cover nearly all of the continent.

Look at a globe map of North America. You see that North America does not end with Mexico. A narrow strip of land continues south and east to South America. This land bridge between the two continents is called Central America. It is part of North America.

The high chain of mountains that begins in Alaska and Canada continues south through Central America. Many of the people in Central America live in these mountains or in the valleys between the mountains.

Find Costa Rica on the map of North America on page 100. In Costa Rica the Central American land bridge narrows to only 80 miles across. One mountain in Costa Rica is so high that a person can see both oceans from its top. Farther south and east in Panama the distance between the Atlantic and the Pacific becomes 40 miles and less. At the narrowest point in Panama only 28 miles separate the two oceans.

The Crossroads of the World. Panama has been called the "crossroads of the Americans." It has been a crossroads for thousands of years.

The first American Indians to enter South America probably came through Panama. The first white men in Central America crossed Panama to reach the Pacific Ocean. From there they sailed down the west coast of South America.

Years later roads and railroads were built across Panama and the rest of Central America.

Some of the early explorers and road builders had a wonderful dream. They hoped that men could dig a **canal** across Central America. A canal is a ditch to carry water. Ships could then sail quickly from

These ships are crossing the Panama Canal. Notice that each section of the locks is like stairsteps. These locks will raise the ships about 85 feet (26 meters).

110

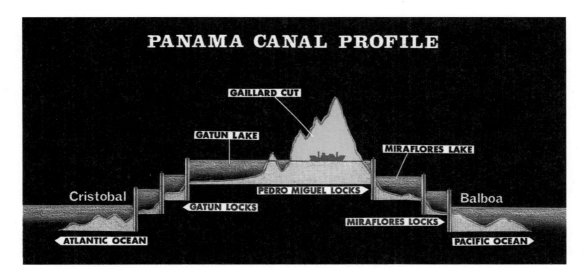

PANAMA CANAL PROFILE

GAILLARD CUT

GATUN LAKE

MIRAFLORES LAKE

Cristobal

PEDRO MIGUEL LOCKS

GATUN LOCKS

Balboa

MIRAFLORES LOCKS

ATLANTIC OCEAN

PACIFIC OCEAN

This diagram shows the different sections of the Panama Canal. A city is located at each end of the canal. Cristobal is near the Atlantic end of the canal, and Balboa is on the Pacific end. Why do you think cities grew up near this canal?

one ocean to another. The only other way ships could reach the Pacific Ocean was to sail thousands of miles around the tip of South America. That trip took months. Storms along the South American coast made the trip dangerous.

Some men from France asked permission to dig a canal across Panama. The land was rough and hilly. A thick forest covered the land. The hot weather year around discouraged the workers. During the rainy season, mud began to fill their ditch. Their machinery began to rust in the hot, wet climate. Worst of all, millions of mosquitoes carried diseases that killed hundreds of workers. Because of the mosquitoes, part of the coast of Central America is called the Mosquito Coast.

Then American workers took over the job. They coated the swamps with a thin film of oil. This killed most of the mosquitoes. Finally, in 1914 ships began to use the new

Panama Canal. Now ships from many nations around the world sail through the canal each day. Can you see why the Panamanians (pan′ ə mā′ nē ənz) call their country "the crossroads of the world"?

In the famous Gaillard Cut, train tracks were laid to take workers to their jobs when the Panama Canal was being built. Many workers died of disease and accidents while building this canal.

111

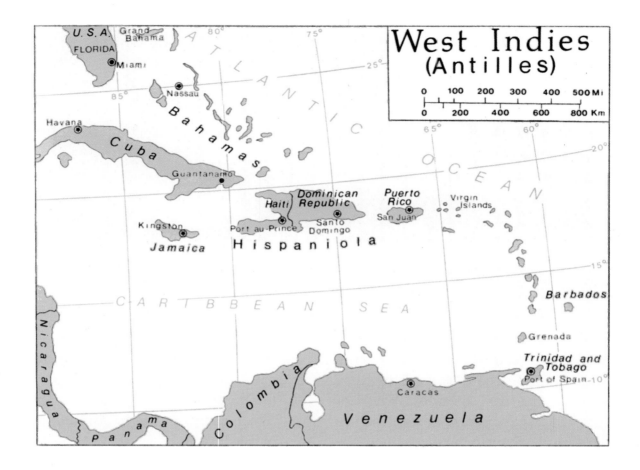

The Isthmus of Panama. Most of the country of Panama is also called the Isthmus of Panama. An **isthmus** (is′ məs) is a narrow strip of land that joins two larger pieces of land. The Isthmus of Panama joins North America and South America. Anyone who wants to go by land to South America must cross this isthmus.

Stepping-Stones to South America

Look at the map of the West Indies on this page. Find Florida in the United States. Now find Venezuela in South America. What do you see between Florida and Venezuela?

Like stepping-stones, a large string of islands lies between North America and South America. We use two names for these islands—the West Indies or the Antilles (an til′ ēz). How many large islands can you count? There are hundreds of smaller islands. Some are so small that only a very large map could show them.

If God would drain all the water from the ocean around the West Indies, you would see that they are a great chain of underwater mountains. The mountaintops rise out of the water to form islands. Most of the islands are very mountainous. Cuba has the largest areas of flatland found in the West Indies.

Sometimes the larger "stepping-

112

stones" near Florida are called the Greater Antilles. The smaller islands reaching to South America are the Lesser Antilles.

What Do You Say?

1. Why do we call Central America a bridge to South America?

2. a. What country is called the "crossroads of the Americas"?
   b. What makes this country a crossroads?

3. The West Indies are called the _____ to South America.

What Does the Bible Say?

1. How did the land bridge between North America and South America come to be? Find the answer in Jeremiah 51:15.

2. What will finally happen to the islands in the ocean? (Read Revelation 16:20.)

Using Globes and Maps

1. Trace a map of North America. Trace another map of South America. Looking at your two outlines, how are these two continents shaped alike? How are they different?

2. On a globe point out the Western Hemisphere and the Eastern Hemisphere. Which continents are in each?

3. Draw a map of North America. Ask your teacher to help you with this. Draw the western and eastern mountains on your map like this: ∧∧∧ On your map write the names of the three largest North American countries.

New Words and Terms

From the list of new words and terms, fill in the blanks in the sentences on page 114.

Western Hemisphere   canal
Eastern Hemisphere   prosperous

113

manufacturing   maize
Sierra Madre   plains
tierra caliente   canyons
American Indians   oasis
archaeologists   *tierra fria*
tierra templada   adobe
materialistic   thatch
sombrero   mestizo
Central America   slum
New World   machete
West Indies   Antilles

1. People who live in Africa live in the a. _____ _____ , but people who live in South America live in the b. _____ _____ . We also say that people who live in North and South America live in the c. _____ _____ .

2. Large areas of flatland are called a. _____ , but steep-sided river valleys are called b. _____ .

3. The first people to live in the Americas were the a. _____ _____ . b. _____ have found the remains of things made by these people long ago.

4. Another name for corn or Indian corn is _____ .

5. A place in the desert where water is close to the surface is an _____ .

6. Making things by machine is called _____ .

7. People who have a lot of money and are very a. _____ often become b. _____ , caring too much for the things money can buy.

8. A mountain range in Mexico is called the _____ _____ .

9. In Mexico the hot lands are called the a. _____ _____ , the higher, warm lands are called b. _____ _____ , and the coolest lands are called c. _____ _____ .

10. The walls of many buildings in Mexico are made of a. _____ and the roofs are made of b. _____ .

11. A _____ is a special wide-rimmed hat worn in Mexico.

12. A person who is part Indian in Mexico is called a _____ .

13. A _____ is a long, sharp knife for chopping.

14. The poor part of a city is often called the _____ .

15. A _____ is a ditch that carries water.

16. _____ _____ is the narrowest part of North America between Mexico and South America.

17. Two names for the islands between Florida and South America are a. _____ or b. _____ _____ .

Thinking Together

1. What do you think would be the best name for the people who lived in the Americas before the white man came? Why?

2. How are North America and

114

South America alike in shape and in their landforms?

3. What are some natural resources God has given your state or province? Name five or more.

4. Where might you expect to find water in a desert?

5. What landforms would you expect to see on a trip from Laredo, Texas, to Mexico City?

6. a. What are the needs of many people in Mexican villages? b. What is the most important need?

7. Suppose you stood for most of the day on a street corner in Mexico City. a. How would you know the city is rich? b. How would you know that many people are poor?

8. In what way is Central America like a bridge?

9. Why is Panama called the "crossroads of the Americas"?

10. Why are the West Indies called "stepping-stones"?

For You to Do

1. Draw an outline map of North America showing the borders of the countries. Fill in the names of the ten countries on the mainland.

2. Find an article on *American Indians* in an encyclopedia. See if you can find the answer to these questions: How many Indians were in the Americas when Columbus discovered the land? How many American Indians are there today? How many are in your country?

3. Read an encyclopedia article on your favorite of the vegetables first raised by American Indians. Write a report of at least 75 words on what you read. Tell how the vegetable is raised. Tell other interesting facts you discover.

4. Think about your house. What natural resources were used to build it? If you do not know what natural resources some things were made of, ask your parents or your teacher. What natural resource is used to heat your house?

5. Ask your teacher to help you make an outline map of Mexico. Draw the mountains on the map. Color the lowlands green, the mountains brown, and the great Plateau of Mexico yellow. Use the landform map on page 102 to help you.

6. What are tortillas? Read about them in an encyclopedia. From what are they made? How often do Mexicans eat them?

7. Look at a map of North America. a. What is the name of the ocean to the east of North America? b. What is the name of the part of this ocean between the West Indies and Central America?

7. On to South America!

The second great continent we will study is South America. This continent is about twice as large as the United States.

Which direction would you go from your house to reach South America? Did you know that much of South America is east of any place in North America? The map below shows you.

The line on this map helps you see that most of South America is east (really southeast) of North America. Only the very western edge of South America is farther west than New York City and Montreal, Canada.

This fourth-grade girl shows you the eight main directions. She is pointing north. Her shoes are pointing in what direction? On which side of her is west? East? Name the four in-between directions.

On the map, a line has been drawn north and south through the Americas. The line passes through Montreal and New York City. These cities are in eastern North America. How much of South America is east of those two cities?

South America is south of North America. It is also east of North America. Any place that is south and also east of another place is south-east of that place.

The Equator and the Hot Lands. Look at the map on page 118. Do you see the line marked "equator" that

In-Between Directions

In Unit 1 we learned the four directions: north, south, east, and west. These directions help tell us how to go from one place to another.

You just learned that South America is south and east of North America. This "in-between direction" is called *southeast*.

There are four in-between directions. A place that is north and also east of another place is *northeast*. A place that is north and also west is *northwest*. A place that is south and west is *southwest*. A place that is south and east is *south-east*.

The four in-between directions will help you tell directions better. You will be able to find places more quickly when you know the direction more exactly.

Find a map of the United States and Canada which shows the states and provinces. Answer each of the following questions with an in-between direction. Florida is _____ of Oregon, Indiana is _____ of North Carolina. New Brunswick is _____ of Quebec. Manitoba is _____ of Nevada.

Children who live in South America, Central America, and other places near the equator, must look high over their heads to see the sun. Much further north, we see the sun much lower in the sky.

crosses northern South America?

The **equator** (i kwāt′ ər) is a very important line on a map or globe. It is exactly halfway between the North Pole and the South Pole. Every place north of the equator is in the Northern Hemisphere. Every place south of the equator is in the Southern Hemisphere.

At the equator the sun shines overhead, or nearly overhead, at noon all year. The sun's warm rays shine straight down. They keep lands near the equator warm or hot all year. Usually the closer you go to the equator the warmer the weather is. In lands near the poles the sun is always very low in the sky. The

Here is a map of South America. Practice naming and locating the different countries until you are familiar with them. Also observe the network of streams and rivers which drains this continent.

slanted rays of the sun do not warm the ground so much. Usually the closer you go to the poles the cooler the weather becomes. Later you will learn why a few places near the equator are cool.

If you could visit South America and walk or ride across the equator, would you see a line marked "equator"? No! Unless someone had posted a sign you would not know exactly when you crossed the equator. The equator is a line found on maps and globes to show you the places that are exactly halfway between the two poles. The equator is not marked on the earth, of course. But the places halfway between the poles are real places!

A teacher once asked her geography class: "Could a monkey hang on the equator by his tail?"

"No," exclaimed one student, "because it is too hot!"

The student knew that lands near the equator are usually hot. But he still imgained that the equator was a real line or rope.

One country in South America has a name which tells us that the equator runs through it. That country is Ecuador (ek′ wə dȯr). In Spanish *ecuador* means "equator."

Looking at South America

Look at the map of South America on page 118. In some ways South America is like North America. The continent is very wide in the north. Further south it becomes narrower and narrower.

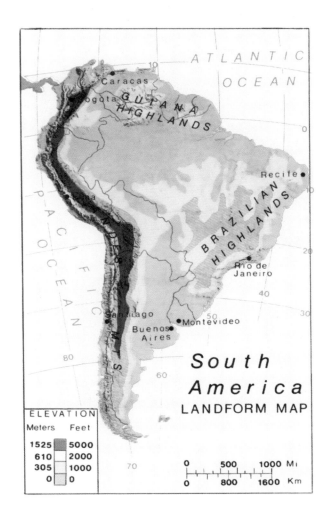

The landform map of South America on this page shows that the two Americas are alike in other ways. Do you see the long chain of mountains all along the western coast of South America? North America also has a long chain of western mountains. The western mountains of South America are called the Andes (an′ dēz). The tallest mountains in the Americas are in the Andes. The Andes are the longest chain of mountains in the world. They stretch as an unbroken wall for 4,500 miles (7,240 kilometers).

The tallest mountain in the

This picture was taken high in the Andes Mountains of South America. What kind of roof does the house have? Notice how steep the mountains are. Why is there snow on the highest peaks when this place is near the equator?

Andes is Mount Aconcagua (ak′ ən käg′ wə) on the border between Chile and Argentina. This mountain rises over 22,000 feet (7,100 meters) above sea level.

The landform map also shows that central South America has vast lowlands as does North America. The map also shows lower mountains in the eastern part of the continent. These mountains are much lower than the Andes but higher than the mountains of eastern North America.

The Greatest River on Earth. You have learned that the longest mountain chain in the world is found in South America. The greatest river in the world is also found in South America. This river is called the Amazon (am′ ə zän′).

The Amazon is not the *longest* river, but the *greatest*. More water flows in the Amazon than in any other river. If the Amazon could be drained of its water, the waters of ten Mississippi Rivers could be put into it with room to spare! At many places the river is so wide that a person cannot see across.

The Amazon is 4,000 miles (6,400 kilometers) long. That is farther than the distance from New York to California. The Nile River in Egypt is the only river in the world that is longer than the Amazon. It is only a little longer.

The creeks and streams of nearly half of South America flow into the Amazon. All the vast area that has streams draining into the Amazon is called the Amazon **basin**. If you follow the waters of any stream or smaller river in this basin, you will finally reach the Amazon.

What Do You Say?

1. a. Name the four main directions. b. Name the four in-between directions.

2. Exactly where is the equator?

3. Draw an outline map of South America. In it draw the Andes Mountains and the Amazon River.

What Does the Bible Say?

1. Read Luke 13:29. From what directions will the people come who enter heaven?

2. Only two in-between directions are named in the Bible. What are they? (Read Acts 27:12.)

Resources God Gave South America

God has given South America many rich resources. Many of these have not been discovered or used.

The most useful resource in South America has been the soil. Much rich farmland awaited the early settlers. Unfortunately, much of it

This map shows where the great rain forest in South America is located. This rain forest stretches all the way from the Atlantic Ocean to the Andes Mountains, not so far from the Pacific Ocean.

121

Angel Falls in Venezuela is the highest waterfall in the world. Jimmy Angel from the United States was the first known white person to see this waterfall. He flew over it in 1935.

tops reach 200 feet (65 meters). We call such forests **rain forests**. Can you guess why?

Some people call the rain forests of South America "jungles." Actually only certain parts of the rain forests are jungles. A jungle is a thick growth of trees and vines which is almost impossible to walk through. Jungles form along the rivers or wherever the sunshine can break through to the ground.

South America has many large rivers to carry all its extra water to the sea. Some of these rivers are useful for travel and trading by boat. At some places along the rivers the water tumbles over rocks and high cliffs. Thus it moves from highlands to lowlands.

Llamas are beautiful animals valued for their warm fur and for their work as beasts of burden in the Andes Mountains of South America.

has been worn out. Farmers took crops from the soil year after year. They did not use fertilizer to keep the soil productive.

Water is another one of South America's important resources. Much of the continent receives plenty of rainfall. Some places receive very heavy rainfall. Over 100 inches (250 centimeters) fall each year. The heavy rain causes thick plant growth. Thick forests grow in such wet places. Sometimes the tree-

Angel Falls in Venezuela drops 3,212 feet (979 meters). This falls is more than 1,000 feet (300 meters) higher than any other falls in the world.

South America has other very important resources such as oil. Venezuela, Ecuador, Argentina, and Brazil have large supplies of oil. These countries need oil for running factories, machinery, cars, and electric generators.

This continent also has many rich mineral resources. Chile sends out or **exports** more copper than any other country. Chile also has all the world's known supply of nitrate. Nitrate is a natural fertilizer. Diamonds are mined in Brazil. Iron and tin are other important mineral resources in South America. One thing South America does not have enough of is coal.

Hot Lands—Cold Lands

You have already learned that lands near the equator are usually warm or hot. At noon the sun shines high in the sky.

Many children who live in South America have never wiped frost from a window. Some have seen snow but have never played in it! How can that be? Come with me to the mountains and you will see.

The Indian's Friend—The Llama

Do you think of animals when you think of natural resources? Probably not. But in South America an animal is one of the most important blessings God has given the Indians. This animal is the wooly llama (läm′ ə).

Llamas live in the Andes Mountains. There are millions of llamas living in the Andean countries.

Llamas thrive well on the scanty grasses of the highlands. They almost seem to like the cold weather there. Llamas could not stand the heat of the lowlands.

Indians in South America use the llama in many ways. Llamas are good burden bearers. They can climb over rocky, slippery paths too rough for other animals.

A llama can carry about 100 pounds (45 kilograms). It will not let anyone overload it. If someone loads too much on it, the llama promptly sits down and waits for the load to be removed. Angry llamas will even spit in people's faces.

The llama provides the Indians with meat. Llama wool is woven into heavy cloth. In this way the llama helps keep the people warm. Even llama dung is useful when dry. The Indians use it for fuel because few trees grow high in the mountains.

Up! Up! Up! Let's visit the Andes Mountains. We will leave from Lima (lē′ mə), Peru. This city is near the west coast of South America. A railroad has been built from Lima into the mountains.

We leave Lima and head east. The view of the mountains is almost breathtaking. They rise like a steep wall from the low hills outside Lima.

The tops of the Andes are covered with snow! Children who live in Lima can see snow on the mountains. But snow never falls in Lima. Most have never been high in the mountains to play in the snow!

Lima, Peru, is only a few hundred miles from the equator where the weather stays warm or hot all year. "How can there be snow so close to the equator?" you ask. The

Potatoes are a delicious and healthful vegetable. They grow in many parts of the world. Where do these potatoes come from?

This field of potatoes in the state of Maine is in bloom. Where did the first potatoes come from? Name some places besides Maine where they grow. Do they grow in your area?

lowlands in Central and South America are warm or hot—*tierra caliente*. The higher the land, the cooler the air.

As we start up the mountains, the air soon begins to feel cooler. People begin to put on their sweaters and jackets. The train track becomes steeper and the train slows down. If something would fall out the window on one side of the train, it would tumble thousands of feet down the mountainside.

The railroad crosses the mountains below the **snow line**. Above the snow line it is below freezing almost all the time.

You are on the highest railroad in the world. The man who had it built claimed that he would lay the tracks on air if necessary! The workers did not do that, of course. They did need to blast the side of the mountains. They had to build bridges and tunnels.

The railroad crosses the mountains at a low place, or **pass**. Here at three miles (almost five kilometers) above sea level, you must still look up to see the mountaintops.

Our train now whines down steep hills and around sharp curves into a great valley. At the bottom of this valley we are still two miles above sea level. The valley weather is like spring all year. We are in the *tierra fría* of Peru.

Potato—Mountain Vegetable

The valleys high in the Andes Mountains are the home of the white potato. Thousands of years ago potatoes grew wild in the highlands. The millions of Indians who lived there learned how to raise them. Potatoes grew better than corn or almost any other food crop. The cool weather did not hurt them.

The first white men who came to the Andes and to Peru were hunting silver and gold. They did not find as many of these riches as they had hoped! But they did find the potato.

Soon the potato spread around the world. Potatoes became a very valuable crop in many lands. The people in Ireland were soon raising potatoes as their main crop. Early Irish settlers in the United States brought potatoes with them. Did you ever hear them called Irish potatoes? We may also speak of Idaho potatoes or Maine potatoes. But remember, potatoes first came from South America.

Lands in the South. Turn to the landform map of South America. Find all the countries that lie partly in the Andes. Name them. Find the countries that are at least partly in the Amazon basin. Can you find any countries not in the Amazon basin or in the Andes?

The Amazon basin is mostly very low and flat. South of the basin are hilly lands and then more flatlands.

In northern Argentina the flatlands east of the Andes are called the Pampa (päm´ pə). The Pampa is a grassland hundreds of miles wide. Some of the best land in South America is found in the Pampa. This part of South America reminds visitors of the Great Plains of North America.

South of the Pampa lies a dry land of hills, lowlands, and plateaus called Patagonia (pat´ ə gō´ nē ə).

Many sheep graze on the flat grasslands of the Pampa region of Argentina. Do you know what region of North America is much like this part of South America?

The first white men to visit Patagonia met tall Indians who wore big boots stuffed with straw. The white men kept talking about the Indians' big feet. They named the land Patagonia, which means "big feet."

South of "big feet" land lies the large island called Tierra del Fuego (tē âr′ ə del fwā′ gō). This island is about the same size as the states of Maryland and New Jersey put together. Tierra del Fuego means "land of fire" in Spanish. The first white man to see this island saw the fires Indians had built at night to keep warm. They called the island the "land of fire."

What Do You Say?

1. Name some natural resources God has given South America.

2. How is the llama an important resource in South America?

3. a. Where might you find snow in the warm lands near the equator? b. Why would you find snow there?

4. How did white potatoes get from South America to the United States?

What Does the Bible Say?

1. Finish this verse. "The earth is _____" (Psalm 24:1).

2. Read Job 28:1, 2. List the natural resources named in these verses. These can all be found in South America.

Ecuador—Land of the Equator

Ecuador is a small country on the west coast of South America.

Lowlands lie along the Pacific Ocean. The Andes Mountains cover much of the rest of the country. A steaming rain forest covers eastern Ecuador. This rain forest is a small part of the one that covers much of the Amazon basin.

The map on page 121 shows where the South American rain forests are found. Can you find the part that is in eastern Ecuador? Only four countries in South America have no rain forests at all. What are they?

Many different peoples live in Ecuador. Most of the white people live near the Pacific Ocean and in Quito (kē′ tō), the capital. Many of the white people are rich. Most of the rulers are white.

Many of the people who live in the Andes are Indians. Long ago Indians from the Andes ruled much of South America. Today the Indians are very poor people. They try to farm the steep hillsides in the Andes. The land is rocky and much of it has been worn out. The land has become poor because of hundreds of years of farming and because of too little fertilizer.

East of the Andes lies the rain forest. In the rain forest every day is hot. Thunderstorms drench the land almost every afternoon. Very few people live in the rain forest. The great forest is too hard to clear. The rains wash many of the minerals from land cleared for farming.

Mostly Indians live in the rain forest. They live in tiny clearings

Find the equator on this map of South America. Near to what city in Ecuador does the equator come? What does the name "Ecuador" mean?

127

These are ruins of the ancient Inca city of Machu Picchu (ma′chu pek′ chu). This city stood on a mountain about 8,000 feet (2,400 meters) high.

along the rivers. They have no machinery, no electricity, no modern conveniences. They live much as their forefathers lived for hundreds of years.

The following story tells of missionaries who set out to bring the Gospel to a tribe of forest Indians in Ecuador. What can you learn about the rain forest? About the people? About their needs?

Mission to the Aucas

In the jungles of eastern Ecuador lives a tribe of Indians called the Aucas (ȯ′ käz). Few people had ever seen Aucas until the early 1950s. The Aucas lived deep in the jungles where there were no roads.

The Aucas were a fierce tribe. They did not like anyone coming into their lands, especially white men.

Many years ago white men had come by boats to search for rubber trees in the thick forest. The cruel rubber hunters killed some of the Indians and captured others as slaves to work for them.

The rubber hunters finally left the rain forest. The Indians, especially the Aucas, did not forget.

Some people said that the white man would never be able to make friends with the Aucas.

But five missionaries in Ecuador believed that the Aucas could be reached.

First of all, the missionaries had to find out exactly where the Aucas lived. Aucas lived in small groups of perhaps 50 at the most. They lived in small jungle clearings. The missionaries flew over the jungles and rivers looking for the Aucas. At first they could see nothing.

Finally on a very clear day the

missionaries flew over the jungles again. This time they saw some smoke rising through the trees. They passed over the place and saw a small clearing and one long house. Indians were walking about the clearing. The missionaries had seen their first Aucas.

In the days ahead they passed over the Aucas' clearing a number of times. They gradually flew lower, being careful not to frighten the Indians. They began to drop gifts of pots and pans, machetes, and clothing. Finally they flew so low the Indians could see their faces. They called to the Indians in their own language, *"Biti miti punimupa*—I like you; I want to be your friend." The missionaries had learned these words from a woman who had once lived among the Aucas.

The Aucas were soon smiling and waving. The missionaries felt the time had come to land and meet the Aucas. But where could they land? Trees 150 feet (45 meters) tall grew down to the edge of the river.

Finally a few miles away they found a sandbar along a river. Dirt and sand had piled up near the edge of the river, making a flat runway barely large enough for their plane to land.

The excited missionaries landed and set up a camp. They waited and waited. After a few days the first Aucas appeared—a man and two women. The Aucas seemed friendly. The missionaries had learned how to say different things to the Aucas such as, "I like you. We are friends. What is your name?"

The missionaries nicknamed the first Auca they met "George." George seemed very friendly. He motioned that he would like to take a plane ride. One of the missionaries gave him a ride over his own village. He leaned out the window waving and yelling to his friends.

The Aucas stayed overnight, then disappeared into the forest. Would they tell other Aucas? Would others return? Would they remain friendly?

Two days later the missionaries were killed on a beach. No one knows exactly what happened. Their bodies showed the marks of lance wounds.

This Auca Indian village is in a jungle clearing along a river. Do you see the long boat used by the Aucas?

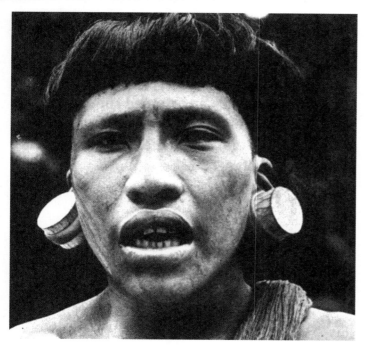

Here is a picture of the first Auca Indian met by missionaries. The missionaries nicknamed him "George." A hole was cut in each of his earlobes. The opening was gradually stretched by larger and larger pieces of balsa wood. These were worn much like some people wear jewelry.

Apparently a group of unfriendly Aucas had attacked them by surprise.

Later the wife and sister of one of the dead missionaries were able to go in and work among the Aucas.

The Aucas are only a few of the many millions in South America who need to know about Jesus Christ. More Indian tribes live deep within the rain forest awaiting the Good News of Jesus Christ. Many Indians and white people who have heard about Christ do not know Him or follow Him. The Gospel is needed in the jungles, in the mountains, in the cities throughout the Americas.

This open Bible is written in the language of the Auca Indians of Ecuador. Notice that the same alphabet that is used for English was used to spell this language. Do you see any letters that look different from ours?

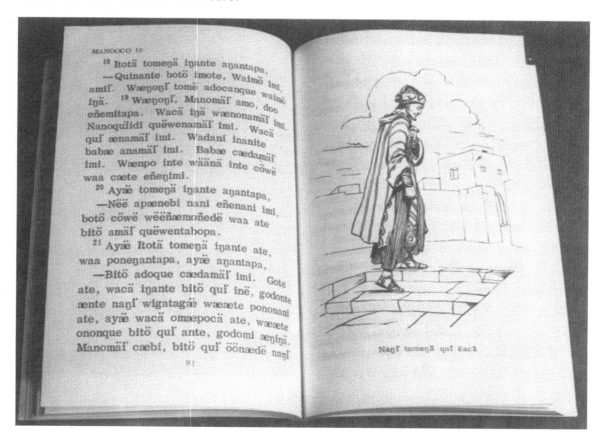

What Do You Say?

1. Which of the following would you expect to find in the rain forests of South America: rain, snow, dry weather, tall trees, cool weather, good roads, Indian villages?

2. How did missionaries try to make friends with the Auca Indians?

3. What do you think might have happened if the missionaries would have killed some Aucas when the Aucas attacked them?

Using Globes and Maps

1. On a globe point out the Southern Hemisphere and the Northern Hemisphere. In which hemisphere is most of South America?

2. Draw a map of South America. Draw mountains at the right places on your map.

3. On an outline map of South America, write the names of all the countries. There are 13 countries in South America.

What Does the Bible Say?

1. Read Isaiah 55:10. What is the reason God sends rain and snow?

2. Read Matthew 5:44. Name four things Christians are to do for their enemies.

New Words and Terms

Write a definition for each of these words.

1. northeast
2. northwest
3. southwest
4. southeast
5. equator
6. basin

7. rain forests

8. export

9. llama

10. snow line

11. pass

12. Pampa

13. Aucas

Thinking Together

1. In what direction are the following places from where you live? Look at a map of the United States and Canada. Use the four main directions plus the in-between directions. Toronto, Canada; Denver, Colorado; Miami, Florida; Toledo, Ohio.

2. Why is it good to have the equator marked on maps?

3. In what ways is South America different from North America?

4. a. What is a rain forest? b. Can you think of any problems people might have who live in a rain forest?

5. How does the weather change when you travel up a high mountain?

6. How can we help people by being kind to them and never fighting back?

7. Can you give a Bible verse that the missionaries obeyed when they treated the Aucas kindly?

For You to Do

1. Make a map of your classroom. Ask your teacher to show you which end is north. Label the four main directions and the four in-between directions.

2. Check "river basin" and "Mississippi River" in an encyclopedia. List the states that are in the Mississippi River basin. Include the states that are partly in the Mississippi basin.

3. Find "tropical rain forest" in an encyclopedia. From your reading, name three important things to remember about a rain forest.

4. Trace or draw a map of South America using penciled blocks. Ask your teacher for help.

5. a. Check a dictionary to find out what *martyr* means. b. What martyrs did you learn about in Chapter 7?

Europe North and South

Unit 3

What you will learn . . . in unit three

Do you like to visit faraway places? We are now ready to visit the continent of Europe. Europe is several thousand miles east of North America.

Have you ever heard people talk about Europe? Perhaps you know someone who has been there. People in Canada and the United States feel especially close to people in Europe. Do you know why?

Many of the early settlers in America came from Europe. We call these people who lived before us our **ancestors**. Our parents and grandparents are some of our ancestors. Our grandparents had parents and grandparents before them. And these ancestors had ancestors before them. Do you know how long ago your ancestors came to your country? From what country did they come?

People in Europe feel especially close to America too. Many Europeans can say, "I have relatives in America." Many people visit back and forth between Europe and America.

In this unit you will study the land of our ancestors. If your ancestors came from Africa or Asia, just wait. We will soon study those lands too.

We have studied North America and South America, the New World. From here on, this book will describe the Old World of Europe, Asia, and Africa.

8. Europe—The Land God Made

Are you ready to visit the interesting land of Europe? Europe is one of the smallest of continents. Only Australia is smaller. All of Europe is only a little larger than the United States without Alaska.

Look at the map of Europe above. You can see that Europe looks like a giant peninsula connected to Asia. In dividing Europe from Asia, **geographers**, people who study the earth, usually choose the Ural Mountains in Russia as the dividing line. Europe and Africa are separated by

water. Europe and North America are separated by water. But Europe and Asia are not separated by water. They border each other for hundreds of miles in the country of Russia.

Some geographers say that Europe and Asia are actually one continent. They call Europe and Asia together, **Eurasia** (yü rā′ zhə). Can you guess how this name came to be?

Like other peninsulas, Europe is surrounded by water on three sides. The Arctic Ocean lies to the north,

135

If you could place the continent of Europe on top of North America, this is what it would look like. This continent is larger than the United States but smaller than Canada.

the Atlantic Ocean to the west, and the Mediterranean (med′ ə tə rā′ nē ən) Sea to the south.

Four large peninsulas and many smaller ones jut out of Europe. On the map of Europe on page 135, find the Balkan Peninsula. You will find it in southeastern Europe between the Black Sea and the Mediterranean Sea. Greece is the most famous country on the Balkan Peninsula.

The Apennine (ap′ ə nīn′) Peninsula looks like a boot jutting out into the Mediterranean Sea in Southern Europe. What country is on this peninsula?

The Iberian (ī bir′ ē ən) Peninsula is found between the Mediterranean Sea and the Atlantic Ocean. Spain and Portugal are the two countries on the Iberian Peninsula.

Look at the northernmost part of

Europe. Do you see the largest peninsula in all Europe? It lies between the Baltic Sea and the Atlantic Ocean. This Peninsula is called the Scandinavian (skan′ də nā′ vē ən) Peninsula. Norway and Sweden are on this peninsula.

How Far North? Look at a globe or a map that shows both North America and Europe with the Atlantic Ocean between. You can see that southern Europe lies about as far north of the equator as do North Carolina and Virginia in the United States. The British Isles are as far north as Labrador and the Hudson Bay in Canada. Norway is as far north of the equator as Alaska and southern Greenland. What kind of climate would you expect to find in Europe?

Many North Americans are surprised when they learn how warm Europe's climate really is. In Europe the climate is so warm that orange trees can grow in areas as far north as the state of Kansas. Orange trees would be killed by the cold that far north in the United States.

Some places in Norway have more rain than snow in January. Places that far north in Canada and Alaska have bitter cold and snow in January. What makes Europe so warm? Let's find out.

The Warm Seas. Look again at the map of Europe. You remember that Europe is like a giant peninsula with oceans and seas on three sides.

Most places in Europe are not very far from the sea. Except in European Russia, almost no place in Europe is more than 400 miles (640 kilometers) from the sea.

God has made water to hold heat and to cool off more slowly than land. Did you ever notice that the ground freezes before rivers and ponds do? The seas around most of Europe remain free from ice all winter. The water helps to keep the nearby land warm. This is one way God takes care of the people in Europe.

The North Atlantic Drift. Some oceans and seas on earth could not keep Europe warm. Some seas are cold and choked with ice. But a large river of warm water flows through the Atlantic Ocean from the Gulf of Mexico all the way to Europe. A river of warm or cold water that moves through the ocean is called an **ocean current**.

The ocean current that begins in the Gulf of Mexico is called the Gulf Stream. Near the equator it has been warmed by the direct rays of the sun. As the Gulf Stream nears Europe, it spreads out. Near Europe it is known as the **North Atlantic Drift**. The warm waters of the North Atlantic Drift wash the Atlantic coast of Europe.

The North Atlantic Drift warms the winds blowing across it. These winds help keep the land near the ocean much warmer than land that far north in America.

Bright winter sunshine warms the waters of the Mediterranean Sea.

Like the North Atlantic Drift, the Mediterranean helps keep southern Europe warm in the winter.

God created warm seas. He also planned for ocean currents to carry this water far to the north. Without this wonderful plan, much of the world would be too cold for crops. God made the sea and He controls it.

Psalm 95:5a

Psalm 89:9a

"The sea is his, and he made it."
"Thou rulest the raging of the sea."

What Do You Say?

1. Who are *ancestors*? Name some of your ancestors.

2. a. What is Eurasia? b. What two words were put together to make the word *Eurasia*?

3. Name the four largest peninsulas in Europe.

4. What makes northern Europe warmer than northern North America?

What Does the Bible Say?

1. When the Bible talks about our ancestors, it often uses the word "fathers." a. Read Joshua 24:2. What had the ancestors of the Israelites done years before? b. Read Acts 7:30-32. Who are the ancestors named in verse 32?

Climates in Europe. The winters of northwestern Europe are fairly

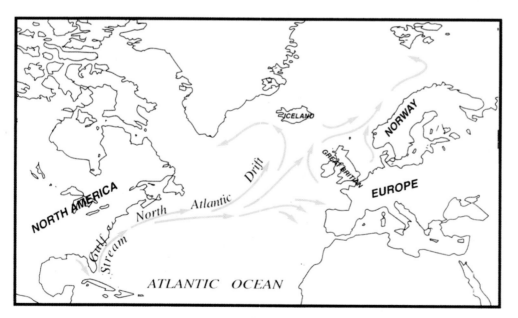

This map shows you the location of the Gulf Stream. These warm waters from near North America move far north in the Atlantic Ocean. What are these warm waters called when they near Europe? What do they do for the weather in Europe?

The Alps are some of the highest mountains in Europe. These beautiful mountains are part of the Alps in the little country of Switzerland.

warm, and summers are not too hot. Plenty of rain usually falls throughout the year. Moist ocean breezes bring this weather.

In most of Europe, the nearer the ocean you are, the warmer the winters are and the cooler the summers. Far away from the ocean, winters are colder and summers are warmer.

London, England, is on lowland not far from the ocean. In January the temperature averages about 45° F (7° C) in the day and about 35° F (2° C) at night. In July the temperature seldom goes above 90° F (32° C).

The lands around the Mediterranean Sea have a climate that is very different from that of northern Europe. Summers are hot and dry. Winters are mild and rainy. The Mediterranean is like a huge, warm lake. It captures much warmth from the bright southern sun. When winds blow over these waters, they bring warm weather to southern Europe. Sometimes hot air from the great deserts of northern Africa blows across the Mediterranean. At such times the air is hot, dry, and dusty. But in winter moist winds from the northwest bring rain.

In the parts of northern Europe away from the Atlantic Ocean, the winters are cold and the summers are cool. The highest mountains of Europe also have cool or cold weather all year.

The Shape of the Land

Europe has many different landforms, from high mountains to flat plains. High mountains border the ocean in parts of Great Britain and in much of Norway. Very little lowland lies between the mountains and the ocean.

Lowlands and plains spread

across much of Britain and northern Europe from France through Russia. These lowlands are sometimes called the North European Plain. This plain is widest in Russia.

South of the North European Plain the land becomes hilly and mountainous. High mountains stretch almost all the way across Europe from east to west. Between France and Spain these mountains are called the Pyrenees (pir′ ə nez′). From France and Switzerland east the mountains are called the *Alps*. The Alps stop much of the cold air that pours across Europe from the north in winter. Lands to the south stay warmer in winter than lands to the north.

Much of Europe south of the Alps and near the Mediterranean Sea is hilly or mountainous. Mountain areas are cool in winter. Lowlands near the Mediterranean Sea are warmer.

The land in much of southern Europe is hilly. This picture was taken near the Mediterranean Sea looking toward the mountainous land found in Italy. In some places in southern Europe the hills and mountains come to the edge of the sea.

3. How do the Alps help keep lands in southern Europe mild in winter?

What Do You Say?

1. Why does water help keep nearby land warm in winter?

2. a. Describe the climate in Mediterranean lands in winter. b. In summer.

What Does the Bible Say?

1. From where does rain come? Find an answer in Job 5:8-10.

2. The mountains and the wind have much to do with the weather in southern Europe. What does Amos 4:13 say about the mountains and the wind?

Using Globes and Maps

1. Use thin white paper and trace the outline of Europe from one of the maps in this text. On your traced map name all the large peninsulas and islands and the oceans and seas around Europe. Include at least the following: Scandinavian Peninsula, Iberian Peninsula, Balkan Peninsula, Great Britain, Iceland, Sicily, Atlantic Ocean, Arctic Ocean, Mediterranean Sea, North Sea, Baltic Sea, Black Sea, Caspian Sea.

2. On a map of Europe with major cities marked, use the scale of miles or kilometers to find how far it is from the following cities to the nearest sea or ocean: Madrid, Spain; Paris, France; Berlin, Germany; Moscow, Russia; Bergen, Norway.

3. Refer to a relief map of Europe in an encyclopedia. Trace or draw an outline map of Europe and show the major mountain systems of Europe. They are the mountains of Norway and Sweden; the Ural Mountains of Russia, along the Asian border; the Pyrenees, between France and Spain; the Alps, from southern France to Austria and then southeast into Slovenia; the Apennines in Italy; and the Carpathians in Slovakia and Romania. Use symbols like this to show the mountains:

New Words and Terms

Match the words with the descriptions following.

1. _____ ancestors
2. _____ geographer
3. _____ Eurasia
4. _____ Balkan Peninsula
5. _____ Scandinavian Peninsula
6. _____ Apennine Peninsula
7. _____ Iberian Peninsula
8. _____ ocean current
9. _____ Gulf Stream
10. _____ North Atlantic Drift

a. Europe and Asia considered as one continent.

b. The warm waters of the Gulf Stream as they near Europe.

c. A boot-shaped peninsula in southern Europe.

d. A river of warm or cold water that moves through the ocean.

e. An ocean current that begins in the Gulf of Mexico.

f. A person who studies the earth.

g. People who have lived before us such as our parents and grandparents.

h. A peninsula in Europe where Spain and Portugal are located.

i. A peninsula in southeastern Europe.

j. A large peninsula in northern Europe.

Thinking Together

1. Why do people in Europe feel especially close to people in North America?

2. If you wanted to visit two or three European countries farthest from the sea, where would you visit?

3. From their earliest history Europeans have traveled much on the sea. Why do you think this is?

4. a. What does the Gulf Stream or the North Atlantic Drift bring to Europe? b. What might the climate be like if there were no warm ocean current?

5. Why did God plan for warm seas and warm ocean currents?

For You to Do

1. Some in your class will no doubt know from what country their ancestors came. Make a list of these places. Mark them on a map.

2. Find a country in Europe that is the same distance north of the equator as your state or province. From an encyclopedia read about the climate in that country. How is it different from the climate where you live? If you live farther south than any country in Europe, find a country or city in Africa that is as far south as you live. Find out what the climate is like there.

9. Land of the North

Now let us visit Europe's far north. The people who live here call their land *Norge* (nȯr′ gə). *Norge* means "North." We call their land Norway, "the land of the north." The people who live there are Norwegians (nȯr wē′ jənz).

Look at the map of Europe on page 135. Find Norway. Norway is part of the large peninsula called Scandinavia. With what other country does Norway share the peninsula?

Norway is a long, narrow coun-try from north to south. It stretches about 1,100 miles (1,770 kilometers). At one place in the north, Norway is only four miles (6½ kilometers) wide. In the south the country is about 250 miles (400 kilometers) wide. Norway is a very mountainous land. There is so little level land in Norway that only four of every 100 acres of land can be used for farming. About 22 of every 100 acres is wood-land. The rest is too steep, too rocky, or too icy for plants to grow.

Norway is a land of mountains.

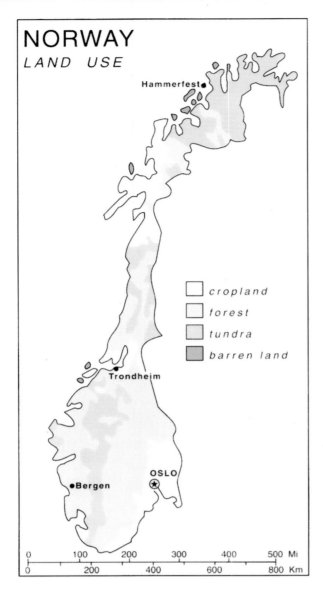

NORWAY
LAND USE

Hammerfest

☐ cropland
☐ forest
☐ tundra
☐ barren land

Trondheim

OSLO ★
● Bergen

| 0 | 100 | 200 | 300 | 400 | 500 Mi |
| 0 | 200 | 400 | 600 | 800 Km |

How much of Norway can be used for farming? Which part of the country has the most farming land?

It is also a land of the sea. Along much of the coast the mountains rise steeply from the sea. Most of Norway's people live near the sea or in the few lowland areas.

One of the first things that a visitor sees are the thousands of islands along the coast of Norway. There are at least 150,000 of them! These rock islands are called **skerries** (sker′ ēz). Some are only small rocks sticking out of the water. Other islands are large. Hundreds of people live on them. The Norwegians call their coastal islands the "skerry fence."

The "skerry fence" around Norway helps protect the coast from the high winds and storms of the open ocean.

Land of the Midnight Sun

How would you like to go out and play ball or go hiking at midnight? You could do it in northern Norway without floodlights or flashlights. The sun shines day and night for weeks in the far north.

At North Cape, the northernmost place in Norway, the sun begins shining all day and all night in the middle of May. It does not set until the end of July. The people of Norway call the northern part of their country "The Land of the Midnight Sun."

In winter the sun does not rise for many weeks in The Land of the Midnight Sun. At North Cape the sun sets in mid-November and does not rise again until near the end of January. Norwegians call this "the dark time."

Years ago a lady was traveling by ship to northern Norway. One morning the stewardess asked, "Will you have breakfast?"

The lady replied, "Thank you, I'll wait until the sun rises."

"Then, madam," came the answer, "you will stay in bed for weeks, for the sun will not rise before the middle of January!"

144

Thousands of islands are found off the coast of Norway. While some of these islands are quite large, many are just rocks sticking out of the water. What do the Norwegians call these islands off their coast?

What Causes the Midnight Sun?

What causes the midnight sun in summer and the midday darkness in winter in Norway?

The sun can be seen at midnight because the earth is always tilted as it circles around the sun. Many globes are made with rods through them and are tilted in the same way the earth itself is tilted.

As the earth circles around the sun, it is always tilted the same way. During part of the year the North Pole is tilted toward the sun. At that time of the year, places north of the

equator have long hours of daylight. As you travel farther north there are more hours of daylight. In the far north the sun shines all day and all night. This is summer in the Northern Hemisphere.

Do you see the dotted line on the map of Europe on page 135? This line is called the *Arctic Circle.* All places north of the Arctic Circle have at least one day of midnight sun each year. No place south of this line has a midnight sun.

During winter in the Northern

Hemisphere the North Pole tilts away from the sun. During this time of the year all places north of the Arctic Circle have days or weeks of darkness.

Find Hammerfest on the map of Norway on page 144. It is almost at the northern tip of the country. Hammerfest is far north of the Arctic Circle. In winter the sun does not shine there for many weeks. The people in Hammerfest are glad to see the sun rise again. In early February they have a special holiday called "Sun Coffee Day." What do you think they do on this day?

In parts of Norway south of the Arctic Circle the winter days are very short. In Oslo, the capital of Norway, the sun rises about 9:30 in the morning on Christmas Day. It sets about 3:30 in the afternoon. How many hours of sunlight does this make?

June 21 is the longest day of the year in Norway and in most other parts of the Northern Hemisphere. On that day the sun shines about 18 hours in Oslo. The short night does not get completely dark. Norwegians have a midsummer festival to celebrate the long hours of sunlight.

What Do You Say?

1. a. What does the name *Norway* mean? b. Why is this a good name for that country?

2. When does the sun shine all night in northern Norway?

3. What happens in midwinter at all places north of the Arctic Circle?

4. a. How many hours of sunshine does Oslo, Norway, have at Christmastime? b. How many hours of sunlight does Oslo have in late June?

What Does the Bible Say?

1. a. What kind of weather do you think about when you hear the word *north*? b. What does the Bible say comes from the north? Find the answer in Job 37:9. (Remember that this is true only in lands north of the equator.)

2. Some Norwegians are unhappy when the long, dark winter days come. They wish for warm weather and sunshine. But what should we remember about day and night, summer and winter? (Read Psalm 74:16, 17.)

Along Norway's coast, steep mountains come down to the edge of the water. Norwegians must make use of every bit of more level land found here and there along the fjords.

In and Out on Norway's Coast

Look at the map of Norway. Notice the crooked coastline. Dozens of little arms of the sea reach far inland like watery fingers. These "fingers" are called **fjords** (fyordz).

Some of the fjords in Norway reach inland as far as 200 miles (320 kilometers). A fjord is almost too beautiful to picture with words. The water in most fjords is very deep. Steep mountains rise from the water on both sides of the fjord. People must travel in and out of fjords by boat or by air. The land is too steep for roads to be built along most fjords.

A ship captain once decided to surprise some visitors to a Norwegian fjord. He sailed so close to the side of the fjord that the passengers could lean out and touch the mountainside. He knew that the mountain dropped steeply into the sea. He knew that the water was very deep right up to the shore.

Here and there along the fjords are little bits of flat land where a few people have built their homes. At the end of a fjord one usually finds a larger area of lowland. Sometimes small villages have been built at the end of fjords. Only a few fjords have enough flat land along them for building cities.

This prosperous farm is one of the few lowland regions of Norway.

Life Along a Fjord

Hans Olsen lives with his sister Ingrid and his parents beside a beautiful fjord. Their home is in a small village. Each home is sturdy, built of wood from the nearby forests.

The villagers have cleared much of the land around their houses and on the steep hillside behind the village. These hardworking Norwegians farm in the summer. In the winter they fish and cut lumber.

The short, rainy summers are good for field crops such as hay, oats, barley, and potatoes. Families grow many vegetables in their gardens.

This photo shows hay drying on racks near a stone church in Norway. Why do the Norwegians dry hay this way?

Potatoes, turnips, and greens do well. Corn needs longer and warmer summers than are found in Norway.

Seasons Along the Fjords. In summer, Hans and some of the other young boys take the cows and goats to green pastures high on the mountains. Here the weather is too cool for trees. The short, warm summers are just right for thick grass. The boys live in little wooden huts. They watch the cows and goats and milk them too. Then they make cheese and butter.

At least once a week one of the village fathers visits the huts. He brings down the butter and cheeses. Boats sail up the fjord to buy these products. They will be sold in cities elsewhere in Norway.

As autumn comes and snow begins to fall in the high mountains, the boys bring the cattle down to the village. The farmers gather in the hay and oats to feed the animals during the long, dark winter.

Hay does not dry well on the ground in the cool, damp air. Farmers put the hay up on racks or wires to dry.

Winter along the fjords of Norway is almost as busy as summer. The cows must be milked. The cheese and butter must be made. The farmers need to repair farm equipment for the next year.

In winter Hans learns how to use his father's woodworking tools. He hopes to make simple wooden blocks and toys to sell. Perhaps when he is older, he will be able to make chairs and tables.

Ingrid spends many long winter hours knitting and embroidering. She makes beautiful mittens, scarves, and sweaters. She embroiders mottoes. She sells these to make extra money.

For many of the men and older boys, winter is a time to cut wood in the forests. Most homes in Norway are built of wood from the fine forests. In Norway, forests cover four of every ten acres or hectares of land. Much wood is also used for firewood. In many parts of Norway, timber is cut to make paper.

A few of the men in the village where Hans lives go out on fishing boats in January. They fish around the islands off the coast. The men fish much of the time from January until April. Then it is about time to begin spring plowing. And so another busy year begins for the Norwegian farmers.

Riches in Norway's Forests

God has covered much of the land in Norway, Sweden, and Finland with rich forests. The people of Norway use their trees for many different things. They even use the sap from their trees.

In the winter men cut thousands of trees in the forests of Norway. More and more logging roads have been built for hauling out the timber. But much of Norway's timber is dragged to the nearest river. In the winter the rivers are covered with thick ice. Loggers roll the logs onto the ice. The logs lie there until spring.

In spring the ice begins to melt. *Creak, crack, crack, snap!* The logs begin to move, slowly at first, then faster and faster. Water from melted snow runs into the rivers. The water

Norwegians are used to an abundance of snow in the long, cold winters. Some people still use skis to get from one place to another as many Norwegians did long ago.

rises. The high, rushing waters move tons of logs down the rivers to the sawmills.

At the sawmills big electric saws quickly cut a log into chunks. The chunks of wood are crushed into a mush or pulp. This pulp is pressed between big rollers to make paper.

God has given Norway many valuable natural resources. One of them is trees. Here is a picture of just some of the things made from Norway's trees. How many of these things can you name?

Norway makes and sells thousands of tons of paper each year. Some of this paper is even sold across the ocean in the United States.

Paper is not the only thing the Norwegians make from wood. Many of the big logs that come down the rivers will be turned into other valuable products. Some of the wood is used to make beautiful chairs, tables, and wooden toys. Did you know that cloth can be made from wood? Some of Norway's wood is treated and made into rayon, a strong, shiny cloth.

Wood is also used to make some of the strongest plastics known. Thin cellophane and camera films are made from wood. Most Norwegian homes, even those in the cities, are built of wood. Wooden houses last a long time in the cool climate of Norway.

Even the resin or sap which oozes from some of the pines in Norway can be used. Resin is used in making varnish, paints, and soaps.

What Do You Say?

1. Which of the following is the best description of a fjord?

a. a large lake near the coast

b. an arm of the sea reaching far inland

c. a wide river leading to the sea

2. Which season would you enjoy most on a Norwegian fjord? Why?

3. Name at least five things Norwegians make from wood.

What Does the Bible Say?

1. You have learned in this chapter that many of the Norwegians are hard workers. Hard work is good for everyone. The Bible teaches many things about work.

a. What does 1 Thessalonians 4:11 ask us to do?

b. What does the Bible say about a person who does not work? (Read 2 Thessalonians 3:10.)

2. We should thank God for the natural resources He gives. Psalm 104:24 tells about the resources God gives. Fill in each blank with a word. "O LORD, how manifold are thy works! in wisdom hast thou made them all: the a. _____ is full of thy b. _____ ."

Power From Water!

Do you remember reading about the electric saws in Norwegian sawmills? The sawmills of Norway are electric for two important reasons. First, Norway used to have very little oil or other fuel as a source of power. Not long ago the Norwegians found oil under the shallow waters of the North Sea to the south. Until then Norway had to buy from other countries any oil that it used.

The people of Norway needed fuel. Where would they find it? God had given them plenty of another kind of power—water power. The people could not burn water or run big motors with water itself. But they could use water to make electricity, and electricity can run machinery. Plenty of inexpensive electricity made from "water power" is the second reason Norwegian sawmills are run by electricity.

In Norway plenty of rain and snow falls. Hundreds of waterfalls tumble down the steep mountainsides. Electric power stations are built beside the falling water. The fast-running water turns giant wheels. The wheels spin machines, called generators, that make electricity.

Electricity made by water power is called **hydroelectricity**. *Hydro* means "water."

Many electric plants in the Americas are powered by expensive fuels such as coal and oil. These fuels are burned to make steam to spin the

This picture shows the famous Seven Sisters Waterfalls in Norway. How many of the seven falls can you find on this picture?

machines that make electricity. The burning of coal and oil sends dirty smoke into the air.

In Norway the hydroelectric plants send no smoke into the air. Most of Norway's machinery and trains run on electricity. They make no smoke either.

Because of water power, the air in Norway is much cleaner than in many parts of the United States. Smoke and dirt in the air are called **pollution** (pə lü′ shən). Norway has some pollution from gas-burning automobiles and trucks. But mostly the

151

air is very clean.

As long as God sends rain and snow, Norway will have plenty of water to turn its generators. Other countries may run out of oil, coal, and natural gas. But Norway is not likely to run out of water power.

"Thou visitest the earth, and waterest it: thou greatly enrichest it with the river of God, which is full of water."

Psalm 65:9

God's Blessings From the Sea

When God made people, He gave them power over the fish in the sea. "And God blessed them, and God said unto them, Be fruitful, and multiply, and replenish the earth, and subdue it: and have dominion over the fish of the sea."

Genesis 1:28

The Norwegians have had do-minion or power over the fish of the sea for many years. They have long been a people of the sea. Indeed, most of Norway's people live near the sea. Much of the land away from the sea is too rough or too mountainous to live on.

Fish is one of the favorite foods of Norway. There are fishing villages along many of the fjords. Trondheim and Bergen are two cities with large fish factories. In the winter many farmers earn extra money by fishing.

Many kinds of fish are found in Norway: herring, cod, mackerel, flounder, and salmon. Certain kinds of fish are caught in different seasons. January to April is cod season. The codfish swarm into the waters along the coast to lay their eggs. January is a dark, cold time to set out fishing, but that is when the fish are biting. The weather out among the islands is above freezing even in the middle of the winter. Even this far north the warmth of the North Atlantic Drift can still be felt.

These Norwegian fishing boats are being readied to do more fishing.

Out to Catch the Cod

In January dozens of fishing ships set out from towns and cities along the coast of Norway. A group of ships called a **fleet** travels together. A government hospital ship goes along with each fleet.

Cod are caught in three different ways. Some are caught on long lines baited with pieces of fish. Most fishermen, however, use nets.

Sometimes they drop the nets from their ships. When the nets fill with fish, the men haul them in. Some fishermen use small boats for fishing instead of dropping nets from larger ships. They leave the main ship in these smaller boats. They stretch a net between the two boats. They pull up the nets full of squirming cod and dump them into a larger boat.

Some of the cod are packed in ice and shipped fresh to the fish factories. Some of the fish are split, cleaned, and hung up to dry in the cool, salty air. Some are salted and laid out on rocky islands to dry. Dried cod will keep for months and even years without spoiling.

Frozen, dried, and salted cod are brought into factories in the larger cities. At Bergen, Norway's second largest city, dozens of fishing boats come and go.

Bergen has a large open-air fish market. Almost every day thousands of Bergensers come to market to buy fresh fish. They like their fish fresh. Not many buy fish on Mondays because the fish were caught on Saturday.

Large factories in Bergen and other cities prepare most of the fish catch to be sold in other countries. Anything that a country sells to another country is called an export. Norway exports many fish along with paper and oil.

Anything which a country buys from another country is called an

These fish are drying on racks along Norway's coast.

import. Norwegians cannot grow all the food they need, so they import food along with tools, machines, and other factory-made goods.

What Do You Say?

1. What is hydroelectricity?

2. Why is the air in Norway cleaner than that of the United States?

3. Name two ways the oceans around Norway help this country earn money?

What Does the Bible Say?

1. We know that God sends the rain and the snow that make the rivers. Man can use the rivers for making electricity, for sources of drinking water, and for irrigating fields. What does Job 28:25 say that God does to the water?

2. Read Genesis 1:26. What does this verse say about man and the sea? (*Dominion* means "rule" or "control.")

Life in Lapland

One of the most interesting parts of Norway to visit is the northernmost part. There live a sturdy people called the Lapps. Lapps also live in the northern parts of Sweden and Finland. A few live in Russia.

The Lapps of Norway live in Finnmark County. Sometimes people call all the lands where Lapps live *Lapland*.

The Lapps look somewhat like people from Japan or China. Their ancestors are believed to have come from the east thousands of years ago. The Lapps are among the shortest people in Europe. Most reach only about five feet (150 centimeters). The Lapps may be short, but they are strong, muscular people.

The Lapps speak their own language and follow their own special ways of life. They are, however, learning new ways and becoming more like other Norwegians.

A Cold, Harsh Land. Norway's Finnmark County and all of Lapland is cold. Winter lasts nine months. Summer is much like spring in warmer lands.

Lapland has few trees because of the cold wind that blows over the land. Trees that do grow are in sheltered places. Even these trees are small because they have little time to grow in the short summers. Some grasses, flowers, and mosses also grow during the short summers. Mosses grow especially well. One kind, reindeer moss, is very important to the Laplanders.

The "Cattle" of Lapland. Reindeer are the "cattle" of Lapland. Ordinary cows could not stand the long, cold winters without shelters. Reindeer can live very well outside. They live off the short plants that grow on the tundra around them. They especially like reindeer moss. When snow covers the ground, they dig for food.

For hundreds of years the Lapps have been herders of reindeer. The reindeer give them milk, cheese, and meat to eat. Reindeer skins are used for tents and for clothes.

Changes in Lapland. Today the Lapps are divided into three groups.

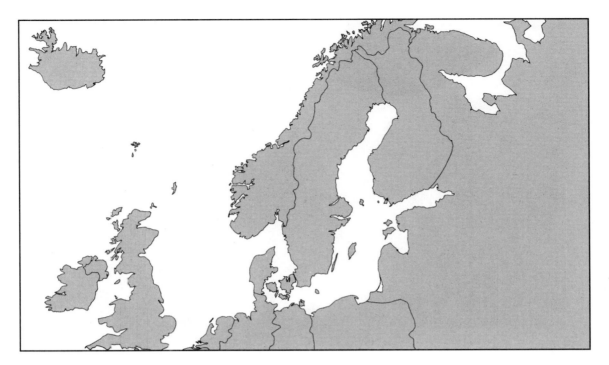

The shaded area near the top of this map is sometimes called Lapland. Most of Northern Europe's Lapps live here.

These groups are the Mountain Lapps, the Sea Lapps, and the River Lapps.

Only the Mountain Lapps still live as nomads. They live in tents and move about searching for food for their reindeer. They eat mainly reindeer meat, milk, and cheese.

The Sea Lapps live near the ocean and fish for a living. Many of them live in little villages. Their houses are often made of wood covered with sod.

The River Lapps live in towns and villages along the rivers of Lapland. They fish, hunt, and keep reindeer, cattle, and sheep. Some of the River Lapps do a little farming. But the cold climate and very short summers keep farming from becoming a big business.

One of the greatest changes in Lapland took place in recent years. In the 1960s a schoolteacher in Lapland bought a snowmobile. The Lapps were excited about the little machine that could go almost anywhere in the snow. Some believed it would help them round up their reindeer. Soon many were buying the machines. Some people called them the "iron reindeer." Now the Lapps could travel quickly from one place to another. Men began to herd reindeer with their snowmobiles.

The coming of the snowmobile was not all good, however. Snowmobiles are expensive to buy. Expensive gasoline must be imported to "feed" the iron reindeer. Some of the Lapps can hardly afford the machines, but they buy them anyway.

155

This picture shows a Norwegian Lapp with a harnessed reindeer. How can you tell from this picture that Lapland is a cold place? The reindeer is about 3 1/2 feet (107 centimeters) high at the shoulder. It weighs about 300 pounds. Unlike most deer, both the male and female reindeer have antlers.

The snowmobile has made it possible for a few men to round up more reindeer. This has forced some of the men to leave their families and friends to look for work elsewhere.

The use of the snowmobile has helped cause groups of herders to become angry with each other. With their snowmobiles some have greedily rounded up more than their share of reindeer. Herders need large herds to earn enough money to pay for the "iron reindeer."

Some fear that the snowmobile will play a big part in ending the old way of life. Others feel it is a change the Lapps must accept. Certainly the snowmobile in Lapland teaches us some lessons. Not everything that is new is good. Some new things may be very helpful but can be used in wrong ways. Not all changes are for the best.

What Do You Say?

1. Where is Lapland?

2. What kind of "cattle" do the Lapps have?

3. a. What important change has taken place in Lapland in recent years? b. Name some problems this change has brought.

What Does the Bible Say?

1. Some Lapps, you remember, be-

156

This frame structure is used by Lapps of Norway. Notice the grass growing on the roof.

came greedy for more land and more reindeer. The Bible calls greed covetousness. Read Exodus 20:17. What things should we not covet?

2. Hebrews 13:5 speaks about covetousness (greed) also. Instead of being greedy, how should we be?

Long Ago in Norway

People have lived in Norway for hundreds of years. No one knows

This map shows the places where early explorers from Norway traveled. What name do we give to these explorers?

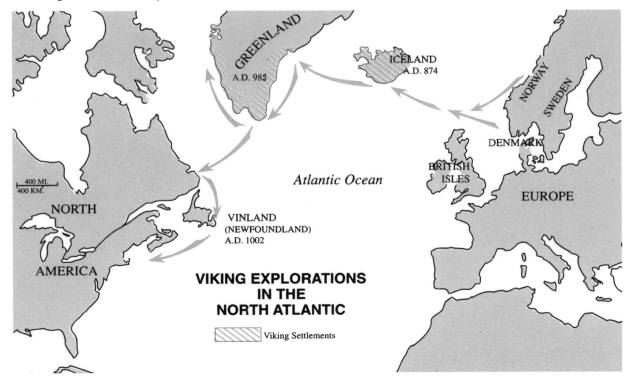

GREENLAND
A.D. 985

ICELAND
A.D. 874

NORWAY

SWEDEN

DENMARK

BRITISH
ISLES

EUROPE

Atlantic Ocean

NORTH

AMERICA

400 MI.
400 KM.

VINLAND
(NEWFOUNDLAND)
A.D. 1002

**VIKING EXPLORATIONS
IN THE
NORTH ATLANTIC**

Viking Settlements

A Viking ship probably looked something like this. What did the Vikings use these ships for?

when men first came to the land of fjords and of the midnight sun.

The earliest people in Norway were **heathen**. This means they worshiped false gods. They knew almost nothing about the true God.

The people of Norway were at one time called *Norse* or *Northmen*. Both words mean "people of the north." In many parts of Europe the Norse were also called *Vikings* (vī′ kingz). This name may have come from the Norse word *vik*. A vik was a bay along the coast. The Vikings lived mostly along the coasts of Norway, Sweden, and Denmark.

The Norse believed in many gods. Female gods were called goddesses. The Norse also imagined that the earth and sky were the home of many giants. The giants and the gods often fought each other.

The Norse thought they could hear their gods all around them. Thor (thȯr) was the Norse god of thunder. Thunder was supposed to be his voice. Black clouds were his brow. Lightning was the flashing of his hammer as he fought the giants.

The Norse liked to tell stories about the gods, giants, and human heroes. These stories are called *sagas* (säg′ əz).

The sagas told of the cruel deeds of the gods. The gods fought with each other and with the giants. One of the sagas told of the end of the world. It said that the gods will kill each other, all the giants, and all but two people.

We know that the true God is not cruel. The Bible says, "Far be it from God, that he should do wickedness; and from the Almighty, that he should commit iniquity." **Job 34:10**

"The LORD is gracious, and full of compassion; slow to anger, and of great mercy. The LORD is good to all: and his tender mercies are over all his works." **Psalm 145:8, 9**

God will not be killed or die at the end of the world. He will live forever. "From everlasting to everlasting, thou art God." Because He will live forever, we can live forever also. **Psalm 90:2b**

No Better Than Their Gods. The Norse behaved much as their gods did. They built speedy ships and sailed to faraway lands. They robbed villages, killed the people, and burned what was left. No place along the coast of Europe was safe from the cruel Vikings.

Churches in Europe had special prayers for God's help. They prayed, "God, deliver us from the fury of the Northmen."

Vikings conquered and ruled England and part of France. This part of France was named Normandy because of the Northmen who settled there.

Viking warriors were known for being fierce and cruel. People in many parts of Europe feared them.

Some Vikings settled in England, France, and other countries. They did not go back to Norway, Sweden, and Denmark. Some of them became Christians and quit their stealing, killing, and burning.

Unfortunately some of the Norse who became Christians did not act like Christians. One such man was King Olaf I.

Olaf was a fierce Viking. He fought against and burned villages along the coasts of France and England. Finally he professed to accept Christianity. He quit his dirty work and sailed back to Norway. There he became king.

In Norway Olaf treated his friends kindly. But he was cruel to his enemies. He tried to force the people of Norway to give up the old gods. "You must accept Christianity," he demanded. He made many enemies.

Olaf fought a sea battle against the Swedish. When he saw that he was losing the battle, he leaped from his ship. No one ever saw him again. He was only 31 years old.

Had King Olaf I been a true Christian, he would have been kind to his enemies. He would have won the people to Christ by sending preachers to bring them the Gospel.

The Bible says, "Love your enemies, bless them that curse you, do good to them that hate you, and pray for them. . . . That ye may be the children of your Father which is in heaven. . . . For if ye love them which love you, what reward have ye?"

Matthew 5:44b-46a

159

Some Norse Words We Use

The Norse who came to England brought their religion and their language with them. The English borrowed some words and ideas from the Norse.

Most English words that begin with sk- come from Old Norse. The word *sky* meant "cloud" in Old Norse. What does it mean in our language? *Skirt* was the Norse word for "shirt." What does this borrowed word mean in English? *Skin, skill,* and *scrape* are also words that came to us from the Norse. Some other Norse words in English are *aye* (meaning "yes"), *nay, ill, die, fro, they, their,* and *them.*

The Norse brought to England their names for the days of the week. The English borrowed four of these. *Tuesday* is named for Tyr (tir), the Norse god of war. *Wednesday* was named for Odin or Woden, the chief Norse god. *Thursday* was Thor's day. (Thor, you remember, was the god of thunder.) Frigg, the goddess of love, gives us the word *Friday.*

What Do You Say?

1. a. Who were the Vikings?
   b. Give two other names for them.

2. In what ways did the Vikings behave as their gods did?

3. Name at least six words that have come to us from the Norse.

What Does the Bible Say?

1. What does the Bible say about gods like Thor and Odin? Find two answers by reading Psalm 96:5 and Psalm 135:5.

2. Finish this verse. "If it be possible, as much as lieth in you, _____ " (Romans 12:18).

Using Globes and Maps

1. Look at the map of Europe on page 135 and answer these questions about Norway: a. What two countries share the Scandinavian Peninsula? b. Does any other country in Europe have land that reaches as far north as does Norway? c. What ocean lies north of Scandinavia? d. West? e. What large sea lies southeast of Scandinavia?

2. On the map of Norway on page 144 find Oslo, Bergen, Trondheim, and Hammerfest. a. Which is the capital? b. Which are along fjords away from the main ocean? c. Which are along the main ocean?

3. Place a lamp on a table or desk. Walk around the light holding a globe always tilted in the same direction. This will show how the sun shines more on the Northern Hemisphere for part of the year.

4. On a world map or globe find where the Arctic Circle crosses Canada and the United States.

5. On a large piece of paper trace a map of Norway from the map on page 144. Place on it the names of these cities: Oslo, Bergen, Trondheim, Hammerfest. Draw a dotted line where the Arctic Circle crosses Norway. Label the following: Arctic Ocean, Atlantic Ocean, North Sea.

New Words and Terms

Choose the best of the three choices to finish each sentence.

1. *Norge* is the Norwegian word for _____ .
   a. a kind of refrigerator   b. Norway   c. the Midnight Sun

2. *Scandinavia* includes _____ .
   a. Norway and Sweden   b. Norway, Sweden, and part of Russia
   c. only Norway

3 *Skerries* are _____ .

a. large islands near Norway   b. ferries across Norway's many fjords
c. small, rocky islands

4. The *Land of the Midnight Sun* includes _____ .

a. all of Norway   b. the northern part of Norway
c. most of Scandinavia

5. The *Arctic Circle* has _____ .

a. at least one day of midnight sun each year
b. six hours of daylight in the winter
c. no days of midnight sun

6. A *fjord* is _____ .

a. an automobile made in Norway   b. a large, inland lake
c. a little arm of the sea that reaches far inland

7. *Hydroelectricity* is made from _____ .

a. water power   b. coal power   c. horse power

8. A *fleet* is _____ .

a. a small group of ships   b. a large group of ships   c. only one ship

9. *Exports* are _____ .

a. things one country buys from another
b. things one country sells to another
c. things sold inside a country

10. *Imports* are _____ .

a. things one country buys from another
b. things one country sells to another
c. things sold inside a country

11. Smoke and other dirt in the air causes _____ .

a. fog   b. pollution   c. clear weather

12. *Lapland* includes parts of the following countries:

a. Norway, Sweden, Finland, and Russia
b. Norway, Sweden, and Denmark
c. Norway and Denmark

13. The land of the far north where only short grasses will grow is called
_____ .

a. Lapland b. fjord c. tundra

Thinking Together

1. Why have Norwegians called their country "the land of the north"?

2. Why have Norwegians long been a people of the sea?

3. If you lived in Norway, which would you enjoy most, January or July? Why?

4. Why are winters in Norway a busy time in spite of the darkness and cold?

5. List at least four ways the Norwegians use the wood from their forests.

6. List three or more ways wood is used in your community.

7. a. What is pollution? b. Give ways you or your parents could help stop pollution of the land or air around you.

8. a. In what ways were the Vikings no better than their gods? b. How does the true God teach us to live?

For You to Do

1. Write a report on the different seasons in your community. You may include in your report changes that take place in weather, in the work people do, and in the plant and animal life.

2. Read an article on forest products in an encyclopedia. List at least twenty forest products.

3. Cod, herring, and salmon are three of the most important fish caught in Norway. Read an article in an encyclopedia on one of these fish and write a short report. Include answers to the following questions: Where do the fish live? When do they lay their eggs? How much do they weigh? What countries catch the most of these fish? Also draw a picture of the fish you have chosen.

10. Italy—The Boot-Shaped Peninsula

Norway, you remember, is the northernmost country in Europe. Now you will study Italy, one of the southernmost countries in Europe.

Find Italy on the map of Europe on page 135. Italy is easy to find because of its shape. The country is on a peninsula shaped like a boot. The "boot" hangs down into the Mediterranean Sea from Europe. Can you find the "heel" and the "toe" of the Italian "boot"? The boot looks as though it is kicking the large island near the toe! The name of this island is Sicily.

The island of Sicily is also a part of the country of Italy. Find the island of Sardinia (sär din′ ē ə) off the west coast of Italy. This large island is also part of Italy. The island of Corsica (kȯr′ si kə) just north of Sardinia belongs to France.

Italy is a mountainous land. Three-fourths of Italy is up and down with hills and mountains. In the north the Alps rise like a high wall between Italy and the rest of Europe. South of the Alps is the Po River. The Po flows through the plains of Lombardy (lom′ bärd′ ē). This is the largest lowland in all of Italy.

South of the lowlands are more mountains. These mountains are called the Apennines (ap′ ə nīnz′). The Apennines are a chain of mountains that stretch all the way to the "toe" of the Italian boot. The Apennines are not as high as the Alps, but the land is rough and the mountainsides are steep.

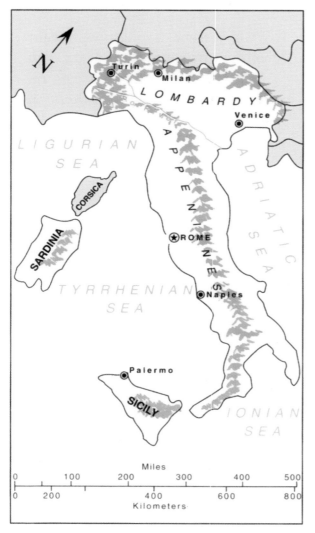

Italy

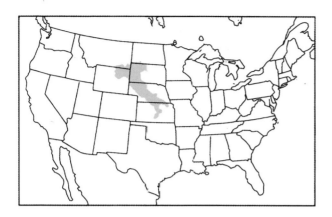

This map shows how Italy's size compares with the United States. It also shows you how far north Italy is compared with places in North America.

Italy is surrounded on three sides with the warm waters of the Mediterranean Sea. The parts of the Mediterranean Sea around Italy have special names you should remember. Find the arm of the Mediterranean just east of Italy. It is called the *Adriatic* (ā´ drē at´ ik) *Sea*. The part of the Mediterranean Sea between Italy and Greece is called the *Ionian* (ī ō´ nē ən) *Sea*. The *Tyrrhenian* (tə rē´ nē ən) *Sea* lies to the west of Italy between Italy and the islands of Sardinia and Sicily.

Small Land—Many People

On this page see the map of Italy laid on top of a map of the United States. This map helps you to see the size of Italy. Italy is so small that the country would fit into the United States 31 times. Italy is about the same size as the state of New Mexico.

As small as Italy is, it has more than 34 times as many people as does New Mexico. It has more people than the entire western half of the United States!

What Do You Say?

1. If you saw a map of Italy without the names of the country or its cities, how could you tell it was Italy?

2. Name the parts of the Mediterranean Sea around Italy.

3. How many countries the size of Italy would fit into the United States?

What Does the Bible Say?

1. Name a book in the New Testament written to people who lived in Italy. Hint: The book is named for a large city in Italy.

2. The Mediterranean Sea is mentioned in the Bible but not by that name. What is it called? (Read Joshua 1:4.)

165

This quiet little town lies on a sunny hillside in central Italy. What are the mountains of central Italy called?

Sunny Italy

Look at Italy and Norway on the map of Europe on page 135. Do you think Italy would be warmer than Norway? Why?

If you guessed that Italy is warmer than Norway, you were right. It is much farther south. You can see on the map on page 165 that Italy is as far north as Kansas, Nebraska, and the Dakotas in the United States. These states have long, cold winters. But Italy is warmer than these states. The climate in much of Italy is like that of southern California.

Most of Italy has long, hot summers. The summers are dry with only a few thunderstorms. In the summer, hot, dry winds from the vast deserts of Northern Africa blow across the Mediterranean. Sometimes the hot south winds are filled with very fine dust blown from the desert. Italians call the hot, dusty wind a **sirocco** (sə räk′ ō). The sirocco makes people feel very uncomfortable. Some Italians think people are more cross with each other when the *sirocco* blows. More fighting and murders seem to take place too.

The Bible gives a different cause for fighting and killing. "From whence come wars and fightings among you? come they not hence, even of your lusts [selfish desires] that war in your members?"

James 4:1

Winter in Italy is very different from summer. Winter is cooler than summer but often very pleasant. Winter also brings nearly all of Italy's rainfall.

Winters in the mountains may be cold and snowy, but they are usually short. Along the coast, winters are usually warmer with almost no snow. In Rome a usual January day may find the temperature up to 50° F (10° C) or more. In the north at Milan, January temperatures average about 29° F (−2° C) at night and 40° F (4° C) in the daytime. The temperature at Milan has been as low as 5° F (−15° C). But in Milan, as in all Italy, winters are short.

People from England, Germany, and other lands like to take vacations in Italy during the winter. They especially go to the south where winters can be quite warm.

The Climate and the Crops

Italy has most of its rainfall in winter when few crops grow well. The summer months are hot and dry. Most crops must be irrigated.

The soil in many parts of Italy is poor. Mountain land is especially poor. Long ago much of Italy was covered with forests. People cut down the forests for buildings and fuel. Heavy rains washed away much of the good topsoil. Today there are not many forests in Italy. The people are learning that they need to plant trees on the hillsides. They are finally learning what the Bible has said all along. God wants man to care for the earth, not spoil it.

"And the LORD God took the man, and put him into the garden of Eden to dress it and to keep it." **Genesis 2:15**

The Italians try to make use of all the land they have. The lowlands are covered with fields of wheat, corn, rice and other crops. Wheat is Italy's most important crop. But even with all the wheat grown in Italy, tons of it must be imported from countries such as the United States and Canada.

Other important crops in Italy are olives and grapes. To use all the land, the farmers will sometimes plant corn, wheat, or some other crop between the rows of grapes and olives.

Sheep graze on the barren hillsides of Italy. Long ago, forests covered much of Italy. Since the trees are gone, only grasses and short bushes grow.

Here is a grove of olive trees in Italy. Olive trees live to be very old. The trunks become large and odd-shaped as the tree grows older.

The Blessings of the Olive

Many crops would not grow well in Italy and other Mediterranean lands without irrigation. But God has blessed the Mediterranean lands with the olive tree. Olives do well in Italy's rainy winters and dry summers. They will not bear much fruit in wet countries.

Italy harvests more olives than any other country in the world. Most of Italy's olives are crushed and pressed to make olive oil. Farmers allow the olives to ripen until they turn black before pressing them. Each ripe olive is more than one-third oil. Olives are also very healthful to eat. Most people think they taste best if harvested just before they ripen and turn black.

Many Italian foods are prepared with olive oil. The olive oil has a much stronger taste than the vegetable or corn oil your mother may use.

What Do You Say?

1. The climate of most of Italy is called the Mediterranean climate. The climate in southern California is also sometimes called Mediterranean. Why do you think it is called this?

2. What has man done to make much of Italy's land poor?

3. Why does the olive tree grow well in Italy's climate?

What Does the Bible Say?

1. Palestine (Israel) has a Mediterranean climate much like that of Italy. Read Song of Solomon 2:11. What does this verse say about rain in Palestine?

2. How did the Bible writers feel about olive trees? (Read Hosea 14:6.)

3. Only once does the Bible speak of trees talking. (Read Judges 9:8, 9.) What reason did the olive tree give for not becoming king over the trees?

Farming in the North

The Po Valley in northern Italy is the richest farming region in Europe. Fields of wheat and corn and loaded apple trees remind visitors of America.

Farmers in crowded northern Italy use every bit of the land they can. It is not unusual to see grapevines growing between rows of apple trees. Tomatoes, melons, and other vegetables may be grown in vineyards among the grapevines.

These farmers are doing **intensive farming**. They raise as much as possible in a little space. They put much fertilizer and work into the land. Later in this book you will learn about more places where intensive farming is done.

Much of the farming in Italy is intensive. Still Italy must import much of its wheat. Some of this wheat is imported from the United States. Later in this chapter you will learn why the Italians need so much wheat.

Farming in Southern Italy. Farming in southern Italy is very different from farming in the north. For one thing southern Italy has very little lowland. Farmers must farm the hillsides.

Winter rains sometimes wash some of the good topsoil from the hills. Farmers in southern Italy

This beautiful scene from the rich Po Valley is not far from Bologna, Italy. How is farming life different in the Po Valley region than in southern Italy?

have learned a way to stop much of this erosion. They build low stone walls around the hills. Then they fill up the spaces behind the walls with soil. This makes a good flat place for planting crops. Behind the level ground the farmers build another wall to hold soil higher on the hill.

Farmers terraced this hillside near Genoa in northern Italy. Vegetables and fruit vines and trees are planted on these leveled places. Without terracing, few crops could be grown on such a steep hillside.

These walls with level ground behind them look like giant steps on the hillsides. These steps are called terraces. In some places the hills and mountains are terraced all the way to the top. Farming on terraces is called **terrace farming**.

Terrace farming requires much hard work. The farmer must collect and haul stone to build the stone walls. Then he must level the soil behind the walls. The farm work must be done by hand. Tractors cannot be used on the narrow terraces. Farming on terraces is also intensive farming.

Italy, the Manufacturing Nation

For most of its history Italy has been a nation of farmers. Today seven of every ten acres of land is farmed. But far less than half the people are farmers today.

Many of the people in Italy work

in factories. Most of Italy's factories are found in the northern part of the country. These factories manufacture tiny calculators, machine parts, cars, trucks, and many other things.

Did you ever see a Fiat (fē′ ät′) car? Fiats are made in Turin (tür′ in) in the Po Valley. Find the city on the map of Italy. Fiats are probably Italy's most famous manufactured product. They are used in Italy and are also exported to many countries.

Can you guess now in which part of Italy the people are the most prosperous? If you guessed "the north" you were correct. The best farmland and the most manufacturing are in the north. People there make about twice as much money as the people in the south. Many of them can afford cars. Some who do not have enough money for a car have little motor scooters called *Vespas*. The word *vespa* in Italian means "wasp." Can you guess why a little motor scooter might be called a *vespa*?

What Do You Say?

1. What is intensive farming?
2. Why is terrace farming necessary in parts of Italy?
3. Name at least three products manufactured in Italy.

What Does the Bible Say?

1. Italian farmers work hard to plant and harvest their crops. But they must depend on God for rain and sunshine. According to Psalm 104:13, 14, what does God do for all farmers?

2. Write 1 Timothy 6:17. It is a verse that is good for anyone who earns money to remember. It reminds us that what we have God has given to us.

These Fiats have been loaded on a train to be shipped to dealers.

This photo shows earthquake damage in southern Italy. What causes such earthquakes?

Terremoto—Earthquake

The date was November 23, 1980. The time was 7:34 in the evening. Many Italians were sitting down to Sunday supper.

Without a warning the ground began to shake. Walls began to crack. Soon hundreds of buildings fell. In about 40 seconds the shaking stopped.

People ran into the streets crying, "*Terremoto! Terremoto!*" (*Terremoto* means "earthquake" in Italian.) But buildings fell on many people before they reached the streets.

The center of the terrible earth-quake was in the mountains east of Naples. Find Naples on the map of Italy. The most damage was done in the "ankle" of the Italian "boot." Rome, one hundred miles to the northwest, felt the quake. In Rome people fled from an airport control tower as it began to sway back and forth. The tower did not fall.

In one city a group of mostly women and children were attending a church service. The church collapsed and killed 50 people. The priest who was in charge of the service escaped alive. He said, "It was the end of the world, enough to drive you mad."

Of course it was not the end of the world. But many Italians must have felt that way. For many it was the end of their lives.

The earthquake in Italy seems little when we think about the great earthquake when the world really does end. "And every island fled away, and the mountains were not found."

velation
20

The earthquake in Italy was one of many that will come as the world becomes older and comes to an end. The Bible warns, "And there shall be famines, and pestilences [diseases], and earthquakes, in divers [many different] places. All these are the beginning of sorrows."

tthew
7b, 8

The worst damage in the Italian earthquake took place in the little villages that cling to the steep mountains. One of the hardest hit was the poor farming village of Sant' Angelo dei Lombardi (sänt än' jel ō dā ē lom' bär dē). Before the quake 4,000 people lived there. All but a few of the buildings fell. Hundreds were killed. Later, one thousand were still missing. Some other villages nearby were completely destroyed.

What Made the Ground Shake?

Earthquakes can take place anywhere in the world. But some places have more quakes and

This map shows you places where earthquakes happen most often. Earthquakes happen in many other places, but they are more common in the areas shown on the map. Can you find Italy on this map? Look for its shape on the part of Europe where earthquakes occur.

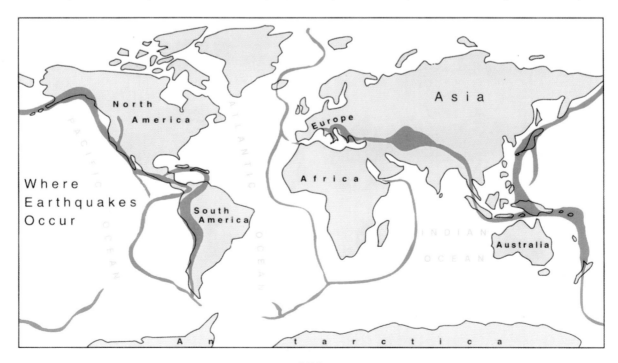

173

stronger quakes than others. Italy lies along part of the great Mediterranean earthquake belt.

Italy has had many earthquakes over the years. Earthquakes have brought much sorrow and suffering to Italy. In 1908 an earthquake killed 75,000 people on the island of Sicily. In 1915, 30,000 people were killed by an earthquake in the hill country east of Rome.

Scientists have not been able to tell exactly when an earthquake will happen. They believe large sections of the earth's crust move. The layers of rocks are bent and squeezed. Pressures build up under the ground. Finally the layers of rocks break, causing an earthquake.

The break in the ground is called a fault. Faults are often under the ground. Sometimes they can be seen on top of the ground.

But scientists are quick to say that they do not understand all of what happens deep under the earth. No one has ever seen exactly what happens many miles below the ground.

We do know that God controls the earthquakes. Job said, "[God] shaketh the earth out of her place, and the pillars thereof tremble." **Job 9:6**

Sometimes God sends earthquakes to judge people for their sins. We do not know why God allowed the earthquake in Italy.

This diagram shows you the different directions the earth can move during an earthquake. Sometimes the ground moves in more than one direction in the same earthquake. This makes the damage even worse.

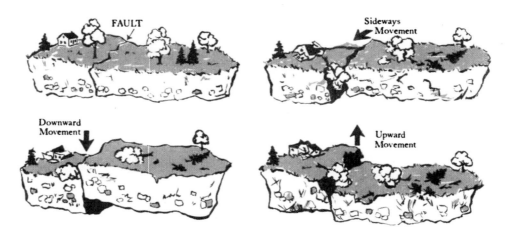

What Do You Say?

1. a. What happens to the ground during an earthquake? b. What happens to buildings?

2. The earthquake has been called "Italy's sorrow." What do you think this means?

What Does the Bible Say?

1. Sometimes God has sent earthquakes at special times. What happened to Jesus just before the great earthquake in Matthew 27:50-54?

2. What happened at the time of the earthquake recorded in Matthew 28:2?

3. What happened at the time of the earthquake in Acts 16:26?

The Poor South

The 1980 earthquake hit southern Italy, one of the poorest parts of the country. The south is more crowded than the north. The soil is poorer in most places. The land is hillier. Floods, droughts, and earthquakes bring much suffering to the south.

The south is a much drier land than the north. Much of the north has 40 or more inches (100 centimeters) of rain each year. Much of the south has less rainfall each year. Nearly all this rain falls in the winter.

The north has many rivers that

Which areas of Italy have the most rainfall? Which have the least? At what time of year does Italy have most of its rainfall?

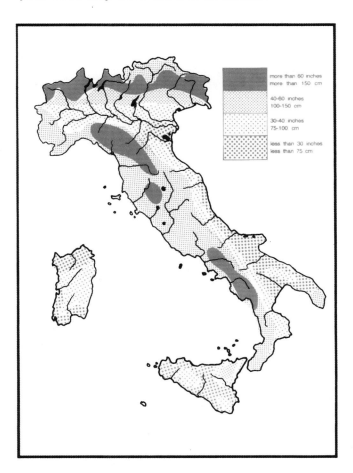

These Alps lie in northern Italy. People who live in the northern part of the Po Valley can see the snow-capped Alps in the distance.

flow all year. Heavy snows in the Alps melt in spring and summer. Snow-fed rivers rush down the mountainsides. The rushing water can be used to make electricity. Many hydroelectric stations have been built in the Italian Alps. When the water reaches the valley, it can be used to irrigate dry fields. The same water is used twice.

The rivers in southern Italy are very different from those in the north. The Apennine Mountains are not as high as the Alps. Less rain and snow fall on them. In spring, melted snow fills southern rivers. The rivers flood and destroy homes and farmland. Not enough snow or rain falls to supply the rivers with water all year. Many southern rivers dry to just a trickle

in the hot summer sun. Some dry up completely.

Imagine a hydroelectric station on a southern river. In spring and early summer it would produce electricity. Then it would need to close for the rest of the year.

Imagine a farmer trying to irrigate from a southern river. Just when he needs the water most, the river dries up!

Life in a Southern Village

Most visitors in Italy spend their time in or near the big cities. They see little of the countryside except as they ride along the superhighways between cities. One such highway stretches from Turin in the north to Naples in the south. Can you guess why this highway is called the Sun Highway?

If you want to see how most southerners live, you must leave the cities and superhighways. Some hard-surfaced roads connect the larger towns. Many villages are found along dirt or gravel roads.

The farmers of southern Italy live in villages. Each farmer owns or rents land on the nearby hillsides. But some farmers must walk several miles to reach their fields.

Village farmers must work hard on the steep hillsides. Steep land means terraces must be built. This means hard work. The farmer builds the holding walls of stone. He does his work with no machines to help him. Terraces must also be

176

repaired after the spring rains and floods.

Most of these farmers can barely raise enough corn, beans, and other vegetables for their families. Each farmer hopes to grow enough on his fields to sell. He can then use the money to buy the things he cannot raise.

Most village houses are made of mud brick dried in the sun. A house may have only two or three rooms. The family may share their rooms with a few chickens or with a goat.

The government in Rome has tried to help the poor people of the southland. But what it sends is not enough. Billions of lire (Italian money) have been spent for machinery, fertilizer, food, and other helps. Factories have been built in the south to give the people more work. With all the help, southerners make only about half as much money as northerners.

How many of these pasta products can you name? How many have you ever eaten? What country is most famous for its pasta? (See page 178.)

These children are from a village in southern Italy.

The people of southern Italy are dark-skinned, almost olive-colored. Many of the people in the north are light-skinned and look very much like people from England or Germany. More and more olive-skinned people are moving into the north. They look for better jobs and homes. They hope they will be happier in the north with more money.

But many people in northern Italy are not happy. Big homes, Vespas, Fiats, and plenty of lire to spend have not brought lasting happiness. The Bible says, "For a man's life consisteth not in the abundance of the things which he possesseth." **Luke 12:15b**

Food in Italy

Italians enjoy eating! Many of their special foods have become famous around the world.

Who in America has not eaten spaghetti or pizza, two favorite Italian dishes? Other Italian foods you may have tried are macaroni, lasagna (lə zän′ yə), and ravioli (rav′ ē ō′ lē).

Most of these dishes include pasta (päs′ tə), a favorite food in Italy. **Pasta** is a dough made mostly of finely ground hard wheat and water. The Italians cannot raise enough wheat for all their pasta. They must import tons of wheat from other countries.

Did you know that tons of durum wheat are shipped from North Dakota to Italy each year? Durum is a hard wheat that makes especially good pasta.

The Italians form pasta into many different shapes. The pasta is then dried for future use. Spaghetti and macaroni are made from pasta pressed through holes and dried with hot air. Sometimes a visitor to Italy can see pasta drying on racks in the hot sun.

Lasagna is pasta in wide strips. It is usually cooked with cheese and meat.

Ravioli is little cases of pasta dough filled with a sauce or meat. Italians also mix eggs in pasta and make egg noodles.

Italy is famous for other foods besides pasta. People in northern Italy like minestrone (min′ ə strō′ nē). Minestrone is a thick soup made with macaroni, dried beans, and other vegetables.

Italy is also famous for many kinds of cheese. One kind is Parmesan (pär′ mə zän′) named after the town of Parma. It is a dry cheese with a sharp flavor. In America this cheese comes grated to sprinkle on spaghetti and other dishes.

People in southern Italy eat different foods than those in the north. Their meals are very starchy with bread, pasta, and dried beans. They usually cannot afford to eat as much meat as northerners. Southerners as well as northerners eat tomatoes, melons, corn, and other vegetables. Most Italians use olive oil for cooking.

Some of the poorest people in the south must eat mainly soups and lentils. Lentils look like tiny, flattened peas.

What Do You Say?

1. Name at least three things that make farming hard in southern Italy.

2. How do the northern Italians use their river water twice?

3. Why are many rich people in northern Italy unhappy?

4. Name at least three Italian dishes made from pasta.

The famous Colosseum in Rome now stands in ruins. But two thousand years ago the Romans watched many games here. Animals and people fought to the death. Christians were fed to the hungry lions in the Colosseum.

What Does the Bible Say?

1. The Italian government is doing much to help the poor. Many people wrongly believe that helping the poor is mainly the government's job. But the Bible says much about the Christian's duty to the poor. Name two things we can share with the poor according to Luke 3:11.

2. Read Matthew 19:21. What did Jesus ask the rich young man to do for the poor?

Italy Long Ago

You read earlier that visitors like to come to Italy because of its sunny weather. Another reason many come to Italy is because of its history. Italy has a long and interesting history. In most parts of Italy you can see old buildings. Some of them are 2,000 years old.

The city of Rome has dozens of very old buildings. Most of them are partly fallen down. We call them **ruins**.

The ruins in Rome remind us that all the things man builds will one day fall. Only what is done for God will last. "The earth also and the works that are therein shall be burned up." "But the word of the Lord endureth for ever."

2 Peter 3:10b

1 Peter 1:25a

Two thousand years ago much of Italy was prosperous. Rome was

179

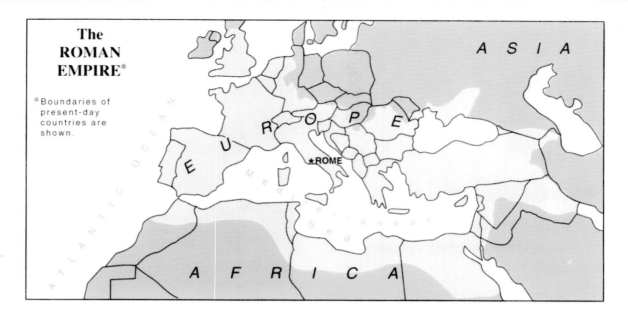

The ROMAN EMPIRE*

*Boundaries of present-day countries are shown.

This map shows you how much of Europe, Asia, and Africa was once ruled by the Romans in Italy. These lands were called the Roman Empire. Was Norway part of the Roman Empire? What sea was completely surrounded by the Roman Empire? The Romans once called this sea "our sea."

a strong city. The Romans had conquered all of Italy. Then they moved on to conquer all the lands around the Mediterranean Sea.

The Romans called the Mediterranean Sea "our sea." Can you guess why? Rome and all the lands she controlled were called the Roman Empire.

We call the days of long ago **ancient times**. *Ancient* means "old." We use the word *ancient* to speak of the Roman Empire and all history before that time. Our own days are called **modern times**. *Modern* has to do with the new or the present time.

Traders from the Roman Empire brought back many riches from the lands they conquered. They brought grain by ship from Egypt. Egypt was called the "breadbasket" of the Roman Empire. Roman traders brought perfumes and drugs from Arabia.

Gold came from Africa, silk from China, and spices from India.

Yet not everyone in the country of Italy was rich in the days of the Roman Empire. Many farmers were very poor. High taxes and low prices for their crops kept them from making much money on their farms. The cities were crowded, and many people were out of work. Prices for food kept going up, making life hard for the poor.

Christians in Ancient Italy

Most of the people in Rome were very ungodly. They worshiped ancient Roman gods or no gods at all. Many were unhappy. They wanted something better. One Roman in early Christian times said, "I believe in nothing beyond the grave." Another man asked this to be written on his grave, "I lived not. I lived. I live no more. I do not care."

Christians began to arrive in ancient Rome. They came on excellent highways Roman soldiers had built. These roads made travel easy from Rome to many parts of the Empire. In those days people sometimes said, "All roads lead to Rome."

The good roads were part of God's plan. They were free for anyone to use. The early Christians used these good roads to go from place to place. They spread the good news of Jesus Christ as they traveled across the Empire and to Rome itself.

The Christians brought a message of hope to the sinful people of Rome. Their message was, "For as in Adam all die, even so in Christ shall all be made alive."

Corinthians 22

People in Italy today still need the Gospel of Christ. Many say they are Christians. They were baptized as babies. They may go to church once in a while. But millions do not really know Jesus Christ. They have not let Him change their lives. Many people fight, curse, murder, and commit other sins.

Christians Begin to Suffer. Long before Christians came to Rome, many people no longer believed in the old gods. The Roman rulers knew that people needed to worship something. The rulers began to tell the people, "We are gods. Worship us." Altars were built for the sacrifices demanded by the rulers.

The people found the rulers or emperors easy to worship. They could not see the old gods, but they could see the emperor.

Christians refused to worship the gods or the emperor. They believed in the only true God and His Son Jesus. Some of the rulers were angry. They did not mind that the Christians worshiped Christ. But why could they not worship the emperor also?

One of the emperors was named Trajan. He wanted to make sure the Christians obeyed him. One of his helpers named Pliny wrote this letter:

"For now I have done as follows with all persons brought before me accused of being

In this picture is shown part of the Appian Way, the famous Roman road. It is still used over two thousand years after it was built.

This is a statue of the Roman Emperor, Trajan. He was an emperor in Rome during the time when the early Christians were being persecuted.

Christians. I have asked them in person if they are Christians and if they admit it, I repeat the question a second and third time, warning them of the punishment that awaits them.

"If they hold fast, I order them away to be executed [killed]. For . . . I believe their stubbornness should be punished.

"I thought I should let go any who said they were not Christians when they had repeated after me a prayer to the gods and had made offerings of wine and incense to your statue . . . and had insulted the name of Christ.

"I understand that any true Christian cannot be made to do any of these things."

The Emperor Trajan wrote back to Pliny:

"You have done the right thing, dear Pliny, in your handling . . . of persons accused of being Christians. . . . These people must be hunted out. If they are taken before you and the charge against them is proved,

Many Christians in Rome hid in underground tunnels called Catacombs. This picture shows a hollowed-out place in the wall, where they sometimes buried their dead.

they must be punished. . . . They set the worst kind of example and are fully out of keeping with the spirit of our time."

Christians were not following the spirit of those days. They were different from other Romans. In the Christian home there were no statues of the gods. There were no altars for sacrifices to the gods.

Some Romans thought Christians were atheists, people who do not believe in any god. Christians are not atheists, of course. They believe in the only true God.

Others thought Christians were against the government because they refused to sacrifice to the emperor. Certainly, they thought, Christians must hate him! But Christians did not

The ruins of an ancient marketplace of the Roman Empire still stand today in the city of Rome. Tourists can visit this market, the Colosseum, and many other reminders of the Romans of long ago. These buildings also remind us that only God's Word will stand forever.

This drawing from the Martyrs Mirror shows a Christian being attacked by a lion in the Colosseum at Rome. What else did the Romans use the Colosseum for?

hate the government. The Bible taught them to obey the rulers if at all possible. "Put them in mind to be subject to principalities and powers, to obey magistrates, to be ready to every good work."

Titus 3:1

But Christians said, "If the government asks us to disobey God, we must obey God rather than men." They could not worship the emperor because Jesus had said, "Thou shalt worship the Lord thy God, and him only shalt thou serve."

(Acts 5:29)

Matthew 4:10b

What Do You Say?

1. What does *ancient* mean?

2. How did Roman roads help the early Christians?

3. Why did Christians in ancient Rome refuse to worship the gods or the emperor?

4. Name one way in which Christian homes in ancient Rome were different from other homes.

What Does the Bible Say?

1. The Roman rulers in Jesus' time were called *Caesars* (sē′ zərz). What did Jesus say should be rendered [or given] to Caesar? To God? (Read Mark 12:17.)

A Christian Family Suffers

Ancient Rome was a large city. A million or more people must have lived there in early Christian times. The rich lived in large houses. But most of the people lived in crowded apartment buildings. These apartments were called *insulae* (in′ sü lī). *Insulae* means "islands."

Many of the insulae were not kept in good repair. In some cases owners propped the side of their insulae with poles to keep them from falling. The Christians were often among the poorest of the people. Many, no doubt, lived in insulae.

Rome was also a very wicked city. Some people came to the city for the fun and games. Others came because they hoped to be rich.

The Roman emperors knew that plenty of food and plenty of games would make the people happy. Racetracks and arenas for sports events were built to please the people. The racetracks were called *circuses*.

In the arenas trained men fought each other. Sometimes fierce wild animals fought. The people screamed with delight.

Finally, Christians were fed to hungry lions in the arena called the Colosseum (kăl' ə sē' əm). It is said that the sand in the Colosseum was dyed red from the blood.

The *Martyrs Mirror* tells of a Christian family that suffered for Christ in Rome. They lived about A.D. 164. The mother's name was Felicitas, meaning "happiness."

Felicitas' husband had died, but she was blessed with seven sons. One thing she had to be happy about was that all seven sons were Christians.

People who knew Felicitas and her family were impressed with their lives. Of course, the family refused to go to the games, fights, and theaters. They were too busy serving the Lord to waste their time at such places. Felicitas spoke about Jesus to the women she met. Many became Christians. The boys spoke about Christ to the men they met.

Not everybody in Rome liked Felicitas and her sons. The priests of the old Roman gods hated Christians. When people became Christians, they no longer went to the heathen places of worship. The priests reported Felicitas and her sons to Publius, the man who ruled the city.

Publius ordered Felicitas and her sons to come to his own house. He hoped to cause them to give up their Christian faith. He begged them to worship the Roman gods and the emperor. He promised them money and other gifts if only they would follow the old religion. Kind words did not work. Next he tried to scare them, "I'll punish you! I'll kill you!"

"I am not scared by your threats," Felicitas answered. "For the Holy Spirit is working in my heart. He gives me a living power. He will help me to stand for the faith no matter what you do to me."

Publius saw that he could not easily scare her. He answered, "Very well, if you want to die, die by yourself. But have pity on your sons and tell them to save their own lives, at least, by sacrificing to the gods."

Felicitas turned to her sons, "Remain steadfast in faith and in your confession of Christ. For Christ and His saints are waiting for you. . . . Fight bravely for your soul, and show that you are faithful to Christ."

Publius became angry. Some of his men hit Felicitas in the face with their fists. She kept on encouraging her sons, "Fear neither tortures . . . nor even death itself, but die willingly for the name of Christ."

Publius then took each son and talked to him alone. They all stood for Christ.

At last Publius sent a message to the emperor, the ruler of the Roman Empire. "None of them will listen, and I cannot make them sacrifice to the gods.'

The emperor sent back the terrible word, "Kill them. The mother must first watch all her sons die, then she shall be put to death."

—Adapted from *Martyrs Mirror*

That is exactly what happened in the year A.D. 164.

Hundreds of Christians were killed in ancient Rome and Italy before the terrible persecution finally ended.

The city of Rome has not known such religious persecution since. Today there is religious freedom in Rome. People may worship very much as they please. Christians are no longer killed in the arenas. But people in Rome still need the Gospel preached to them. Who will take the message to this city?

What Do You Say?

1. What happened to Christians in the Colosseum at Rome?

2. In what two ways did the ruler of Rome try to force Felicitas to worship the old gods?

3. What promise did Felicitas give her sons if they would stay faithful to Christ?

would not worship the ruler when commanded to do it. They knew they must obey God first. (Read Acts 5:29.) Now fill in each blank below with a word from this verse.

If men ask us to do something that is wrong, we ought to _____ _____ _____ _____ _____ .

2. What does Revelation 2:10 promise to those who are faithful unto death?

What Does the Bible Say?

1. In this chapter you learned that Christians in ancient Rome

Using Globes and Maps

1. Draw or trace a map of Italy. Mark the following cities: Rome, Milan, Naples, Venice, Geneva,

Palermo (Sicily).

Label the following areas: Alps, Apennines, Po Valley, Sicily, Sardinia, Tyrrhenian Sea, Ligurian Sea, Adriatic Sea, Ionian Sea.

2. Find Italy on a globe. Also find it on a map of Europe.

New Words and Terms

Fill in the blanks with the best word to complete the sentences. Choose from the list below:

sirocco	terrace farming
Apennines	ancient times
earthquake	intensive farming
pasta	Tyrrhenian Sea
insulae	Ionian Sea
ruins	Adriatic Sea
lire	modern times
fault	

1. A chain of mountains called the _____ stretches the length of the Italian "boot."

2. The _____ _____ lies just east of Italy.

3. The _____ _____ is found between Greece and Italy.

4. The sea west of Italy near Sicily and Sardinia is called the _____ _____ .

5. A hot, dusty wind from Northern Africa that sometimes reaches Italy is called a _____ .

6. Raising as many crops as possible in a little space is called _____ _____ .

7. The ground shakes during an _____ .

8. Farming on steps of level ground made on hillsides is called _____ _____ .

9. A large break or crack in the ground along which earthquakes take place is called a _____ .

10. Italian "dollars" are called _____ .

11. Italians enjoy eating _____ made from hard wheat flour and water.

12. In Italy you can see many _____ of buildings from long ago.

13. We call history in the days of the Roman Empire and before _____ _____ .

14. Our own days are called _____ _____ .

15. _____ were apartment buildings in ancient Rome.

Thinking Together

1. Do you remember what you

187

learned about water in Chapter 8? Italy is almost surrounded by water. How does that fact affect its climate?

2. The climate of Italy is sometimes called a Mediterranean climate. Why do you think it has this name?

3. Why has the soil become poor in parts of Italy?

4. How could the Italians make their land richer again and keep it from washing away?

5. Why is intensive farming important in Italy?

6. In what two ways is northern Italy richer than southern Italy?

7. What do scientists think causes earthquakes?

8. Name two reasons why the southern Italians could use more water in their rivers.

9. Why do you think the ancient Romans called the Mediterranean Sea "our sea"?

For You to Do

1. Read about Italy in an encyclopedia. What fruits and vegetables are farmed in different parts of Italy? Make a map of Italy and write on it the names of different foods in the places where they are grown. Be sure to include olives, grapes, other fruits, wheat, corn, and rice.

2. Bring some samples of pasta products to show to the class. These might include spaghetti, macaroni, noodles, or lasagne noodles. Make a chart showing pasta products. Glue a sample of each pasta product on the chart. In old magazines find a picture of a dish using each form of pasta. Paste these beside or below the pasta product.

3. The Bible says much about olives and olive oil. Look up the following verses. In your own words tell what each passage says about the olive. Genesis 8:10, 11; Leviticus 24:1-4; Psalm 128:3; James 3:12.

4. Almost every year a severe earthquake hits some place on the earth. Find a report from a newspaper or a newsmagazine of a recent earthquake.

5. In an encyclopedia find an article about the Roman Empire. Try to find a map of the Roman Empire when it was at its largest. List the modern countries in Europe that were once a part of the Roman Empire.

Homelands of the Slavs

Unit 4

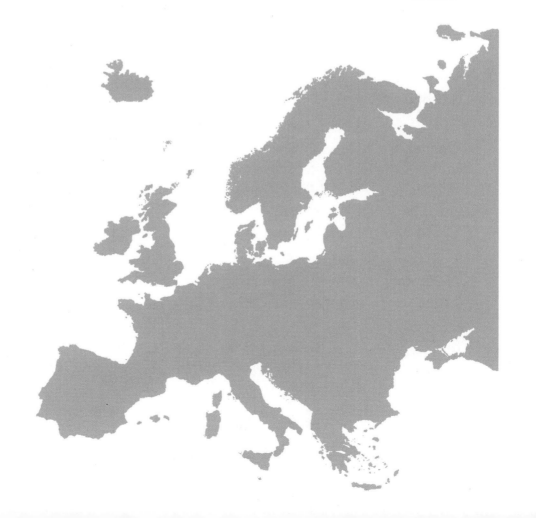

What you will learn . . . in unit four

You are about to study lands and people who are not very well-known to the rest of the world. These are the lands of **Eastern Europe**—Poland, the Czech (chek) Republic, Slovakia (slō väk′ ē ə), Albania, Romania, Bulgaria, Russia, Slovenia (slō vē′ nē ə), Croatia, Bosnia, Kosovo (kō′ sō vō), Serbia, Montenegro, Macedonia, Moldova (mōl dō′ və), Estonia, Latvia (lat′ vē ə), Lithuania, Belarus (bel′ ə rüs), and Ukraine.

We do not know these people well partly because harsh governments have ruled their countries for many years. The people have not been able to travel to the rest of the world as freely as you and I can. Until recent years people from other countries were not as free to travel in Eastern Europe.

We will spend much of this unit studying the largest country in the world. This country is partly in Eastern Europe and partly in Asia. This country is called Russia.

Above all else, the people of Eastern Europe need the Gospel of Christ. Christians in some of these lands had to suffer for their faith for many years. Their governments said, "There is no God." Now Christians can worship freely in most of these lands. Bibles, Christian literature, and material aid can be sent to them freely.

Jesus Christ came to save all people, including the people of Eastern Europe. Here is John 3:16 in Russian, the language of at least half the people of Eastern Europe:

Ибо такъ возлюбилъ Богъ міръ, что отдалъ Сына своего единороднаго, дабы всякій, вѣрующій въ Него, не погибъ, но имѣлъ жизнь вѣчную.

11. Eastern Europe and the Slavs

Did you enjoy studying Norway and Italy? Both are large countries in Western Europe. But they are only a small part of the continent.

People who study the history and geography of Europe sometimes divide the continent into two parts. These parts are Western Europe and Eastern Europe. **Western Europe** includes Germany, Austria, Italy, and all countries west of them. All countries to the east of these are in **Eastern Europe.**

People in North and South America usually know more about Western Europe than they do about Eastern Europe. Many people on both continents came from Western Europe. But did you know that millions of people have come to the Americas from Eastern Europe? More have come from Russia than any other country in Eastern Europe. Large groups of Polish Americans live in some cities. A large percentage of the residents of Philadelphia have Polish ancestors.

Eastern Europe is the homeland of many of our ancestors. What is this land like?

Eastern Europe—The Land God Made

Look at the map of Eastern Europe on page 192. The map shows the

East Europeans to U.S. 1820-1995	
Poland —	734,895
Czech Rep. & Slovakia —	155,459
Romania —	241,459
Former Yugoslavia —	156,529
Bulgaria —	75,963
Former Soviet Union —	3,747,189

Millions of people have come to Canada and the United States from eastern European countries. This chart shows how many came to the U.S. from six of these countries between 1820 and 1995.

borders or **boundaries** of the countries.

The line that separates Eastern Europe from Western Europe is manmade. Sometimes it follows mountains or rivers that God made. At other times it cuts across fields and open countryside. Sometimes countries bought land. Unfortunately, boundaries were often decided by war.

The lands of Eastern Europe look much like those of Western Europe. Some of the same plains and mountains in Western Europe stretch into Eastern Europe. Do you remember the great North European Plain which we studied about in Unit 3?

Eastern Europe

This map shows the countries of Europe as they were in the 1990s. The darker countries are what we call Eastern Europe. They were once ruled by communists. Six of these countries that border Russia and Romania were once united with Russia in the communist country called the Soviet Union. A country called Czechoslovakia has now become the Czech Republic and Slovakia. The country called Yugoslavia broke into several little countries, the largest of which are Serbia, Croatia, and Bosnia.

This plain continues through Eastern Europe.

In parts of Western Europe this lowland is only 50 miles (80 kilometers) wide. In Poland, which is in Eastern Europe, it widens to 300 miles (480 kilometers). European Russia is almost all plains. The plains stretch from the Arctic Ocean to the Black Sea, over 1,500 miles (2,400 kilometers)!

In Russia you could travel all day across the flatland and see no hills as tall as a house. Other than trees, the houses are the highest things that can be seen.

The mountains of Western Europe also continue into Eastern Europe. Sometimes the word *Alps* is used for these mountains. The mountains of Croatia and Bosnia are called the Dinaric (di nar′ ik) Alps. The Carpathian (kär pā′ thē ən) Mountains stretch from Slovakia through a corner of Ukraine and through Romania. These mountains are shaped like a huge horseshoe. The southern part of the Carpathians is often called the Transylvanian (tran′ sil vā′ nē ən) Alps.

The Climate in Eastern Europe

The map on page 192 shows how far north Eastern Europe reaches. Much of it lies as far north as Canada and Alaska. Do you remember the way God planned to protect most of Europe from the bitter cold?

Yes, He made the Gulf Stream and the North Atlantic Drift. He sends breezes from the warm ocean to help keep the land warm in winter. God spoke and all these good things were made. He still cares for His marvelous creation. "The voice of the LORD is upon the waters . . . the LORD is upon many waters."

Psalm 29:3

The people in Eastern Europe can feel some of the warm Atlantic breezes. But they feel more of the cold blasts of air that sweep west from deep within Asia. The farther from the ocean a European lives, the less he feels its warm breezes.

In Paris, France, the average high temperature on a January day is 42° F (6° C). Paris is not far from the Atlantic. At Berlin, Germany, the average is 35° F (2° C). Berlin is

This scene is from the hilly lands near Prague, the capital of the Czech Republic. Prague lies in the midst of a mountainous region including southern Germany and Austria.

193

farther from the Atlantic. Still farther east at Warsaw, Poland, the January temperature averages 32° F (0° C). At Moscow (mäs′ kaů) deep inside Russia, it is a chilling 21° F (−6° C).

Summers in Eastern Europe are warmer than those in much of Western Europe. In summer, Western Europe is cooled by the breezes that blow from the Atlantic Ocean. Eastern Europe is warmer because it is inland away from these ocean breezes. The warm summers help make up for the colder winters.

The People of Eastern Europe

The people of Europe are very much alike. Most Europeans have brown or blond hair and light skin. Europeans may look alike, but in one important way they are different.

Europeans speak many different languages. Each country has its own language. A little country such as Switzerland uses four languages. No less than 50 languages are spoken in Europe.

Can you imagine what it would be like if each of our states or provinces used a different language? If you wanted to trade with people of another state, you would need to learn their language. The states and provinces would not get along nearly as well together if they used different languages. Europeans have this problem.

Most Western Europeans speak languages that came from a Germanic language or from Latin. German, English, and Norwegian are **Germanic languages**. Many words in these languages look or sound much alike. French, Spanish,

---

JOHN 3:16

Russian

Ибо такъ возлюбилъ Богъ міръ, что отдалъ Сына своего единороднаго, дабы всякій, вѣрующій въ Него, не погибъ, но имѣлъ жизнь вѣчную.

Polish

Albowiem tak Bóg umiłował świat, że Syna swego jednorodzonego dał: aby wszelki, kto wierzy weń, nie zginął, ale miał żywot wieczny.

Czech

Nebo tak Bůh miloval svět, že Syna svého jednorozeného dal, aby každý, kdož věří v něho, nezahynul, ale měl život věčný.

Romanian

Fiindcă atît de mult a iubit Dumnezeu lumea, că a dat pe singurul Lui Fiu, pentruca oricine crede în El, să nu piară, ci să aibă viaţa vecinică.

Hungarian

Mert úgy szereté Isten e világot, hogy az ő egyetlenegy szülött Fiát adná, hogy minden, valaki hiszen ő benne, el ne veszszen, hanem örök életet vegyen;

194

and Italian are three languages that came from an old language called Latin. Latin languages are also called **Romance languages**.

In Eastern Europe most of the people are **Slavs**. The Slavs are divided into a number of different countries and speak several different languages that are much alike. With a little practice, people who speak different **Slavic languages** can understand each other. Germanic languages are not so much alike.

Slavs have lived in Eastern Europe for many hundreds of years. At one time they lived close together and all spoke the same language.

What Do You Say?

1. Into what two parts is Europe often divided for study?

2. Name four ways in which the boundaries of countries are set.

3. A certain town in Europe has an average January temperature of 40° F (4° C). The average in another town is 28° F (−2° C). Which town would likely be in Eastern Europe? Why?

4. Most of the people in Eastern Europe speak one of the _____ languages.

What Does the Bible Say?

1. What four things does Acts 14:15 say that God made?

2. What can we expect to stay much the same while the earth remains? (Read Genesis 8:22.)

3. Read Acts 17:26a. Fill in the blanks. God "hath made of one a. _____ all b. _____ of men for to dwell on all the face of the c. _____ ."

Who Are the Slavs?

No one is sure where the Slavs came from. Perhaps they came to Europe from Asia. One of the first places the Slavs settled in Europe was along the Vistula (vis′ chü lə) River in Poland. From Poland the Slavs moved slowly east and south. Today the Slavs of Poland, Slovakia, and the Czech Republic are called Western Slavs. Those of Russia, Belarus, and Ukraine are the Eastern Slavs. Those of Bulgaria, Croatia, Serbia, and Slovenia are Southern Slavs.

Strangely, most Hungarians and Romanians are not Slavs, though Slavs live all around them. The ancestors of the Hungarians came from Asia long ago. Some of the ancestors of the Romanians came from Italy.

Today the homeland of the Slavs

is in Eastern Europe and northern Asia. Over 300 million Slavs live in these lands. Millions more live in other lands, especially in North America.

The Sad Story of the Slavs

The Slavs have suffered more than any other European people. The Slavs usually have wanted to live quietly in their farming villages. But enemies have often conquered them.

Many years ago Slavs were taken as slaves by other nations. Our English word *slave* comes from the word *Slav*. But Slavs will be quick to tell you that *Slav* does not mean

This map shows you about where the first Slavs are believed to have lived. The arrows show you the lands to which many of the Slavs then moved.

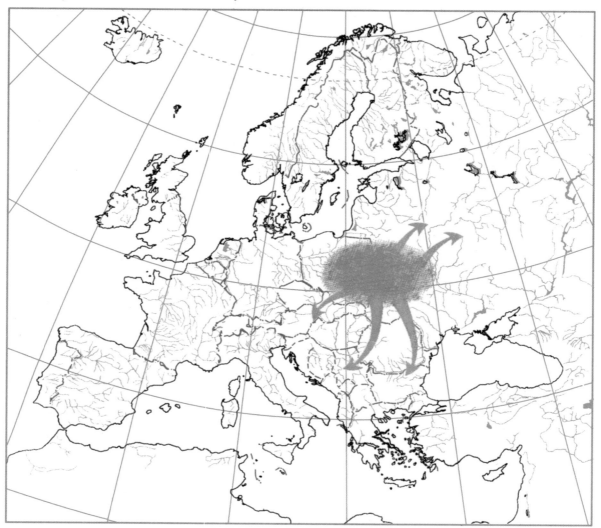

Homeland of the Slavs

"slave" in their language.

The word *Slav* means "glory" in the Slavic languages. For example, the Russian Christians often say "*Slava Bogu*," which means "glory to God."

Over 800 years ago the Slavs were ruled by fierce tribes from Asia. After that the Turks from the south ruled the Southern Slavs. More recently the Slavs have suffered under the Germans.

The Slavs have fought each other too. Poland was once a powerful nation that ruled over many other Slavs. The Russians have also fought wars with Poland and other Slavic countries.

Millions of Slavs live in the Americas because their parents or grandparents or other ancestors fled the wars and fighting of their homelands.

The Bible tells us what causes people to hate each other and fight. "From whence come wars and fightings among you? come they not hence, even of your lusts that war in your members?" Lusts are selfish desires for things that do not belong to us.

mes 4:1

Eastern Europe is sometimes called the **"marchland of Europe,"** for many armies have marched across the land conquering the people.

The Slavic lands, as well as Hungary and Romania, are also called Europe's **"shatter zone."** These nations have been shattered or broken by many wars.

Poland probably has suffered

These two Polish girls are dressed in Polish clothing of many years ago. Today the Poles usually wear the same type of clothing as other Europeans do. They dress up in old-fashioned clothing for special holidays.

more than any other nation in the shatter zone. About 200 years ago three other nations divided Poland among themselves. The name "Poland" did not appear on a map of Europe again for over 100 years.

Only a few years after Poland again became a nation, Germany and the Soviet Union or Russia divided the country between themselves. Today Poland is again a nation. The

197

Russians have sometimes controlled them. But the Poles want to rule their country without the Russians telling them what to do.

The Southern Slavs are divided into many little countries. Wars often began in these and other countries of southeastern Europe. For over 45 years most of these countries were united into a nation called Yugoslavia. Yugoslavia means "land of the Southern Slavs."

Bible for the Slavs

The early Slavs were pagans. They worshiped many gods. Like the Norwegians, they worshiped the gods of the sky, the fields, and the forests.

One of their gods was Perun, the god of thunder. His name is now the Russian word for thunder.

Over a thousand years ago the Slavs first heard about Christianity. They were slow to accept any new religion.

Two brothers, Methodius and Cyril, set out from Greece to teach the Slavs about Christianity. The brothers found that the Slavs had no written language. How could anyone read God's Word with no alphabet?

Cyril is believed to have invented a special alphabet for the Slavs. He borrowed some letters from the Greek alphabet. He made some new letters for Slavic sounds not found in Greek.

Today most of the Slavs still use Cyril's alphabet. It is called the **Cyrillic** (sə ril′ ik) **alphabet**.

Cyril prepared a Bible for the Slavs. His own Bible was in the Greek language. Chapter by chapter he had to decide how to put God's Word into the Slavic language. He worked many, many months translating the Bible for the Slavs. To *translate* means to change from one language to another.

Cyril knew the Slavs needed to have the Bible in their own language to know the truth that could set them free. Jesus said, "And ye shall know the truth, and the truth shall make you free."

John 8:32

Slavs in Need of Christ. Today the Slavic people still need the Gospel. Millions do not know God. The communist governments taught them that there was no God.

Faithful Christians who lived in Slavic countries often suffered because they followed Christ. They could not have Christian day schools to teach their own children. In some

The Russian Alphabet

Russian letters		Sound
А	а	ā
Б	б	b
В	в	v
Г	г	g
Д	д	d
Е	е	ye
Ё	ё	yo
Ж	ж	zh
З	з	z
И	и	ē
Й	й	ē (shorter)
К	к	k
Л	л	l
М	м	m
Н	н	n
О	о	ȯ
П	п	p
Р	р	r
С	с	s
Т	т	t
У	у	u
Ф	ф	f
Х	х	kh
Ц	ц	ts
Ч	ч	ch
Ш	ш	sh
Щ	щ	shch
Ъ	ъ	y (before vowel)
Ы	ы	i
Ь	ь	y (after consonant)
Э	э	e
Ю	ю	yü
Я	я	yä

This is the Cyrillic alphabet used in writing Russian. The "sound" column tells you about how each letter is pronounced. The first letter is the capital; the second is the small or lowercase letter. Who invented this alphabet? Why?

countries Christians met in secret if they wanted to pray and study the Bible together.

Today most of these people are free to worship God as they wish and teach their children from the Bible.

We think of Eastern Europe and the Slavs. We think of their need for Bibles and for Christian literature. When we think of the Slavs, we often think of the largest Slavic country. We will study this large country next.

What Do You Say?

1. Name the three main groups of Slavs and tell where they live.

2. a. Where is the "shatter zone" of Europe? b. Why is it called a shatter zone?

3. a. Who invented an alphabet for the Slavs? b. What is the alphabet called? c. Why did he invent it?

What Does the Bible Say?

1. You learned in this chapter that

199

wars and more wars have been the sad lot of Eastern Europe. Sinful people often take the way of war when they become greedy. The Bible points to a better way. Fill in the blank: " _____ is better than weapons of war" (Ecclesiastes 9:18a).

2. Read Matthew 24:6. What problem in Eastern Europe is mentioned in this verse as a sign of the last days?

3. The Slavs, as well as millions of other people, now have the Bible in their own language. God wants mankind to hear the Word and obey it. Revelation 1:3 speaks of the need to hear the Word God has given us. Fill in the blanks: "a. _____ is he that b. _____ , and they that hear the c. _____ of this prophecy, and keep those things which are written therein."

Chapter Eleven Review

Using Globes and Maps

1. Find Europe on a globe or on a flat map. Show which part is Western Europe. Point to Eastern Europe. Name the countries of Eastern Europe.

2. On a large map of the world, find the east-west direction line nearest Moscow in Russia. Follow this line west into North America. In what country are you? Are you north or south of where you live?

3. Look at Eastern Europe on the map on page 192. a. Which country is the farthest south of the Eastern European countries? b. Which is the farthest north (near the Baltic Sea and Finland)?

4. Make an outline map of Eastern Europe. Fill in the name of each country.

New Words and Terms

Here are the definitions of twelve people, places, and things you have learned about in this chapter. Go back through the chapter and find out what each one is.

1. Another name for Eastern Europe given it because of the armies that have marched across the land. _____ _____ _____

2. To change or turn from one language to another. _____

3. A river in Poland close to the homeland of the Slavs. _____

4. Germany, Austria, Italy, and other European countries west of them. _____ _____

5. German and similar languages found in Western Europe. _____ _____

6. A range of mountains in Slovakia. _____ _____

7. Poland, the Czech Republic, Hungary, Slovenia, and Europe east of these countries. _____ _____

8. The border or limits of a country. _____

9. A people who live in much of Eastern Europe. _____

10. An alphabet invented for the Slavs. _____ _____

11. A name for Eastern Europe given because so many of its countries have been broken by war. _____ _____

12. European languages that came from the Latin language. _____ _____

God that could serve as boundaries between countries. The text names just two.

3. a. Why is Eastern Europe colder in winter than Western Europe? b. Why is it warmer in summer?

4. Name one way Eastern Europeans are like Western Europeans. Name an important way that they are different.

5. The peoples of Europe speak more than 50 different languages. How do you think this has divided them and kept them from working together?

6. In Genesis 11:9 read the story of the beginning of different languages. Why did the many languages cause the people to scatter over the earth?

7. a. From where did we get our word *slave*? b. What does this say about the history of the Slavs?

8. Name at least two ways in which the Cyrillic alphabet helped the Slavic people.

Thinking Together

1. Give one reason why so many Slavs live in North America.

2. Name four landforms made by

For You to Do

1. Do you know of any people living in your community who came from Eastern Europe? Do you

know anyone whose parents or grandparents came from Eastern Europe? See if you can find out why they came to America.

2. In an encyclopedia read about one of the Eastern European countries other than Russia. Be prepared to share at least six interesting facts about this country or its people.

3. Read about the Cyrillic alphabet in an encyclopedia. Look under "Russian language" or "Cyrillic alphabet." How many letters are in this alphabet? How many letters look just like letters in our alphabet? Make a copy of the capital letters in the Cyrillic alphabet.

4. In your community someone may have a copy of a Bible or Testament in a European language other than English. If possible, get permission to bring it to class. You would most likely find a Bible in German, French, Spanish, or Italian. Perhaps someone in the class will locate a Bible in a Slavic language such as Russian.

12. Russia—Nation on Two Continents

You cannot study Eastern Europe or northern Asia without studying the world's largest nation. More than four of every five of its people are Slavs.

This gigantic country has had different names during its history. The correct name today is *Rossiya* or *Rossiya Federatsiya*. In our language this name is Russia or the Russian Federation. For almost 70 years, from 1922 to 1991, this country was known as the Union of Soviet Socialist Republics. Its abbreviation was U.S.S.R. Often the country was called the Soviet Union. **Soviet** means "a committee" or "a council." A **socialist** is one who believes that the government should own the land and businesses.

The country we call Russia today was one of the republics or states of the Soviet Union. It was by far the largest of them. In the early 1990s the republics became separate countries. Russia still has more than 75 of every 100 square miles or kilometers of land found in the old Soviet Union.

In this book we will call this country Russia. When speaking of Russia between 1922 and 1991 we will often use the name Soviet Union. We call the people who live in Russia *Russians*. The Slavic language spoken in their country is called *Russian*.

Big! Bigger! Biggest!

If you had to use one word to tell about Russia, what word would you choose? Perhaps the best word is *big*! Almost everything about Russia is big. It is the largest country in the world. From east to west the country

This is the flag of Russia today. This was the same white, blue, and red flag used by Russia from 1699 to 1918. During communist rule, the Soviet Union used a red flag with a hammer and sickle in the corner. The red stood for revolution and blood. The hammer stood for factory workers and the sickle stood for farm workers.

is about 5,000 miles (8,000 kilometers) wide. From north to south Russia is about 2,500 miles (4,000 kilometers) wide.

Russia is almost twice as large as the United States. It is almost as large as South America. One of every ten acres (hectares) of land on earth is found in Russia.

Russia covers the eastern part of Europe and the northern one-third of Asia. Russia is larger than the continents of Europe, Australia, or Antarctica.

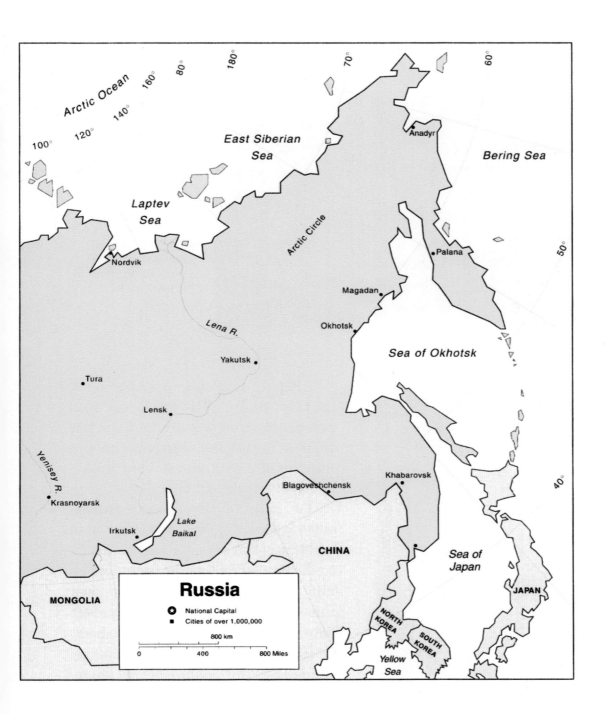

Many of the world's largest things are found in Russia. This country has the tallest mountain in Europe and the longest rivers in Europe and Asia. It has the largest forest, the largest swamp, and the deepest lake in the world.

Natural Resources in a Big Land

You would expect a country as large as Russia to have plenty of natural resources. Yes, God has blessed the world's largest country with plenty of the resources it needs.

Forests, lakes, and swamps cover the warmer parts of Siberia. In the far north, the ground stays frozen most of the year and no trees can grow.

Lake Baikal is the deepest lake in the world. It is 5,712 feet (1,741 meters) deep at its deepest point This lake also contains more water than any other freshwater lake in the world. Why do you think it holds so much water?

Russia has all it needs of many metals and fuels such as coal, petroleum, iron ore, and natural gas. Russia leads the world in the production of nickel and natural gas.

During its existence the Soviet Union mined more **manganese** (mang′ gə nēz′), than any other country. Most of the manganese was found in Ukraine which is now an independent country. Manganese is a very important metal used in making steel from iron ore. Steelmakers use about thirteen pounds (five kilograms) of manganese in each ton of steel. Manganese removes harmful gases from the steel and makes it stronger.

Russia is one of the world's leading lumber producers. Thick, dark forests spread for thousands of miles across the land. Much of the lumber is cut in the European part of Russia. The Asian part has much larger forests, but they are too far from the

206

These are some of the natural resources found in Russia. Can you name them? What is caviar? Find out what it is in a dictionary or encyclopedia.

people who use most of the lumber and paper made from wood.

Many Russians, like many Americans, are proud of their big country and its riches. God warns people not to trust in those riches but to trust in Him.

"Charge them that are rich in this world, that they be not high-minded, nor trust in uncertain riches, but in the living God, who giveth us richly all things to enjoy."

1 Timothy 6:17

What Do You Say?

1. What was another name for Russia between 1922 and 1991?

2. Name at least five ways that Russia is "big."

3. What are some of the natural resources with which Russia is blessed?

What Does the Bible Say?

1. God allows countries such as

207

Russia to grow larger and larger. He allows the nations to fall and other nations to take their place. Read Job 12:23. Fill in the blanks. "He [God] a. _____ the nations, and destroyeth them: he b. _____ the nations. . . ."

2. God has blessed Russia with many natural resources. Why does God give these natural resources? Find the answer in 1 Timothy 6:17.

The Land God Gave

Russia is blessed with much farmland. It has more farmland than the United States has. Some of the best farmland in the world is found in Russia.

The richest farmland in Russia is called the **black earth belt**. This region stretches across Ukraine and southern Russia. It is a wide region in European Russia. This region becomes narrow in Siberia.

In some places the black earth is as much as five feet (one and two-thirds meters) deep! This soil is much like the good prairie or grassland of the United States.

Rich soils grow beautiful crops in other parts of Russia. Even some desert soils produce good crops if they can be watered.

The soils of the far north in Asia and Europe are not very rich. They are frozen most of the year. In the short summers only the top few inches thaw out. The soil often stays wet on top because melted snow and rain cannot soak in very far. Similar soil is found in northern Canada and Alaska.

Landforms in Russia. You would expect many different landforms in a large country, especially the largest country in the world. Visitors to Russia, however, are often surprised to see almost nothing but flatland. Only near the borders of the country and in the far eastern part do you see many mountains.

Nearly all the European part of Russia is a vast plain. The Caucasus (kô′ kə səs) Mountains are found in the far South. Mount Elbrus (el brüz′) is the highest mountain in Europe. Find this mountain on a classroom map or atlas map of Russia. The mountain lies between the Black Sea and the Caspian Sea.

Between Europe and Asia are the Ural (yür′ əl) Mountains. These are the low mountains like the Appalachians of North America. The Urals are not wide. Each road that crosses the Urals has a sign that points west to Europe and east to Asia.

As soon as you cross the Urals you are in the part of Russia called Siberia. Siberia stretches from the Urals for over 3,500 miles (5,650

This huge tea farm is in the hilly part of Ukraine, once part of Russia. In other parts of Ukraine, the land is flatter and is covered with vast fields of grain.

kilometers) to the Pacific Ocean. The part of Siberia nearest the Urals is called the West Siberian Plain. It is over 1,000 miles (1,600 kilometers) wide. This plain is almost as flat as a tabletop. Because water drains very poorly, this area has the largest swamps on earth.

East of the West Siberian Plain is the Central Siberian Plateau. This land is higher than the plains, but much of it is flat.

The far eastern part of Siberia is called the East Siberian Highlands. This is a beautiful, wild land of steep mountains and rushing streams. Few people live in any part of Siberia, especially in the East Siberian Highlands.

Br-r-r-r, It's Cold!

Russia is famous for its cold cli-mate. The winters in most of the country are long. Summers are warm or sometimes hot, but they are very short.

For many years Hungary bor-dered Russia. It is said that a Hungarian farmer once saw some Russian surveyors checking his land. He hurried home to tell his wife. "They say our farm is going to be in Russia now."

"Why should that matter?" asked the wife. "We will get along just as well in Russia as in Hungary."

"Oh, no," answered her hus-band. "You do not want to live in Russia. You could freeze to death there."

Of course, we know that chang-ing boundaries will not change the weather, but we do know that

The Seasons in Russia

NOVEMBER	DECEMBER	JANUARY	FEBRUARY	MARCH
1 2 3 4	1 2	1 2 3 4 5 6	1 2 3	1 2 3
5 6 7 8 9 10 11	3 4 5 6 7 8 9	7 8 9 10 11 12 13	4 5 6 7 8 9 10	4 5 6 7 8 9 10
12 13 14 15 16 17 18	10 11 12 13 14 15 16	14 15 16 17 18 19 20	11 12 13 14 15 16 17	11 12 13 14 15 16 17
19 20 21 22 23 24 25	17 18 19 20 21 22 23	21 22 23 24 25 26 27	18 19 20 21 22 23 24	18 19 20 21 22 23 24
26 27 28 29 30	24 25 26 27 28 29 30 31	28 29 30 31	25 26 27 28	25 26 27 28 29 30 31

APRIL	MAY
1 2 3 4 5 6 7	
8 9 10 11 12 13 14	1 2 3 4 5
15 16 17 18 19 20 21	6 7 8 9 10 11 12
22 23 24 25 26 27 28	13 14 15 16 17 18 19
29 30	20 21 22 23 24 25 26
	27 28 29 30 31

JUNE	JULY	AUGUST
1 2	1 2 3 4 5 6 7	1 2 3 4
3 4 5 6 7 8 9	8 9 10 11 12 13 14	5 6 7 8 9 10 11
10 11 12 13 14 15 16	15 16 17 18 19 20 21	12 13 14 15 16 17 18
17 18 19 20 21 22 23	22 23 24 25 26 27 28	19 20 21 22 23 24 25
24 25 26 27 28 29 30	29 30 31	26 27 28 29 30 31

SEPTEMBER	OCTOBER
1	1 2 3 4 5 6
2 3 4 5 6 7 8	7 8 9 10 11 12 13
9 10 11 12 13 14 15	14 15 16 17 18 19 20
16 17 18 19 20 21 22	21 22 23 24 25 26 27
23 24 25 26 27 28 29	28 29 30 31
30	

Which is the longest season in Russia? Which are the shortest seasons?

winters can be bitterly cold in Russia.

One of the coldest places in the world is found in central Siberia in the Siberian Plateau. The area near the town of Yakutsk (yə kütsk′) is called the **"cold pole"** of Russia. There the temperature in January stays below –50° F (–46° C) much of the time. The ground is frozen so deeply that water pipes must be laid on top of the ground and wrapped in insulation. They would burst underground. The cold air will freeze an uncovered finger in a couple of minutes.

In some parts of Siberia, schoolchildren get a holiday when the temperature drops below –50° F (–46° C). Would you like to live in Siberia?

Mild weather in Siberia lasts only a short time—about three months. People in Siberia like to say, "We have nine months of winter and then it's summer, summer, summer."

The short Russian summers can be surprisingly warm. The temperature has climbed as high as 100° F (38° C) in Siberia. Much farther west in Moscow the average afternoon temperature in July is 76° F (24° C). Sometimes Muscovites (as residents of Moscow are called) sweat through hot spells of 90° F (32° C).

Even southern Russia can have cold weather. This is because the southern part of the country is as far north as Pennsylvania and Oregon. The northern part of the Caspian (kas′ pē ən) Sea, the largest lake in the world, freezes over in winter. But the summer sun is so hot that eggs could almost be fried on the hot sands along the Caspian Sea.

One strange thing about the climate in Russia is the short spring and fall seasons. In many parts of the country these seasons are only from one to two months long.

In Moscow, winter holds its icy grip until April. By June the weather is warm and summer has come. Farmers must raise their crops quickly, for winter soon returns. By September snow and cold returns to Siberia. Snow flurries reach Moscow by the first week of October. Winter weather arrives by November.

The flat Russian plains allow the cold wind to sweep down from the north for many months. The people seem to have become used to the cold. They bundle themselves in fur coats and caps, as well as sheepskin boots. Of course, they enjoy the short summer when it comes.

What Do You Say?

1. a. Name the region in Russia which has very good soil. b. What region in the United States and Canada has soil which is similar?

2. Which word best describes most of the land in Russia: hilly, flat, mountainous, steep?

3. a. Describe the winters in Siberia. b. Describe the summers.

What Does the Bible Say?

1. You have read about the good soil in the black earth region of Russia. Read Zechariah 8:12. a. What does the good earth (soil) give? b. What do the heavens give?

2. In some parts of Russia the soil is good, but there is not enough water for plants to grow. But in most parts of the black earth region, there is enough moisture for crops. Read Psalm 104:13, 14. a. What does the Lord do "from his chambers" or from heaven? b. What does He do on the earth for men and animals?

3. In Russia clear, cold weather usually comes from the north.

Read Job 37:22. In Bible lands, from where does fair weather come?

Using Globes and Maps

1. On a globe find Russia. Put your finger on the eastern and western ends of Russia. Notice how far around the northern part of the earth the country stretches.

2. Russia is the largest country in the world. The second largest in land area is Canada. The third largest is China. The fourth largest is the United States, and the fifth largest is Brazil. Find each of these countries and tell what continent it is on.

3. On an outline map of Russia, draw in and label the following: North European Plain, Ural Mountains, Caucasus Mountains, West Siberian Plain, Central Siberian Plateau, East Siberian Highlands. Use an atlas map, a classroom map, or an encyclopedia map to find these places.

New Words and Terms

Write a definition for each of these terms.

1. soviet
2. socialist
3. Soviet Union
4. manganese
5. black earth belt
6. Caucasus Mountains
7. Ural Mountains
8. West Siberian Plain
9. Central Siberian Plateau
10. East Siberian Highlands
11. cold pole
12. Caspian Sea

Thinking Together

1. You have read about many "big things" in Russia. Name some of

the "big things" in your own country, such as rivers, lakes, and natural resources.

2. Name some of the most important natural resources in your country. An encyclopedia article on your own country will help you learn about these resources.

3. People and nations who are rich need to remember God's warnings about riches. Read Matthew 19:24 and fill in the blanks. "It is easier for a a. _____ to go through the eye of a b. _____ , than for a c. _____ man to enter into the d. _____ of e. _____ ."

4. a. How do the vast flatlands in Russia help the people in farming? b. in traveling?

5. How do people in lands with cold winters prepare for the cold and protect themselves from it?

For You to Do

1. You have read about the great size of Russia. Find out how large your country is. How far does it measure from east to west? From north to south?

2. Read an article in an encyclopedia about a natural resource such as soil, coal, petroleum, iron ore, water. List four important uses of the natural resource you choose.

3. Find out the average low temperature in your community in the winter. Talk to your parents or some elderly person who has always lived in your community. What is the coldest they have seen? How does this compare with the usual January temperature at the "cold pole" in Siberia?

13. The Russian People

Russian History Helps Us Understand. Before we look at the Russian people and their needs, we must take a look backward. Russian history helps us understand the Russians and the way they live.

It is very hard for us to understand the people of Russia. For one thing, the country is far away. Its people do not speak our language. They do not even use our alphabet. Until recently the Russian government allowed visitors only in certain places. Russians were not allowed to visit freely in other countries.

This is the bell tower of Ivan the Great, ruler in Moscow at the time when Columbus discovered America. Ivan freed Russia from the rule of the Mongols from eastern Asia.

During their history, the Russian people have often suffered much. Harsh rulers often mistreated the people, especially the poor. The Russians have not always had freedom of religion either. Under communism Christians in Russia suffered much. No wonder the Russian people are different from us in many ways.

Long Ago in Russia.

Nobody knows how long people have been living in Russia. People no doubt lived there in Bible times.

At least 1,200 years ago the first Slavs were settling in Russia. For many years their most important city was Kiev (kē′ ef′). Kiev is in the country called Ukraine (yü krān′).

About the year 1200, fierce tribes from deep in Asia conquered Kiev. These tribes were called **Mongols** (män′ gōlz). They forced the Russians to pay them high taxes.

The group of Mongols who conquered Russia and Eastern Europe were called the **Golden Horde**. Perhaps they were called this because their leader slept in a magnificent gold-colored tent. A horde is a large group of people who wander from place to place. Golden Horde also became the name of the Russian lands that were conquered by the Mongol hordes.

Empire of the Golden Horde

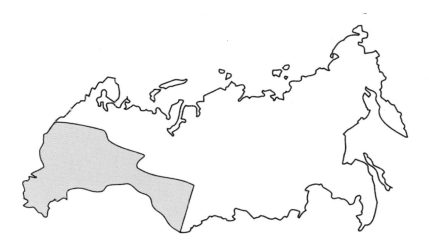

This map shows in dark blue the part of Russia once ruled by the Mongols or the Golden Horde from deep inside Asia. They ruled Russia for 240 years until 1480.

In 1480 the Russian leaders of Moscow threw off the rule of the Golden Horde. Moscow then became the leading city in Russia. All the lands ruled by the princes of Moscow were called Muscovy (mə′ skō′ vē).

The rulers of Moscow became more and more powerful. They began to call themselves **czars** (zärz). *Czar* comes from the word *Caesar*. Caesar was the name of the rulers in ancient Rome about 2,000 years ago.

Most of Russia's Czars were harsh rulers. They made the poor people pay high taxes. Their laws forced the poor to work almost like slaves for the rich landowners. The poor were bound to the land of the rich and could not move away to find a better life.

The Bible warns rulers and rich people of the sin of making life hard for the poor. "Oppress not the widow, nor the fatherless, the stranger, nor the poor."

Zechariah 7:10a

The poor farmers in the days of the czars were called **serfs.** This word means "servant" or "slave."

Finally a czar named Alexander II freed the serfs. What a time of rejoicing that must have been! At last the people could move from place to place. Each family received a small piece of land to call their own.

Hiding the Truth

Not all czars in Russia treated the serfs cruelly. You already learned that Alexander II freed the serfs. Another ruler who tried to help these poor people was Catherine the Great.

Catherine had heard that the serfs were living in miserable huts with little to eat and ragged clothing. *I will take a trip to learn the truth about my people,* she decided.

Catherine was doing what the Bible says rulers should do.

Proverbs 25:2b

"The honour of kings is to search out a matter."

Rich landowners did not want Catherine to find out the truth. They knew the route she planned to travel. They falsely beautified some of the buildings she would see. Some peasants were dressed in good clothes. They had to stand along the roadside as Catherine's carriage passed by.

Catherine did not see the peasants who were in rags. She did not see their miserable little huts.

The rich landowners sinned. They were lying to Catherine the Great. Covering up the truth is lying, and it hurt the poor serfs.

"He that oppresseth [wrongs] the poor reproacheth [shows disrespect for] his Maker: but he that honoureth him hath mercy on the poor."

Proverbs 14:31

Catherine the Great rode through Russia to see the poor people. What things were hidden from her along the road she traveled? Why?

Free Serfs—More Problems! The freeing of the serfs did not solve all of Russia's problems. The freed serfs and their families were terribly poor. The rulers gave each family a small piece of land. The serfs then became known as **peasants** (pez′ ənts). This word is a name used for poor farmers in many European countries.

Many of the Russian peasants were not happy with the small pieces of land they received. They became greedy for more. Greed is a common sin among the rich and the poor. The more people have, the more they seem to want.

"Woe unto them that join house to house, that lay field to field, till there be no place. . . ."

Isaiah 5:8

How Much Land Does a Man Need?

Leo Tolstoy, a famous Russian writer, told a story about the dangers of greed. He had heard this story as it was told by Russian peasants. He retold it for his readers.

One day a lady from the city visited in the home of a peasant named Pahom. The conversation turned to the dangers of city life.

Pahom boasted that country life was the most satisfying if only a person could own enough land.

Soon afterwards a rich lady who lived nearby had land for sale. Pahom decided to buy 20 acres (8 hectares) from the woman. He and his wife scraped and saved and borrowed until they had enough money to make the first payment.

Pahom rejoiced to have so much land he could call his own. His fields were rich. The first crop was very good.

All was not well, however. He began to have problems with his neighbors. Their animals would get into Pahom's fields. Pahom also believed that some neighbors had been stealing from him.

Soon Pahom wished for more land somewhere else. He had made enough money on his 20 acres to buy 40 acres (16 hectares) somewhere else. Again he moved. Soon Pahom wished for more land. He bought another farm of 120 acres (48 hectares). Again he wished for more.

At last Pahom heard of a place where a man could buy all the land he wanted. This was on the wide grasslands far to the south. Only a few wanderers, or **nomads,** lived there. These nomads were called Bashkirs (bash′ kirz). They lived in tents and moved around with their animals. They did not farm the land.

Pahom met with the Bashkirs. They let him know that he could have all he wanted.

"And what will the price be?" asked Pahom.

"Our price is always the same," answered the Bashkir chief, "one thousand rubles (rü′ bəlz) a day." A ruble was a Russian coin. The Russians speak of rubles in the same way we speak of dollars.

"A day? What measurement is that?" said Pahom. "How many acres would that be?"

"We sell it by the day," answered the chief. "As much as you can go around on your feet in a day is yours. The price is one thousand rubles a day. But there is one condition: If you don't return on the same day to the spot from where you started, your money is lost."

The next morning Pahom rose up early. He and the nomads met on a low hill. At sunrise he set out to walk around his land. He carried a spade. Once in a while he dug a hole and piled up the sod. This marked the boundary, or the outside edge, of his farm.

Greed made Pahom walk many miles before he turned to make the first corner on his land. He kept seeing beautiful grassy meadows and a moist hollow, good for planting flax. Pahom wanted all he saw.

It seemed like no time until the sun was halfway down in the western sky. Pahom saw that he must hurry to return to where he started. He ran faster and faster. His heart beat like a hammer.

There is plenty of land, he thought, *but will God let me live on it? I have lost my life. I shall never reach that spot.*

Pahom feared he would die, but he rushed on. He did not want to lose the land. The nomads would laugh at him. He reached the hilltop just as the sun was setting. He fell to the ground exhausted. He had arrived just in time.

Pahom's servant rushed forward to help his master. But Pahom did not get up. He was dead.

How much land did Pahom really need? The servant picked up a spade and dug a grave for Pahom. Six feet from head to toe was all the land he needed!

"Take heed, and beware of covetousness [greed]: for a man's life consisteth not in the abundance of the things which he possesseth." "For what is a man profited, if he shall gain the whole world, and lose his own soul?"

Luke 12:15b

Matthew 16:26a

—Adapted from "How Much Land Does a Man Need?" by Leo Tolstoy (1881)

Pahom sets out to mark out his land on the vast plains of Russia. Why is he hurrying?

How much land did Pahom really need? What was Pahom's greatest problem?

What Do You Say?

1. Name four reasons why it is hard for us to understand Russia and its people.

2. After 1480, _____ became the leading city in all Russia.

3. a. What did Catherine the Great set out to see in Russia? b. What did she see?

4. a. What great problem did the Russian serfs have after they were free? b. What great sin were some of these freed serfs guilty of?

What Does the Bible Say?

1. Read Hebrews 13:5. What does this verse say to a person who is tempted to be greedy?

2. Rich landowners lied to Catherine the Great by telling her that the serfs were living in good conditions. What does Ephesians 4:25 say the Christian should do?

A New Russia

The serfs were free in Russia after 1861. But the hatred between the poor and the rich grew worse and worse.

Greed, hate, and murder finally led to a great war. We call this war the Russian Revolution. New leaders began to rule the country. They murdered the czar and his family.

The new leaders in Russia were **communists** (käm′ yə nəsts). These communists believed in socialism, the idea that the government should own land, factories, and other businesses. The communists also said that people should share their wealth equally with each other.

At first the Russian communists promised more land to the peasants or poor farmers. The peasants were excited. They helped the communists to take over Russia.

In a few years the peasants were sadly disappointed. The communist rulers took all the land from the rich and poor alike. Farmers who tried to keep their farms were killed or sent to labor camps in Siberia.

What Is Communism? The word communism comes from the word *common.* Communists say people should own everything together and share with each other. A farmer in a communist land usually does not own his own land or machinery. The land and the machinery are shared in common by a large group of farmers. Each one receives food and

These buildings are part of the famous Kremlin in Moscow. The Kremlin contains beautiful palaces, towers, paintings, jewels and crowns worn by the Czars. The Kremlin is the place where the Russian government meets.

clothing for his family.

In most communist countries people are forced to share things in common. Communist governments have taken the land from the people and have taken over private businesses. Many of the people did not really want communism. They were forced to accept it.

The Bible teaches Christians to share with each other and with others. Christians share because they love others and because they want to share. Christians do not force other people to share.

"Every man according as he purposeth in his heart, so let him give; not grudgingly, or of necessity: for God loveth a cheerful giver."

2 Corinthians 9:7

In communist countries people own some things such as their clothing and their furniture. Some people own their own homes. They do not usually own land or factories. The government owns these things. The people usually work for the government. The government pays their wages. Farmers are given little plots of land to raise some fruit and vegetables for themselves. The government takes what it needs of the crops and other things made in communist countries.

People in communist countries are not free to change jobs whenever they choose. In some places the people must get permits to change jobs, to move across the country, or even to move from one apartment to another.

Early communist leaders looked forward to a time when the government would "wither away." They imagined that people in a communist country would learn to love each other. They believed people would want to share and to help each other. They thought that, later on, a government would no longer be necessary.

In communist countries governments never withered away. They remained until new noncommunist governments rose to take their place.

The communists who took over Russia did not believe in God. Many believed that they did not need any god because the government gave them work, food, clothing, and shelter.

Even in noncommunist countries, many people believe they can live without God. They do not think about God when they have plenty to eat and plenty of money to spend.

"They spend their days in wealth, and in a moment go down to the grave. Therefore they say unto God, Depart from us; for we desire not the knowledge of thy ways. What is the Almighty, that we should serve him? and what profit should we have, if we pray unto him? . . . And do ye not know . . . that the wicked is reserved to the day of destruction? they shall be brought forth to the day of wrath."

Job
21:13-15,
29b, 30

The Soviet Union

In 1917 communists took over in Russia. In 1922 they changed the name of their country to the Union of Soviet Socialist Republics (abbreviated U.S.S.R.). The country was also called the Soviet Union. People from this country were sometimes called Soviets. When we remember the Soviet Union, we think of communism. Communists ruled there from there from 1917 to 1991.

Many years of communism greatly changed Russia. People became used to not owning property. Many blindly followed the teaching that there is no God. Christians in the Soviet Union had many hard times. At times the police broke into homes and other places where worship services were being held.

Communist governments in Eastern Europe began falling in the late 1980s. Communism ended in Poland and Romania before 1990. Others took control of Hungary in 1990 and Albania in 1992.

In the 1980s the communist rulers in the Soviet Union began to grant more freedoms. Christians were persecuted less. A man named Yeltsin who wanted change was elected president of the Russian Republic (part of the Soviet Union.) He began to challenge the communist government. Other republics of the Soviet Union declared independence. The communists tried to regain power in August of 1991 and failed.

On December 25, 1991, the Soviet Union ended. It had divided into 15 countries. By far the largest one is Russia. Russia is three times larger than the other fourteen put together!

We will now study about how life was in the Soviet Union and how it has changed in Russia today.

The people of Moscow are happy for their subway called the Metro. Almost five million people ride on it every workday. Many of the 70 Metro stations look like fancy palace rooms.

What Do You Say?

1. What is a communist?

2. Name some things people in a communist country may own.

3. What do communists believe about God?

What Does the Bible Say?

1. Acts 4:32-34 tells of early Christians who shared all things in common.   a. Pick out the words which show that they did this willingly.   b. How was

222

this different from the kind of sharing in a communist country?

2. Acts 2:44, 45 also tells of Christians sharing. How did they know how much to share with each person (verse 45)?

Chapter Thirteen Review

Using Globes and Maps

1. On a map of Europe find the Russian capital, Moscow. Use the scale of miles or kilometers to find how far it is from Moscow to Oslo, Norway. From Moscow to Rome, Italy. To measure the distance, lay the edge of a piece of paper on the scale. Mark 50 miles, 100 miles, 200 miles, and so on across the paper until you have marked at least 2,000 miles. Now measure the distances with your paper scale of miles.

2. On a globe find out the shortest way to travel from Moscow to New York (or Montreal). Through what countries would you travel? To find this route, cut a string long enough to reach about halfway around your globe. Hold one end of the string on Moscow. Stretch the string in different directions until you find the shortest distance to New York (or Montreal).

New Words and Terms

Mark each sentence as either true or false in the blank before it. If the statement is false, correct it.

1. _____ *Kiev* was once the leading city of Russia.

2. _____ *Mongols* were a tribe from Western Europe.

3. _____ *The Golden Horde* was a tribe of Mongols.

4. _____ *Moscow* is now the capital city of Russia.

5. _____ *Czars* are the communist leaders of Russia.

6. _____ *Serfs* were rich farmers in old Russia.

7. _____ *Nomads* are wanderers.

8. _____ The inside of a country is called its *boundary*.

9. _____ A *communist* says that people should own all things together.

Thinking Together

1. What are some needs that both Russians and Americans have?

2. Describe the life of the poor under Russia's czars.

3. Just as rich landowners deceived Catherine the Great, many people today do not tell the truth. Following Christ is the only way people can learn to tell the truth. What does Jesus Christ say about Himself in John 14:6?

4. Name some ways Christians can share with other people. How is true Christian sharing different from "sharing" under communism?

For You to Do

1. Read an encyclopedia article about the Russian czar, Peter the Great. Name at least three changes he brought to Russia.

2. Make a time line of Russian history. Draw a line 10 inches long. Mark the beginning of the line with the year 1000. Place large dots along the line at each inch. Mark the first dot 1100, the second dot 1200, and so on until 2000. The space between each dot stands for 100 years. Draw a line one inch long straight down from each of the following dates: 1000, 1200, 1300, 1480, 1760, 1917, 1991. If a date is between the dots marking each 100 years, you will need to figure where to draw your lines. Below each line write what happened on that date in Russia. The dates and happenings are: Russia ruled from Kiev (1000), Russia ruled by Mongols (1200), the Golden Horde (1300), Moscow conquers the Golden Horde (1480), Catherine the Great (1760), Communists take over (1917), End of Communism in Russia (1991). (If you use the metric system, mark each dot two centimeters apart.)

14. Life in Russia During and After Communism

Communism Changed Russia. Life under communism, you remember, is very different from life in North America. Russian communists believed that the government should own most things such as factories, farms, and machinery. The government first promised plenty of land for the poor farmers. Later the government took all the land away from the poor and the rich. They did not feel that they were doing wrong. *Anything is right,* they thought, *if it helps communism.*

But the Bible says, "Righteousness exalteth a nation: but sin is a reproach to any people." Taking advantage of people is sin no matter who does it or why it is done.

Farming During and After Communism.

The government in the Soviet Union owned the farms. Farmers worked together. They shared the land and the machinery.

Communists liked to say that the farmers owned everything together. They shared things in common. Remember that the name *communism* comes from the word *common.*

These were two kinds of farms in the Soviet Union. Either kind of farm often covered thousands of acres or hectares.

The majority of the farms were **state farms.** Hundreds and some- times even thousands of people lived on state farms which the government operated. Most of the people lived in large apartment buildings. They came to work each day and received weekly pay much as factory workers did.

The second type of farm was the **collective farm.** On a collective farm the families often lived in separate houses. The houses were built together in villages. The village farmers worked together on the land around their village. A few of the men were chosen to run or manage the farm. The government paid the farm for the crops it raised. The farm managers used this money to pay for machinery, fertilizer, seeds, and other farm needs. The money that was left over was divided among farm families. This is their pay.

The largest country in the world is Russia. It is a large and important country, but to many people it is an unknown country. This chapter may remove some of your questions about this country.

Comparing Farm Sizes

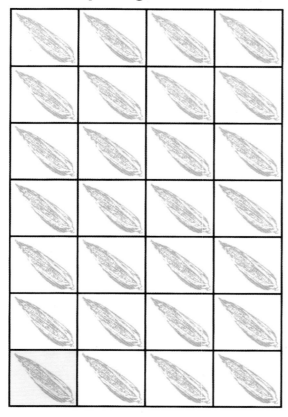

Farms in Russia are very large. The entire chart above represents the size of an average Russian farm. The single ear in the lower left corner represents the size of a farm in the United States. Almost 28 average U.S. farms would fit into one Russian farm. Farm size is beginning to change in Russia. Why is this so?

The state farms under communism in the 1980s averaged 112,000 acres (45,320 hectares) each. Collective farms average 10,600 acres (4,249 hectares) each. The average farm size in the United States in the 1980's was about 390 acres (158 hectares). The difference was so great because most American farmers own or rent their own farms. Usually one or two families operate one farm. These are called **private farms.**

When communism ended, the new rulers wanted to break up the state farms and collective farms and divide them among individual farmers. But not many Russian farm workers had enough money to start farming by themselves right away. By 1996 only four of every 100 acres (hectares) of farm land were owned by farmers. It will probably take many years to switch to mostly private farms.

This picture shows the inside of the famous GUM department store in Moscow. Why is it difficult sometimes for shoppers to find what they are looking for in this and many other stores in Russia?

These farm women are selling produce in Moscow in an open air market. Vegetables bought here are usually fresher and better than those bought in larger grocery stores.

Shopping in Moscow—Russian Style

Urie and Lina are a brother and sister who live in Moscow, the capital of Russia.

They live in a three-room apartment with father, mother, baby Vanya, and Babushka. *Babushka* (bə büsh′kə) is Russian for *grandmother.*

Today Urie and Lina are allowed to go shopping with Babushka. They are excited about the sights and the sounds of the big city.

Babushka makes sure to take along the big handbag she uses for shopping. Russian stores often do not give shoppers bags for purchases. People take their own bags from home.

As the three walk down the street, they see dozens of shops and stores. Moscow has some of the largest stores in Russia. One of the largest department stores in Russia is in Moscow. This store is called GUM (güm). In Russia, GUM is short for Government Department Store.

In one of these stores Urie notices a long line of people waiting in line.

"We must get in line," Babushka says. "No doubt they are selling something that is hard to get. You know how often we have shortages of things we need."

The three step to the end of the line. Babushka questions the lady in front of her, "What are they selling?"

"Sweaters," the lady answers. "I've been looking for a new sweater for weeks."

"Babushka," asks Urie, "why are things we need sometimes hard to get?"

"Who knows this time?" Babushka shrugs. "Back in the days of communism, the government told factories what to make and how much to make. The government did not always know what the people needed. Sometimes they felt that weapons and big machinery were more important than refrigerators and other things we need in the home. Factories today still do not know what all we need. Perhaps they cannot always get the materials they need to make these things. Since the days of communism most things are more expensive than they used to be. Some people wish we were back in those days. But then Russians would not have as much freedom to go to church, to travel, and to own land and houses."

Babushka does not need a sweater. "Let's go," she says. "We do need vegetables." They hurry to one of the many open air markets. These are much like farmers' markets in North America. Here farmers who own their own gardens or farms bring extra fruit, vegetables, and sometimes meat to sell. Here one can usually buy fresher food than in stores that get their food shipped in from larger farms.

Now it is Lina who has a question, "Why are the vegetables better here than in the grocery stores we sometimes go to?"

"You asked a good question, Lina," Babushka chuckled. "Farmers who own their own land and people who have extra from their backyard gardens bring their things to market here. In the grocery stores most of the food comes from big farms, some of them far away. Many of the people who bring things to market live closer by. And as in the days of communism, it seems that people who have their own gardens and truck patches take better care of their land than people who go to work each day at some big farm that is not their own."

Babushka fills her shopping bag with fresh carrots, beans, a cabbage, and other foods the family needs.

On the way home the children beg, "May we stop at GUM?"

"All right," sighs Babushka, "but we mustn't buy anything. We don't have time to wait in line!"

At GUM they discover that Babushka was right. Some people are looking at goods they want. Others stand in line to tell the salesclerk what they want. In another line people pay for their purchases. In a third line they pick them up.

The three do not stay long at GUM. Soon Mama and Papa will be home from the factory, and supper will need to be prepared.

Babushka will probably go shopping again the day after tomorrow.

What Do You Say?

1. What was a state farm in communist Russia?

2. What was a collective farm?

3. Why are things people need sometimes hard to find in Russian stores?

4. Where are the vegetables raised that are found in Russian farmers' markets?

What Does the Bible Say?

1. You learned that the communists believe that anything is right as long as it helps communism. According to Psalm 19:8, what is the standard for deciding whether something is right or wrong?

Families in Russia

Urie and Lina live with their parents and grandmother. This is not unusual in Russia. Sometimes aunts and uncles and even cousins live in the same house. This happens mainly because of the shortage of houses and apartments. This has not changed much since the fall of communism.

We call such large families **extended families.** They extend, or go beyond, the usual family of mother, father, and their children.

Often in Russia both the father and mother work. Grandmother or some other member of the extended family stays home to prepare meals and to take care of the little children. Some people send their children to nurseries and kindergartens for preschoolers. Under communism, the government provided nurseries to encourage mothers to work away from home. From age six through seventeen children go to school.

Many Russians live in apartment buildings. Some of the more expensive apartments have little balconies where people can sit and where flowers can be planted.

Going to School in Russia

During the many years of communist rule in Russia, Christian families could not send their children to Christian schools. The government owned schools. The schools taught only what the government wanted the children to learn. Only

Apartment buildings, in Russia's large cities, are huge. Often these buildings are drab or not very colorful.

229

This is a photo of a Russian schoolroom taken before 1990. Whose picture is on the wall? Why is it there? Why would it not be there today?

communists could teach in the schools.

Teachers carefully taught the children that there was no God. Instead, they honored a man named Lenin. Lenin was the first communist ruler in Russia. A picture of Lenin hung in each classroom.

Even children in nurseries and kindergartens saw pictures of Lenin on the wall. They learned to call him "Father Lenin."

People could visit Lenin's tomb in Moscow. His body was preserved so that people could actually see it.

One young communist told of going to see Lenin's body on his first visit to Moscow.

"The first place I went was the tomb of Lenin. There I got in line and stood patiently for several hours, until it was my turn to go in. . . . I stood close, quietly looking at the body of the man about whom I had studied so much and who was a god to me. . . . I bowed my head and prayed to him. Yes, it was a prayer. I cannot describe it in any other way. I prayed, 'Help me, Father Lenin, in my life.

Give me the guidance and direction I need. Help me to have the understanding to follow your teachings. . . . Lead me and guide me. Help me, Father Lenin.'"

But his faith in Lenin's teaching did not meet the need of his heart. Later this man became a Christian. He learned to worship God as his Father. The Bible says, "Call no man your father upon the earth: for one is your Father, which is in heaven." **Matthew 23:9**

Lenin is dead. A dead person is not able to help anyone. Jesus Christ is no longer in the grave. He rose from the dead because He is God. He is alive forevermore and able to help all who trust in Him.

"Jesus said . . . I am the resurrection, and the life: he that believeth in me, though he were dead, yet shall he live." **John 11:2**

Today the Russian government is working to remove the influence of communism in the schools. No longer do pictures of Lenin hang on the walls. Children are no longer taught that there is no God. Bibles are even permitted in many Russian public schools.

People used to line up to enter the tomb of Lenin in Moscow. Why was he considered to be important?

What Are Russian Schools Like?

Russian children attend school from ages six through seventeen. They go to the same school through grade nine. From then on they can choose between a secondary school where they can prepare for college and a vocational school where they can learn a trade such as carpentry or certain kinds of factory work.

In secondary school, students must pass exams to move from one grade to the next. At the end of secondary school students receive a certificate, something like a diploma. If they have done well, they will receive a gold or silver medal.

Students are graded with numbers. After each subject, they find a number between one and five. Five is the highest grade, like an A on your report card.

In school, children study many of the same subjects you do. They study geography, history, and math. In fourth grade they begin to learn a foreign language. English is the most widely taught foreign language. Some study French and German.

Games and exercises have long been an important part of each school day. Under communism, the government wanted each young person to grow up strong and healthy. Healthy people can better serve communism.

Today many people exercise because it is fun or to be stronger or healthier. But the Christian should try to keep a strong, healthy body for a better reason. The Christian serves

What tells you that this American fourth-grade room is in a Christian school?

God with his body.

"Know ye not that . . . ye are not your own? For ye are bought with a price: therefore glorify God in your body, and in your spirit, which are God's." I Corinthians 6:19, 20

In communist schools in Russia the children were taught that God is not real. One communist teacher greeted her students each morning with, "Good morning, boys and girls. How are you today? Remember, there is no God."

Teachers and children sometimes made fun of those who did believe in God. They tried to make them feel foolish.

The Bible says, "The fool hath said in his heart, There is no God." "The fear of the LORD is the beginning of wisdom." Psalm 14:1a Psalm 111:10a

New Textbooks in Russia. Since the fall of communism, many new books are being published to replace textbooks prepared by communists. Of course this takes time and money to do. Under communism, even dictionaries taught communist beliefs in some of the examples they gave.

One dictionary used the word *vera* which means "faith" this way: "*Faith* in the revolutionary cause." *Poshchada* means "mercy." A communist dictionary used it this way: "No *mercy* to the enemies of the people." The dictionary used *znamya* or *banner* this way: "To hold aloft the *banner* of Lenin."

Can you think of some examples of how a Christian might use these words?

What Do You Say?

1. What are extended families?

2. Name two wrong things communists in Russia taught school children.

3. a. Name four subjects school children study in Russia. b. What is the favorite foreign language?

4. a. Why did communists consider games and exercise important? b. Why should Christians take good care of their bodies?

This is a drawing of a Christian named Dirk Willems saving his enemy from drowning in an icy river. The enemy had chased Dirk across the ice and had fallen through. Dirk returned to help the man. In your own words, describe what Dirk did, using the word "mercy." How might communists use the word "mercy"?

What Does the Bible Say?

1. What is faith according to Hebrews 11:1?

2. Read Proverbs 14:21. Write the phrase that uses the word *mercy*.

3. Copy Psalm 60:4. Every Christian banner should display a message of _____.

4. Read Jesus' words in Revelation 1:18. What does He say about His life and death? These words cannot be said of Lenin.

The Church in Russia

Christianity came to Russia and the other Slavs in the time of the brothers, Cyril and Methodius. This was more than one thousand years ago. For hundreds of years, the main church in Russia was called the Russian Orthodox Church. Orthodox church buildings were usually very fancy with paintings, statues, crosses and other decorations. Priests who wore special robes led the services with reading and chanting in a language called Old Church Slavonic. This was similar to the Slavic language into which the Bible was first translated.

The Russian Orthodox Church was the main church in Russia when communists took over in 1917. Other churches such as Baptist, Pentecostal, and Mennonite also existed in Russia.

The communists were **atheists** (ā′ thē ists). Atheists believe that there is no God. Communists said that religion was the "opium of the people." Opium is a drug that stops pain and makes people sleepy.

The communists felt sure that when communism provided people with food, places to live, and other things they needed that they would no longer need religion. They would trust in communism.

The communists destroyed many churches or turned them into barns or community centers. They turned many Orthodox churches into museums. They arrested or killed church leaders who would not follow communism. Many Christians fled the country. Others were sent to prisons and to labor camps where many suffered and died.

The communist government only permitted churches that would support communism. In Moscow, a city of millions of people, only one Protestant church (a Baptist church) was open for services.

Christians in Russia and other communist countries in Eastern Europe suffered most in the 1930s and again in the 1950s. Many Christians met in secret.

In the 1980s communist leaders allowed more and more freedom of worship. But many still met in secret. The government began to allow many persecuted people to leave in order to live in other countries. Many fled to the United States to find religious freedom. Large numbers left the part of the Soviet Union called Ukraine. Today, Ukraine is a separate country from Russia.

Finally, when communism ended in Russia and the countries that were united with Russia, the governments allowed religious freedom. The communists had believed that religion would fade away because communism would supply all the people's needs. They were wrong. As soon as communism fell, church attendance shot up. After more than 60 years of "no God" teaching, millions began attending church. New churches were built. Christian books were again published. Sunday schools and Christian schools opened. Christians from other countries were free to send books, Bibles, and other Christian literature to Russia.

For years Christians around the world had been praying for the Christians in communist Russia and nearby countries. They had prayed for them as they suffered. They also prayed that the terrible persecution would end.

We are told that many Russian Christians prayed for the Christians in countries with religious freedom. They prayed that the "free" Christians would be true to Christ and not forget Christ because of

Here is a picture of some Christian literature ready to be sent to a country where Christians once suffered under communism. What happened that allows this material to be sent? What did Christians do for Bibles before they could be sent so freely?

their freedom and prosperity.

With new freedom in Russia, will Russian Christians be able to stand for Christ? Christians everywhere still need to pray for each other. Sometimes freedom and material things can be just as dangerous as persecution.

An early Christian writer once said, "The blood of the martyrs is the seed of the church." Sometimes churches that face persecution grow and spread more than churches that have many freedoms.

We must also remember that many Christians are still being persecuted in other parts of the world. China, parts of Southeast Asia, Cuba, and several other small countries are still communistic. More than one of every five people on earth is still living under communism. Christians in many noncommunist countries are also suffering.

Standing for Christ. Under Russian communism, Christians often had to meet in secret if they wanted to worship together. They met in homes, barns, or even in forests. Sometimes these Christians were called the *underground church,* not because they met under the ground, but because they met in secret.

Sometimes underground Christians in Russia would meet together at birthday parties and holiday dinners. The police would not accuse them of having a church service. Each person would take his turn giving a testimony, a reading, a Scripture, or encouragement.

When communist soldiers did break up Christian meetings, they might imprison the minister or other leaders. Christians were sometimes beaten or jailed. The police would destroy all the Bibles and Christian literature they could find. The following story tells what an underground church meeting must have been like.

Christians at Worship

For many years Christians were persecuted by the communist government of Russia. Christians often met in secret to worship God together.

Come with me to such a Christian worship service in Moscow in the 1960s. This service is not in a fine church building, but in a common house. The house looks much like every other house along the narrow street. It is a small, wooden, frame house with a wooden, shingle roof.

You see no cars parked in front of the house. Few Christians in the Soviet Union could afford cars. No one is standing outside talking before the service begins as we are free to do in North America. This would let the police know about the meeting. They might rush in and stop the service.

As we enter the main room of the house, we see that twenty or twenty-five people are already there. The windows are covered with blankets so no one can see inside. People whisper to each other as we wait for more to come. Soon two or three more slip into the house. It would be dangerous for many people to be seen on the street at the same time.

As soon as the service begins, the people sing very softly. Only a few people have songbooks. The communist government does not allow hymnbooks to be printed. Those who have songbooks or handwritten copies of songs hold them high. The people sitting nearby crowd around to see the words.

Few people have Bibles either. As the minister reads, some follow along in notebooks. They have copied whole books of the Bible into their notebooks. Would we love the Bible enough to spend many hours making copies of it?

Suddenly someone standing near a window along the street gives a signal. Everyone sits very still. We can hear each other breathing. There is a sound of footsteps. Policemen are patrolling the streets. Will they discover the Christian meeting?

Everyone knows very well what might happen. The police might break in and take Bibles, songbooks, and tracts. The communists claim that these writings are against communism. Some of the believers might be arrested, especially the leaders.

Finally the sound of footsteps fades away. The minister continues the sermon he had begun earlier.

After the message, many give their testimonies of how God has helped them. They tell of witnessing for Christ and suffering for Him.

The service ends with prayer. The believers leave as they came. One or two leave. A few minutes later more leave. Many of them whisper, "Pray for us."

Believers in communist Russia especially loved God's promises to those who are persecuted:

"Blessed are ye, when men shall revile you, and persecute you, and shall say all manner of evil against you falsely, for my sake. Rejoice, and be exceeding glad: for great is your reward in heaven."

Matthew
5:11, 12a

What Do You Say?

1. Name some things Christians and their children suffer in the Soviet Union.

2. Name some new freedoms Christians have since the fall of communism.

3. Why did persecuted Russian Christians often share hymnbooks and Bibles?

What Does the Bible Say?

1. Communists in Russia promised to follow Lenin and obey the Communist Party. God's people cannot make such promises. They promise to follow the teachings of God's Word. The Bible calls promises we make *vows*. Read Psalm 116:17, 18. a. What does the psalmist promise to

offer to God? b. Where will he pay his vows?

2. Read Luke 6:22, 23. According to verse 23, why did Christians in the Soviet Union rejoice even when they were persecuted?

3. Read 2 Timothy 3:12. Who is certain to suffer some kind of persecution?

Chapter Fourteen Review

Using Globes and Maps

1. Using the map on pp. 204 and 205 of your textbook, make a list of all the countries that used to be a part of the Soviet Union. Be sure to include the one that is far larger than all the others.

New Words and Terms

Write a one-sentence definition for each of the following:

1. state farms
2. collective farms
3. private farms
4. GUM
5. extended families
6. atheist
7. underground church

Thinking Together

1. Communists believe that anything is right as long as it helps communism. How should Christians decide whether something is right or wrong?

2. Name three different kinds of farms Russians have known during and since communist rule. Why is it not always easy to divide up all the large farms in Russia?

3. a. What does the word *babushka* mean in Russian? b. Find this word in an English dictionary. What does it mean? We have borrowed this word from the Russian language.

4. In North America, extended families are rather unusual. Sometimes a grandparent will live with a family, but aunts and uncles usually do not. Can you think of some ways that the extended

family could be a good thing?

5. A grade school teacher in communist Russia once asked the children to pray to Jesus, asking Him for candy. They received none. She asked them to pray again, this time to Lenin. While they were praying, she secretly brought out some candy. The children opened their eyes and saw the candy. a. What was this teacher trying to teach the children? b. Read the last ten words of Jeremiah 9:6. Of what sin was this teacher guilty? Check the word in your dictionary if you do not know what it means.

6. Why were the churches that met in secret in communist Russia called the "underground church"?

7. Why did persecuted Russian Christians pray for the Christians in "free" countries? What does persecution sometimes do for a church?

For You to Do

1. You can be thankful that you do not go to a school that is not Christian or that teaches that there is no God. Make a list of all the things you learn about God in a school day. You might include devotions, Bible class, prayer before lunch, the times you heard about God in different classes.

2. Pretend you are writing a dictionary for Christian schools. Write a sentence using each of these words in a Christian way: mercy, love, happy.

3. Imagine that you are in a country such as China where Christians are being persecuted today. You do not have a Bible of your own. Someone loans you a Bible so you can copy part of it in a notebook. Let us say you want to copy a short book, such as 1 John. How much time will you need to copy it? Some verses are long, some are short, but the average length is about 22 words. Carefully print a verse this long and see how many minutes you need to do it. Now multiply the number of minutes times 105 which is the number of verses in 1 John. This will tell you about how long it would take to copy 1 John. Suppose you wanted to copy the entire Bible. There 30,442 verses in the Bible. How long would it take to copy all these if they averaged as long as the verses in 1 John?

Exploring Asia

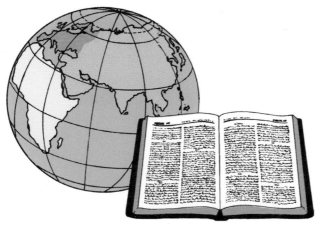

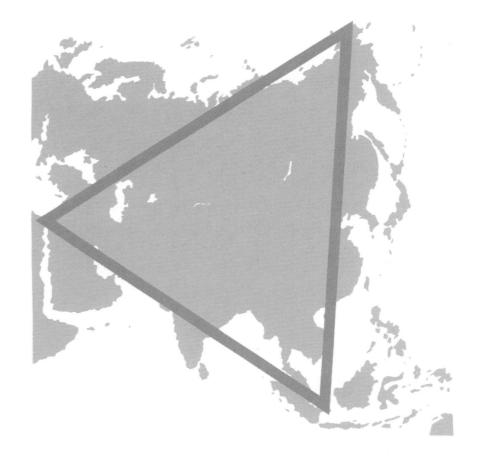

Unit 5

What you will learn . . . in unit five

We are about to study parts of the largest continent on earth, the continent of Asia. Asia has more land than North and South America put together.

This vast continent we are about to study is shaped something like a gigantic triangle with two sides about 6,500 miles (10,500 kilometers) long and the third side some 4,500 miles (7,300 kilometers) long.

The most important thing about Asia, however, is not its size or its shape. The most important thing about Asia is its many people. About three out of every five people on earth live in Asia. In the late 1990s the world population reached about six billion. Over three billion of these people lived in Asia.

Billions of people live in Asia, but there are probably fewer Christians there than on most of the other continents. We need to remember that Asians, as well as all people, need to hear the Gospel of Jesus Christ. The Bible says, "Declare his glory among the heathen, his wonders among all people" (Psalm 96:3).

15. The Lands of Asia

Asia—The Largest Continent

In the last unit we studied about Russia, the country with the most land. You may remember that well over half of this gigantic country is found in Asia. Most of the Soviet people, however, live in the part that lies in Europe. We studied mainly that part of the country.

In the next two units we want to look closer at Asia and some of the countries besides Russia found there. But first, let us consider the continent of Asia as a whole.

In many ways Asia is gigantic. If you could divide the world's land into three equal parts, Asia would cover one of those parts. Thus we say that one-third of the world's land is found in Asia.

Asia stretches some 5,400 miles (8,700 kilometers) from the cold area near the North Pole southward almost to the equator. Asia's greatest east-to-west measurement is about 6,000 miles (9,700 kilometers).

The Landforms of Asia

The word *gigantic* also describes the landforms of Asia. Where can you find the largest plain or area of flatland on earth? In Asia, of course. Find the Western Siberian Plain on the map of Asia on page 242. This great flat plain is 1,000 miles (1,600 kilometers) wide from east to west and stretches for over 1,000 miles from north to south.

But Asia is not all flatland by any means. More of this continent is covered by mountains and other highlands than by plains. The largest group of mountains in the world is found in Asia. Part of this great **mountain system** is sometimes called the "rooftop of the world." From the rooftop of the world, mountains spread westward, east, and northeast into many parts of Asia. The mountains in the highest part of this "rooftop" are the

Much of southern and eastern Asia is very crowded with people. This large crowd is from Bombay, India. Can you name some parts of Asia that are not crowded?

241

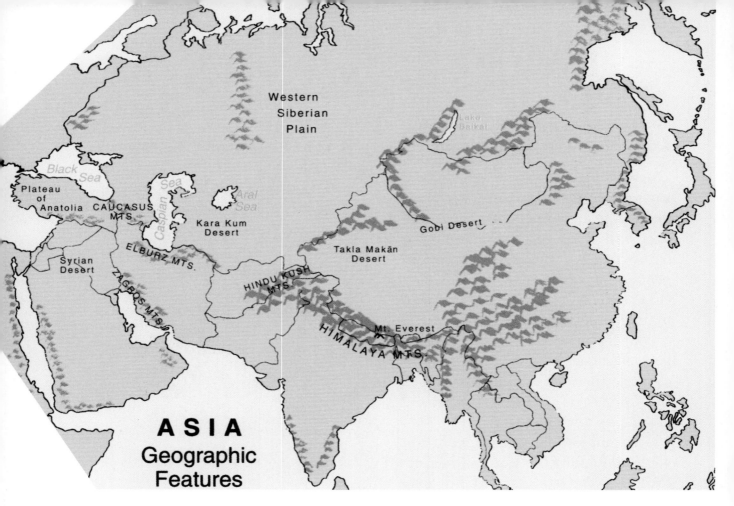

ASIA
Geographic Features

Himalayas (him′ ə lā′ əz). They lie just north of India.

Many of the mountains in Asia are three or four miles (five or six kilometers) above sea level. Sixty-seven mountain peaks in Asia are higher than any mountains on any other continent! Seventy-six of the one hundred highest mountains in the world are found in Asia. The highest mountain in the world is Mount Everest on the border between Nepal and Tibet (part of China). This mountain towers almost 5½ miles (8.9 kilometers) above sea level.

Such great mountains remind us of what the Bible says about God's great power. "O God of our salvation . . . which by his strength setteth fast the mountains; being girded with power."

Psalm 65:5b, 6

Asia is also known for its vast deserts. None are as large as the Sahara in Africa, but at least nine great deserts are found in Asia, especially in the central and southwestern part.

The largest lake on earth is on the border between Asia and Europe. This lake is called the Caspian Sea. It is over four times larger than Lake Superior, the largest lake in North America. The world's fourth largest lake, the Aral Sea, is also found farther east in Asia.

242

The Climates of Asia

On a continent as large as Asia we could expect vastly different climates. The far north of Asia, called Siberia, is a frozen land most of the year. In parts of Siberia the ground thaws only several inches down in the short, cool summer. The mainland of Siberia reaches to within 875 miles (1,410 kilometers) of the North Pole. Outside of Antarctica, the coldest temperatures ever recorded were in Siberia. During winter the temperature may drop to 90° F (68° C) below zero or more. Much of the time, winter temperatures stay around 50° F (45° C) below zero.

The mountains which stretch across the center of Asia help keep the cold air of Siberia from pushing into southern Asia. Southern Asia is a vastly different land with a vastly different climate. Much of southern and southeastern Asia stays warm

These pictures show some of the many landforms found in Asia. The above photo is of the Thar Desert of India and Pakistan. The picture below is of the Himalaya Mountains, the highest mountains in Asia and in the world. The last picture is from the dry, windswept plains of central Asia.

243

all year. Dense jungles cover much of this area where people have not cleared the land.

Much of Asia is too dry, too rough, or too cold for crops. The best land is found in the river valleys and in southern Asia where it is warm enough and wet enough to grow crops. One of the unusual things about Asia's climate is what we call the **monsoons**. Monsoons are winds that blow steadily from a certain direction for a long period of time. The winter monsoons bring dry, cooler air to much of southern and eastern Asia. The summer monsoons blow from the ocean and bring heavy rains to much of southeastern Asia. In some parts of Asia, the people think of monsoons as rains, not winds. To them, the dry winter winds are not monsoons; only the steady summer rains are monsoons.

Sometimes the monsoons fail to bring the needed rains. Severe droughts sometimes come to India and eastern China. In other years the rains may be so heavy that floods do much damage to villages and crops.

There are various races of people in Asia. The boys eating ice cream belong to the Asian Geographical Race. They are Chinese. The bareheaded man is of the African Geographical Race found in both Africa and Asia. The Arab man on the next page is an Asian of the European Geographical Race. The lady holding her girl is a member of the Indian Geographical Race.

Most of the people in Asia live in lands that God has blessed with rainfall or with rivers for irrigation. "[God] made a decree for the rain, and a way for the lightning of the thunder." **Job 28:26**

The driest region of Asia is

found from western India and Pakistan to the Arabian Peninsula and between the Indian Ocean and the Caspian Sea. People in this area live mostly along the rivers and in the few areas where enough rain falls to support them.

The People of Asia

Another way that Asia is big is in the number of people who live there. About three out of every five people on earth live in Asia. That means that over three and one-half billion people live on the largest continent. But all these people are not spread evenly over the continent. Much of Asia is too cold, too dry, or too mountainous for many people to live there. So most of these three and one-half

billion people are crowded into the warm, moist lands that border the Indian and Pacific Oceans. Some of the most crowded places on earth are found in eastern and southern Asia. In parts of China over 3,000 people live on each square mile of land.

The billions of people who live in Asia come from several different races and speak hundreds of different languages. A **race** is a group of people who are somewhat alike in their appearance, such as skin color, hair color, size, and shape. For many years the world's people were said to be divided into three races—the white, black, and yellow races. The names *Caucasian, Negroid,* and *Mongoloid* were also used for these races.

There are many differences in people who might be considered part of the same race. Because of this, many scholars now speak of **geographical races.** This way of describing races is based on where people live as well as the way they look.

Many of the people of Russia, for example, have light-colored skin and

Languages of Asia

Language	Speakers	Country or Countries
Mandarin Chinese	999 million	China, Southeast Asia
Hindi	457 million	India
Arabic	230 million	Western Asia, Africa
Bengali	204 million	India, Bangladesh
Malay-Indonesian	164 million	Malaya, Indonesia
Japanese	126 million	Japan
Urdu	104 million	Pakistan, India
Punjabi	95 million	Pakistan, India
Korean	76 million	Korea
Telugu	75 million	India

This chart shows the ten largest language groups of Asia. Some of them are spoken in other places besides Asia—Arabic, for example. These were the number of speakers to the nearest million in 1996. Someday God may want you to learn another language so that you can share the Gospel with people in other lands.

light hair. We say they are of the *European geographical race.* The majority of people in India have black hair and very brown skin. They are called the *Indian geographical race.* At one time, the Russians and the Indians were all said to belong to the white race.

Most of the people of China and Southeast Asia are said to be of the *Asian geographical race.* They were once called the yellow race. But most of these people have brown skin, not yellow. The people of the Asian race also have a fold of skin over the corners of their eyes which causes their eyes to appear slanted.

A few people of the *African geographical race* live in Asia. They are black. They have lived in Asia for many hundreds of years. No one is sure where they came from or when they came to Asia.

Languages in Asia

Asians speak hundreds of languages. In one state in India it is said that there are 275 different languages. A **language** is a way of speaking or writing that is very different from another way of speaking or writing. People who speak different languages cannot understand each other very well. For example, Spanish, French, and German are languages so different from English that we cannot understand them unless we study them.

Some of the languages of Asia are spoken by millions of people. Other languages have only a few hundred speakers. Chinese is spoken by more

246

people than any other language on earth. But the ways of speaking Chinese are so different from place to place that some speakers of Chinese can hardly understand each other. Differing ways of speaking the same language are called **dialects**.

Asia—The First Home of People

The Bible is clear that the first people lived in Asia. A river flowed out of the Garden of Eden where God placed the first people. This river divided into four parts. One of these parts was the Euphrates (yü frā′ tēz) River. The Euphrates is one of the great rivers of southwestern Asia. Hundreds of years later, after the Flood of Noah's day, Noah's ark landed on the mountains of Ararat (âr′ə rat′). These mountains are located in the Asian country we call Turkey. From this Asian land, people spread around the world. Even scientists who do not believe the Bible usually agree that the first people lived in Asia.

Apparently the American Indians came directly from Asia. They were in America before the white people came. They have dark skin, black hair, and eyes that look like the Asian geographical race. People who study races call them the *American Indian geographical race*.

Many people who spread out from Asia over the earth have forgotten God. We know from God's Word that Noah believed in the one true God. But later, people began to worship the sun, moon, stars, images, and other things. Beliefs about the true God were mixed with the false teachings of those who were forgetting God.

Some beliefs in Asia and around the world, however, still point back to the true God. Stories about a great flood in man's early history have been discovered among many people around the world. These point back to the true story of the great flood the Bible tells about.

We will learn more about Asia in the chapters which follow. The first land we will study about in Asia is China. China has more people than any other country in the world. China has more land than any other country except the Soviet Union and Canada.

What Do You Say?

1. a. In what ways is Asia the largest continent? b. How many of the world's people live there?

2. a. Name some of the "big" things found in Asia. b. Why do you think the high mountains of central Asia are called the "rooftop of the world"?

3. a. Name three very different climates you would find in Asia.

b. What keeps the cold of Siberia from sweeping even farther south into Asia?

4. a. What are the monsoons in Asia? b. What do they do for southern and eastern Asia during the summer?

5. a. What is a race? b. A geographical race? c. Name three main geographical races found in Asia.

6. a. What is a language? b. Why would it be difficult for many Asians to understand each other?

7. Where is the "home" from which all people of the earth have spread out?

What Does the Bible Say?

1. Read Psalm 65:6. What do the mountains of the earth show about God?

2. What does the Bible say in Genesis 3:20 about the beginning of all people?

3. Read Acts 10:34, 35. How should we treat all people no matter what their color? Why?

China—The Big Land

What do you think about when you hear the word "China"?

Some people think only of how different China is from North America. They imagine China as a strange land where people wear white to funerals and red to weddings. Perhaps they think of the Chinese workers who nearly always wear blue and of the women who often wear trousers.

Some people think about the beautiful buildings in China with the curved, tiled roofs. Perhaps they think of beautiful Chinese paintings of misty mountain scenes with Chinese temples perched on steep hillsides. Some, no doubt, think of the giant pandas that come from the mountains of western China. Still others think of the Chinese people whose eyes appear to be slanted.

Many of these things are true of China, but China is much more. Not everything in China is strange either. China is a beautiful land, somewhat like parts of North America. China also includes people. Well over one billion people live there, and they are much like you and me. They need food, clothing, and shelter. They have joys and sorrows just as we do.

"He [God] giveth to all life, and breath, and all things; and hath made of one blood all nations of men for to dwell on all the face of the earth."

Acts 17:25b, 2

The most important way the

Chinese are like us is that they need Jesus Christ. Life for Christians in China has been very difficult. The communist leaders put so many Christians to death that few were left. Still, there are some Christians. And in recent years, more have been coming to Jesus. Today there is a great need for pastors in China.

In the following chapters we will study the gigantic land called China. We will study its people and their needs. The unit ends with a story of how Christians suffer in China today.

The panda is a bear-like animal found in the mountainous parts of China. Today, pandas are found in many zoos around the world. Bamboo shoots and leaves are the favorite foods of pandas.

Which Country Is the Largest?

In Unit 4 you studied about the country with the most land. This country is Russia. Russia is the largest country in the world in land area.

In this unit we will study the country with the most people—China. China is the country with the largest **population.** The number of people in a city or country is called its population.

Steep, tree-covered mountainsides may be found in the southern part of China where the weather is warm and rainy. Chinese paintings often show such steep mountainsides.

Interestingly, both of these largest countries are found on the same continent—Asia. China is large in land area too. Only two countries in the world have more land than China. They are Russia and Canada. China is just a little larger than the United States.

Find China on the map on page 251. China is in eastern Asia. Sometimes China and other lands in eastern Asia are called the **Far East.**

They are as far east in Asia as a person can go. They are very far to the east of Europe!

China stretches from the Pacific Ocean into the heart of Asia. It is more than 4,000 miles (6,400 kilometers) across the country. North to south, China is over 2,300 miles (3,700 kilometers) wide.

On the north, China borders Russia and Mongolia. On the west it borders Russia, Kazakhstan, Kyrgyzstan, Tajikistan, Afghanistan, Pakistan, and India. To the south, China's next-door neighbors are Nepal, Bhutan, India, Burma (Myanmar), Laos, and Vietnam. The Pacific Ocean borders China on the east.

This is a Chinese pagoda or place of worship. The pagoda, like many other older Chinese buildings, has beautiful, curved roofs.

The Other Side of the Earth. You know that China and its neighbors are in Asia. Where is Asia from North America? Did you ever hear anyone speak of digging down to China? Even if a North American could dig straight down through the heart of the earth and come out the other side, he would not dig to China. He would come out somewhere around Australia. China is, however, on the opposite side of the earth from North America. If you travel halfway around the world from North America either to the east or to the west, you will find yourself in eastern Asia.

When it is night in North America, it is daytime in China. Children in Oregon are getting home from school as the children in eastern China are going to school. When morning comes to eastern America, it is evening in China.

CHINA

⊕ National capital

• Major cities

Russia

Kazakhstan

Mongolia

CHINA

Pakistan

Nepal

Bhutan

India

Bangladesh

Myanmar
(Burma)

Laos

Vietnam

Harbin •

Shenyang
(Mukden) •

North Korea

Beijing
(Peking) ⊕

South
Korea

Japan

Tianjin •
(Tientsin)

Lüshan

• Tai-yuan

He

Huang

• Shanghai

Wuhan •

Kiang

Chongqing •
(Chungking)

Yangtze

Xi

Jiang

Guangzhou
(Canton)

Taiwan

Landforms in China. China is a vast land with many different landforms. China has some of the highest, most mountainous land in the world as well as some of the flattest land.

Much of western and southern China is very mountainous. The highest mountain on earth is found in southern China. This mountain, you remember, is called Mount Everest.

In northeastern China you find China's largest area of lowland. Here the great Huang He (hwäng′ hə′) flows hundreds of miles across flatlands. (*Huang He* means "yellow river.") But China has much less flat-land than either Canada or the United States. Most of China is at least hilly.

Many beautiful Chinese paintings show buildings perched on almost unbelievably steep hillsides or mountains. Some westerners used to think the artists were not showing the land correctly. But visitors to China are amazed to see steep land much like that shown in paintings.

The beauty of the Chinese countryside should remind us of the One who made it for people to enjoy.

"For the LORD is a great God. . . . In his hand are the deep places of the earth: the strength of the hills is his also. The sea is his, and he made it:

251

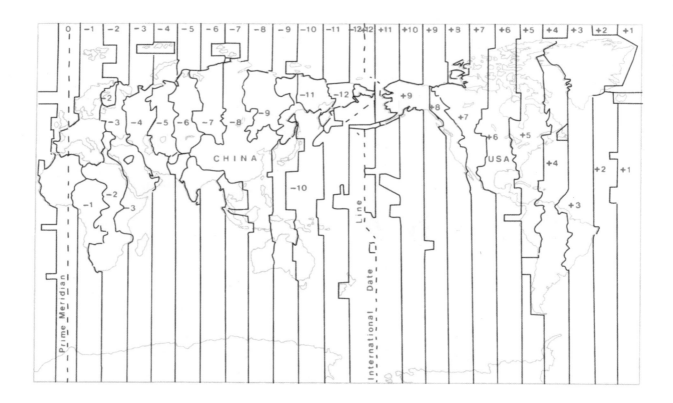

World Time Zones

This is a time zone map of the world. There are twelve time zones in the Western Hemisphere (+1 through +12) and twelve in the Eastern Hemisphere (0 through -12). The plus twelve and the minus twelve are together in one time zone. Each zone is one hour different from the zone beside it. All of China is in the -8 time zone. Ontario, Canada and the eastern United States are in the +5 zone. To find out how many hours it is between the eastern United States and China, begin counting with zone +6 and count to your left unto you reach -8. Count +12 and -12 as only one zone. You will discover that the difference between the eastern U.S. and China is eleven hours. How many hours difference is there between Alaska and China?

and his hands formed the dry land. O come, let us worship and bow down: let us kneel before the LORD our maker."

What Do You Say?

1. Name some ways the Chinese are much like people in your country.

2. Name something China has more

of than any other country.

3. In what part of Asia is China?

4. a. What would be the shortest way for you to fly to China? To find this out, use a globe. Stretch a string from your state or province to Beijing, the capital of China. b. Over what ocean or seas does this string pass? c. Over what countries?

5. a. Name some landforms found in China. b. Find a landform map of China and Canada in an

encyclopedia. Which would you say has more flatland, Canada or China?

What Does the Bible Say?

1. China is one of the greatest of nations. It has the most people and the highest mountains. But what is greater than all these things? (Read Psalm 113:3-5.)

2. Read Revelation 4:11. a. Why has God created all things? b. What should people in China, North America, and around the world do because of all that God has created?

Chapter Fifteen Review

Using Globes and Maps

1. Find Asia on a globe. Notice how near the North Pole it reaches.

Also notice how close the southern tip of the continent is to the equator.

2. Look at the map on page 242 of the landforms of Asia a. Where are the greatest mountains and highlands of Asia found? b. Where are the greatest lowlands found?

3. On a globe take a string and put one end of it where you live and the other end on Beijing, the capital of China. First stretch your string in a westerly direction to China. Measure the string distance from your area to China, and then stretch the string around to China in an easterly direction. Which is longer? Do you see why we say China is on the opposite side of the earth from North America?

4. Draw a map of Asia on a large sheet of paper. To help you draw your map, you may trace or draw a grid of blocks lightly in pencil on a small map and then draw a larger grid on your paper. Draw the lines you see on the small map in each block on your map. Erase the blocks on the small map as well as on your map. You will have a large map of Asia that is quite accurate.

New Words and Terms

Write definitions for these words and terms.

1. rooftop of the world
2. monsoons
3. race
4. geographical race
5. population
6. Far East
7. mountain system
8. language
9. dialects

Thinking Together

1. How does the word "big" describe Asia?
2. a. Describe some of the different climates found in Asia. b. Why are so many different climates found there?

3. a. In which parts of Asia do the greatest number of people live? b. How has God provided so that many people could live in these parts of Asia?
4. a. Name two large geographical races found in Asia. b. What do people of the two races look like?
5. a. Which language in Asia is spoken by the most people? b. Which language is spoken by more people—English or Chinese?
6. Name some ways China is much like the United States and Canada and some ways it is different.

For You to Do

1. Read an encyclopedia article about Asia. Find at least three facts about its land and its size which you are not told in this chapter.
2. a. List the seven continents in order of their size, the largest first. b. Now list all the continents in order of the number of people each has. Notice the differences in your two lists.

254

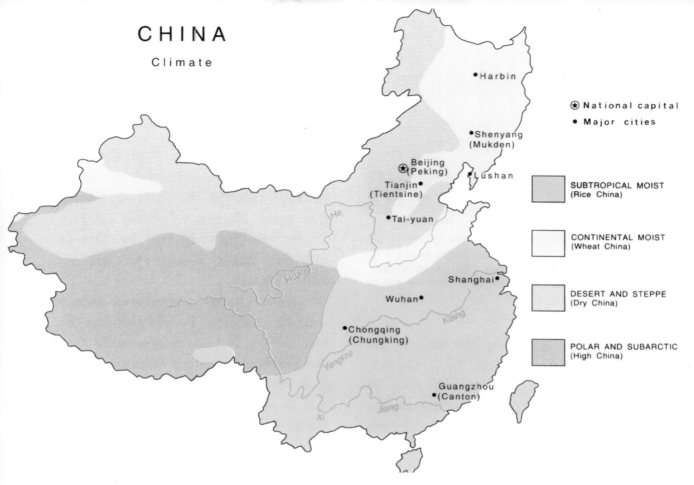

CHINA

Climate

⊛ National capital
• Major cities

SUBTROPICAL MOIST
(Rice China)

CONTINENTAL MOIST
(Wheat China)

DESERT AND STEPPE
(Dry China)

POLAR AND SUBARCTIC
(High China)

This map shows the climate regions of China. The subtropical moist climate is sometimes called Rice China. The continental moist climate region is Wheat China. The desert and steppe climate is Dry China. The polar and subarctic climate is in High China.

16. God's Gifts to China

God Gives China Good Climates.

China is a huge country. You would expect many different climates in a country so large. China is about as far north of the equator as the United States and southern Canada are. It is not surprising that China has some of the same climates we have.

One way to describe the climates of China is to divide the country into four parts: High China, Dry China, Wheat China, and Rice China. We call these parts the climate regions of China. The map above shows where these four regions are found.

High China. High China is the western part of the country. This is a mountainous land with deep valleys between the mountains. It would be correct to say that High China has many different climates. The higher

255

This flat field is in Wheat China. In fall and winter the land in Wheat China is often dry and brown. The people can grow wheat and soybeans in summer if there is plenty of rain.

into the mountains one travels, the cooler the climate. The highest mountains are covered with snow all year. The high plateau or flatland of Tibet in the west has cool summers and very cold winters. This plateau is a very windy land. The valleys in High China are often much warmer than the nearby mountains. Mountains all around protect the valleys from the cold winds that blow from the north.

Dry China. North of High China is Dry China. Some of the driest deserts in the world are found here. Two of the most famous deserts of Dry China are the Gobi (gō′ bē) Desert and the Takla Makan (tä′ klə mə kän′) Desert.

Rain clouds sometimes sweep over the deserts. People can see the rain falling, but the rain usually does not reach the ground. It **evaporates** or dries up in the warm, dry air.

In some parts of Dry China nothing grows. The land is covered with bare sand and rocks. In other parts with more rainfall, some grass and scrubby bushes grow.

This is High China. Notice the snowcovered mountains in the distance. Why do you think not many people live in this part of China?

This picture is from Dry China. How can you tell that the climate here is very dry?

256

In most of Dry China, winter winds bring very cold weather from Siberia. There are few mountains between Dry China and Siberia to keep the cold from pouring in. But in summer, Dry China is one of the hottest places on earth. The temperature rises well above 100° F (37° C) almost every day.

Wheat China. East of Dry China is a land watered by great rivers and more rainfall. This northeastern part of China is sometimes called Wheat China. What does this tell you about the crops raised there? Wheat China is a land with cold winters and warm summers. Wheat grows well, and it is the most important crop in this part of China.

In the winter, Wheat China is dry and cold. The land looks much like Dry China. But spring brings more rain, and the land becomes green. Warm summers ripen many crops such as soybeans, corn, and vegetables in addition to wheat.

Wheat China is not always green in summer, however. Every few years too little rain falls. The land remains dry and brown. People may go hungry. But in other years Wheat China has too much rainfall. The rivers swell and flood the fields. Many crops are ruined and many people drown in the floods.

The mighty Yellow River, called the Huang He, does the most damage in years of flooding. The Huang He brings fine yellow soil from parts of Dry China. This fine soil piles up in

These steep hills and rice fields or paddies are found in Rice China. What is the weather like there for most of the year?

the riverbed as it flows through the flatlands of Wheat China. The river slowly rises. The people build up the banks of the river to hold back the floods. In places the Huang He is higher than the nearby countryside. When floodwaters break through the man-made banks, they flood the land for miles around.

The Huang He is sometimes called **China's Sorrow.** Many have been the sorrows of those who live along its banks, especially when floods take thousands of lives.

Rice China. Rice China lies south of Wheat China and east of High China. Can you guess why this southeastern part of China is called Rice China? Yes, rice is the main crop there.

The fact that rice is grown in most of southeastern China says much about its climate. Rice China is the wettest part of China. Rice needs much more water than wheat. The greatest river in all China waters the northern part of Rice China. This is the Yangtze (yang′ tsē′) River, the third longest river in the world. In the southern part of Rice China flows the shorter Xi Jiang (shē′ jyäng′) River. This river drains the mountains of the far south. It has been said that Rice China is one of the most well-watered lands on earth.

The rice growing in southeastern China tells us still more about the climate. The climate is warmer than in the rest of China. Rice needs about six months of warm growing weather. Rice China has a long growing season much like the southeastern United States. Wheat China is brown for many months out of the year. But green is the color of Rice China. Grasses and other plants stay green most of the year.

The southernmost part of Rice China stays green all year. Oranges, sugarcane, and many vegetables grow, even in winter. In this part of China, two crops of rice are grown each year on the same land.

Gifts of Food From China

China is a land of farmers. About eight out of ten people in China work on farms.

and tangerines also spread from China around the world. In what part of China do you think they were first raised?

Peaches

Apricots

Nectarines

Oranges

Many of the fruits and vegetables we enjoy were raised first in China. When you eat peaches, thank the Chinese! Peaches and their cousins, apricots and nectarines, were developed in China. Oranges

Another fruit first raised in China is the Chinese gooseberry. We know this vine fruit as kiwi (kē′ wē). This fruit has been raised in New Zealand and in the United States in recent years. It tastes something like a strawberry and has far more vitamin C than oranges have.

Tangerines.

Kiwi Fruit

Some useful and delicious vegetables have come to us from China. Chinese cabbage is a lettuce-like plant. Mung beans are a Chinese bean we use to make bean sprouts. Onions and rhubarb both came from Mongolia, on the border of Dry China.

Chinese Cabbage

Mung Beans

Probably the most valuable vegetable from China is the soybean. Most North Americans probably do not think of soybeans as a vegetable. Most of our soybeans go for cattle feed. But many northern Chinese eat soybean curds almost every day. To make curds, they cook the dried beans to a mush. Then

Onions

Rhubarb

they skim off the thick cheeselike curds. This can be made into cakes and even dried for later use.

The ancient Chinese considered soybeans a sacred grain, along with rice and wheat. But it is actually a bean, not a grain. And the bean inside the fuzzy pods is probably the world's most valuable bean. Soybeans are higher in protein than almost any other vegetable. One hundred acres of soybeans provide ten times more protein than the beef cattle that could be fed on the same amount of land.

In North America many people are discovering that soybeans make a delicious and healthful garden vegetable.

Soybeans

Rice

We eat soybeans in ways we may not know about. A large portion of the vegetable oil, margarine, mayonnaise, and salad dressing we use are made with soybean oil. Soybean meal is used in cereals, mixed with meats, and sometimes used in the place of meat.

The next time you eat any of these delicious fruits and vegetables that first came from China, thank God "who giveth us richly all things to enjoy."

1 Timothy 6:17b

Unusual Foods of China. We have borrowed many delicious foods from the Chinese. But the Chinese also eat other foods that have never become popular in other parts of the world.

One unusual Chinese food is Ming eggs. Ming eggs are duck eggs. These eggs are hard-boiled, then soaked in limewater for 40 days. The eggs turn black inside. People who are used to Ming eggs say they are delicious!

Bird's nest soup is another unusual Chinese food. This food is very expensive. One kind of swift, a bird common in China, makes its nest of its own saliva, or spit. When the saliva hardens, the nests look like white saucers. The whiter the nest, the more delicious the soup made from it.

What Do You Say?

1. Name the four main regions of China. What is the climate like in each?

2. a. Name the three greatest rivers of eastern China. b. Which is named after its muddy water? c. Which is the longest? d. Which is the farthest south?

3. a. Make a list of the fruits and vegetables that have come to us from China. b. Which of these have you never eaten?

4. Name two interesting foods used in China that we do not eat.

5. Find an article on soybeans in an encyclopedia. Name several products made from soybeans or soybean oil which are not used for food.

What Does the Bible Say?

1. God made many different kinds of climates even within one country like China. He created the

earth and all that is in it, including the climates. What is the purpose of this creation? (See Isaiah 45:18.)

2. In this section you studied about many delicious foods. Read Psalm 104:14-16. a. Name the different foods mentioned. b. Why were they created? c. What do they do for people?

Who Are the Chinese?

Have you ever met anyone from China? If you have, at first glance you may have thought his eyes appeared to be slanted. But actually, the eyes of Chinese people are no more slanted than yours. A fold of skin on the upper eyelid causes the slanted appearance. Notice the close-up picture of a Chinese person.

As you remember, most of the Chinese belong to the Asian geographical race. This race is sometimes called the **Mongoloid** (mong′ gə loid′) race or even the yellow race. People of this race have folds of skin above their eyes. They have light brown or sometimes slightly yellow skin. They have pads of fat over their cheekbones. The Chinese have very dark and usually straight hair. Ninety-four of every one hundred people in China belong to the Asian geographical race. Many other people in eastern Asia are of the same race as the Chinese.

People have lived in China for thousands of years. Since the people of the Asian race first came to China, few people of other races have moved in. Most Chinese today are descendants of people who lived in China 4,000 or more years ago.

How Many People? As you know, China has more people than any other country in the world. Only a few times has anyone ever tried to count them all. A counting of people in a country or part of a country is called a **census.** A census in such a

This child is from China. Why do her eyes look slanted? She belongs to the Asian geographical race.

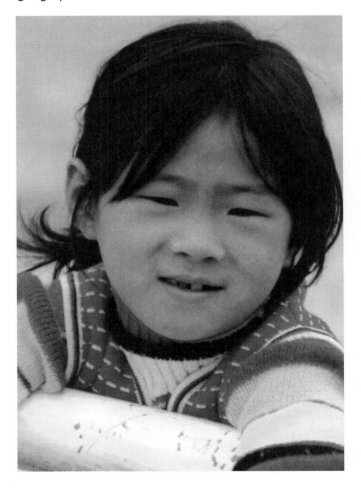

261

large country as China probably does not count nearly all the people.

Well over one billion people live in China. The population of the whole world is around six billion.

This means that more than one out of every five people on earth lives in China. Four times more people live in China than in the United States.

How Many Is One Billion?

More than a billion people live in China. One billion is a very hard number to imagine. Most of us can understand a thousand for we can count to a thousand in a few minutes. A million is a thousand thousands. A billion is another way of saying a thousand million.

If you could line up a billion marbles four to an inch, the line of marbles would stretch almost the length of the border between the United States and Canada. If a billion people could stand in a line, the line would reach around the world fifteen times!

Could you count to a billion? Never! You would need to count over 1,100 every hour, every day, for over 100 years!

If all the people in China were lined up in a row, they would make a line of people stretching around the world fifteen times!

Understanding the Chinese

Many people around the world know very little about China. For many, China is just another land far away. The people look different. They speak a different language. Their way of doing things is often different from ours.

Another reason many know little about China has to do with the history of China. For many years Chinese rulers kept the country closed to outsiders. Few Chinese visited other lands either. Even fewer people visited China. Even in modern times, China was closed to most outsiders for about twenty years during the 1950s and 1960s.

We are learning more about China in recent years. There is much to learn about such a vast country. But even if you visit China today, the government does not allow you to go just anywhere you wish.

The Beautiful Chinese Language

Along the sides of this page are some Bible verses in Chinese. Can you read them? You can see that the Chinese do not use the same alphabet we do. Besides, the spoken language is very different from English.

Chinese is probably the oldest language on earth that is still spoken. Anyone who can read modern Chinese can read Chinese books 2,000 years old.

Nearly everyone in China today speaks Chinese. But there are many ways to speak Chinese, just as there are many ways to speak English. You may find the English spoken in Scotland or in Australia a bit difficult to understand. Different ways of speaking the same language, you remember, are called dialects.

In China, there are many dialects. The people in Beijing (bā zhing'), the capital of China, speak Mandarin Chinese (man' də rin). About eight of every ten Chinese speak Mandarin. In the south, around the city of Guangzhou (güang jō') or Canton (kan' ton'), the people speak Cantonese (kan tə nēz'). There are many other Chinese dialects in southern China. The Cantonese speakers cannot understand some of the southern dialects around them.

Most Chinese words are only one syllable long. Chinese sounds a bit like singing because of something called **tone**. Tone includes how high or low the voice is when a word is spoken. In Chinese a word may change meaning if spoken with a different tone. The word *li* (lē) spoken in a high tone means "monkey." *Li* spoken in a low tone may mean "plum." In English we could say "plum" in a high or low voice, and it would still mean a kind of fruit.

Chinese writing is even more unusual than the spoken language. Chinese is written with no alphabet. Each beautiful sign you see in the Bible verses here stands for a word or a group of sounds. These Chinese signs began with picture writing. Over the years the pictures slowly changed. Each picture has become a group of beautiful marks made with a tiny brush. The chart on page 264 shows how some pictures slowly changed into the signs used today.

The same picture writing is used all over China. The picture sign for *river* stands for "river" all over China. In different parts of China people say "river" differently, but the written

263

sign is the same everywhere. Having the same written language helps to keep the Chinese people united even when they speak differently.

Chinese picture writing works a bit like the numerals or number pictures we use. when you see "3" what do you think about? You think the English word *three*. A French Canadian thinks the French word *trois* (trä). A German thinks *drei* (drī). A Mexican thinks *tres* (träs). When someone from the Chinese city of Guangzhou sees the word for *mother*, 母親, he says *mochun* (mō′ chən). But someone from Beijing who sees the same word says *mu-ch'in* (mü′ chēn).

The written Chinese language is very difficult, even for the Chinese. The Chinese use thousands of pictures in writing. A person needs to memorize at least 4,000 picture signs just to read a newspaper. To read some books, a student has to learn 20,000 or more pictures. Learning to read Chinese takes years of hard work. The Chinese cannot use small typewriters as we do. They must use huge machines with thousands of symbols.

The communist rulers of today's China have tried to make their language easier to learn and use. They have tried to make some of the picture signs simpler. They have also been teaching the use of an alphabet. They use the same alphabet we use for English. Their reason was partly so they could spread their communistic ideas better. In spite of this, most newspapers and books are still printed in the beautiful Chinese writing that has been used for thousands of years.

要以爲希奇風隨着意思吹你聽見風的響聲卻不曉得從那裏來凡從聖靈生的也是如此尼哥底母問他說怎能有這事呢耶穌回以色列人的先生還不明白這事麼我實實在在的告訴你我們所知道的我們所見證的是我們見過的你們卻不領受我們的見

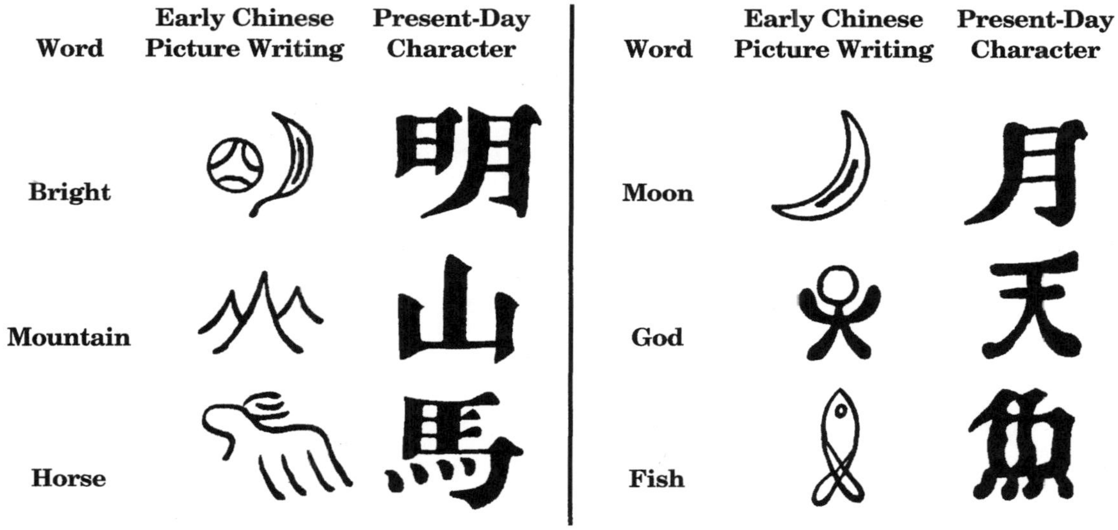

Word	Early Chinese Picture Writing	Present-Day Character		Word	Early Chinese Picture Writing	Present-Day Character
Bright		明		Moon		月
Mountain		山		God		天
Horse		馬		Fish		魚

The chart above shows you how the Chinese once drew pictures to stand for words or ideas. Slowly the pictures changed to the writing characters the Chinese use today. Can you tell that the new characters look something like the old ones?

264

What Do You Say?

1. a. To what race of people do most Chinese belong? b. What do people of this race look like?

2. a. How many people live in China? b. How many people live in the whole world? c. How could you explain one billion to someone?

3. Name two reasons why many people do not understand the Chinese.

4. a. How is Chinese writing different from our writing? b. Why is it hard to learn to read the old way of writing Chinese?

5. a. How are the communists trying to make Chinese easier to read? b. Why?

What Does the Bible Say?

1. The one billion Chinese are a very large and very important part of the world's people. What is God's will for all these people according to I Kings 8:43?

2. Chinese is one of thousands of languages spoken around the world. Read Psalm 19:1-3. a. What is it that speaks to people of all languages on earth? b. What does it tell about?

Long Ago in China

China is an old, old country. The ancient Chinese believed that the first people lived in China. Indeed, they thought China was in the middle of the earth. For that reason they called their land *Zhongguo* (jŭng güō′) which means "Middle Country." This name is still used by the Chinese for their country. To the ancient Chinese, other lands beyond the great deserts and high mountains seemed far away.

The ancient Chinese believed they were the most civilized people on earth. A people who are **civilized** have progressed in science, art, and inventions. The Chinese had built large cities and good roads long before people in Europe did. The Chinese learned to make paper and to burn coal for fuel long before people in the rest of the world knew of such things.

Before the time of Christ, the wealthy in China were using beautiful plates, cups, and saucers. Many hundreds of years passed before the rest of the world used such fine tableware. Today we still call our best

The Temple of Heaven in Beijing, the capital city of China. The emperors of China used to go to this temple to pray for a good harvest. How do Christians seek for a good harvest?

their country from enemies. The Chinese also trusted in something else for safety. They trusted what today is called the *Great Wall of China*.

The Great Wall. The Ancient Chinese often fought enemies coming from the deserts and grasslands of the north. These enemies were called Mongols (mong′ gəlz). The Chinese began to build a long wall across the northern part of their land to hold

You are looking through the window in one of the towers of the Great Wall of China. On the distant hillside you see another section of the wall. Why did the Chinese build this great wall?

dishes *china* after the country where they were first used. No wonder the ancient Chinese thought they were the most civilized people on earth!

Understanding Chinese History. Chinese history helps us better understand the Chinese people. You already understand why the Chinese believed they were the most civilized people on earth.

Over two hundred years before Christ, China was already a powerful country. Chinese armies protected

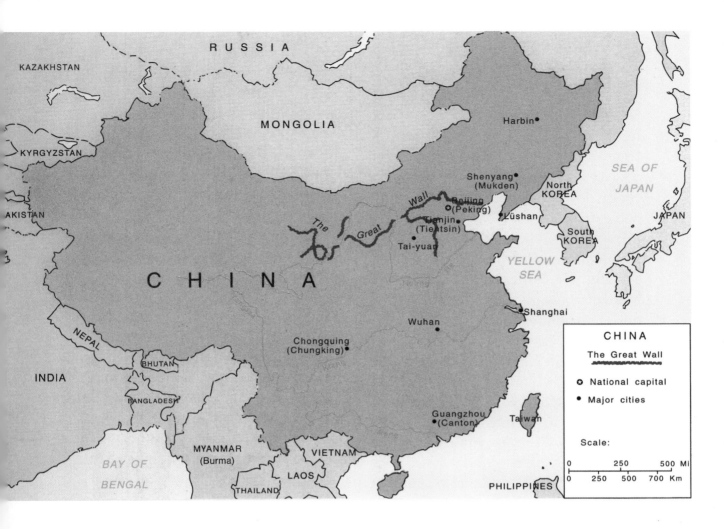

back the Mongols. The wall began near the Yellow Sea. It crossed the flatlands, then the hills and mountains. When it was finished, the wall was about 2,150 miles long (3,480 kilometers). Sections extending out from the wall at various places added another 1,800 miles (2,900 kilometers). A wall this long in the United States would reach from New York City to the Rocky Mountains.

The Great Wall of China is about 25 feet (7 ½ meters) wide at the bottom. It is also about 25 feet high. The Great Wall of China is the only man-made object that has been seen by people traveling in space!

The Chinese ruler who finished the Great Wall was very proud. He believed his kingdom would last forever. He was wrong, of course. Only twenty years after he began to rule, enemies sneaked across the Great Wall. They killed the Chinese ruler who had boasted, and his great kingdom ended.

Many other rulers rose and fell in China. They trusted in their armies. Some even trusted again in the Great Wall.

God's Word says, "There is no king saved by the multitude of an host: a mighty man is not delivered by much strength."

Psalm 33:16

267

For a thousand years after the Great Wall was built, fierce tribes of Mongols would enter China. Much fighting and killing always drove them back.

At last the time came when the conquerors beyond the Great Wall came to stay. The Mongols did not kill large numbers of Chinese. They did not force the Chinese to live or behave as Mongols. Rather, the Mongols became much like the Chinese they had come to rule.

China—The Land of Surprises. In the days of the Mongol rulers about 700 years ago, a young man traveled from Italy to China. His name was Marco Polo. Perhaps you have heard of his adventures.

Young Marco, his father, and his uncle traveled three years to reach China. In those days Europeans called China *Cathay* (ka thā′). At last the Polos reached the palace of the great Kublai Khan (kü′ blī kän′). The Khan was the Mongol ruler or **emperor** of Cathay. An emperor is a powerful ruler who rules a very large country. The lands ruled by an emperor are sometimes called his empire.

The Polos lived in China for about 18 years. They learned the language. They spent much time traveling and working for the great Khan. Young Marco learned much about China. Finally the Polos returned to Italy. Later Marco wrote a book about his travels. The book was called *Description of the World*.

Many people in Europe did not believe the stories in Polo's book. Polo told of the almost unbelievable riches of the Great Khan. He wrote of the Khan's magnificent palace and his jewel-covered robes. Polo wrote of the wonderful Chinese highways with rows of trees or stones to mark the way when snow covered the ground. Marco found rest stops about every 25 miles on Chinese highways.

Polo wrote too of the black stones he saw the Chinese burn for fuel. The "black stones" were coal. The people in Europe did not yet know about using coal for fuel.

Again Polo wondered at the paper

These are some of the things Marco Polo saw on his trip to China. What are they? Why was Marco surprised when he saw these things?

money used in China. The special stamp or seal of the emperor made the money valuable. Europeans were still buying and selling with heavy coins of gold, copper, and even lead.

But Polo's stories were true. China was indeed a land of surprises.

Chinese Inventions

Earlier you studied about the foods the Chinese first raised. Did you know that the Chinese gave us many other useful things? They gave us some very helpful inventions. An **invention** is something new that people make out of the natural resources God has given.

Paper From China. What would we do without paper? We use it for much more than books, Bibles, and letters. Boxes, paper bags, and wrappings of all kinds have been made of paper. When you think of paper, you should think of the Chinese.

Some people think the Egyptians invented paper. They did make paper from the papyrus plant. But the Chinese were the first to make paper from wood. About 100 years after the birth of Christ, a man in China named Ts'ai Lun (tsī′ lün) invented paper. He chipped up some of the inner bark of a mulberry tree. He moistened the chips and pounded them into thin sheets—the world's first paper made of wood. Today, most paper is still made of wood chips.

Later the Chinese learned to make paper from rags and even from old fishnets. Rag paper is still used for writings people want to keep a long time. Papermaking slowly spread from China to other parts of the world. One thousand years after Ts'ai Lun invented it, the first paper made of wood was manufactured in Europe.

Until paper came to Europe from China, sheepskins were used for writing material. This kind of "paper" was called **parchment**. It is said that it took the skins of at least 300 sheep to make one copy of the Bible. Few people could afford such a book!

The Chinese were the first to use paper for books, for kites, and for paper money. The next time you use paper for these or other uses, remember to thank God for the Chinese.

Printing Follows Paper. Long ago people wrote books by hand. When new copies were needed, men called scribes had to write a new copy by hand.

The invention of paper in China led to another great invention called printing. Over one thousand years ago the Chinese began to carve whole pages of words on wooden blocks. The words stood out higher than the rest of the block. These raised words were coated with ink. Sheets of paper were pressed against the blocks. When the paper was lifted, a new copy of the page was

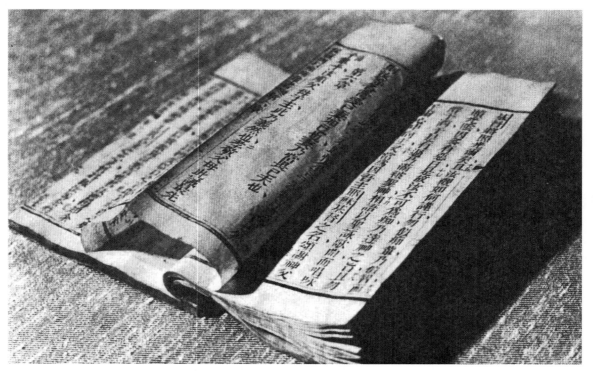

Above is a picture of a beautiful book of Chinese writing printed many hundreds of years before the invention of printing presses in Europe. The picture below is of an early printing press in Europe.

printed on it.

One Chinese inventor discovered that a little block of wood could be carved for each Chinese word symbol or picture. The words could be arranged to make sentences. But this discovery was not very useful in China because of the thousands of blocks that would be needed to print even a few pages. But this invention was passed on to other people. Finally, a German named Gutenberg used this invention with an alphabet. He made little blocks with letters on them. The blocks could be moved around to make pages of words, then rearranged and used again and again.

Other Famous Chinese Inventions.
Another Chinese invention was gunpowder. At first they used it only for fireworks. Later it was used in war to kill and to destroy. Gunpowder has changed the world, but it has not always been a blessing.

Another wonderful Chinese invention is Chinese porcelain (pȯrs′sə lən), or chinaware. You may remember that the wealthy in China used beautiful plates, cups, and saucers long before Europeans did.

Porcelain or china is usually white and allows light to shine through it. It is the finest kind of pottery. This lovely invention did not come to the rest of the world until several hundred years ago.

Early in their history, the Chinese learned to make silk cloth. It is believed that the first silk cloth was made over 4,000 years ago.

the caterpillars are fed fresh mulberry leaves. When grown, the silkworm (caterpillar) spins a soft, delicate cocoon around itself. The cocoon is made of one single thread wrapped around the caterpillar hundreds of times. The thread is called silk.

Chinese workers unwind and twist together a number of these

Beautiful silk threads come from the cocoon of the silk moth. Chinese silk farmers prepare special places for the moths to lay their eggs. When the eggs hatch, they become furry little caterpillars. Every few hours

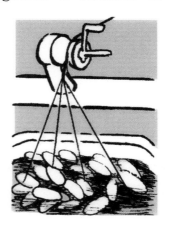

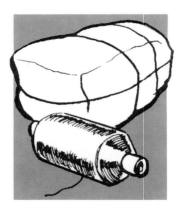

threads to make stronger threads. These threads are spun into silk cloth. Silk cloth is shiny, lightweight, and beautiful. It is prized by wealthy people all over the world.

Still another invention that is believed to have come from China is the compass. More than a thousand years ago the Chinese discovered that certain rocks were magnetic. Iron and certain other metals are attracted to them. It was discovered that a piece of magnetic stone attached to a cork and floated on water would turn itself and the cork in a north-south direction. Sailors discovered that magnets taken along on ships could show which direction was north. The other directions could be figured out. In modern times ships use radio signals, radar, and other equipment to tell directions. Even with all this equipment they also use compasses.

What Do You Say?

1. a. Why did the ancient Chinese call their country the "Middle Country"? b. How did they feel about their country?

2. How can knowledge of Chinese history help us?

3. a. What was the purpose of the Great Wall of China? b. Did it serve its purpose well?

4. Name at least two things Marco Polo saw in China that people in Europe knew nothing about.

5. a. Name at least five Chinese inventions b. Which do you think was most important? c. Why?

What Does the Bible Say?

1. a. Do you think we should look on our country as the center of

272

the earth? b. What does Psalm 24:1 say about the whole earth?

2. What is the danger of trusting in weapons, walls, and our own strength instead of in God? (Read Psalm 20:7, 8.)

3. The Bible mentions paper only twice. a. Read Isaiah 19:7. What was this paper made of? b. What other writing material is mentioned in 2 Timothy 4:13? c. What have you learned that parchment is made of?

Chapter Sixteen Review

Using Globes and Maps

1. a. Draw a map of China or trace a large map of the country. You may use the map on page 255. Mark off, color, and label each of the four climate regions. From an encyclopedia article on China, find and label on your map the ten largest cities in the country. b. In which climate regions are these cities found? c. Why do you think this is so?

2. On the map you have just drawn, mark the location of the Great Wall of China. Mark it like the symbol shown on page 267.

New Words and Terms

Write definitions for these words and terms.

1. Mongoloid
2. census
3. billion
4. language
5. tone
6. China's sorrow
7. Middle Country
8. civilized
9. emperor
10. invention
11. porcelain
12. parchment

Thinking Together

1. a. Describe the physical appearance of most of the people of China. b. About how many people live in China? c. What

portion of the total number of people in the world is this?

2. What are some reasons why many people do not really understand the Chinese?

3. a. What are some things that make Chinese a very different language from English? b. How have the communist leaders tried to make Chinese simpler?

4. You learned that the Great Wall did not really help the Chinese to protect themselves from enemies. Why would a Great Wall do even less good today?

5. a. Which Chinese invention do you think has been the most helpful for the entire world? b. How many ways can you think of that this invention is used in your country?

For You to Do

1. Try growing some Chinese plants from seeds, starting them indoors in cups. Mung beans make bushy plants with beautiful blossoms. Chinese cabbage can be started indoors and set outside early in spring. Soybeans are fuzzy plants

with tiny blossoms close to the stalk.

2. If you live near large grocery stores, you may be able to find a sample of many Chinese fruits and vegetables to bring to class. Soybeans are hard to find in grocery stores. Perhaps someone in your class can bring some from home.

3. Bring some of the following items for a class display of Chinese objects or inventions (neatly label each item):

> paper made of wood
> paper made of rags
> something printed (a book or
>   tract)
> a piece of china (be very
>   careful)
> silk cloth
> a rubber stamp
> a compass
> Chinese pictures or wall
>   hangings

17. China Today

China Today—A Different Land

Seven hundred years have passed since the Polos first told the rest of the world about China. China has changed in many ways. But in some ways China has not really changed.

Today, powerful emperors like the great Khan no longer rule. The land is not so closed to the outside world. Many people travel to China. Many Chinese, especially students, travel to other countries.

The ancient Chinese believed that their kingdom was at the center of the earth. The Chinese still think of their land as the greatest and most important land on earth. Of course, many people who live in the United States and Canada probably feel that way about their country too.

China's Rulers Today

For thousands of years China was ruled by emperors. These men had the power of life and death over the people. About 100 years ago the emperor began to lose much of his power. Finally, the last Chinese emperor was overthrown in 1911. This emperor, Henry Pu-yi, was only a six-year-old boy.

Between 1911 and 1949, China suffered from terrible fighting among its people. China also suffered from wars with other countries. In

The Chinese emperors of old were rich and powerful. They dressed in expensive robes while many people were very poor.

1931, nearby Japan took the northeastern part of China, called Manchuria (man chür′ ē ə). In 1937 Japan attacked the rest of China. Two years later most of eastern China was ruled by the Japanese.

The United States and other countries fought against Japan and conquered it. At last China was freed from the foreigners. The land enjoyed peace, but not for long.

Even before the Japanese had left, the Chinese had begun to fight again among themselves. This time Chinese communists fought against others who wanted a free China. Those who wanted a free China were

This is the flag of communist China. The stars stand for the communist party and its members.

called the Nationalists. The Nationalists had sometimes been cruel to the people. Many believed the communists would certainly be better rulers.

In 1949 the Nationalists were driven from China. They fled to the island called Taiwan (tī wän′). The Nationalists still rule Taiwan.

Communist rule began with a strict and sometimes harsh ruler called Mao Zedong (maủ ze dȯng′). He ruled from 1949 until 1976. He was often called Chairman Mao. After Mao died several men tried to become China's chief leader. Finally, in 1981 Zhau Ziyang (zaủ zē yäng′) became premier or main leader. He ruled until 1989.

In the 1990s Deng Xiaoping (dung shaủ ping′) was a powerful ruler.

When the communists took over in 1949, many people rejoiced. One of the first things the communists did was to take most of the land from the rich landowners. They divided the land among millions of poor farmers. Many people owned land who had never had land before.

In 1956 the government told the farmers they could farm better if they would put their little plots of land together. The communists forced the farmers to work together in bands or groups. Soon China had thousands of large government farms called **communes** (kom′ yünz).

The farmers on a commune were made to work in groups called **brigades** (brig ādz′). They usually ate in a large dining hall rather than together as families. Many of the women had to work in brigades too. The children stayed in nurseries or went to school while their parents worked. If a brigade ran out of farm work, they were given other work. Some brigades helped build bridges, factories, and other buildings.

City dwellers too were organized into brigades to work at large factories and at other work in the cities.

Many Chinese were very unhappy with the new way of life. The Chinese have always had strong families. Loyalty to families was more important to them than loyalty to rulers.

The communists soon learned that communes did not work well. Families needed to be together. The people did better work if they could at least have tiny plots they could call their own. Finally the leaders decided to allow most families to live in houses they could call their own. During their free time they could tend small vegetable gardens of their own. But most of their work would still be done on the large government-owned farms.

Life on a Chinese Farm

Long ago Chinese farms were very small. Each farmer tended his own little plot that might not be larger than one acre (one-half hectare). In many cases farmers did not own their own land at all. Rich landowners with hundreds of acres controlled most of the land. Many farmers worked hard for rich landowners. The landowners often kept their workers poor. The landowners took most of the food. The workers barely had enough food to last from one year to the next. When there was too little or too much rain, these poor people were the first to suffer.

Communism changed all this. Nearly all Chinese farmland was organized into large government farms or communes. A commune usually included several villages and all the farmland between. Commune leaders or managers assigned each person his job.

As we noted, the communes by themselves did not work. So the individual families can now tend little plots of their own. They can sell any extra food they raise. It is said that one-third of China's food is raised in these little backyard plots.

A Chinese Farm. How would you like to visit a commune in China? You could see for yourself how the farmers and their families live.

Let us visit a commune through words and pictures. Every commune is different. Some are rich. Others are poor. On some, almost everything is done by hand. Other communes use modern farm machinery.

Life has changed very little along the Grand Canal even since the communists took over China. These people are washing clothes in the canal. The Grand Canal is over 1,000 miles (1,600 kilometers) long. It is the longest man-made waterway in the world.

Life on a Chinese commune is busy and often hard work. This man is carrying water in wooden buckets. The buckets are balanced on his shoulders with a pole. Can you tell what any of the crops are which are growing beside the walkway?

We will visit with Wang Ting-yi and his family. We will call him Ting-yi (tingJ yë). In China, what we would call the last name, or surname, comes first. Wang (wong) is the family name. The given name is placed last. Yi is Mr. Wang's "milk name." We would call this his first name.

Ting-yi lives with his wife and two children. Grandfather and Grandmother Wang also live with them. The extended family you learned about in Russia is even more common in China.

Home—Simple but Enough. Ting-yi's family lives in a very small house. The walls are made of clay. The house has two rooms. One is a living room or family room. Here the family eats, especially when it is too cold to eat outside. Here the family meets to talk and to entertain company. Some of the Wang family must sleep in this room also.

In the family room, along the wall, is an interesting Chinese invention called a **k'ang** (jyang). The k'ang is a raised bench or platform all along one side of the room. It has cloth-covered mats on it. People may sit on the k'ang instead of using chairs. It is also used for sleeping at night. An interesting thing about the wonderful k'ang is that a small fire can be built under it in cold weather. The smoke and warm air pass under the k'ang before it finds its way outside. This makes the k'ang warmer for sitting or sleeping.

The kitchen for the Wangs is an outdoor shed they share with two other neighboring families. The families cook their meals together and sit outside on wooden benches to eat.

The only other room in the Wang house is an attic where some of the family sleep and where jars of grain are stored for the winter.

278

Work at the Wangs. The Wangs live in a village of about 2,000 people. Their village and ten other villages work together as a commune. The villages are divided into production teams of about 50 to 60 people.

Both Ting-yi and his wife work on a production team. In spring and summer they are busy working in the fields. They tend the rice plants and later harvest rice and other crops. In fall and winter they work on bridges, repair buildings, and repair irrigation ditches. Sometimes they may be assigned to kill all the rats and mice they can find. Sometimes school children band together also to kill mice, grasshoppers, and other pests.

While the Wangs are out work-

The k'ang is very important in a Chinese house. What uses does the k'ang have? How is it used to keep people warm?

ing, their children are in school. Grandmother and Grandfather stay at home. The grandparents take care of the chickens, ducks, and pigs. They also work in the family garden plot. Here is grown most of the winter's supply of food for the family.

The children and their parents arrive home in the late afternoon. No one has time to waste. All willingly do their chores.

For Mrs. Wang, there are clothes to wash, there is food to fix, and sometimes there is clothing to make. Grandfather again feeds the pigs. He collects leftover cabbage leaves and stalks as well as other vegetable stems and tops.

Grandmother catches a chicken for butchering and helps Mother finish the day's housework. In her extra moments, she braids garlic and onion bulbs by hand for drying.

Sometimes after supper the family has time to sit and relax after their work. This is about the only time in their busy day that they have time to talk together.

Life is so busy in China that people have little spare time to travel or go to games and amusements. Most people would not have the money to do these things even if they had time. Chinese Christians who want to meet together for worship must meet very early in the morning or late in the evening. There is little time for Bible reading and memory work. You will learn more about Christians in China a little later in this chapter.

Rice—Food for Millions

The Chinese were the first to grow soybeans and a number of other good vegetables and fruits. But the favorite of all foods grown in China is rice. Rice was first grown somewhere in eastern Asia, perhaps in China.

No unit on China, India, or any other country in Southeast Asia would be complete without telling the story of rice.

To grow properly, rice needs plenty of warm weather and water during the growing season.

Plowing the paddy for seeding.

Rice has been called Asia's "staff of life." Many Chinese and other Asians eat rice three times a day. Half the world's people eat rice as their main food. In some parts of China the people say, "Have you had your rice?" We would say, "Have you had something to eat yet?"

Rice is a cereal grass. It is somewhat like oats, rye, wheat, and barley. But rice grows in places too warm or too wet for these other grains.

Seeding.

Rice grows two to six feet tall depending on the type of rice, the soil, and the weather. The plants produce heads called **panicles** (pan′ i kəlz) much like the oat plant does does. Rice is usually

Pulling the seedlings. Clumps are tied with straw.

grown in flat fields or on terraced hillsides. While the rice is growing, the fields are kept flooded with water.

Rice grows in the northern part of the Yangtze River Valley and from there south. The well-watered Yangtze Valley is the best rice growing region in China. Rice growing starts in April in the Yantze Valley. The grains to be planted are soaked in water until the sprouts are about an inch long.

Workers carefully set the seedlings close together in special seedbeds prepared in the corner of the fields. The seedbeds are fertilized well to help the young plants get a good start. When the seedlings are six inches high, workers are again busy in the fields. They pull up the seedlings in bunches of five or six. They set them out in the fields in neat rows. The fields have been flooded with water and plowed while under water.

After the plants are set out, they grow rapidly. About a month after they are set out in the fields, the plants begin to bloom. In another month or so, the rice begins to ripen. The fields are drained of their water with drainage ditches.

Harvest begins when the plants bend over with yellow heads of ripening grain. Most of the harvesting in China is still done by hand. The rice stalks are cut with a curved knife called a scythe (sīth) and stacked in

These heads of rice are beginning to ripen. What are these heads called?

bundles. Threshing boxes are moved to the fields. A threshing box is made of wood. It has a frame of wooden slats on the top. The farmer picks up a bundle of rice and hits the heads against the slats. The grains fall between the slats into the box below. After the rice is threshed, it is tossed into the air so that the wind can carry away the chaff and straw.

The rice is then hulled in a hand mill. The hull is not good to eat. Hand mills are used to polish the rice as well. The polishing removes the brown bran coating and leaves white grains.

Farmers in Asia can raise more rice on a plot of land than any other grain. With a billion people in China, the land needs to be used to the best advantage.

Rice is one of the most healthful grains to eat, especially if the bran is left on it. Polishing rice removes many of the vitamins and minerals in rice.

Weeding.

Reaping.

Threshing.

Polishing.

281

This rice has been cut and stacked in the rice paddies.

People in Asia would be much healthier if they would eat brown rice (rice with the bran on it).

You may wonder why the Chinese remove the healthful bran. For one thing, the oil in the bran soon spoils if rice is not kept in a cool, dry place. Many Asians do not have places to keep brown rice from spoiling. Also brown rice must be cooked much longer than white rice before it becomes tender. Fuel for cooking is very scarce in most of Asia. White rice does not take as much fuel for cooking.

The Chinese make good use of the rice plant. The grain is not the only useful part. The hulls from the

Chinese farmers beating out sheaves of rice. The grains fall into the large wooden bin.

This man is cleaning the rice grains before the rice is stored. Notice the broom he is using to separate the grains from the chaff.

rice and the straw may be used for fuel. The straw is also used for bedding, for making thatched roofs, and for weaving sturdy baskets.

What Do You Say?

1. What happened to China between 1911 and 1949?

2. a. What year did the communists take over China? b. How did the people feel about their new rulers, at first? c. What did the communists later do that many did not like?

3. a. What is a commune? b. Why did the early communist communes in China not work?

4. a. Why are the Chinese not as tempted as North Americans to spend time traveling and finding amusements and entertainments? b. How does the amount of spare time the Chinese have affect the Christians?

5. a. What kind of climate is necessary for growing rice? b. List at least six steps in growing and harvesting rice in China.

6. Name five uses of the rice plant in China.

What Does the Bible Say?

1. China has suffered many wars during its long history. Where do wars come from? (See James 4:1, 2.)

2. Communism teaches that one's love and obedience belong to the government first, before love for family or for God. a. What does the Bible say about love for family? b. For God? c. For the government? (See the following Scriptures: Colossians 3:18-21; Matthew 10:37; Exodus 20:3; Romans 13:1, 5-7; Acts 5:28, 29.)

283

3. The Bible speaks of several different grains, but not rice. Most often the word *corn* is used to describe grains such as wheat. Read Psalm 65:9-13.   a. Who sends the right climate for grain to grow? b. What should we do because of these blessings?

Ancient Chinese Religions

The Chinese have long been very religious, but not many have ever been Christians. Only within the last 150 years have there been many Christians in China. About 1900 there were probably more Christians in China than at any other time. Even then, only about one of every two hundred people claimed to be Christian.

The Chinese have mostly followed three false religions: **Buddhism** (bü′diz əm), **Confucianism** (kən fyü′shə niz′ əm), and **Taoism** (daủ′ iz əm). All three of these religions began before the time of Christ.

Buddhism. Buddhism is the oldest of these three religions. It began with a man called Buddha. *Buddha* means "the enlightened one." Buddha believed that he had somehow received a special light to help him live a peaceful life.

Some of the teachings of Buddha were good. He told people to avoid evil. His followers were to say nothing that would hurt anyone.

The Chinese have many statues of Buddha, the man who started the Buddhist religion in India and China. Why do Christians not accept the teachings of Buddha?

Buddhists were to hold no jobs that would injure another.

Many of the teachings of Buddhism are false. The people are taught to have faith in Buddha. They must follow his teachings. One of his false teachings was that there are many gods. Another was that after people die, they are reborn on the earth to live as another person or perhaps as an animal.

Buddhists in China and other far eastern lands worship in temples. Each temple has one or more statues of Buddha.

284

Confucianism. The second religion of ancient China is named for a man we call Confucius (kən fyü′ shəs). The Chinese call him Kung Fu-tze (kəng′ fə′ dzə). Confucianism is very different from most religions. It has no temples, no churches, no priests or ministers, and no worship services. Confucianism is something a person merely believes in. Confucius taught people to love their neighbors. He taught them to love their families more than the government. Followers of Confucius taught people to worship their dead grandparents and other ancestors.

This is a painting of the famous Chinese philosopher Confucius. What did he teach?

The ideas of Confucius were passed on through teachers called philosophers. They taught their ideas in Chinese schools. They shared them with anyone who would listen.

Taoism. The third Chinese religion was Taoism. The poor and the uneducated liked Taoism better than Confucianism because Taoism taught that there were many gods. Taoism gave the people more to worship than did Confucianism. Taoism also taught life after death. Some Taoist teachers claimed to do miracles, even healing the sick.

One of the strange things about these Chinese religions is that a person could believe in all three at once. In fact, the ordinary person would worship some of the gods of Buddhism and Taoism. He would also follow some of the teachings of Confucianism such as ancestor worship.

None of these religions claimed to be the only way to God. No one minded if a person believed in all three.

At last Christianity came to China. Some of the Chinese wanted to add Christianity to their other beliefs. They wanted to make Jesus Christ just another god. Many Chinese did not like a religion that claimed to be the only way.

True Christians in China dared not mix Christianity and other religions. They remembered the words of Jesus: "I am the way, the truth, and the life: no man cometh unto the Father, but by me."

John 14:6

285

Something else also seemed to keep many of the Chinese from accepting Christianity. You may remember that the Chinese never liked outsiders. Some even called Europeans and Americans "foreign devils." Anyone who became a Christian could expect to be made fun of. Neighbors might say, "You are just a slave of the foreign devils."

A New Religion

The communists took control of China in 1949. The communists told the people, "There is no God. Throw away your old beliefs." The communists worked to do away with the "four olds"—old customs, old thinking, old habits, and old ideas. Soldiers even marched through the villages smashing old things.

Buddhism, Confucianism, Tao-ism, and Christianity were among the four olds. Communists especially hated Christianity, for it was a religion brought to China by foreigners. Christianity also taught obedience to Christ above all.

The communists taught people to love the government most. In school the children learned to disobey their parents if what their parents asked did not agree with the government.

Communism soon became like a religion to many people. The first communist ruler of China, Mao Zedong, wrote a book of his thoughts and sayings. Millions of these books were printed. They were called the "Little Red Book" because of their red covers. Many people carried copies of the Little Red Book. People studied it and memorized it. Many

Mao Zedong was the first ruler of communist China. How do you think this poster picture of him is supposed to make the Chinese feel about their ruler?

meetings were held to discuss it. In many ways the Little Red Book was like a Bible—a communist Bible.

Mao died in 1976. The Chinese communists still follow many of his teachings. During his rule the communists closed most churches. They forced the preachers to go to work camps. They had to work so hard that they hardly had time to preach.

Some ministers who claimed to be Christians did not try to stand for the truth. One minister said, "From the heart I can say sincerely that I fervently love communism and accept the teachings of the communist party."

One woman was nearly blind. When the communists took over, she received help for the first time. After an operation she could see again. Whom did she praise? Not God! She praised communism. This is one way the communists have stolen the love of many people away from God.

During the rule of Mao, soldiers, called the Red Guard, searched the villages. They were looking for anyone guilty of the "four olds." Many Christians and others had to march through the streets. The communists laughed at them and made fun of them in front of everyone.

One certain pastor had to march through the streets. The Red Guard asked the people to come out and criticize him. The people would not say anything bad about their minister. But the Red Guard kept trying to find some wrong thing they could blame on the pastor. They asked him to accept communist teaching. He could not do that. To do so would deny Christ. The pastor made a speech. He encouraged the people to stand for the truth. The Red Guard put him into jail. They said his crime was being an enemy of the people and having no feeling for them.

The years between 1967 and 1973 have been called the "silent years" in China. Visitors to China heard very little about Christians there. Some believed that the Christian church had died out.

How happy Christians in other lands were to learn that in the 1980s hundreds of Christians were still witnessing in China!

God Is Still at Work in China. The church that still lives in China is very different from the church in other parts of the world. Very few church buildings can be found anywhere. The home is the center of the Christian church. Several families may get together to study and worship in one another's homes.

There is a great need for ministers among the churches of China. Most of the preachers were taken away many years ago. Some groups are growing larger and are choosing new ministers. Some believers are traveling from village to village as Bible teachers.

Chinese Christians, especially pastors and teachers, need more Bibles and other Christian literature. Stories have been told of Bibles being torn into sections and passed around. Then more people can read God's Word. In some places it is still dangerous to be caught with a whole Bible.

In some places there is more freedom. Stories reach the outside world saying that most of the people in some villages are Christians. In some places the rulers do not seem to complain about Christian meetings. But things could change almost overnight. New rulers could take over.

This page from a Chinese Bible shows John 3:3-19. The Chinese begin reading at the top right-hand side of the page. They read from the top to the bottom of the column.

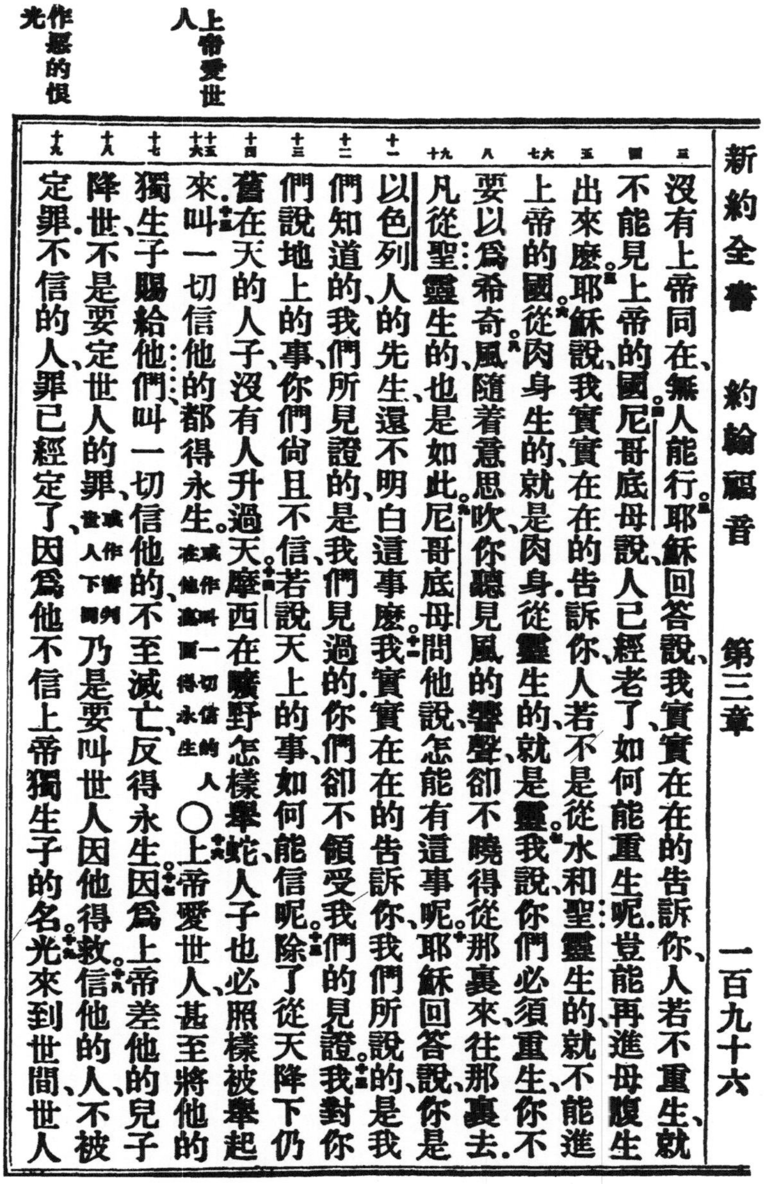

新約全書　約翰福音　第三章　一百九十六

上帝愛世人

作惡的恨光

三 沒有上帝同在、無人能行。耶穌回答說、我實實在在的告訴你、人若不重生、就
四 不能見上帝的國。尼哥底母說、人已經老了、如何能重生呢、豈能再進母腹生
五 出來麼。耶穌說、我實實在在的告訴你、人若不是從水和聖靈生的、就不能進
六七 上帝的國。從肉身生的、就是肉身、從靈生的、就是靈、我說你們必須重生、你不
八 要以爲希奇。風隨着意思吹、你聽見風的響聲、卻不曉得從那裏來、往那裏去、
九十 凡從聖靈生的、也是如此。尼哥底母問他說、怎能有這事呢。耶穌回答說、你是
十一 以色列人的先生、還不明白這事麼。我實實在在的告訴你、我們所說的、是我
十二 們知道的、我們所見證的、是我們見過的、你們卻不領受我們的見證。我對你
十三 們說地上的事、你們尚且不信、若說天上的事、如何能信呢。除了從天降下仍
十四 舊在天的人子、沒有人升過天。摩西在曠野怎樣舉蛇、人子也必照樣被舉起
十五十六 來、叫一切信他的都得永生。(或作叫一切信的人在他裏面得永生)○上帝愛世人、甚至將他的
十七 獨生子賜給他們、叫一切信他的、不至滅亡、反得永生。因爲上帝差他的兒子
十八 降世、不是要定世人的罪、(或作審判世人下同)乃是要叫世人因他得救。信他的人、不被
十九 定罪、不信的人、罪已經定了、因爲他不信上帝獨生子的名。光來到世間、世人

Christians could suffer terrible persecution again. The communist leaders, of course, still do not believe in God.

What Can We Do? What can we do to help the Christians in China? The communist government may never allow missionaries into their country. We can pray that someday they will permit Bibles and other Christian literature to be sent. The most important thing we can do is to pray that the Chinese Christians will be true to Jesus Christ even if persecution comes.

What Does the Bible Say?

1. How many religions can a Christian follow and still be a Christian? (Read Acts 4:12.)

2. What does the Bible itself say about how we should study it and use it? (Read Psalm 119:11, 97; 1 Timothy 4:13; and 2 Timothy 4:2.)

Chapter Seventeen Review

What Do You Say?

1. a. Name the three religions of ancient China. b. Name at least one error in each religion.

2. a. Why did some Chinese people want to add Christianity to their other religions? b. Why did true Christians not do this?

3. a. How is communism like a religion? b. How was the "Little Red Book" used like a Bible?

4. How have Christians suffered in China?

New Words and Terms

Match the following words with the correct definition.

1. brigades   5. Buddhism
2. commune   6. Confucianism
3. k'ang   7. Taoism
4. panicles

_____ a. A raised bench or platform along the wall in a Chinese home. It may be used as a place to sit or as a bed.

_____ b. A Chinese religion that teaches ancestor worship.

_____ c. Groups of workers on a Chinese commune or farm.

_____ d. A Chinese religion that teaches belief in many gods, worship of the man who began the religion, and the belief of being reborn into this life as another person or as an animal.

_____ e. A Chinese religion that teaches belief in many gods and life after death.

_____ f. Heads of rice including the bran.

_____ g. A farm in China where the people live, work, and eat together. This may include two or more villages and the land between.

Using Globes and Maps

1. Find an article in an encyclopedia or another book on communism. Find out which countries in Asia are still communistic besides China. Make a map of Asia and color these countries red. Place the names of the countries on your map.

Thinking Together

1. a. Name some ways China has changed in recent years.

   b. Do you think all of these changes have been good? Why?

2. Why was it easy for the Chinese to accept communism when it first came to China?

3. a. Why did the communes which the Chinese communists first organized not work well?

   b. What changes did the rulers make in commune living.

   c. What does the Bible say about the importance of the family? (Read Genesis 2:24; Ephesians 5, 22, 23; and Ephesians 6:1-4.)

4. a. How important is rice to most of the Chinese in southern China?

   b. What could the Chinese do to make rice a more healthful food.

   c. Why to the Chinese not do this?

5. a. Name the three main religions of ancient China.

   b. Which one did the poor and uneducated like best?

   c. Why?

   d. Why was it hard for many Chinese to accept Jesus Christ?

The Middle East— Crossroads of the World

What you will learn . . . in unit six

Some people call the lands we will study in this unit the "crossroads of the world." You can understand this better by looking at the map of the Middle East on the next page. Do you see that Africa, Asia, and Europe all come together in the part of the world we call the Middle East?

For many years people in Europe and America did not think much about the Middle East. The land was mostly desert. The people were poor. But today much has changed. The world pays attention to what goes on in the Middle East. Many of its countries have become very rich and powerful. Half of the world's oil or petroleum comes from the Middle East. "Wars and rumours of wars" are happening all the time in the Middle East. Some people are afraid that war there could spread to other countries and stop the supply of oil.

God's people, however, receive comfort from Jesus' words. "But when ye shall hear of wars and commotions, be not terrified: for these things must first come to pass; but the end is not by and by."

Matthew 24:6

Luke 21:9

292

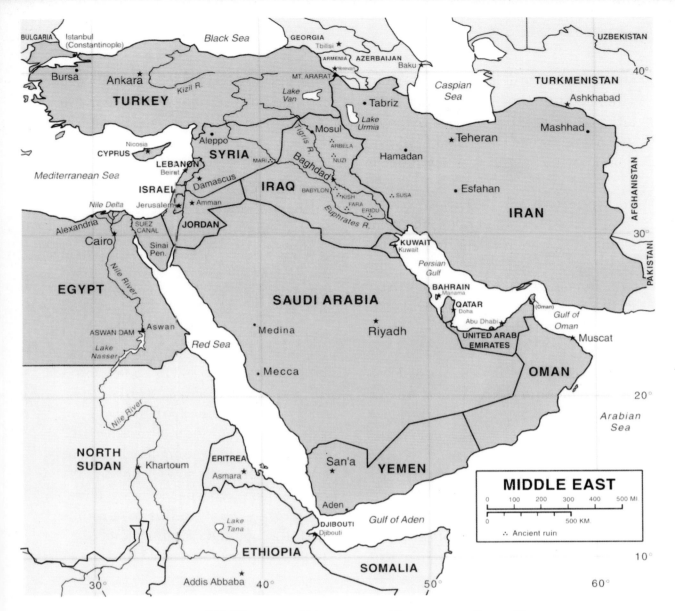

18. The Lands of the Middle East

Where Is the Middle East?

Geographers have trouble agreeing which countries should be listed as part of the Middle East. In this book we will consider the Middle East to stretch from Iran in the east to Egypt in the west. North to south, the Middle East stretches from Turkey to the southern tip of the huge Arabian Peninsula. Some geographers would say that more countries in northern Africa are part of the Middle East. But we will study Africa in another unit.

Why do we call these lands of

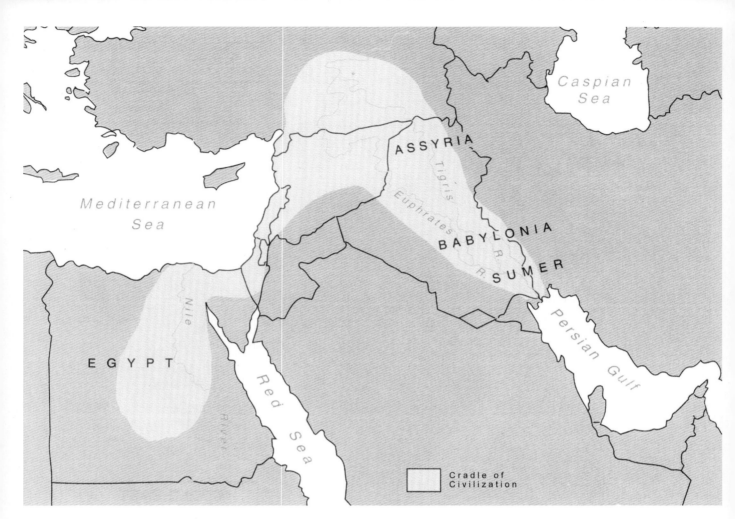

A large section of the Middle East is where the first great countries of the world began. We call this area the "cradle of civilization." Name the three great rivers that early people settled around.

southwestern Asia the Middle East? What are they in the middle of? What are they east of?

Hundreds of years ago the people of Europe began to travel to other parts of the world. They traveled east to reach the countries of Asia. Europeans called India and China the Far East because they were so far from Europe. The lands of Southwestern Asia were called the Near East because they were closer. In modern times the Near East is usually called the Middle East. It is found in the

middle of the Eastern Hemisphere.

Most people know the Middle East as the part of the world where great nations of long ago began. Part of the Middle East is called the **Cradle of Civilization.** Find this Cradle of Civilization on the map above. Here farming, science, and cities began.

We know from the Bible that God placed the very first people in the part of the world we call the Middle East. God made the Garden of Eden beside the Euphrates (yü frā' tēz) River. This river is in the country we call Iraq (i rak′). We know that Noah's ark settled on a mountain in the Middle East. This mountain, called Ararat (âr′ ə rat′) is in the country we call Turkey.

The Middle East is important for still another reason. Here God first spoke to people telling them to worship only one God. God spoke to Abraham, Moses, and others. The Middle East became the birthplace of Christianity.

Not everyone in the Middle East accepted Christianity, however. Many people hated Christians and did not want to accept Jesus as their Saviour. Perhaps this is why two other major world religions also were born in the Middle East. We will learn more about these religions later.

In this unit we will also learn why the Middle East is such a troubled land today. We will learn about the one natural resource that has suddenly made some countries in the Middle East among the richest nations on earth.

We will begin our study of this important and interesting part of the world by studying its geography. What is this land like?

Mountains, Plains, and Plateaus

Many, many different landforms can be found in the Middle East. Tall, steep mountainsides look down on flat, treeless plains. Other parts of the Middle East are covered with hills and low mountains. The northernmost countries of Turkey, and Iran, are especially mountainous.

The highest mountain in Turkey is Mount Ararat which rises 16,945 feet (5,200 meters) above sea level. The mountains of Iran rise still higher. The highest mountain in Iran is Mount Demavend (dem′ ə vend′). This mountain is 18,934 feet (5,809 meters) above sea level. The

This plain in Israel lies near the village of Endor. This plain is flat to slightly hilly. Some of the plains in the Middle East are completely flat. Why would these plains be easier to farm than steep or mountainous land?

295

A roadway cuts across a mountainside in Iran. Why would such a roadway be difficult to build?

This mud-brick village is on the desert Plateau of Iran. Plateaus are not always flat, but the land is high above sea level. Mountains found on a plateau are usually not high mountains.

Hindu-Kush mountains of Afghanistan rise still higher to about 25,000 feet (7,600 meters) above sea level.

Not all of the Middle East is mountainous, of course. Large parts of the highlands between the mountains are fairly flat. Some parts of the highlands are hilly. Such highlands are called **plateaus.** The word *plateau* means "flat." (The word *platter* is related to the word *plateau*.) But do not make the mistake of thinking that all plateaus are flatlands. Few of them are. But they are usually more level than nearby mountains.

The central part of Iran lies between high mountains. It is called the Plateau of Iran. Most of central Turkey is a hilly plateau called the Plateau of Anatolia (an′ ə tō′ lē ə). Anatolia is an old name for Asia Minor or Turkey. What is the land like in the picture of the Plateau of Iran on this page?

Most other Middle Eastern countries also have some mountains. But none are as high as the mountains in the north. Most Middle Eastern countries also have a narrow strip of lowland along the ocean. Mountains or hills rise farther inland. The Plain of Sharon in Israel lies along the Mediterranean Sea. This plain is only 20 miles (32 kilometers) wide at the widest.

The largest areas of lowland in the Middle East are in the valleys of great rivers. The Nile River valley in Egypt is only a few miles or kilometers wide at places. But as the

The Elburz Mountains lie north of Tehran, the capital of Iran. These are among the highest mountains found in the Middle East.

Nile near the Mediterranean Sea, it spreads out to form a lowland over 150 miles (240 kilometers) wide.

The largest lowland in the Middle East is the valley of the Tigris (tī′ grəs) and Euphrates Rivers in the modern country of Iraq. This is the valley where history began. "And a river went out of Eden to water the garden; and from thence it was parted, and became into four heads.

. . . And the fourth river is Euphrates."

Genesis 2:10, 14b

The Tigris and Euphrates River Valley is about 600 miles (970 kilometers) long and about 200 miles (320 kilometers) wide. The Nile River is the longest river in the Middle East. The next two longest rivers are the Tigris and the Euphrates. No other rivers in the Middle East are nearly as long.

The lowest place found in the Middle East and in the world is along the shore of the Dead Sea in Israel. It is nearly 1,300 feet (390 meters) below sea level. The cliffs on the left rise some 2,500 feet (806 meters) above the Dead Sea.

Here are some more cliffs found in the Middle East. These cliffs in Turkey are where Christians once hid when they were persecuted.

What Do You Say?

1. a. What is the Middle East in the middle of? b. What is it east of?

2. Name some ways the Middle East was important long ago.

3. a. In what parts of the Middle East are the highest mountains found? b. Where are the largest lowlands found?

4. a. What is a plateau? b. Name two large plateaus found in the Middle East.

5. Name the three longest rivers in the Middle East.

What Does the Bible Say?

1. On the map of the Middle East on page 293 find Israel and its capital, Jerusalem. How does Ezekiel 5:5 describe Jerusalem's place in the Middle East?

2. The Middle East has long been a land of "wars and rumours of wars." How does Jesus say Christians should treat their enemies? (Read Matthew 5:43, 44.)

3. God spoke to His people in the Middle East many times, telling them to worship Him only. Read about one of these times in Deuteronomy 6:4-7. a. How were God's people to love Him? b. How were they to make sure that their children worshiped the one true God?

Lands of Little Water

One of the greatest needs of every country in the Middle East is water. Most of the land is desert. Most geographers say that at least four of every five acres of land, or four of every five hectares, in the Middle East is desert. Deserts are very dry lands. Less than ten inches (twenty-five centimeters) of rain falls each year in a desert. Some of the world's deserts are found in cold places such as Siberia. These places are sometimes called cold deserts.

But usually when we think of deserts, we think of hot deserts such as those found in the Middle East. Almost all of northern Africa is a hot desert. This desert stretches from the Atlantic Ocean to the Red Sea. The

After this desert soil in Egypt is plowed, watermelons will be planted here. What important gift from God besides soil and sunshine will be needed to make the melons grow?

This rocky land has no plant life. It is found in the desert between the Nile River and the Red Sea in Egypt. The children of Israel probably fled across land like this when they left Egypt in the time of Moses.

desert continues across the Middle East into Afghanistan, Pakistan, and India.

During much of the year the hot deserts of the Middle East have daytime temperatures over 100°F (38°C). Sometimes the temperature rises above 130°F (54°C). Nights become surprisingly cool because desert air is so dry. It does not have enough moisture to retain the daytime heat.

What Makes a Desert?

The world's largest desert stretches across northern Africa 3,000 miles (4,900 kilometers) from west to east. The desert continues into southwestern Asia another 2,000 miles (3,200 kilometers). This vast desert is 1,000 miles (1,600 kilometers) wide at places. Much of this desert in Africa is called the Sahara (sə hâr′ ə). In Syria and Iraq the desert is called the Syrian Desert. In southern Arabia the desert is called the Empty Quarter. Since most of the Middle East is desert, it is often hard to tell where one desert ends and the next begins.

Have you ever wondered why such large deserts are found in the Middle East and nearby lands?

Look at the map of the world's deserts at the bottom of this page. You will see that most of these deserts are about the same distance north or south of the equator. The moving of hot air has much to do with deserts at these places. Near the equator the hot air rises. As it rises, it cools and loses much of its moisture as rainfall. So the lands close to the equator often have heavy rainfall. The hot, dry air moves away from the equator. About 1,000 to 1,500 miles (1,600 to 2,400 kilometers) from the equator this warm air falls back toward the earth. Many of the world's deserts are found where this dry air descends to the earth.

Still other reasons can be found for the large deserts in Africa and Asia. Most winds in that part of the world blow from west to east. These winds blow across large stretches of land. The air does not pick up moisture as it would if the winds blew across large bodies of water. This adds to the dryness of the region.

In the southwestern part of the Arabian Peninsula, there is a region with more rainfall than the nearby desert. This is caused by winds blowing from the Indian Ocean during

This map shows some of the world's great deserts. On what continents are the largest of these deserts found?

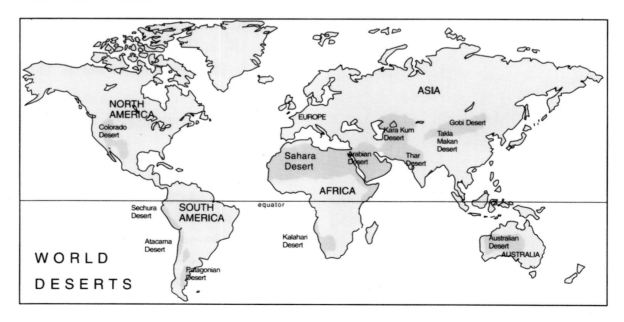

WORLD DESERTS

NORTH AMERICA
Colorado Desert
EUROPE
ASIA
Kara Kum Desert
Gobi Desert
Takla Makan Desert
Sahara Desert
Arabian Desert
Thar Desert
AFRICA
equator
Sechura Desert
SOUTH AMERICA
Kalahari Desert
Atacama Desert
Australian Desert
AUSTRALIA
Patagonian Desert

300

part of the year. The mountains of southwestern Arabia force the winds to rise and drop much of their moisture on the mountains. By the time the air reaches central Arabia, it is dry.

Parts of the Middle East near the Mediterranean Sea receive some rainfall during the winter. Winds blow across the warm sea toward the land. In the summer, winds blow from the dry desert toward the sea. Almost no rain falls in these lands during the long, hot summers.

Look at the rainfall map of the Middle East on this page. How much rain falls near the Mediterranean Sea?

On page 302 find the monthly rainfall chart for three Middle Eastern cities—Beirut, Cairo, and Baghdad. Can you tell which one is closest to the Mediterranean Sea by its winter rainfall? Now find the cities on the map on page 293 to see if you are right.

Nearby mountains also have much to do with rainfall. In the Middle East, mountains are often found near the sea. When moisture-bearing winds reach the mountains, the air rises and cools. Rain or snow falls on the mountains. Since the air has lost its moisture, lands beyond the mountain are left dry. The same thing happens along the west coast of North America. Moist winds from the Pacific Ocean drop their moisture on the mountains near the ocean. Drier lands and even deserts are found inland on

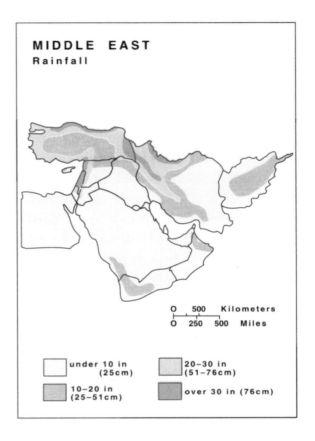

MIDDLE EAST
Rainfall

0   500   Kilometers
0   250   500   Miles

under 10 in (25cm)

10–20 in (25–51cm)

20–30 in (51–76cm)

over 30 in (76cm)

This map shows that the most rain falls in the northern part of the Middle East. These rainy areas are near the highest mountains of the region. Compare this map with the one on page 293 showing the names of the countries in the Middle East. Which countries have the most rainfall?

the eastern side of the mountains.

Still another reason for deserts is people. People do not cause deserts by themselves. But what people do to the land can cause deserts to expand. Sometimes too many people and their grazing animals live in the dry grasslands near the edge of deserts. The animals eat the grasses and other plants too close to the ground, killing them. The people may cut down the bushes and trees for their

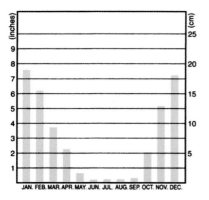

Beirut, Lebanon
Annual Rainfall: 35.1 inches (89 cm)

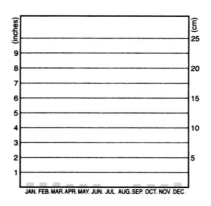

Cairo, Egypt
Annual Rainfall: 1.1 inches (2.8 cm)

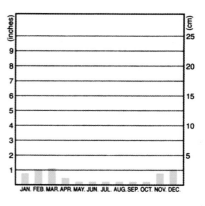

Baghdad, Iraq
Annual Rainfall: 5.5 inches (14 cm)

These charts show how much rain falls each month in three cities of the Middle East. Which has by far the most rainfall? Which has the least? In what part of the year does the most rain fall in all of these places?

animals or for fuel. The hot sun and drying winds help the desert to soon take over the nearby grasslands. Unless a lot of rain falls, land lost to the desert will not grow many plants again.

some of the parts of the great desert of North Africa and Asia.

5. How can people and their animals cause deserts to expand?

What Do You Say?

1. How much rain usually falls in a desert?

2. How long and how wide is the great desert that stretches across Africa and a large part of Asia?

3. Name at least three reasons why such large deserts have formed in these places.

4. Name and tell the location of

What Does the Bible Say?

1. The Bible speaks of deserts and sometimes uses the word *wilderness* to describe them. Read Deuteronomy 32:8-10. What, according to v. 10, did God do for His people in the desert long ago?

2. What desert is named in Exodus 19:2? Find it on the map of the Middle East on page 293. (Hint: It is a part of Egypt.)

302

Natural Resources in the Middle East

A **natural resource** is anything around us that God has given for our use. Soil and water are natural resources. Plants and animals are also natural resources. Oil, coal, and metals are other natural resources. Even air and sunshine are often called natural resources.

When you think about the Middle East, what natural resources do you think about first? If you have heard or read very much about the Middle East, you will probably say, "Oh, yes, oil is the most important natural resource in the Middle East."

It is true that more oil (petroleum) has been found under the deserts and shallow seas of the Middle East than in all the rest of the world put together. More than one-half of the world's oil comes from the Middle East.

But most people in the Middle East know that there is a natural resource much more important to them than oil. What do you think it is? A deputy minister of water in Saudi Arabia says that this most important natural resource is water. He said, "We cannot afford to let a single drop go to waste." He realizes that the oil wells will some-day start to go dry. But his country will still need water. The people of the Middle East must work together to use their valuable water wisely. Even the prices of oil and water in Saudi Arabia tell us how important water already is. Gasoline is cheap, only thirty or forty cents a gallon. But bottled water may cost as much as five dollars a gallon!

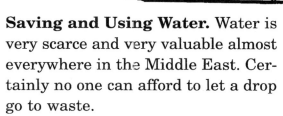

Saving and Using Water. Water is very scarce and very valuable almost everywhere in the Middle East. Certainly no one can afford to let a drop go to waste.

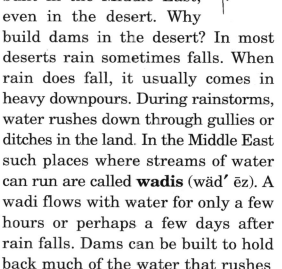

Some countries in the Middle East are using much of their oil money to find new water supplies or to save the water they do have. Many dams have been built in the Middle East, even in the desert. Why build dams in the desert? In most deserts rain sometimes falls. When rain does fall, it usually comes in heavy downpours. During rainstorms, water rushes down through gullies or ditches in the land. In the Middle East such places where streams of water can run are called **wadis** (wäd′ ēz). A wadi flows with water for only a few hours or perhaps a few days after rain falls. Dams can be built to hold back much of the water that rushes

down the wadis. Dams help keep the water from rushing away into the sea or sinking into the desert sands.

Middle Eastern countries are also exploring the deserts for large underground pools of water. An underground layer of rock or sand containing water is an **aquifer** (ak′ wə fər).

Well-drilling machinery and electric pumps make it possible to pump water from aquifers that lie deep underground. Some of the huge aquifers in the Middle East lie 1,000 or more feet (more than 300 meters) under the ground.

It is amazing to think of large aquifers under deserts. No one knows for sure how these aquifers form. **Geologists** (jē äl′ ə jəsts) who study the land and rocks have made some good guesses. Some of the water that falls in sudden desert storms probably sinks into the ground and reaches the aquifers. Perhaps some of the water could flow underground from far-away mountains where more rain falls. Some geologists believe that the aquifers formed thousands of years ago when the Middle East was wetter than it is now.

Scientists and farmers have discovered that it is not good to pump too much water from the aquifers of the Middle East. In some places much pumping has caused the water level to drop. The aquifers do not

This wadi lies between two mountains in the Sinai Peninsula. Many wadis are found in the Middle East. At one time rivers may have flowed through some of these wadis. Today water flows in them only after the few heavy rains that come to the desert.

refill as rapidly as in wetter lands.

The Oases of the Middle East. An **oasis** is a place in the desert where water comes near the surface of the ground. Sometimes the water flows from wells or springs. Sometimes the water flows up from wells like a fountain and no pump is needed. Such a well is called an **artesian well.** Many artesian wells are found in the Middle East. But in many other places, the water must be drawn or pumped from shallow wells. Most of the oases in the Middle East have been used for hundreds and even for thousands of years. Now with drilling rigs and pumps, new oases can be made where only barren rock and sand had once been.

Some oases are very small. An

oasis may have only a few trees and a watering hole for weary travelers and their animals. Other oases may cover thousands of acres (or hectares). The picture here is from the huge al-Hasa (al ha′ sə) Oasis in Saudi Arabia.

Water flows from this artesian well. No pump brings the water to the surface of the earth. Pressure that God has placed under the earth forces the water up. Many places in the Middle East and in other parts of the world have artesian wells.

Saving the al-Hasa Oasis

Al-Hasa is the largest oasis in Saudi Arabia. It covers hundreds of acres (or hectares). About fifty villages are found in this oasis. Some years ago the oasis was in danger of turning into desert. Windblown sand began to cover many of the villages. Some of the mounds of sand that were taking over at al-Hasa were twenty feet (six meters) high. Mounds of windblown sand are called dunes.

The Saudi Arabian government spent millions of dollars to rescue this beautiful oasis from turning into desert. Tamarisk trees were planted on the sand dunes to hold the sand down. Tamarisks are low bushes or trees that can grow where little else does. Tamarisks can be planted in salty soil and in sand.

Irrigation specialists built 820 miles (1,330 kilometers) of concrete water ditches to carry water to the fields at al-Hasa. Ditches or other water carriers are called **aqueducts** (a′ kwə dəkts). Before the aqueducts at al-Hasa were built, farmers dug ditches in the soil so that water could flow to the fields. Much of this water sank into the ground and was lost before it ever reached the fields.

Al-Hasa also needed better ditches for draining the fields. If water is left standing on desert soil, salts from under the ground can rise to the top of the soil. Few crops can be grown in salty soil.

Without money from the sale of oil, Saudi Arabia could not do such a good job of conserving water and saving the oases. Now Saudia Arabia will be prepared to farm the land and grow valuable crops.

A man is climbing a date palm tree. Notice how straight the trunks of these trees are. Can you find the clusters of dates hanging below the feathery branches?

A Tree for Every Need

An unusual but very useful natural resource in the Middle East is a tree called the date palm. This tree needs plenty of moisture and so grows well in oases. But the date palm also needs hot, dry weather. The fruit will spoil if rain falls when it is ripening.

Most North Americans know the date only as a very sweet dried fruit used in cakes, cookies, and candies. For us dates are expensive.

But did you know that dates are the daily food of many people in the Middle East? For some, the date is their main food. In some parts of the Middle East the date is called the **"cake of the poor."** Dates are necessary to help keep the people alive.

People in the Middle East eat the date fresh or dried. The fruit is high in vitamins and minerals, and it has lots of sugar for energy. Dried dates have more sugar than any other fruit. The high sugar content keeps them from spoiling easily. Not only do the people eat dates, but cattle are fed dates which have been pressed into cakes.

Dates grow in clusters. About how many dates do you think may be found in one cluster? How are dates a blessing from God to the people of the Middle East?

The seeds of the date can be ground up, roasted, and brewed into a drink like coffee. The seeds may be used for cattle feed as well. The syrup from dates can be made into sugar, vinegar, alcohol, and even a sweet, refreshing drink. The buds on the date tree may be eaten as a vegetable.

Almost every part of the date palm is useful. The trunk of this tree grows straight and tall. It is almost the same size all the way to the top. The straight trunks may be used for lumber in a land where few other trees grow.

The leaves of the date palm may be used for weaving mats and baskets. The tough centers of the leaves may be used to make crates, furniture, and baskets. In parts of the Middle East, people live in little houses built almost entirely from the date palm. Woven mats of palm leaves cover the walls. The mats keep out the hot sun and any rain that might fall.

Even the stalk that bears the fruit of the date palm is not wasted. The stalks may be used for ropes and for fuel. Can you think of a more useful tree?

Growing the Date Palm. People who grow date palms pull off the young shoots that appear near the bottom of the trunk. These are planted to start new trees.

The date palm may grow to be 40 to 100 feet (12 to 30 meters) tall. The top of the tree has beautiful, feathery branches that sway gracefully in the wind. The dates hang in big clusters among the feathery branches. A cluster of dates weighs about 26 pounds (11 kilograms). Two hundred or more dates may grow in a cluster. A healthy date palm produces 100 to 200 pounds (45-90 kilograms) of dates each year. The dates are a beautiful red or gold color as they ripen on the tree.

Egypt and Iraq are the world's largest producers of dates. But dates are grown in almost every country of the Middle East. Most dates used in North America come from the Middle East. They can be grown, however, in the hottest parts of California, Arizona, and Texas.

The date palm has been very important in the Middle East for thousands of years. The Bible mentions this tree and simply calls it the palm tree. You may remember that people cut down branches of this tree to wave before Jesus as He rode a donkey into Jerusalem. People often cut down branches of the date palm to honor rulers by waving the branches before them.

Ships of the Desert

We have studied the importance of water and trees as natural resources in the Middle East. Now we will study about an animal that is a natural resource. This animal is the camel. God made the camel to be especially useful in the desert.

The camel can go for days, even weeks, without drinking water. It gets some water from its food. The

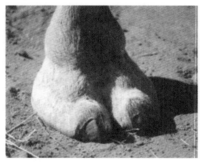

The photo above is a closeup of a camel's foot. How did God make the camel's foot so the camel can walk well in the deserts? The photo to the right shows you its bushy eyelids and narrow nose openings. How do these help the camel to work in the desert? In the top photo the standing camel shows you the long legs that help camels to move swiftly and the rough knee pads that help them kneel in the rocky deserts.

camel's body is made to store water in its fat so that the animal does not need frequent drinks. The camel can eat almost anything. In the Middle East, camels eat dates, grass, and whatever grains are available. Hungry camels have been known to eat bones, meat, skin, and even tents!

The camel has special eyelids and eyelashes to keep out sand and the glaring sunlight. The animal holds its head high to see out from under its heavy eyelashes. With its head held high, the camel has a proud look.

Most camels used in the Middle East have one hump on their backs. Some camels from other parts of Asia have two humps. People used to believe that the camel stored water in its hump. This is not exactly correct. The hump stores fat. Of course the fat has a lot of water in it. The fat stored in the camel's hump gives it energy. If the camel is starving, the hump becomes smaller.

Camels have been used for thousands of years in the Middle East. They carry people and loads of 400 to 500 pounds (180 to 225 kilograms). Most camels can travel about 25 miles (40 kilometers) in one day. Camels have special pads on their feet which help them walk across soft sand. Camels are such good desert travelers that they have been called **ships of the desert.**

The people in the Middle East use the camel for far more than travel, however. Camels provide milk, cheese, and meat. Fat from the camel's hump can be melted and used like butter.

Camels lose much of their hair each spring. The desert people collect the hair to make heavy cloth and blankets. Camel skins make good leather for shoes, water bags, and other containers. Even the camel's manure is not wasted. It is very dry and can be used for fuel. Sometimes camel dung or manure is the only fuel to be found in a land where few bushes or trees grow.

The Bible refers to camels more than 60 times. They are mentioned as early as the days of Abraham, about 4,000 years ago. Years ago some people who did not believe the Bible said that camels were not used this long ago. No one had found any mention outside of the Bible of camels used in the Middle East 4,000 years ago. But now ancient records have been found showing that camels have been used for at least that long in the Middle East.

Today camels are not used as much as they once were. Trucks and airplane travel have replaced the camel in many places. The change from camels to trucks, planes, and other vehicles has taken place because of another natural resource found in the Middle East. We will study about that resource in the next section.

What Do You Say?

1. a. What is a natural resource? b. What is the most important natural resource in the Middle East? c. Why is this resource so important?

2. a. What is an aquifer? b. Name three ways geologists think water may have reached the aquifers under the deserts of the Middle East.

3. What did the government of Saudi Arabia do to keep the al-Hasa Oasis from becoming desert?

4. a. Name at least ten ways the date palm may be used. b. Why are dates sometimes called the "cake of the poor"?

5. If a desert dweller had a herd of camels and some date palm trees, how could these meet all his needs for food, drink, clothing, and a place to live?

What Does the Bible Say?

1. Read Psalm 65:9, 10. a. What important natural resource do these verses name? b. From where does this resource come?

2. a. What is the name of the oasis mentioned in Exodus 15:27? b. How many wells were found there and how many palm trees?

3. Read Genesis 24:61; I Kings 10:2; Matthew 3:4. Name three ways camels were used in Bible times.

Black Gold!

What natural resource do you think of when you think of the Middle East? Most people would immediately think of oil. A better name for this resource is **petroleum** (pǝ trō′ lē ǝm).

The word *petroleum* comes from two Latin words which mean "rock oil." At one time many people actually called petroleum *rock oil*. Petroleum is often found in the ground between layers of rock. We often call petroleum "oil" for short. But the word *oil* may also mean vegetable oil or oil from animal fat.

Because petroleum is so valuable, it has been called **black gold.** It was not always so valuable. Only 150 years ago people did not know many uses for petroleum. The kerosene lamp increased the world's use of petroleum greatly. Kerosene is made from petroleum. The invention of gasoline engines, automobiles, and airplanes led to the use of huge amounts of petroleum.

Petroleum is not always black as the nickname *black gold* would suggest. Much of the petroleum in the Middle East is light brown. Some petroleum is almost colorless. Petroleum is a slippery, oily liquid that may be very thin or quite thick.

No one knows for sure how much petroleum lies under the deserts and the shallow seas of the Middle East. But scientists believe that well over half of the petroleum on earth is found in the Middle East. The Middle East gives the world about half the petroleum that is used.

Petroleum is found mostly in underground lakes or ponds between layers of rock. In some places it is found in pools on top of the ground. The ancient people of the Middle East found a thick form of petroleum called pitch in pools above the ground. They used pitch to seal cracks and to keep water out of boats.

The Bible first mentions pitch in Genesis 6:14. God commanded Noah to use pitch to make his ark or boat waterproof. "Make thee an ark of gopher wood . . . and [thou] shalt pitch it within and without with pitch."

Genesis 6:14

Noah and the other people of long ago did not know about the vast stores of petroleum that lay beneath their feet. Even if they had known about all this petroleum, they would not have known how to use it.

Petroleum is found under the desert in Egypt, Iran, Iraq, Saudi Arabia, and some other countries of the Middle East. Petroleum is also found beneath the shallow waters of the Persian Gulf between Iran and Saudi Arabia. The little country of Kuwait at the northern end of the Gulf is said to be on top of a huge lake of oil. Saudi Arabia alone has half of the petroleum found in the Middle East. We will learn more about this country in Chapter 20.

Uses of Petroleum

Petroleum as it comes from the ground is called **crude oil.** By itself, crude oil is not very useful. People once used it for greasing machinery and even for medicine. Petroleum must be heated to very high temperatures to separate it into useful parts. A little more than half of every barrel of oil can be made into gasoline. Kerosene and heating oil are two other valuable fuels taken from petroleum. Some other parts of petroleum are used to make grease and oil to keep motors running smoothly.

Petroleum also gives us many other useful things besides fuel. Rubbing alcohol, ammonia, petroleum jelly, fertilizers, insect killers, and even medicines can be made from petroleum. Petroleum forms a large portion of many paints we use. Certain plastics are made from it. Many of the clothes we wear, as well as the tires on your bike or car, are probably made at least partly from oil. Real rubber is not used as much as it once was.

Take a look around your house and discover how many ways petroleum is used. Vinyl floor coverings are made of petroleum. The soft carpet in your living room is probably made of it. Even if your house has a hardwood floor, the wax you put on the floor is made of petroleum. The paint and woodstain are likely petroleum products. Almost everything that is not made of metal or wood will be made of plastic or some other petroleum product. Look around your schoolroom to see the many uses of plastic.

If people keep using petroleum in such large amounts, someday it may all be used up. This should teach us to use carefully and wisely the natural resources God has given. In the chapter on Saudi Arabia you will learn about how that country is trying to prepare for the day when the petroleum is gone.

What Do You Say?

1. a. What is petroleum? b. Why is *petroleum* a better name than *oil* for this natural resource?

2. a. How much of the petroleum used in the world comes from the Middle East? b. How much of the petroleum in the Middle East is found in Saudi Arabia?

3. a. What is crude oil? b. How can it be made into many useful products such as gasoline?

4. Name some uses of petroleum in your home or school. Think about fuels as well as many other uses.

5. Find out how the electricity you use is made. Is petroleum used to make any of it? If so, then petroleum is being used in more ways at your home than you might have thought.

What Does the Bible Say?

1. a. According to Exodus 2:3, how was pitch (petroleum) used?

b. What can happen to pitch according to Isaiah 34:9b? c. What does this tell you about a possible use of petroleum?

2. Look up each reference and find what was used for fuel in Bible times. Many of these things are still used for fuel in the Middle East.
   a. Leviticus 1:7
   b. Ecclesiastes 7:6
   c. Matthew 6:30
   d. Matthew 25:4, 8

Chapter Eighteen Review

Using Globes and Maps

1. Look at the map of the Middle East on page 293. a. Which countries have the longest rivers? b. Name the three longest rivers in the Middle East. c. Find and name the seas and gulfs around the Middle East.

2. Draw a map of the Middle East. With a yellow pencil, shade in the places on the map where the most petroleum is found. Check an encyclopedia map showing where the world's petroleum is found.

3. Make a large wall map of the Middle East showing the countries, capitals, and other large cities. Use a different color for each country. Now see activity #1 under *For You to Do*.

New Words and Terms

For each word or term, choose the correct definition.

_____ 1. Middle East
_____ 2. plateau
_____ 3. desert
_____ 4. natural resource
_____ 5. petroleum
_____ 6. wadi
_____ 7. aquifer
_____ 8. geologist
_____ 9. oasis
_____ 10. artesian well
_____ 11. sand dune
_____ 12. aqueduct
_____ 13. ships of the desert
_____ 14. black gold
_____ 15. crude oil
_____ 16. cake of the poor

a. "Rock oil."

b. Water flows through it to thirsty fields.

c. One who studies the earth and rocks.

d. Lands located where Europe, Asia, and Africa come together.

e. Carries water only after a rainstorm.

f. Water bubbles out of the earth here.

g. Formed by wind.

h. Camels.

i. A nickname for petroleum.

j. Something God gives us to use such as water, soil, petroleum.

k. A well-watered spot in the desert.

l. Underground lake.

m. Highland, either level or hilly, between mountains.

n. Petroleum as it comes from the ground.

o. Fruit of the date palm.

p. A dry area with less than ten inches of rainfall each year.

Thinking Together

1. Petroleum is measured in amounts called barrels. A barrel of petroleum is 41 gallons (156 liters). Of course petroleum is not usually stored in barrels today. But we still speak of barrels of petroleum, not gallons or liters. a. Of every 100 barrels of petroleum pumped from the earth, about how many come from the Middle East? b. Of those barrels from the Middle East, how many are from one country? c. What is the name of that country?

2. Why do we call the lands we have been studying the Middle East?

3. Name some things that make the Middle East important to the rest of the world.

4. a. What is a desert? b. How large is the area of desert that stretches across northern Africa into southwestern Asia? c. Name at least four reasons why we have deserts.

5. a. What is a natural resource? b. Name four important natural resources in the Middle East. c. Why do you think water is one of the most important natural resources?

6. Name some things that are being done in the Middle East to use water more carefully.

7. List five important uses of the date palm tree and five uses of the camel in the Middle East.

8. Name five ways petroleum is used in your home, your school, or your community.

For You to Do

1. Plan a bulletin board on the Middle East with the map you made. (See *Using Globes and Maps,* Activity 3, on page 313.) For added interest, place pictures of various places in the Middle East around the border of the map. Make a copy of the flag of each country to place on the map on or near each country.

2. Make a chart naming each country of the Middle East. In separate columns list the capitals, the population, and three or four important natural resources in each country. You can find all this information in encyclopedia articles on each country.

3. Make a desert diorama in a large shoebox or an even larger box. Paint a background of barren, brown mountains. Cover the bottom with sand, rocks, and gravel. A pile of sand at one place can be a sand dune. A green area with date palm trees can be painted on one side of the box. A small tent made of brown cloth and sticks can represent the home of a desert wanderer. You may want to add camel figurines or cardboard camels made to stand up.

19. The People of the Middle East

Many Different Peoples

Over 230 million people live in the Middle Eastern countries we are studying. Most of them belong to the European geographical race. We would probably call them "white" people. But not all "white" people are light-skinned. In fact, most of the people in the Middle East have dark brown skin and dark hair and eyes.

The people in the northern countries of the Middle East are quite

These Arab boys and men are from the country of Jordan. How does their dress seem to be different from the Egyptians selling baskets? Did you know that Jordan and Egypt once were united as one country? This country was called the United Arab Republic.

These Arabs are selling baskets in an Egyptian marketplace. Notice the long robes two of the men are wearing and their headdresses.

different from those in the south. The people who live in Turkey, Iran, and Afghanistan came from northern and central Asia many hundreds of years ago. They are often lighter-skinned than the people of the southern countries. Most of the people of Israel are Jews who came to Israel in the last 50 years. They came from many parts of the world. They have returned to the homeland the Jews lived in some 2,000 years ago. The island of Cyprus is also a part of the Middle East. Most of the people there came from Greece, in Europe.

Most of the rest of the people in the Middle East are called Arabs. Over half of the Middle Easterners are Arabs. The first people to be called Arabs were the people of the huge Arabian Peninsula. Today the people who live in Egypt, Iraq, Syria, and a number of other countries are called Arabs.

It is very difficult to describe exactly who an Arab is, and yet the Arabs are a very important part of the Middle East. To understand the Arabs, we need to understand some Middle Eastern history.

Who are the Arabs? Do you remember Abraham's two sons, Ishmael and Isaac? Isaac was a special son whom God gave to Abraham and Sarah. God made a special promise to Isaac. He said, "And I will make thy seed to multiply as the stars of heaven . . . and in thy seed shall all the nations of the earth be blessed." Through Isaac came the Jewish people and the nation of Israel.

Abraham's other son, Ishmael, was sent away with his mother, Hagar, to live in the desert. Ishmael and Isaac did not get along well as boys. Their mothers, Hagar and Sarah, did not get along with each other either. But because Ishmael was Abraham's son, God made a promise about him also. "As for Ishmael . . . Behold, I have blessed him, and will make him fruitful, and will multiply him exceedingly . . . and I will make him a great nation."

Ishmael's descendants grew up

These men live in Kabul (käb′ ə) the capital of Afghanistan. Nearly all the people of Afghanistan are Muslims. The Afghans are a mixture of Arabs and central Asian people.

in the deserts of Arabia. Several other related tribes also lived in the Arabian Peninsula. Isaac's older son Esau, for example, became the father of the Edomites. Also, remember Abraham's nephew Lot? After the destruction of Sodom, Lot's two daughters each had a son. One became the father of the Ammonites. The other became the father of the Moabites. Both of these tribes of people, like the Ishmaelites and Edomites, lived in Arabia. Other tribes also lived in the area. Descendants of all these tribes came to be known as Arabs.

In the A.D. 600s and 700s the warlike tribes of Arabia joined to form one strong country. This was around

Genesis 26:4

Genesis 17:20

Modern-day Jerusalem is different from most other cities in the Arab world. Three of every four people in the city are not Arabs but Jews. Many Arabs feel that they should have this city because the city once was ruled by the Arabs.

1,300 years ago. These Arabs sent out armies to conquer nearby Palestine. Later on, Arab armies spread eastward to Iraq, Iran, and all the way to India. Arab armies also traveled west to conquer Egypt. They finally conquered all of northern Africa and Spain, which is in Europe.

In most lands conquered by the Arabs, the people accepted the language and some of the customs of the Arabs. Arabs from Arabia also settled in these countries.

Wherever the Arabs conquered, many of the people accepted their religion called **Islam** (is′ läm′). If people did not accept Islam, they had to pay taxes to support the religion.

The spread of the Arabs and their religion has made it difficult to say who are Arabs and who are not. Generally, people who speak the language of Arabia and who follow Arabian customs are called Arabs. Most, but not all Arabs, also follow

the religion of Islam. The people of Turkey, Iran, and Afghanistan accepted the religion of the Arabs. They do not speak **Arabic** (ar′ ə bik), the language of Arabia. They are not called Arabs. Some of the people of Egypt and Lebanon belong to Christian religions. Still they think of themselves as Arabs. They speak Arabic and follow some Arabian customs.

When the Arabs conquered other lands, they conquered Palestine too. Palestine had been the homeland of the Jews. For many years after this, few Jews lived in Palestine. Arabs or people who believed in Islam controlled Palestine until the early 1900s. The British controlled Palestine for a number of years. In 1948 the Jews formed an independent country called Israel. The next day after independence, neighboring Arabs tried to destroy the new country but failed.

Many Jews returned to Israel.

This is an Arab village in Israel. The houses here are some of the better Arab homes. Many of the Arabs in Israel live in crowded shacks and are very poor.

The Arabs do not want the Jews in Israel. "The land is ours," the Arabs say. They believe the Jews have taken their land from them. The Jews, of course, believe they have just taken back what was theirs long ago.

Just as Ishmael and Isaac did not get along as brothers, so their descendants do not get along. Bad feelings have remained to this day. Jews and Arabs living side by side and hating each other is one of the biggest problems in the Middle East today.

Wars and Rumors of War

God said concerning Ishmael, "And he will be a wild man; his hand

This map shows the places where fighting and wars have recently taken place in the Middle East. Most of the people in these places are Arabs or Muslims. They have many beliefs and customs that are alike. Yet these people often fight each other or their Jewish neighbors.

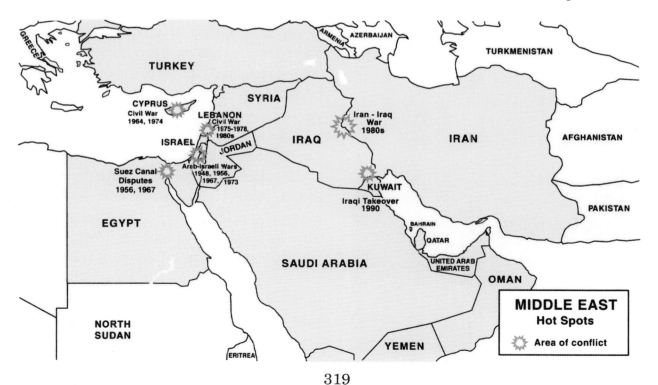

Genesis
16:12

will be against every man, and every man's hand against him; and he shall dwell in the presence of all his brethren."

Ishmael's children, grandchildren, and the many generations since have been a warlike people. The Jews and the Arabs have lived close together for many years. They have fought many wars. But the Arabs have not always had peace among themselves, either.

Hatred and war continue in the Middle East. We hear of wars between Jews and Arabs. We hear of other wars between Arab countries. There are even wars between groups of people within countries.

The Arab-Israeli Conflict. Nine of every ten people in the tiny country of Israel are Jews. We call them Israelis (iz rā′ lēz). Most of the rest

The fertile Bekaa Valley of Lebanon has been the place of many wars. Notice the terraced hillside where crops are planted. How has war affected farming in the Bekaa Valley?

of the people are Arabs.

War has been going on between Israel and nearby Arab countries ever since Israel became a nation in 1948. Large wars broke out between the Israelis and Arabs in 1948 and in 1956. In 1967, the Six-Day War was fought. The Israelis took much Arab land. This made their country three times larger than it had been before.

In 1973, the Israelis fought another war with Egypt and Syria. The Arab-Israeli wars continue. Many thousands have been killed.

The War in Lebanon. One of the saddest wars in the Middle East is one that has been fought in the country of Lebanon. Until about 1958, Lebanon was a peaceful country of beautiful farms and snow-covered mountains.

Nearly all the people of Lebanon are Arabs. About 70 percent of them follow Islam, the religion you will learn about in the next few pages. The other 30 percent call themselves Christians. Many belong to a church that is part of the Roman Catholic Church.

Since 1958, these two groups of Arabs have fought each other. Tens of thousands of people have been killed. Arabs from Israel and other places have come into the country. This has led to still more fighting.

The picture shows farmland in the beautiful Bekaa (bi kä′) Valley in eastern Lebanon. In times of peace this rich valley has given Lebanon half of its fruit and vegetables. But war has destroyed much of the farmland. Many of the farmers have been killed or driven from their land. War has led to hunger and even more deaths because many farmers have stopped farming.

The nations of the Middle East say they believe in God. But they have not learned God's way of peace. Men and women who have hate in their hearts will never live in peace. For God's way of peace is this: "If thine enemy hunger, feed him; if he thirst, give him drink: for in so doing thou shalt heap coals of fire on his head. Be not overcome of evil, but overcome evil with good."

Romans 2:20, 21

What Do You Say?

1. a. From where did the people of Iran come? b. The people of Cyprus? c. What do we call most of the people who live in Israel? d. In Syria?

2. Where did the Arabs first live?

3. a. What is an Arab? b. Why is it sometimes hard to say exactly who an Arab is?

4. a. How are the Jews and the Arabs related to each other? b. How is the disagreement between two brothers still going on after thousands of years?

What Does the Bible Say?

1. a. According to Jeremiah 27:5, who has determined where different groups of people live on the earth? b. What land has God allowed the Arabs to have?

2. You have studied about the two jealous brothers, Ishmael and Isaac. These men were fathers of the Arabs and the Jews. Jealousy between Arabs and Jews has continued until this very day. How does Song of Solomon 8:6 describe jealousy?

3. Read James 3:16. What are the results of envy and strife?

The Religion of the Arabs

Abraham must have taught his son Ishmael to worship the true God. But as time went on, the Arabs began to worship many gods. They made statues of their gods. We call such statues **idols.** The worship of false gods and their statues is called **idolatry.** Most of the Arabs practiced idolatry until about 600 years after Christ was on the earth. A few Arabs became Christians in those days, but most still worshiped idols.

Arabs bowing in worship. Every day, five times a day, Muslims are supposed to stop what they are doing and bow to the ground to worship Allah. The Bible does not ask Christians to pray at certain times of day. But the Bible does say, "Pray without ceasing." This means that we are to pray often and be prepared to pray at any time.

An Arab named Mohammed (mō ham′ əd) knew that Abraham and Isaac once worshiped only one God. Mohammed worked to return the Arabs to belief in one God. At first not many Arabs wanted to give up their idols. But more and more people began to follow Mohammed's teaching. His followers were called **Muslims** or Moslems. The Muslims called their religion Islam. They called their one god Allah (al′ ə). Allah is the Arabic word for God.

One false teaching of Mohammed was that Muslims should force other people to believe in Allah. Mohammed and his followers fought wars to make the Arabs follow Islam. Mohammed called such wars "holy" wars. The word **holy** means clean, pure, or set apart for God. These wars certainly were not holy.

Mohammed and his followers taught that two towns in the desert of Arabia were "holy" cities. They were Mecca and Medina. Find them on the map of the Middle East on page 293. At Mecca was a small building shaped like a cube with all four sides the same size. This building was called the Kaaba (käb′ ə), the Arabic word for cube. Before Mohammed's time, the Arabs had set up many idols at the Kaaba. It was a place of idol worship. Mohammed destroyed all the idols at the Kaaba. He told them to worship Allah alone. He commanded believers in Islam to make special trips to the Kaaba to worship Allah. Mohammed said that Abraham and Ishmael first worshiped Allah at the Kaaba. He said that the two men made a trip to Mecca each year to worship God. In the wall of the Kaaba is a black stone that people said fell from heaven in the days of Ishmael.

Wherever the Arabs went they carried their religion with them. They forced many people to worship Allah. Today most of the people of

322

northern Africa, the Middle East, and many other Asian countries are Muslims. More than one of every ten people on earth today is a follower of Mohammed. Many Muslims are not Arabs.

The Teachings of Islam

The Muslims honor the Bible. They believe that Moses and Jesus were great prophets and teachers. But Muslims believe that Mohammed was the last and greatest prophet from God. Mohammed's followers collected his sayings and teachings into a book. This Muslim "bible" is called the Koran (kə ran′). Muslims also follow other collections of traditions.

The Koran has many verses and teachings borrowed from our Bible. The Koran even calls Jesus the Word of God. But Muslims do not follow all the teachings of Jesus. They do not believe John 14:6 where Jesus said: "I am the way, the truth, and the life: no man cometh unto the Father, but by me."

John 14:6

The Koran allows slavery but tells masters to treat slaves kindly. The Koran allows a Muslim man to have as many as four wives. But most Muslims have only one wife. The Muslims are commanded not to eat pork. Pigs are considered unclean. This teaching comes from the Old Testament. The Koran forbids its followers to drink beer, wine, and such drinks. Some Muslims today break this good rule found in their bible.

The Duties of Islam. The Koran is the most important book in a Muslim's life. When a Muslim child is born, the first words he will probably hear are verses from the Koran. The

This map shows the countries where over half (50 percent) of the people are Muslims. How many Muslim countries are there?

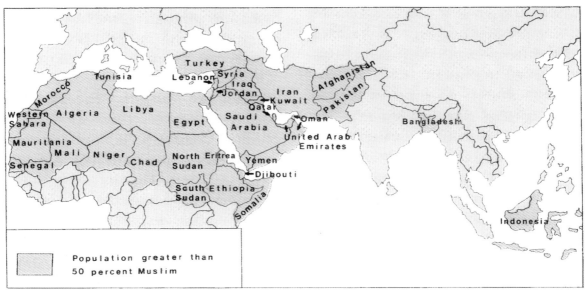

Population greater than 50 percent Muslim

The pages of the Koran, the "bible" of the Muslims, are beautifully decorated. Even the writing itself has a special beauty. The Koran is a little shorter than the Christian New Testament. Many Muslims memorize the entire Koran. Why should Christians memorize Bible passages?

children of Muslims often memorize the whole Koran by age 13. A special celebration is held when a child has memorized the Koran. Did you know that the Koran is almost as long as the Christian New Testament? The Muslims decorate their homes and the things they own with verses from the Koran. The last words a dying Muslim usually hears are from the Koran.

The Muslim's love for the Koran has caused many Christians to think, *Do I love God's Word as much as I should?* The writer of Psalm 119 said, "O how love I thy law! it is my meditation all the day."

Psalm 119:97

Muslims believe that there is one God named Allah and that Mohammed is his prophet. By confessing these things, they hope that someday they will go to heaven.

Christians Among Muslims

Many Christians have lived near or among Muslims since the days of Mohammed. Even in North America we are not far from the Muslims. Almost every large city in the United States and Canada has at least one mosque (mäsk), or place of worship.

Many people wonder why the Muslim religion has spread so far. Part of the reason for the spread of Islam is the teaching of "holy" wars. The Koran promises special rewards in heaven for anyone who dies defending Islam.

Another reason for the spread of Islam has to do with Christianity. Many Muslims remember stories of how Muslims have been mistreated by people who called themselves Christians. Many years ago so-called Christians in Europe fought wars against the Muslims. The Muslims have not forgotten these wars. They think of Christians as their enemies.

Muslims also hate idol worship. They do not understand why some churches have statues of Mary, Jesus' mother, and statues of saints who have died. They think Christians worship these things. Muslims also imagine that Christians worship

The largest Muslim mosque in North America pictured here is in Indianapolis, Indiana. There are over three million Muslims in the United States and hundreds of mosques.

three Gods. They do not believe that God the Father, Jesus Christ, and the Holy Spirit are one God.

Some Muslims have become Christians. They have helped other Christians better understand the Muslims. But the work of winning Muslims for Christ is very hard. Some missionaries to Muslim lands have become very discouraged.

How can Christians best tell Muslims about Christ and salvation in Him? They can begin by showing kindness and doing good to the Muslims. They can show that true Christians do not believe in fighting and killing their enemies. They can explain that Christians truly believe in only one God. Christians can also tell what Christ has done in their own lives. This is probably the best way to tell Muslims or anyone else about Christ.

What Do You Say?

1. Write a complete sentence for each of the following words in which you express the meaning of the word. Underline the vocabulary word in each sentence.
a. idolatry   b. Islam   c. holy
d. Kaaba   e. Koran   f. mosque.

2. a. Name at least three ways Christians can witness to Muslims. b. Why have Muslims thought of Christians as enemies?

What Does the Bible Say?

1. Read 1 John 5:21. What does this verse say about idolatry?

2. a. Read Mark 5:19. What did Jesus tell the man who was healed to do? b. Now read Matthew 5:16. How does this verse tell people who believe in Jesus to let others know they love Him?

3. Muslims believe Mohammed was greater than Jesus. Read Philippians 2:9-11. a. What does verse 9 say about Jesus? b. What two things will every person do someday (vv. 10, 11)?

What Are Arabs Like?

Many of the people in the Middle East are Arabs. But Arabs do not all look exactly alike, nor do they live alike. Not all Americans or Canadians are exactly alike either. But many Arabs have dark skin and hair and speak Arabic. Only where Arabs have mixed with other peoples are their hair, skin, and eyes much lighter.

We will look at the life of an imaginary boy in the Arab land of Egypt. In many ways he is like other Arabs. You will discover some differences as well.

The Egyptian Fellahin. Hussein (hü sān′) is an Egyptian boy who lives in a crowded village less than a mile from the mighty Nile River. Nearly all of Egypt is a great desert. But the Nile River winds like a ribbon of blue through the desert.

A narrow strip of green just a few miles wide along the river shows where people water or irrigate the land. Millions of people are crowded into this narrow strip of well-watered land. In many parts of the Nile Valley, over 2,000 people live on each square mile of land. This is the most thickly settled part of the Middle East.

About half of Egypt's people live in cities. Most of the other half, like Hussein, live in farm villages. A farm worker like Hussein's father is called a **fellah** (fel′ ə). In Hussein's language, Arabic, *fellah* means "a plowman." More than one *fellah* is *fellahin* (fel′ ə hēn′).

The *fellahin* in Egypt live in little villages along the Nile River. So did their fathers, grandfathers, and ancestors for thousands of years. The village houses are crowded together with only a narrow pathway

A boat, called a dhow (daú) sails on the Suez Canal in Egypt. Hundreds of dhows are used on the Suez Canal, the Nile River, and other waterways of Egypt.

between each one. No one wants to waste a bit of space. As much land as possible is used for farming.

Hussein's home is made of mud bricks baked in the hot sun. The roof is held up by palm tree trunks and branches. The roofs are flat on top, for it almost never rains. There is no need for sloped roofs to shed rainwater. Sometimes Hussein and his neighbors can sleep on their flat roofs where it becomes cool at night.

Hussein's home has almost no furniture except for a low table and some mats for resting and sleeping. The floor is bare earth packed hard from the tread of many feet. Often families keep a box or trunk in one corner. There they keep dress-up clothes and other valuables they might have.

The life of the *fellahin* in Hussein's village is very hard. Hussein is already old enough to help his father and the other men irrigate the fields outside the village. They work the ground with hoes and sometimes even break up the clods of soil by hand. They plant beans, corn, rice, and other food crops. They grow cotton for a **cash crop.** A cash crop is a crop that is raised to sell for money to buy other things. Hussein's mother and sisters raise chickens and make butter and cheese to sell in the larger towns.

Part of the hard work in Hussein's village is raising the water from the canal that comes to them from the Nile River. In some villages the people can afford electric pumps to lift the water into their fields. But Hussein's ways of getting the water are almost as old as Egypt itself.

The picture shows the use of the Archimedes' (är′ kə mēd′ ēz) screw, an ancient way of lifting water for irrigation. The Egyptians also use water wheels with buckets on them

The Archimedes' screw is a device to raise water from canals to thirsty fields. As the worker turns the screw, it raises water several feet. The screw is faster than carrying water up the bank in buckets, but much slower than a modern pump. The screws have been used in the Middle East for over 2,000 years. They were invented by a man named Archimedes.

to lift water. Why would an irrigation pump be quicker?

Village life like this is common throughout the Middle East. Water is scarce, and the places where people can live are scattered a long way apart in the desert. Farmers cannot live separated from each other, scattered out across the land as in North America. Middle Eastern villages grow up near springs and oases in the desert and along the few rivers of the Middle East. Many villages do not have enough water to grow as many crops as does Hussein's village. These people must depend on their cattle and camels and on date palms for food.

Arab Clothing. One of the big differences between the Arabs and people in other parts of the world is the way they dress. Many Arabs who move to the cities begin to dress like Europeans or Americans. But most of the farmers in the villages and on the oases dress much as their fathers and mothers did long ago.

One thing that surprises many people about the Arabs is how much clothing they wear. Arab lands are hot. But Arabs are usually dressed from head to toe in long, loose garments that look like robes to us. The Arabs have learned that loose garments which cover as much as possible keep them cooler than if they wear few clothes. The clothing protects them from the hot sun and the drying winds. Arabs must think foreigners very strange for wearing few

clothes in hot weather. When the desert nights become cool, the same garments that keep the people cool in the daytime keep them warm at night.

The Arabs have also learned something from their forefathers about **modesty.** Modesty means keeping our bodies covered in public. Most Arabs would be horrified to think of uncovering their bodies in public as many foreigners do.

Hussein wears a long, striped cotton gown that is long-sleeved and reaches almost to the ankles. In

Egypt this garment is called a **djellaba** (jə lä′ bə). In Saudi Arabia, the long, flowing garment of the working man is called a *thawb* (thaub).

Arabs cover not only their bodies but their heads as well. The fellahin of Egypt often wrap long strips of cloth around their heads. This is called a turban. Some Arab men wear a red cap called a *fez*. In Saudi Arabia men wear a piece of cloth on their heads held on by a rope band.

These two men are Arabs. The man to the left wears the loose-fitting garment and the headdress that have been worn for hundreds of years in the Arab world. The other man, like many city people, wears the headdress with clothing like Europeans and Americans wear.

The Saudis call this headgear a *kef-fiyah* (kə fē′ ə).

Arab women also wear long garments that reach their feet. They nearly always cover their heads. In many places women also cover their faces with a veil. They especially do this in public.

Many Arabs like to show others that they are Arabs. One way they do this is to dress in the kind of clothing Arabs have worn for hundreds of years. Arab men who live in the cities often wear suits like men from Europe. But many of them still wear the *keffiyah*.

Gifts From the Arabs

Europeans and Americans have passed on many inventions and other gifts to the Arabs. Trucks and airplanes, for example, are replacing camels. The Arabs also have received useful gifts from other places. But did you know that the Arabs have passed on to us many gifts? We use them almost every day.

The Gift of Numerals. We can thank the Arabs for giving us our number system. They did not invent it, but brought it to us from India. Before the time of Christ, the people of India learned to count using nine numerals for 1, 2, 3, 4, 5, 6, 7, 8, and 9. About two or three hundred years after Christ was on earth, the Indians added the zero to their nine numerals. Remember that a **numeral** is a sign or picture that stands for a number. The sign that stands for the idea of "three" is 3. This sign is a numeral.

You remember that over a thousand years ago the Arabs conquered many countries far from the Middle East. One of them was India. Arab traders liked the number system used by the Indians. They brought the idea to the Middle East and to all the other lands they conquered. Europeans learned about this way of writing numbers from the Arabs.

One thousand years ago the Arabs wrote their numerals this way: ١ ٢ ٣ ٤ ٥ ٦ ٧ ٨ ٩ ٠ . Which of these numerals look something like the ones we use today?

A thousand years ago the Europeans were still using Roman numerals. The ancient Romans from Italy had used these numerals. Letters of the alphabet were used for different numbers. The Roman numerals worked very well for simple counting and adding. But they were hard to work with when people wanted to multiply or divide.

How would a person go about multiplying these two Roman numerals—XLVIII x XXXVI? Using Arabic numerals is much more simple—48 x 36. Far fewer numerals are needed.

We call our wonderful way of writing numbers the Arabic numerals. Some people call them the Hindu-Arabic numerals. Hindus were the people of India who passed their numerals on to the Arabs.

The Gift of Words. Many words have come into our language from peoples who lived long ago. Over half of our English words came from the ancient Romans. The Romans also gave us our alphabet and Roman numerals.

Many useful words have come to us from the language of the Arabs. What kinds of words have come to us from Arabic? You will not be surprised to learn that some of these words have to do with numbers and math. After all, the Arabs gave us our numerals. The word *algebra* comes from Arabic. Algebra is a special form of math. The word *check,* for paying money, is from Arabic. Other Arabic words include *tariff* (a tax) and *almanac.*

The Arabs were careful students of science and medicine hundreds of years ago. They passed on much of their knowledge to us. Some Arabic words that have come to us have to do with science, such as *alcohol* and *alkali* (a salt).

Another interesting word from Arabic is *alfalfa.* Alfalfa is a plant grown for cattle to eat. Not only is the word a gift from the Arabs, but the plant itself is a gift from the Arab countries. Alfalfa has been raised for thousands of years in the Middle East. The people of the Middle East passed it on to us. The Arabic word for *alfalfa* means "the best fodder." Fodder is chopped plants used as food for animals. Alfalfa really was the best fodder for animals to eat in the ancient Middle East.

Alfalfa provides good food for farm animals. Where was alfalfa first grown? What is the meaning of the word alfalfa?

What Do You Say?

1. a. What do most Arabs look like—their hair, skin color, etc.? b. Why do not all Arabs look like this?

2. What are fellahin, and in what country do they live?

3. Why is the life of the fellahin so hard?

4. Explain the difference between a food crop and a cash crop.

5. Why do most Egyptians live beside the Nile River?

6. Name at least two reasons why the Arabs cover themselves so completely with clothing.

7. Describe the following pieces of Arab clothing: a. djellaba b. thawb c. fez d. keffiyah

8. a. Name two important gifts we have received from the Arabs. b. How have these gifts helped us?

What Does the Bible Say?

1. Read Isaiah 19:4-7. a. What do these verses say would happen to the Nile River? b. What would happen to plant life in Egypt when this takes place?

2. What does the Bible say about how people should dress? (Find the answer in 1 Timothy 2:9.)

3. Reading about Hussein's home should make you more thankful and satisfied with what God has given you. Read 1 Timothy 6:8

331

and list some things you have beyond what this verse mentions.

4. a. Read Isaiah 42:8. What does God say He will not give to graven images? b. What does 1 Corinthians 10:14 say about idolatry?

Chapter Nineteen Review

Using Globes and Maps

1. Draw a map of the Middle East using the block method of drawing you learned earlier in this book. Color each country a different color and print its name. Put the word *Arab* under the name of each Arab country.

2. Choose a country in the Middle East that you would like to know more about. Make a booklet about the country with the name of the country and its flag on the outside. Inside include a map of the country with the capital and large cities shown. On the following pages, write in any interesting information you would like to include, or draw pictures of products of the country. Use an encyclopedia or book on the country to find needed information.

New Words and Terms

From the list of new words and terms, answer each question.

a. Arabs	k. cash crop
b. Islam	l. food crop
c. Mohammed	m. modesty
d. Arabic	n. djellaba
e. idol	o. thawb
f. holy	p. fez
g. Allah	q. keffiyah
h. Koran	r. Arabic numerals
i. mosque	s. alfalfa
j. fellah	

1. What name do the Muslims use for God?

2. What do we call our system of numerals—1, 2, 3, 4, etc.?

3. What is the name of the bible of the Muslims?

4. What is an Egyptian farm worker called?

5. What is the name for the red cap worn by some Arab men?

6. What is a crop grown mainly for food called?

7. What is a crop called which is grown mainly to sell to someone else?

8. What fodder crop was first grown in the Middle East?

9. What is the religion of the Muslims?

10. What long garment is worn by the Egyptian fellahin?

11. In what kind of building do Muslims worship?

12. Which word means "pure and set apart for God"?

13. Who first came from Arabia as a people and now live in many parts of the Middle East?

14. What term describes the practice of keeping our bodies covered in public?

15. What is a statue of a false god called?

16. What do the Arabs of Saudi Arabia wear on their heads?

17. What language is spoken in most of the countries of the Middle East?

18. Who first taught the religion of Islam?

19. What long, flowing garment is worn by men in Saudi Arabia?

alike? c. What language do most Arabs speak?

2. a. What is the religion of most Arab people? b. What does this religion teach about idols? c. About fighting in war? d. About Jesus Christ?

3. a. Why is it so hard for Muslims to accept Christ and become Christians? b. What can people who believe in Jesus Christ do to witness to Muslims?

4. Describe the Egyptian fellahin. In your description, try to answer the following questions: What kind of work do they do? What kind of houses do they live in? How do they dress?

5. Name two reasons why many of the Arabs dress in long, flowing clothing.

6. a. Name two important gifts the Arabs gave to us. b. How often do you use each of these gifts?

Thinking Together

1. a. What is an Arab? b. Why do Arabs not all dress alike and look

For You to Do

1. Read the encyclopedia article on one of the Middle Eastern countries. List ten important facts about the country.

20. Homeland of the Arabs

The Country of Saudi Arabia

The largest block of land in the Middle East is the Arabian Peninsula. On this dry and barren land the Arabs have lived since the time of Abraham about four thousand years ago.

The Arabian Peninsula is somewhat larger than the part of the United States that lies east of the Mississippi River. The peninsula is divided into seven Arab countries. One of these countries, Bahrain (bä rān') is an island just off the east coast of Saudi Arabia. The other six

countries are Qatar (kä' tär'), Kuwait (kü wāt'), the United Arab Emirates (e mir' its), Oman (ō män'), Saudi (sou' dē) Arabia, and the country called Yemen (yem' ən). Yemen was once two separate countries. They became one country in 1990.

Find all seven of these countries on the above map of the Arabian Peninsula. Which is the smallest country? Which is farthest south? Which is by far the largest country?

Saudi Arabia is a large country. Imagine a country as large as

Ontario and Manitoba together. Saudi Arabia may not look so large on a map of the world because we are used to looking at large maps of Canada and the United States. Saudi Arabia is about 1,200 miles (1,950 kilometers) long north to south. East to west it is some 750 miles (1,200 kilometers) wide.

This map shows the Arabian Peninsula placed over the United States and Canada. Notice how many states and provinces are covered or partly covered by the map of the homeland of the Arabs.

Saudi Arabia is named for a family that has ruled the country for much of the last 200 years. The Saud family first ruled the area around the capital city of Riyadh (rē yäd'). By the early 1900s, the Sauds became powerful rulers. By 1925 they ruled most of Arabia. They named their country the Kingdom of Saudi Arabia. The Saud family chooses one of its members to be king.

Saudi Arabia is larger than many states or provinces in the United States or Canada, but it is a vastly different land. We will study the land and the people of this large Arab country.

The Land in Saudi Arabia

Saudi Arabia is a large, dry, and mostly barren land. Some people think of the country as one big, sandy desert, but that is not true. The Saudi Arabians think of their country as divided into many different parts. They speak of a number of different deserts. And not all their country is desert.

Study the map of the regions of Saudi Arabia on page 336. As you continue to read, find each place on the map.

The Eastern Lowlands. If you could travel by jeep or by camel into Arabia from the Persian Gulf, you would think of the country as a flat, rocky desert. Some sandy areas are scattered here and there. But the Eastern Lowlands also has many fertile oases with miles of desert between. The al-Hasa Oasis you have read about is found in this area. In fact, the Saudis call the Eastern Lowlands the province of Hasa. Most of the precious petroleum found in Arabia is found under the Eastern Lowlands.

The Central Plateau. The largest land region of Saudi Arabia is the Central Plateau. This land is called the Najd (najd). This region is hilly

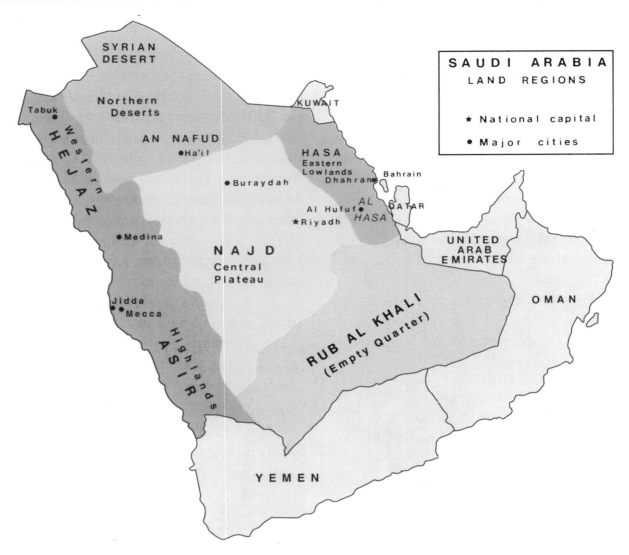

The map shows the land regions of Saudi Arabia, with labels including SYRIAN DESERT, Northern Deserts, AN NAFUD, Western HEJAZ, NAJD Central Plateau, HASA Eastern Lowlands, AL HASA, Highlands ASIR, and RUB AL KHALI (Empty Quarter). Cities marked include Tabuk, Ha'il, Buraydah, Dhahran, Bahrain, Al Hufuf, Riyadh, Medina, Jidda, Mecca, and Qatar. Neighboring countries shown are KUWAIT, QATAR, UNITED ARAB EMIRATES, OMAN, and YEMEN.

SAUDI ARABIA
LAND REGIONS

★ National capital
● Major cities

and much higher above sea level than the Eastern Lowlands. The Central Plateau is all desert with many small oases. The capital of the country, Riyadh, is in the Najd. The Najd is rocky and gravelly with little plant life except on the oases.

The Northern Deserts. Across the northern part of the Central Plateau lie low mountains. North of these mountains is a vast sand desert called An Nafud (nə füd′). Farther north are more deserts and the great Syrian Desert. The Syrian Desert also forms a large part of Jordan, Syria, and Iraq.

The Western Highlands. The Central Plateau becomes higher and higher as we travel west. Finally we reach the highest mountains in Saudi Arabia. These mountains rise from 6,000 to 10,000 feet (1,800 to 3,000 meters) above sea level. These mountains often rise sharply from the Red Sea with very little lowland along the shore. In the south there is more lowland along the sea. But the lowland is seldom wider than 15 or 20 miles (25 or 30 kilometers).

Most of the Western Highlands

336

are also desert. But rich farmland is found in the southern part of the highlands. This region is called Asir (a sir'). This is the only part of Saudi Arabia that is not a desert.

The Empty Quarter. The most mysterious and unknown part of Saudi Arabia is the vast southern desert called the Rub al Khali (rúb al käl' ē). Its name in Arabic means "the empty quarter." This is the driest and hottest of all the Arabian deserts. It is sometimes called "the furnace of the world." Almost nothing grows there, and no people live in the Empty Quarter. Can you see how it gets its name?

These rocky canyons are in the desert land of western Saudi Arabia. Why do you think there is no green on this picture?

The Empty Quarter is almost as large as the state of Texas or the province of Alberta. We can hardly imagine a sandy desert so large. In some places the Empty Quarter is nearly flat. In other places the sand dunes rise to one thousand feet (300 meters) high.

The Empty Quarter lay unexplored until 1940 to 1950. During that time the first good maps were made of the land. Some of the explorers hoped to find the ruins of a beautiful city in this barren land. Some of the desert wanderers of southern Arabia liked to tell stories about a great and wealthy city that lay somewhere in the Empty Quarter. But the explorers were disappointed. They found no such city.

The Climate of Saudi Arabia

Saudi Arabia is a very dry land, but it is home for over 12 million people. God has provided enough natural resources for all these people to live. Saudi Arabia is also a hot land.

Most of Saudi Arabia is true desert. Less than 4 inches (10 centimeters) of rain usually falls in a year. Parts of the country may have no rainfall for two or three years in a row. This is especially true in the Empty Quarter. Asir, in the southwest, is the only part of the country to receive much rainfall. The summer winds from the Arabian Sea and the Red Sea bring from 12 to 20 inches (30 to 50 centimeters) of rain.

Palm trees and grasses grow in the Asir region of Saudi Arabia. Why does more plant life grow in this part of Saudi Arabia than in any other region?

Many small dams have been built along the wadis and in deep mountain valleys to collect as much of this water as possible. The rain often comes fast and hard. Much of it runs off and does little good. Farmers have learned to terrace the hillsides to hold back some of the water. Wadis can become raging rivers for a few hours, or even days, after sudden rainstorms. But for most of the year they are dry.

Farming in Saudi Arabia

In Chapter 18 you were introduced to farming in a desert oasis. You learned about the largest oasis in Saudi Arabia. Until not many years ago the only farming in Saudi Arabia was done on oases or in the mountain province of Asir. But today things are changing. Large aquifers or underground lakes have been found. Pumps can bring this water to places that were only sand and gravel before. Irrigation systems must be used to spread the water on fields.

Near the capital city of Riyadh are dairy farms. Underground water is used for the cattle and for crops. Huge circle-shaped fodder fields are irrigated by long, revolving irrigation arms. The cows are kept in covered buildings where the temperature is kept cool enough for the cows to give the most milk. In other places laying hens are kept in cooled chicken houses much as they are in America.

Saudi Arabians are beginning to use greenhouses to raise crops. A mist of water and large fans keep the temperature just right for growing such things as tomatoes, cucumbers, and melons. Sometimes the vegetables are planted in sand that would not usually grow crops. Water and plenty of fertilizer are added. Some greenhouse farmers are using a modern method of plant growing called **hydroponics** (hī′ drə pän′ iks). They use no soil. The plants grow

338

In a hydroponic greenhouse, the white plastic pipes below the plants carry water and plant foods to the plants. Large, delicious tomatoes can be grown this way.

from plastic tubes with running water in them. Plant food is dissolved in the water. The plants grow rapidly. They produce delicious vegetables without any soil.

Saudi Arabia produces more crops than ever. More land is farmed than ever before. But the country still does not produce enough food to feed all its people. Saudi Arabia must import or bring in over half its food from other countries. More and more food is needed to feed people in the country's growing cities.

3. a. What is the Empty Quarter and where is it located? b. How large is it? c. Why is it sometimes called the "furnace of the world"?

4. a. Where is the only part of Saudi Arabia that is not desert? b. How much rain falls there? c. Find out from your parent or teacher how much rain falls in your community in a year. d. Is this more or less rainfall than the wettest part of Saudi Arabia?

5. Name some new ways of farming that have come to Saudi Arabia.

What Do You Say?

1. a. How long and wide is Saudi Arabia? b. With what part of North America does it compare in size?

2. How did Saudi Arabia get its name?

What Does the Bible Say?

1. The Bible speaks of Arabia a number of times. Read Ezekiel 27:21. What were some of the products of Arabia in Bible times?

2. To whom was the Gospel preached very early in the history of the church? (Read Acts 2:11 and Galatians 1:17.)

3. How does the Bible describe deserts? (See Jeremiah 2:6 and Numbers 20:4, 5). Remember that the word *wilderness* often means "desert" in the Bible.

The People of Saudi Arabia

In 1974 the rulers of Saudi Arabia took a **census.** A census is a count of the number of people who live in a country. This census counted over seven million people in Saudi Arabia. No one is sure how many people live in Saudi Arabia today. But the United Nations guesses, or estimates, that number to be over 19 million people.

Today the people of Saudi Arabia are often called Saudis. The word *Saudi* was once used only for people from the Saud family. This family rules the country of Saudi Arabia. Nearly all Saudis are Arabs. Almost all of them are Muslims. Saudi Arabia is the homeland of Mohammed and the religion he started. Some people live and work in Saudi Arabia who are not Arabs or Muslims. But they are not citizens of the country.

About four million Saudis live in cities. About three million more live in farm villages or on oases. Most of the rest spend at least part of the year wandering in the deserts.

The Bedouin—the Desert Wanderers. Many of the people of Arabia and the Middle East have long been wanderers in the deserts. Abraham lived in a large tent. His family

These scrubby plants come up after a brief shower in the deserts of Saudi Arabia. Desert wanderers depend on such plant life to feed their hungry animals. Many animals starve or are killed to eat in years when the brief rains fail to come.

Interesting Facts About Saudi Arabia

Population: Over 19 million.

Chief Products: petroleum, camels, citrus fruit, dates, goats, cement.

The Most Petroleum: Saudi Arabia has the largest reserves of petroleum of any country in the world.

Size: Saudi Arabia is three times as large as Texas or Alberta.

Little Water: There is no permanent river or lake in all Saudi Arabia.

The People: Almost all the people of Saudi Arabia are Arabs.

A Moslem Country: Almost all Saudis are Moslems. No Christian churches are allowed in the country. Christians may not enter the city of Mecca.

A King Rules: Saudi Arabia is one of the few countries actually ruled by a king.

The Largest: The largest airport in the world is near Jidda, on the west coast of Saudi Arabia.

moved from place to place to seek water and pasture for their animals.

We call such wandering people nomads. Nomads are found in many parts of the world. Nomads are often found where food and water are scarce. Arab nomads are called the **Bedouin** (bed′ ə wən). This name comes from an Arabic word which means "desert dwellers." No one knows for sure how many Bedouin are left in Saudi Arabia. Some have guessed that one-half million or more still wander in the deserts. The government is trying to get the Bedouin to settle in farming villages and on oases.

The Bedouin have a hard life. If desert rainstorms do not come for a long time, some of their animals will starve. The Bedouin often visit villages and oases to find water and food. Sometimes there is trouble between the Bedouin and the village dwellers.

Many people in Saudi Arabia admire the Bedouin. They admire the hard work they do and the difficult life they lead. Most Arabs living in cities remember that their ancestors were once Bedouin.

An interesting custom found among some of the wealthy Arabs in the city is to send their sons for a stay among the Bedouin. The boys learn the ways of desert life and how to work hard. They learn to live without all the nice things money can buy.

The Saud family that now rules Saudi Arabia was once a Bedouin

These Arabs are looking under the hood of their car, an invention that uses much of the petroleum found under the sands of Saudi Arabia. Fifty years ago, most Saudis used camels to ride from one place to another. Times have changed in a country that is now rich.

tribe. Now, of course, the family has settled down to city life. The king of Saudi Arabia lives in a palace, not in a tent. He has palaces in several different cities. His main palace is in Riyadh, the capital of Saudi Arabia. He also has a palace in Mecca where he often goes to worship.

The king of Saudi Arabia still dresses in long, flowing robes as did his Bedouin forefathers. Of course, his clothing is of nicer material than the rough camel hair robes of many Bedouin.

Changing Life in Saudi Arabia

Saudi Arabia is changing fast. Until the 1930s, the country had changed little for hundreds of years. Most of the people were poor farmers or Bedouin.

In the 1930s, the king of Saudi Arabia let an American oil company explore for petroleum. In 1938, the explorers found large underground pools of oil. Ten years later Saudi Arabia was fast becoming a rich nation. In the 1970s, the price of petroleum rose rapidly. Saudi Arabia received billions of dollars every year for its oil.

Saudi Arabia began to build modern buildings in its cities. It built the largest airport in the world at the city of Jidda (jid′ ə). Many of the Bedouin have now moved to the growing cities to find jobs. Their whole way of life has changed.

Petroleum has provided most of the money to spend on all these improvements. The changes in farming would not have happened had it not been for petroleum and the money that comes with it.

Some of the money that has come to Saudi Arabia has been wasted. Some of the so-called farm projects were really gardens for the rich to enjoy. But for the most part, the rulers are trying to prepare the country for the time when the petroleum will run out. The country must prepare to raise more of its own food. When the petroleum is gone, it will not have so much money to buy food from other countries. The country must be prepared to give jobs to its people. It must help them learn to live without so much money.

How will Saudi Arabia be able to do this? Only time will tell. Some people fear that when the oil is gone, thousands of people will be out of jobs. Will some who live in the cities need to go back to the Bedouin life? Will fighting break out between the rich and the poor? This has happened in the past. Saudi Arabia may face hard and dangerous times ahead.

Good Changes—or Bad? We would say that many of the changes that have come to Saudi Arabia have been good. New ways of farming have helped. The people have more and better food. New hospitals, schools, and airports have been built. Trucks, cars, and machinery have made life easier.

But some of the things money can buy are not always good for people. Some Saudis have become very rich and have not shared with the poor as they should. The rich can be seen riding around in sporty or classy American cars.

Money has also brought the movies and television. For a long time many Saudi leaders said no to such things. They were not Christians, but they still realized the dangers. Many movies and TV programs coming to Saudi Arabia from other countries would show people drinking alcoholic drinks. The leaders knew this would cause some of their people to want to drink too. They also knew that Muslims would see people without Arab clothing, and maybe they would begin to dress as foreigners.

But television and movies did come to Saudi Arabia. The leaders have tried to be careful what they let the people see. Still, Saudis have been changed by television. Not all the changes have been good. Many Saudis drink strong drink and dress immodestly in spite of what their forefathers taught them.

One sad thing about these changes is the people who help bring them. Many Europeans and Americans who say they are Christians have brought drinking and other sins to Saudi Arabia. The Saudis do not know that true Christians do not do such things. No wonder Saudi rulers have made strict laws against Christianity. Missionaries may not enter Saudi Arabia to tell about Christ. Christian churches may not be built in the country. No Christian is allowed to enter the city of Mecca. A Christian found there could be punished by death! True Christians can pray that Saudi

Arabia will open its doors to the Gospel. Christians who meet Saudis or who visit Saudi Arabia can be good examples of how Christians should live. Only then can Saudis see that true Christians do not want to bring harmful changes to their country.

What Do You Say?

1. a. About how many people live in Saudi Arabia? b. How many of these live in cities?

2. What is a *census?*

3. a. Who are the Bedouin? b. About how many Bedouin still wander in the deserts? c. What do the others do?

4. a. Name some changes that have come to Saudi Arabia. b. Name some changes that have not been good and tell why not.

What Does the Bible Say?

1. The Bedouin, the nomads of the Middle East, have been around for a long time. The Bible talks about such wanderers who moved from place to place. Name at least two famous Bible people who were nomads.

2. Read Hebrews 11:24, 25. What did Moses choose instead of the pleasures of sin? God will reward those who suffer for Him.

3. The Bible speaks of changes that people can make both for good and for bad. Read each of the following verses and tell what kind of change is being described.

    a. 2 Corinthians 3:18
    b. 2 Timothy 3:13
    c. 2 Peter 3:17

Chapter Twenty Review

Using Globes and Maps

1. Draw or trace a map of the Arabian Peninsula. Using colored pencils, shade each country in a different color. Label the countries in all CAPITAL letters. Show where each capital city is with a large dot or a small star. Write the name of the capital in smaller letters.

2. Make a booklet telling about each of the countries of the Arabian Peninsula. Using stencils, letter the name of the country on one side of a sheet. On the other side draw a small map of the country with the capital labeled. Also draw a flag of the country above or below the map. On a second sheet list the population of the country, its main products, and any other interesting information you can find.

3. In a large, flat metal pan make a sand map of the Arabian Peninsula. Use an encyclopedia article on Arabia or the map on page 334, showing the mountains. Use sand and gravel for the land. Use water with blue food coloring for seas. Use small buttons for the cities. Print the names of countries and cities on small strips of posterboard or heavy paper.

New Words and Terms

From the list in the next column fill in the blanks with the correct word or words.

a. Saud
b. Hasa
c. the furnace of the world
d. Bedouin
e. Rub al Khali
f. nomads
g. Riyadh
h. Najd
i. Yemen
j. census
k. An Nafud
l. Saudi

1. The Rub al Khali in Saudi Arabia is sometimes called _____.

2. _____ are people who wander about rather than living in one place.

3. _____ is the name for a person from Saudi Arabia.

4. The nomads of the Middle East are called _____.

5. A _____ is a count of the number of people in a place.

6. _____ is the name of the large family that rules the country of Saudi Arabia.

7. Another name for the eastern province of Saudi Arabia is _____.

8. The _____ is the desert plateau of central Saudi Arabia.

9. _____ is the capital of Saudi Arabia.

10. _____ is a desert in northern Saudi Arabia.

11. _____ is a country along the southern edge of the Arabian Peninsula.

12. _____ is the largest desert in Saudi Arabia.

6. Name some ways petroleum has helped change Saudi Arabia.

7. How can Christians be good witnesses to the people of Saudi Arabia?

1. a. Name the seven countries of the Arabian Peninsula. b. Which is an island? c. Which is a small peninsula? d. Which is the largest?

2. How large is Saudi Arabia?

3. a. Name the main land regions of Saudi Arabia. b. Name the only part of the country that is not desert. c. How much rain usually falls there each year?

4. Why are the people of Saudi Arabia often called Saudis?

5. a. What is a *nomad*? b. What are the nomads of the Middle East called?

1. Collect pictures from magazines, newspapers, or books that show life in the Arabian Peninsula. Perhaps with what you and your classmates collect, you could make a special scrapbook or bulletin board display. Be sure you have permission before you cut out your pictures. You may need to bring a whole book or magazine to class.

Northern Africa— Lands of the Desert

What you will learn . . . in unit seven

Where can you find the world's largest desert? Where can you find the world's longest river? Where can you find the greatest variety of wild animals? Where are the most gold and diamonds found? Where are most of the world's cocoa beans, tapioca plants, and yams raised?

Only one place on earth answers all these questions—the continent of Africa. Africa is a vast continent. It is the second largest continent after Asia. Africa is larger then the United States, Western Europe, China, and India put together.

We will tell the story of Africa in two units. Why should we spend so much time on Africa? Could we not discuss it in one short chapter? No, because there is so much to tell about the vast continent of Africa and its many different people.

We will begin this unit by looking at the geography of all of Africa. Then we will look at the lands and peoples of the northern part of Africa. In Chapter 23 we will look at one particular country of northern Africa. Then we will learn a bit of the history of northern Africa and what happened to Christians there.

As we learn more about Africa, we will understand its people better. This will help us to love the people of Africa more. May we obey the command found in I John 4:7, 11. "Let us love one another: for love is of God; and every one that loveth is born of God, and knoweth God . . . if God so loved us, we ought also to love one another."

In many parts of Africa, groups of people set out on trips to hunt or photograph Africa's wild animals. We call such a hunting trip a **safari** (sə fär′ ē). We are beginning a safari to learn many interesting things about Africa.

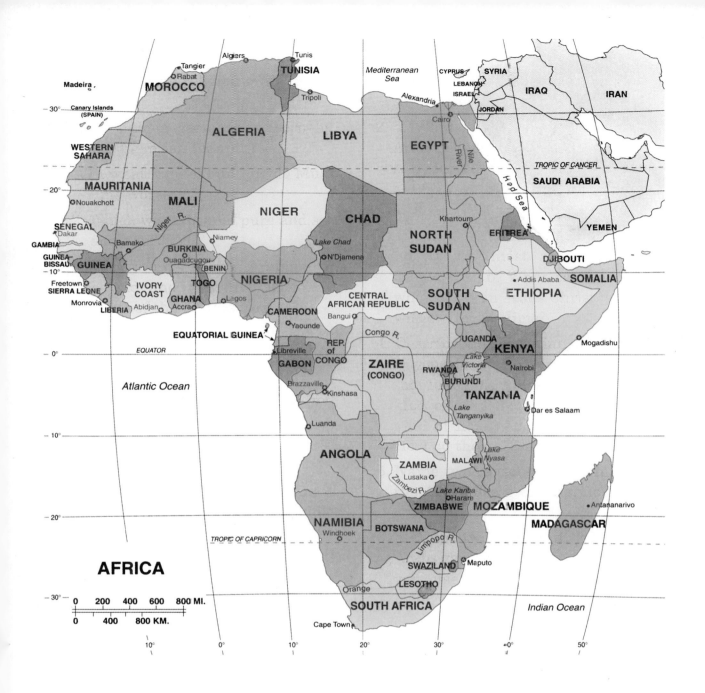

21. The Lands of Northern Africa

A Vast Continent

Africa is indeed a large continent. From its northern tip to its southernmost point it is 5,000 miles (8,100 kilometers). At the widest point, Africa is about 3,000 miles (4,900 kilometers) wide.

Look at the map of Africa on

page 349. How would you describe the shape of this continent? Some people think it looks like a huge, fat question mark. For many people Africa is like a question mark in their minds. They know very little about this second-largest continent.

Find the Atlantic Ocean to the west of Africa. Notice the part of Africa that sticks the farthest out into the Atlantic. This is sometimes called the **bulge of Africa.**

Now look to the southeast of Africa. Which ocean washes the east coast of Africa? Do you see the large island that lies about 240 miles (390 kilometers) southeast of Africa? This

island is Madagascar. It is the fourth largest island in the world. Only the islands of Greenland, Borneo, and New Guinea are larger. Madagascar is almost 1,000 miles (1,600 kilometers) long.

Now look to the northeast of Africa. Find the Red Sea. This long, narrow sea separates Africa from the Arabian Peninsula. You studied about Arabia in the last unit.

Directly north of Africa lies the Mediterranean Sea. This sea separates Africa from Europe. Near the southern tip of Spain, Europe and Africa are only nine miles (15 kilometers) apart.

Another interesting thing about Africa is its even coastline. Very few bays or seas reach into the continent. Compare this even coastline with that of southern Europe just to the north. In Europe many peninsulas jut far out into the oceans and seas.

Only in the last two hundred years have many people from the outside seen the heart of Africa. In the late 1800s, white people first journeyed across Africa by using its great rivers. The first European to climb Mount Kenya did so in 1899. Mount Kenya is the second highest mountain in Africa. Mount Kilimanjaro is Tanzania's highest.

Africa—High and Low. Why was Africa a "question mark" to the rest of the world for so long? The geography of Africa helps tell us why.

This map compares the size of Africa to that of Canada and the United States. Which is larger, Africa or the United States and Canada? Note that the distance across Africa from northwest to southeast is about the same as the distance from Alaska to Florida in North America.

The highest mountains in Africa are found in eastern Africa. These mountains are high, but not nearly as high as many of the mountains in Asia and the Americas.

Mountains and highlands cover much of Africa. In many places the mountains come almost to the sea. Very little lowland lies near the sea around most of Africa. Today people can cross Africa by airplane or by roads. Only a hundred years ago it was hard to travel very far inland in Africa. Ships from other lands tried to travel up Africa's rivers. Not far inland the ships would reach higher land. Here the rivers came tumbling over rocks and steep places. The ships could go no farther.

These places where rivers drop from highlands to lowlands are called **waterfalls.** On some rivers the falls are **cataracts** (kat′ ə rakts′). Cataracts are low falls scattered over a long stretch of river. Ships cannot sail upriver over a falls or cataract. In some places people build canals to take the ships around the falls.

Until one hundred years ago, there were no roads to help people travel across Africa. No roads led from the coasts to the middle or interior of the continent.

Some geographers like to divide Africa into two main parts. They are High Africa and Low Africa. Low Africa is the northern and western part of the continent. High Africa is the eastern and southern part. Study the map of Africa to find these two parts of Africa. In this unit we will be studying a large part of Low Africa.

Most of Africa is made up of plateaus. In Low Africa, the plateau is from 500 to 2,000 feet (150 to 600 meters) above sea level. High Africa, on the other hand, has many plateaus that are 3,000 feet (900 meters) above sea level.

Over most of Africa, the plateaus reach nearly to the oceans. Both Low Africa and High Africa have only narrow strips of lowland along the sea. In some places

351

These two pictures show you the difference between a cataract and a waterfall. At a waterfall, water falls many feet from one level to another. At a cataract, the water falls more gradually over rocks and rough places.

mountain cliffs reach right to the sea. This, of course, is quite different from the Americas. Eastern North America and eastern South America have much lowland near the sea.

Geography of Northern Africa

Look at the part of Africa we will be studying in this unit. The countries in this section are shown in brighter color. How many countries are there in northern Africa? What are their names? Most of these countries lie on low plateaus. Only in Egypt can one travel far inland before reaching hills and higher land.

Most of this huge region of Africa is flat or slightly hilly. High mountains rise in a few places. But these mountain ranges are not nearly as high or long as the large mountain ranges of the Americas or Asia. Mountains are found in only a few parts of northern Africa. The Atlas Mountains are near the Mediterranean Sea in the northernmost part of Africa. The Atlas are the largest group of mountains in northern Africa. They are about 1,500 miles (2,400 kilometers) long and about 200 miles (320 kilometers) wide at the widest. The highest mountain in northern Africa is found here. It is 13,685 feet (4,165 meters) above sea level. The Tibesti (tə bes′ tē) Mountains are located in the northern part of the country of Chad. The Ahaggar (ə häg′ ər) Mountains are in southern

Algeria. These are not large mountain ranges. But they are the only
other really high mountains of
northern Africa.

The land in northern Africa looks
very different from many other lands.
It is a vast desert. A visitor can clearly
see the shape of the land because
there are no forests to cover the bare
ground. If you could fly over northern
Africa, you would see a vast brown
land. Here and there are places that
look something like riverbeds. But
you do not see a drop of water. In some
places you can see vast seas of sand.
You see few rocks and almost no plant
life. These great seas of sand are
called **ergs.** Some of the vast ergs in
northern Africa are fairly flat. Some
are covered with high sand dunes.

Scattered through this desert area
are low places called **depressions.**

The countries of northern Africa are shown
in a darker color on the above map. Make
sure that you are able to name all of these
countries before you finish studying this
unit.

This Egyptian boy is standing
in a sugarcane field. In northern Africa such good crops
can grow only along the few
rivers or on desert oases or
low spots where there is
underground water.

If northern Africa were a wet land, these depressions would be filled with water. But these depressions are nearly always dry. A few of them have shallow, salty lakes. Some of these salty lakes dried up long ago. This left salty places in some depressions. These salty places are called **chotts** (shots).

Some depressions in northern Africa are very large. The largest one is found in Egypt. It is called the Qattara (kə tär′ ə) Depression. It is almost as large as the state of New Jersey! This depression is about 200 miles (320 kilometers) long and about 70 miles (110 kilometers) wide at the widest. The Qattara Depression is also the lowest point in Egypt and northern Africa. It lies 436 feet (133 meters) below sea level. There are a few oases in the Qattara as well as in other depressions. The Egyptian government hopes someday to pump more water into this depression and farm the land.

What Do You Say?

1. Name one reason why we should learn more about Africa.

2. a. What is High Africa? b. Low Africa?

3. Why has it been difficult for people in the past to travel deep into Africa?

4. Describe the geography of northern Africa.

5. What are ergs, chotts, and depressions?

What Does the Bible Say?

1. a. What is the most important thing Christians can share with the poor in Africa or anywhere else? (Read Luke 4:18a.) b. Read Luke 3:11. What are some things we can give to those in need? c. According to Ephesians 4:28, what is one very important reason why we should work?

2. The continent of Africa is not named in the Bible. But many places and people in Africa are named. Read the following verses. See if you can find the location of each place on a map of northern Africa.

   a. II Kings 19:9
   b. Matthew 2:13
   c. Acts 2:10 (Egypt and Libya)

This is a view along the Nile River near Aswan, Egypt. Here the strip of green along the river is very narrow. The desert lies beyond. From an airplane, the Nile resembles a ribbon of blue with a narrow strip of green on both sides. The dry, brown desert lies not far away.

North Africa's Great River

North Africa has very few lakes or rivers. A few short rivers flow from the Atlas Mountains to the Mediterranean Sea. The longest of these rivers is only a few hundred miles long. But northern Africa has one great river that breaks the otherwise rocky, barren land. This river is the mighty Nile that flows north through Egypt. The water in the Nile comes from the rainy lands of eastern Africa. Egypt is part of Africa. You may remember that Egypt is also considered to be part of the Middle East.

If you would travel the three thousand miles across northern Africa, you would fly for hours over dry, brown, barren land. You might begin to think, *Will I ever see trees and green fields and water again?* Just as you almost give up hope, you look ahead and see what looks like a green ribbon in the brown desert below you. As you draw near, you would see that this green ribbon is the irrigated farmland on either side of a river, the Nile. If it were not for the Nile, Egypt would be one vast desert. Few people could live there.

The Nile is an unusual river for North Africa. From where it empties into the Mediterranean Sea, boats can travel southward up the Nile for well over 500 miles (800 kilometers) to the first cataract or falls near the town of Aswan (a swän′). The Aswan High Dam holds back the floodwaters of the Nile and forms Lake Nassar (näs′ ər). **Locks** allow boats to move around the dam and up to the lake level. Once on Lake Nassar, they can travel south up the lake for 300 miles (480 kilometers), well into the country south of Egypt called North Sudan (sü dan′).

In North Sudan, the land slowly rises. Eventually, more cataracts make travel by boat impossible. But the Nile stretches back through the Sudan up many high waterfalls to its **source** in the mountains and

355

This view of Lake Nassar is taken from the Aswan Dam in Egypt. About how long is this lake? What does this lake do to the floodwaters of the Nile River?

The World's Greatest Desert

In Unit 6 you learned that all of northern Africa is desert. You learned that the desert continues across the Middle East all the way to India, deep inside Asia. You learned that different parts of this desert have different names. The same is true in northern Africa. In different countries the desert has different names. In Egypt, for example, the desert east of the Nile River is called the Arabian Desert. Why do you think it is called by that name? Notice what country lies across the Red Sea from this desert.

The desert west of the Nile is called the Western Desert. In Libya (lib′ ē ə), to the west of Egypt, the desert is called the Libyan Desert. But if you would travel across these deserts, you could not tell where one began and the other ended. If it were not for the Nile River cutting through the desert, you could not tell where the Western Desert ended and the Arabian Desert began.

These many deserts are part of one vast desert that stretches all the way across Africa. The Atlantic Ocean washes the western edge of this desert. The desert stretches east for over 3,000 miles (4,800 kilometers) to the shores of the Red Sea. The desert is more than 1,000 miles (1,600 kilometers) from north to south. We call the whole desert the Sahara (sə har′ ə). Sahara comes from an Arabic word which means "desert or wilderness." When the

lakes of High Africa. One of its main sources is Lake Victoria, the largest lake in Africa. The source of a river is the place it starts, usually a spring, small stream, or lake.

The Nile is the longest river in the world. It flows for over 4,000 miles (6,500 kilometers). The river begins over one mile (1½ kilometers) above sea level. It travels about 1,000 miles (1,600 kilometers) to reach land that is fairly flat. Then it flows gently toward the sea with low falls or cataracts here and there. The Nile flows northward nearly all of its route.

No other African river can be traveled so far into the continent. But even this river has rough going when one reaches the higher falls and cataracts. Explorers did not reach the beginning, or source, of the Nile until about 1875.

This man is plowing in the Sahara with a camel. Where do you think the water will come from to irrigate the crops that will be planted here?

Bible speaks about someone going into the wilderness, it is speaking of the desert.

Do you remember the definition of desert? It is a land where less than ten inches (25 centimeters) of rain falls in a year. But much of the Sahara is far drier than this. In many places less than two inches (five centimeters) of rain falls in a year. Some places go for years without any rain. Suddenly, the place

Not all of the Sahara is covered with sand dunes as pictures often show. This part of the desert is rocky and pebbly. Very little plant life grows in most of the Sahara except after brief showers.

357

will have a heavy rainstorm and then no more rain for several years.

Much of the Sahara is so dry and has so little life that caravans of nomads fear to cross it. One such place is the Great Sand Sea in Egypt. Find it on a map of Egypt. There are said to be only about 90 good-sized oases in the entire Sahara. These oases provide enough water for a town or small city. At many other places there are wells in the desert, but they can support only a few people. The Sahara is about as large as the United States. Imagine, if you can, only 90 towns scattered across the whole country. Imagine

These thermometers show the highest temperature ever recorded at any weather station in the world. Where did this take place? How does this compare with the highest summer temperatures in your area? Ask your teacher or parent how warm this is.

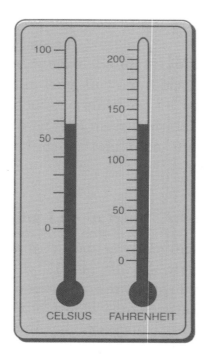

watering holes sometimes hundreds of miles apart! Think how dangerous it would be to travel in such a barren land.

The Sahara is one of the hottest parts of the world. In the summer the temperature is often far above 100° F (38° C) in the daytime. In fact, the hottest temperature ever recorded in the world was in the Sahara. Once the temperature went to 136° F (58° C) at Al Aziziyah (äl ä zē zē′ yə) in Libya. Travelers have discovered that the surface of the ground in the Sahara can sometimes be as hot as 170° F (77° C)! Relief from the heat comes at night. At night the temperature often drops as much as 50 or 60 degrees (10 or 15 degrees Celsius).

You have probably noticed that clear nights at your house are usually colder than cloudy nights. Clouds, haze, and moisture in the air help retain the heat. When it is clear and dry, however, surface heat escapes into the sky at night, and the air becomes cooler.

Relief from daytime heat comes to the Sahara only in the winter. The northern part of the Sahara has temperatures in the 50s and 60s F (10° to 20° C) in the daytime. Farther south it is warmer. At night the temperature may go below freezing in many parts of the Sahara.

Review what you have learned about this great desert. Now you can understand why not many people live there. There is not enough water and food for a large population.

What Do You Say?

1. a. Why do you think northern Africa does not have many rivers? b. Where does the water in the Nile River come from?

2. a. How large is the Sahara? b. How does its size compare with the size of the United States?

3. Why are the nights in the Sahara and other deserts so cool?

What Does the Bible Say?

1. The Bible mentions the Nile River but does not call it the Nile. a. Read Exodus 1:22 and 4:9. What is the Nile called? b. Read Ezekiel 29:3. What did some of the rulers of ancient Egypt (pharaohs) say about the Nile River? c. Who actually made the river?

2. Read Exodus 17:1. What is often difficult to find in a desert?

Resources of the Sahara

For hundreds of years most people thought the Sahara was a wasteland of sand. A book about Africa written around 1959 said that Libya "is a desperately poor country." Only in a narrow strip along the coast and in the few oases could anything grow. The book went on to say that the rest of the country "is either scrubby pastureland or empty desert of no value." Today all that has changed. The Sahara in Libya is not useless wasteland of no value. Petroleum was discovered there in 1959. Now Libya is one of the richest countries in the world!

The story of wealth under the desert sands has been repeated in some other countries of the Sahara. Petroleum has been found especially in Egypt and in Algeria. Algeria and Libya have plenty of oil to sell to other countries, where it is refined and used mainly as fuel. Of the money Algeria gets for exports, nine of every ten dollars comes from the oil it sells. Most of Libya's wealth comes from petroleum as well.

Petroleum fields are not the only riches found in the Sahara. Morocco, Algeria, and Tunisia provide much of the world's phosphate (fos′ fāt′) rock. Phosphate rock can be crushed and used as fertilizer or mixed with other fertilizers. The **phosphorus** (fos′ fə rəs) in phosphate rock is a valuable plant food. Plants and animals need phosphorus for normal growth. Phosphorus helps us grow

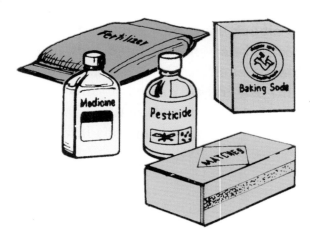

Here are just a few of the things that often contain phosphorus. From what rock does phosphorus come? What three countries of the Sahara provide much of the world's phosphate?

strong and also gives us energy. Phosphorus is an important part of our bones, brain cells, and nerves. Foods that are especially rich in phosphorus are eggs, milk, fish, and peas. Humans and animals get the phosphorus they need from plants. The plants pick it up from the soil. If the soil does not have enough phosphorus in it, the plants will be small and look "sick."

Phosphorus found in phosphate rock has many other important uses. It is used in matches and **pesticides** (pes′ tə sīdz′)—poisons to kill harmful insects. Phosphorus is also used in making certain medicines. Even the baking powder your mother uses contains phosphorus.

Other important minerals are found in the Sahara as well. A **mineral** is a useful substance found in rocks and soil. The Sahara con-

tains minerals such as iron ore, lead, mercury, and zinc. Iron ore is used to make steel. What would we do without good, hard steel bolts and machinery?

Although lead is a poisonous mineral, it can be very useful. The largest use of lead is in making batteries for automobiles, tractors, airplanes, and many other vehicles. Lead is used to make good storage containers for carrying dangerous chemicals. Sheets of lead line the walls of hospital X-ray rooms. This keeps dangerous rays from leaking to other places.

Mercury is used for many important purposes. Many people know that mercury is used in thermometers. It is also used in some electric switches so they work silently. Mercury gas is used in fluorescent lights to help them give off their bright light. Like lead, mercury can be very poisonous, but mixed with silver it may be used for filling holes, or cavities, in our teeth.

Zinc is used to coat other metals to keep them from rusting. Metal coated with zinc is said to be **galvanized** (gal′ və nīzd′). We use galvanized iron or steel to make roof gutters and tank linings. Zinc is even used in making plastics, rubber, and soaps. Plants and animals need zinc for good health. We get some zinc in the food we eat.

One very useful mineral from the Sahara we should mention is salt. Long ago, camel **caravans** (kâr′ ə vanz′) carried loads of salt across the desert. (A caravan is a group of people with their animals or vehicles that travel together.) Some of the salt was used in Egypt. Salt from the Sahara was also taken to African cities south of the Sahara and traded for gold and other valuables.

The soil of the Sahara is also a useful resource. Most people would not think so, for little grows in the Sahara. But if water could be provided, many places in the Sahara would make good land for growing crops. Where wells have been dug to irrigate the desert soil, crops have grown beautifully. But too many wells in the desert can use up the underground water.

There is not enough water to make the desert as useful as it could be. Even so, you can see that the Sahara is not an empty, useless land, as some people might suppose it to be.

What Does the Bible Say?

1. You have learned that in some places desert soil is good for farming. a. What natural resource is usually lacking? b. What does the Bible say can happen in the desert? (Read Isaiah 35:1.)

2. a. What other name does the Bible use for desert? (Read Matthew 3:1 and 4:1.) b. Find this word in your dictionary and write its meaning.

Chapter Twenty-One Review

What Do You Say?

1. a. Why have some people called the Sahara an empty, useless land? b. Name at least five valuable resources found in the Sahara.

2. a. Name some uses of phosphate rock. b. Where in Africa is this rock very plentiful?

Using Globes and Maps

1. Use a map of Canada or the United States. Mark off an area the size of the Sahara. How much of your country would be covered by a desert so vast? If you can find a map of northern Africa drawn to the same scale as a map of North America, draw an

outline of the area in the Sahara. Cut out your outline of the Sahara. Place your cutout on a map of your country. This would show you what a desert the size and shape of the Sahara would look like compared to your country. (A map drawn to the same scale means that the number of miles or kilometers to the inch or centimeter should be the same on both maps.)

2. Draw an outline map of northern Africa. In an encyclopedia find a map of Egypt, Libya, and Algeria. Find as many different names for special parts of the Sahara as you can. (This could include the names of special deserts, ergs, or depressions.) Place the desert names you have found in their proper places on your outline map.

3. In an encyclopedia, try to find maps showing the location of resources in various countries of northern Africa. Draw an outline map of northern Africa and show with pictures or words where various resources are found.

New Words and Terms

Match the following words with the correct definitions.

a. safari
b. bulge of Africa
c. High Africa
d. Low Africa
e. desert
f. ergs
g. depressions
h. chotts
i. Nile
j. Sahara
k. locks
l. phosphorus
m. pesticides
n. mineral
o. galvanized
p. cataracts

_____ 1. A useful substance found in rock and soil.

_____ 2. The low plateau of northern and western Africa.

_____ 3. A valuable plant food found in rock.

_____ 4. Metal that is coated with zinc.

_____ 5. Low waterfalls scattered along a river.

_____ 6. The largest desert in the world.

_____ 7. Poisons used to kill harmful insects.

_____ 8. Low places with salty soil in the Sahara.

_____ 9. Part of Africa that reaches farthest west into the Atlantic Ocean.

_____ 10. Great areas of sand in the Sahara.

_____ 11. The longest river in the world.

_____ 12. A hunting trip.

_____ 13. The high, mountainous land of eastern and southern Africa.

_____ 14. A dry area that usually has less than 10 inches (25 centimeters) of rainfall each year.

_____ 15. Low places in a desert.

_____ 16. Sections of a canal controlled by gates to raise or lower boats to different water levels.

Thinking Together

1. a. What one word could you use to describe the climate of nearly all of northern Africa? b. Can you think of other words that would also describe northern Africa?

2. a. What do we mean by "High Africa" and "Low Africa"? b. How high is Low Africa?

3. How does the lowland near the ocean in Africa compare with the lowlands in eastern North America?

4. Describe the journey of the Nile River from the heart of Africa to the Mediterranean Sea. Include which direction the river flows and how long it is.

5. a. How large is the Sahara? b. List some names used for different parts of this desert.

6. a. How hot does the Sahara often get in summer? b. What was the highest temperature ever recorded in the Sahara?

7. Why are nighttime temperatures cooler in the desert?

8. List at least five resources God has placed in the Sahara and tell how each is used.

For You to Do

1. Prepare a desert scrapbook. Paste in the scrapbook pictures from deserts, especially the Sahara. Plan a section of your scrapbook for pictures or descriptions of desert plants and animals. Include a section showing pictures, if possible, and descriptions of natural resources. You could include in your scrapbook the work you have done in the section **Using Globes and Maps.**

2. In a Bible dictionary or concordance find verses which describe the desert or wilderness. List as many facts from the Bible as you can about deserts.

3. Make a chart showing the name of each North African country. Make columns showing their capitals, populations, resources, languages, and religions.

This desert village in the Sahara is located in the country of Algeria. The houses are made of clay which looks much like the surrounding desert. The villagers get their water from underground wells.

22. The Desert Lands and Their People

The People of the Desert

The people who have lived in the Sahara the longest are called Berbers. Today there are about 15 million Berbers in Northern Africa. Many of them live near the coastland in Morocco, Algeria, and Tunisia. Not as many live in the desert as once did. Many of the Berbers have married Arabs. Many others have accepted Arab customs such as Arab dress. To see something of what the Berbers were once like, one must travel far into the desert.

The Berbers lived in the Sahara region long before the Arabs. In fact, it is believed that they already lived there more than 4,000 years ago. The Berbers had their own language and their own ways of dress and behavior. When the Arabs came, the Berbers fought them at first. Finally they made peace with them and accepted the Muslim religion. But they refused some of the Muslim customs. They did not allow their women to wear the long black robes of Muslim women. Berber women did not cover their faces in public as the Arab women did. We will learn more about the Berbers, especially those in Algeria, in Chapter 23.

The Keepers of the Desert. One special group of people who are related to the Berbers are the Tuareg (twä′ reg′). The Tuareg live in southern Algeria and in the northern parts of Mali and Niger. These people live in the very heart of the Sahara.

The Tuareg are sometimes called the "keepers of the Sahara." For a thousand years they have protected farmers in the desert oases. When enemies would come from other places, the Tuareg would fight them off. In return for this protection, they expected the owners of the oases to pay them with grain, vegetables, and dates.

The Tuareg needed the oases and the farmers who lived there. But long ago no Tuareg would ever consider living on an oasis. They enjoyed roaming about the desert as nomads. They searched for pasture for their animals. It is said that in the Tuareg language there is no word for work. They do not consider wandering the desert and caring for their animals as work. If they had a word for work, they would use it for the farming done on oases.

Today the government is trying to make these desert keepers stay on oases. The Tuareg people, of course, do not like this. This is causing conflict.

Another reason the Tuareg are called the keepers of the Sahara is that they guide caravans across the desert. They have helped many travelers across the Sahara. They have developed an excellent breed of camels for themselves and other desert people.

The Tuareg are sometimes called the "blue men of the desert." Many of them wear long robes that are dyed blue. The dye in these robes

This desert girl is drawing water from a well. She will take the precious water home in large buckets carried by her donkey.

leaves a blue color on their skins. Tuareg men wear cloths called **turbans** (tər′ bənz) wrapped around their heads. They wrap the turban so as to cover their mouths. Only their eyes show. Most Tuareg men will not show their mouths in public. When they eat, they do not remove the turban from their faces. They lift the turban only enough to slip food into their mouths. Tuareg women, however, do not cover their faces, even though many Muslim women do.

The Tuareg live like many other desert people. Their most important food is milk. They buy grain from oasis farmers or from peoples along the edge of the desert.

They seldom eat meat because they need their animals for milk and wool. Only at special feasts do they eat meat. At feasts they eat a favorite dish of steamed wheat called **couscous** (küs′ küs), made especially to be served with meat, vegetables, and a sauce. The Tuareg are fond of young camel barbecued and served with couscous.

No one knows for sure how many Tuareg are left in the Sahara. In the late 1990s their number had fallen to perhaps 300,000. Thousands had died during the 1970s and '80s because of much

The woman is one of the desert people of Mauritania. Like many Arab women, she covers part of her face and her head. The man is a Moor from the country of Morocco. He wears a red cap called a fez.

drier weather than usual in the Sahara and the lands around the Sahara.

Besides the Berbers and the Tuareg, there are other peoples in the Sahara. The Moors are a people of the northwestern Sahara. Most of them live in Morocco. The Moors are part Berber and part Arab. The Moors once spread into Europe and conquered almost all of the country of Spain.

Another group of nomads in the Sahara are the Teda people. The Teda live in the central part of the Sahara near the Tibesti Mountains. The Teda are a black people related to the Africans farther south. The Berbers, Tuareg, and the Moors are lighter-skinned.

What Do You Say?

1. a. Name two reasons why the Tuareg are called the "keepers of the Sahara." b. What is another name for the Tuareg and how did they earn the name?

2. Besides the Tuareg, name several other peoples of the Sahara.

3. What are some foods the Tuareg eat?

What Does the Bible Say?

1. a. How are Tuareg customs of headdress different from many Arabs? b. What teaching does the Bible give about what men and women should wear on their heads? (Read 1 Corinthians 11:4-7.)

The Sahel—Land of the Growing Desert

The people of the Sahara and the lands just south of the Sahara are suffering much today. On the map of Africa on page 349 find the countries of Mauritania, Mali, Niger, Chad, and Sudan. The northern part of each of these countries is part of the Sahara. More than half of each of these countries is desert. Many of the people who live in the northern parts of these countries are nomads. They are much like other people of the Sahara that we have studied.

The region just south of the Sahara is called the **Sahel** (sä hel′). The Sahel is a strip of land from 200 to 500 miles (325 to 800 kilometers) wide. It is found just south of the desert. This land is usually covered with grasses and small bushes or shrubs. More grass and shrubs grow

Thirsty cattle gather at a watering hole in the dry country of Mali. During long droughts in the Sahel, many cattle as well as people die from thirst and lack of food.

here because there is usually more rain here than in the desert.

The Sahel reaches from the Atlantic Ocean in Mauritania and Senegal east to the dry lands of Ethiopia. All of these lands were once called the Sudan. **Sudan** is a word that means "black." Most of the people of the Sahel are black people related to the black Africans farther south. Today Sudan is the name of two countries in North Africa, and the grasslands south of the Sahara are now called the Sahel.

Sahel is an African word that means "shore." If you think of the

This picture from the Sahel in Mali looks quite different from the photo of the watering hole above. Here trucks are leaving a ferry that carried them across a stream in a wetter part of their country. During the dry season and during droughts, the rivers become low or completely dry up.

Sahara as an ocean of desert land, you can understand why the Sahel is like a shore.

Since the late 1960s the Sahel has suffered one period of dry weather after another. Times of dry weather are called **droughts** (drauts).

What Is the Sahel Like? Look at the pictures from the Sahel on page 368. Different parts of the Sahel look different. In the north it is hard to say where the desert ends and the grassland begins. Near the edge of the desert you might find only patches of grass here and there, especially in low, wetter places. As you travel south into the Sahel, you reach a place where the grass covers the ground. Farther south a few bushes grow here and there. Still farther south you will find small trees which can stand the dry weather.

These places with grasses and short trees may have about 20 inches (50 centimeters) of rain each year. Near the southern edge of the Sahel, larger trees grow. Along rivers and lakes, the growth of trees and vines is quite heavy unless people have cut them down. Finally, just south of the Sahel the grassland gradually gives way to thick forest. We will study about these forests in the next unit on southern Africa.

As you might guess, more rain falls in the Sahel than in the desert. In the northern Sahel only about ten inches (25 centimeters) of rain falls each year. The Sahel is much like the desert in that there may be long dry spells between rains. The Sahel usually has a dry season and a rainy season each year. Near the desert, the rainy season may last only one or two months. Farther south the rainy season lasts six months or more. As in most dry lands, the Sahel often has long droughts. Sometimes the rainy season brings very little rain. Then the grass stays dry and brown. If the drought lasts too long, the grasses, bushes, and trees die.

During the 1970s, 80s, and 90s long droughts visited the Sahel. Rivers and lakes ran low or dried up completely. The largest lake in the Sahel is Lake Chad. The Sahara reaches all the way to the northern end of Lake Chad. Much of the area around the lake is almost desert. This lake has been getting smaller and smaller for

This tent dwelling is in the Sahara. The woman on the ground is repairing a tent panel or section. Notice the short trees and scrubby bushes. This shows that there is a little more rain in this section of the Sahara than in some parts.

This caravan of camels is carrying salt across the Sahara. Today, trucks and airplanes are beginning to take the place of camels. The man leading the caravan is one of the Tuareg with his head and most of his face covered with a blue cloth.

many years. It is now about the size of the state of New Jersey. It may have been twice that big years ago. Although it is a large lake, it is very shallow. Few places in it are over 22 feet (6½ meters) deep!

During times of drought, the rivers running into Lake Chad almost dry up. The lake has no outlet to keep its waters moving, so the water is still and **murky**. It is not very healthful for the people who live near the lake.

Many smaller lakes and rivers in the Sahel dry up completely in times of drought. The people of the Sahel often must travel many miles to find water. Many women spend a large part of their day just getting water for their families. The men may drive their herds of cattle for many miles to find precious water.

Is the Desert Spreading? Many places in the Sahel now have little grass. Few bushes are left. When there are few plants to hold the soil, the wind blows it loose. The soil piles up in dunes much like desert sand dunes. When the wind blows from the north, sands from the nearby desert sweep into the Sahel. Soon what was once grassland looks like desert.

In this way the Sahara seems to be growing and taking over what was once grassland nearby. In some places the desert has spread 40 or 50 miles (65 to 80 kilometers) farther south than it was twenty or thirty years ago. People are beginning to

370

wonder if the Sahel will finally become part of the Sahara.

Some scientists tell people not to worry. "The rains will return," they say. After years and years of drought, the people of the Sahel are beginning to wonder. There have been a few years with rain. But the long, hard droughts keep returning.

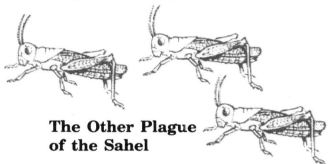

The Other Plague of the Sahel

You have read of the terrible African drought of the 1970s and '80s. We wonder how the people of the Sahel could bear anything more. But every year the Sahelians fear something else. This fear has been around longer than the great drought. This old terror of the Sahel is the **locust**.

Locusts are a type of grasshopper. Most grown locusts are brown and about two inches (five centimeters) long. The locust lays about 25 eggs at a time. They are laid in a little pocket she digs in the ground. These eggs can lie just under the ground for a long time. The eggs wait for rain and warmth. When rain returns, the locusts hatch by the millions.

In the Sahel the people rejoice whenever the rains return. But they may not rejoice for long, for the rains help the locust eggs to hatch.

At certain times, these locusts gather in great groups or swarms. These swarms begin to travel across the land. Scientists do not understand what causes the locusts to do this. Swarming locusts begin to chew almost every green thing in sight.

Locust swarms sometimes cover hundreds of square miles. The cloud of locusts may darken the light from the sun. When locusts swarm down on a field of growing crops there is almost nothing that will stop them.

In the early 1980s, rains began to return to some parts of the Sahel. The locusts began to hatch. But airplanes were used to spread poisonous sprays over wide areas. Locusts were hatching in numbers that promised terrible destruction. Some were saying the coming of the locusts would be as bad as the locust plagues of Bible times. (A plague is any terrible and destructive thing that happens.)

Probably for the first time in history a huge locust plague was stopped. The locusts did not move in great swarms as expected. Some damage was done, but only in parts of the Sahel.

The danger was not over, however. The spray could not reach all the locusts. Plenty survived to lay more eggs. Would the next rainfall bring them back to threaten the land?

To fight off the hungry locusts takes great effort and millions of dollars. The poor countries of the Sahel must depend on other

371

countries to help them. No one knows when the next plague of locusts will strike. No one knows if there will be enough help to keep them from doing what the Bible describes in Exodus 10:15.

"For they covered the face of the whole earth, so that the land was darkened; and they did eat every herb of the land, and all the fruit of the trees . . . and there remained not any green thing in the trees, or in the herbs of the field."

Exodus
10:15

What Do You Say?

1. a. What is the Sahel in Africa?
   b. What does the word mean?
   c. Name the countries where the Sahel is found.

2. a. How have people tried to stop the great locust plagues of northern Africa? b. Why do people still fear a locust plague?

What Does the Bible Say?

1. Read Jeremiah 14:1-6 for a Bible picture of what drought can do. What happened to the plants, animals, and people?

2. a. Read 1 Kings 8:35, 36. What is the reason God sometimes holds back the rain? b. Read Matthew 5:45. How does God show His love and mercy to all?

3. The people who live in desert lands have many different words for *locust*. They have special words to describe locusts that have just hatched, those that are very small, and those that swarm. The Hebrew Old Testament uses a number of words for *locust*. Read Leviticus 11:22 and Joel 1:4. List each different insect. All these are believed to be different words for locusts of different sizes.

5. Moors
6. Teda
7. Sahel
8. Sudan

9. droughts
10. Lake Chad
11. murky
12. locust

Using Globes and Maps

1. Draw an outline map of the countries where the Sahel is located. Check encyclopedia articles on "Sahara" and "Sahel" to see how to draw your map. Mark off the northern parts of these countries that are in the Sahara. Color the Sahara brown. Color the Sahel (the southern part of these countries) yellow. Print on your map the names of the countries and show where their capitals are located. Write "Sahara" and "Sahel" in large letters across these areas on the map.

Thinking Together

1. Name at least three groups of people who live in the Sahara.

2. a. How have the Tuareg usually lived in their homeland? b. How did the Tuareg and the Berbers of the oases depend on each other?

3. In what ways is the Sahel becoming like the Sahara?

4. How is the northern Sahel different from the southern part?

New Words and Terms

Write a short definition or description for each of the following words, places, or people.

1. Tuareg
2. turban
3. couscous
4. Berbers

For You to Do

1. Look up an encyclopedia article on each of the peoples of the Sahara named in this chapter. List interesting details and facts

about them not given in your textbook.

2. From an encyclopedia find out what kinds of animals live in the desert. Make a report on one or several desert animals with unusual habits.

3. Find a recent news article on the condition of the Sahel. (A librarian can likely help you.) Report to your class any new information you find about the problems of the people, drought conditions, or the spread of the desert.

4. Find out what the Bible has to say about locusts. List at least one important fact about them from each of the following verses:

a. Exodus 10:12-15
b. Leviticus 11:21, 22
c. Proverbs 30:27
d. Nahum 3:17
e. Mark 1:6

23. Algeria—Land of the West

Discovering the Land of Algeria

Since the Sudan divided into two countries in 2011, Algeria (al jir′ ē ə) is Africa's largest country. Find Algeria on the map on page 349.

Algeria is in the northwestern part of Africa. The much smaller nation of Morocco lies between Algeria and the Atlantic Ocean.

People from Palestine came to Algeria over 3,000 years ago. These people were called Phoenicians. They called Algeria and neighboring lands the "Isles of the West." To the Phoenicians, Algeria was indeed far to the west. The Phoenicians soon learned about the rain that falls along the coast. They found they could grow many crops there as they had done in Palestine. They also learned that not far inland lay a great desert that we call the Sahara. The Phoenicians thought of the lands along the coast as islands. They were islands between the Mediterranean Sea to the north and the vast sea of sand, the desert, to the south.

The name *Algeria* was not used until many years later. It is interesting that the name *Algeria* means "the islands." The country is named for the small islands found in the harbor of its capital city of Algiers (al jirz′). The name *Algeria* was first used of the islands off the coast. Later it was used of the city near these islands. Finally the name was used for the whole country.

Algeria—a Huge Land. On the map on page 376 you can see that Algeria is shaped much like a large arrowhead. The point of the "arrow" reaches far into the heart of Africa. Algeria is more than three times as large as Texas. That means you could fit three states the size of Texas into Algeria. Algeria is two times as large as the Province of Ontario. From north to south, Algeria stretches for 1,175 miles (1,900 kilometers). At its widest from east to west the country is about 785 miles (1,270 kilometers) wide.

The Land in Algeria. Algeria has three main land regions. Two of

This map shows the size of Algeria compared to the United States. Algeria is one of the largest countries in Africa. The distance across the country from north to south is almost as great as the distance across the United States from north to south.

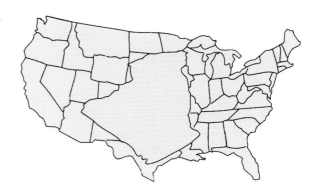

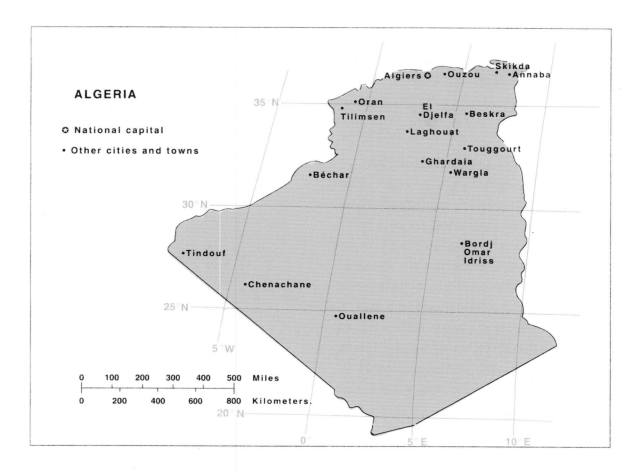

ALGERIA

⊘ National capital

• Other cities and towns

Skikda
Algiers ⊘ •Ouzou • •Annaba
•Oran
Tilimsen   El •Beskra
               •Djelfa
                •Laghouat
                        •Touggourt
               •Ghardaia
•Béchar   •Wargla

                    •Bordj
                    Omar
                    Idriss
•Tindouf

•Chenachane

•Ouallene

0   100 200 300 400 500 Miles
0   200   400   600   800 Kilometers.

these lie in the far north near the Mediterranean Sea. Here live most of the people in the country. As you might guess, most of the rain falls here.

If you could sail on a ship headed for the coast of Algeria, what would you see? You would probably first notice that Algeria's coastline is edged with hills that come right down to the ocean's edge. Beyond the hills, on a clear day, you would see high mountains. These mountains are sometimes snow-covered.

Many people who have traveled by ship to Algeria sail to Algiers, the capital. The city of Algiers rises steeply from the sea. The old part of the city is several hundred feet above the sea. Most of the buildings of Algiers are painted white. The white color helps reflect the heat of the Algerian sun. Because one sees so many white buildings, Algiers is sometimes called "Algiers the White."

This hilly region along the sea is called the **Tell**. *Tell* is the Arabic word for "hill." There is some level land in the Tell region, but most of it is very hilly.

The mountains you would see from the coast of Algeria are the Atlas Mountains. They stretch across Morocco and Algeria to Tunisia. Sometimes the mountains nearest the sea are called the Tell Atlas, and those farthest from the sea along the Sahara are called the Saharan Atlas.

The Tell is only 80 to 200 miles (130 to 320 kilometers) wide. Still, three of every four Algerians live in the Tell. All the larger towns and cities are found there.

The High Plateaus form the second land region of Algeria. These highlands lie between the Tell Atlas and the Saharan Atlas Mountains. The land in this region lies from 1,300 to 4,300 feet (400 to 1,300 meters) above sea level. The nearby mountains are still higher.

The High Plateaus are mostly grasslands with much less rainfall than the Tell. Several million of Algeria's people live here.

South of the Saharan Atlas lies the Sahara. The desert is by far the largest land region in Algeria. About nine of every ten square miles of land in Algeria lie in the Sahara. But only about one million people live there.

Hot and Dry Algeria. Most of Algeria is hot, dry desert. But even the part of the country that has rain is often dry. The Tell and the High Plateaus do receive some rainfall, but almost all of this rain falls in the cooler winter. Winds from the nearby Mediterranean Sea bring this winter moisture to the coastlands of Algeria. Almost no rain falls in the hot Algerian summer.

Most of the other countries around the Mediterranean have the same type of winter weather as Algeria. Other similar climate regions of the world are compared to this area. Any place that has rainy winters and dry summers is said to have a *Mediterranean climate.* Southern California and central Chile have Mediterranean climates.

A few places in the Tell of Algeria receive as much as 40 inches (100 centimeters) of rainfall in the winter. Most places receive less. Algiers receives less than 30 inches (75 centimeters) of rainfall each year.

The Atlas Mountains act as a great wall that keeps rain-bearing winds from visiting the desert. The heaviest rain falls on the mountain slopes that face the Mediterranean Sea. Clouds move farther inland over the High Plateaus. But these clouds have already lost much of their moisture. Only about 10 to 16 inches (25 to 40 centimeters) of rain falls each year on the High Plateaus. The Saharan Atlas drain the clouds of almost all the rest of their moisture.

From about May to October the Tell and the highlands have one long, hot drought. Sometimes the winds blow from the Mediterranean, but they do not bring enough moisture for rain to fall. These winds do raise the amount of moisture in the air. Moisture or water in the air is called **humidity** (hyü mid′ ət ē). When there is a lot of humidity in the air in summer, it feels hotter

This road winds through the Atlas Mountains of Algeria. In this dry part of the Atlas Mountains, only a few grasses and scrubby bushes grow.

than when the air is dry.

At other times during the summer, hot winds with almost no moisture sweep into northern Algeria from the desert. These winds dry up the country. These winds are called the sirocco (sə rok′ ō). You learned about the sirocco when you studied Italy.

You will likely remember that the daytime temperature in summer in the Sahara is usually well over 100° F (38° C). The daytime temperature in the Tell in summer is usually between 90° and 100° F (32° to 38° C). But it actually feels hotter in the Tell than in the Sahara. Does this sound strange? Humidity makes the difference. In the Sahara there is almost no humidity. The Tell, however, receives humidity from the Mediterranean.

The Tell is also much warmer at night than the Sahara. Clouds and moisture in the air help keep the heat near the earth. But in the clear, dry air of the Sahara, you remember, much of the desert heat escapes into the sky at night. And nighttime temperatures there are cool, or even cold.

What Do You Say?

1. a. Why did the ancient Phoenicians call Algeria and nearby lands the "Isles of the West"?

b. What does the name *Algeria* mean?

2. a. How large is Algeria? b. Compare Algeria with the size of a state or province in your country.

3. a. Name the three land regions of Algeria and tell about how much rain falls each year in each region. b. In which region do the most people live? c. Which region covers the most land?

4. a. Which region of Algeria has the hottest daytime temperature? b. Which region often feels the hottest and why? c. Why is the nighttime temperature in the Tell often warmer than the nighttime temperature in the Sahara?

What Does the Bible Say?

1. Palestine, the land of Jesus, has a Mediterranean climate much like that of northern Algeria. What does Song of Solomon 2:11 tell you about the time of Palestine's rainy season?

2. a. Who sends rain according to Psalm 147:7, 8? b. You have studied some natural causes of rain. Read 2 Chronicles 6:26, 27.

What is one reason it may not rain sometimes?

The People and History of Algeria

Algeria became an independent country on July 3, 1962. Independence was something new and different for Algeria. Few times in its long history has the country been free from outsiders. Most of the history of Algeria is a history of people from other lands who have gone there to live. Many have not treated the Berbers and Arabs of Algeria kindly.

People lived in Algeria at least three or four thousand years ago. We do not know who these first settlers were. We do not even know where they came from. They left very little behind them. But they have left one thing that has told us some interesting facts about Algeria and the Sahara long ago.

Unusual Cave Paintings. In southern Algeria near the border of Libya lie the Tassili-n-Ajjer (tä sē lē′ nä jâr′) Mountains. Today these mountains lie in the midst of the hot, dry Sahara. Strangely, the name of the mountains means "plateau of the rivers."

In this dry, rocky land people have discovered over 4,000 cave paintings. These colorful paintings were found on the walls and ceilings of caves. Scientists believe they were drawn about 5,000 years ago. Tuareg guides who live nearby take visitors

Interesting Facts About Algeria

Population: Over 29 million

Size: Algeria is three times larger than the state of Texas.

Where the People Live: Nine of every ten Algerians live within 200 miles (125 kilometers) of the Mediterranean Sea.

Religion: 99 of every 100 Algerians are Muslims. The government provides money to build mosques and to train Muslim leaders.

Valuable Resource: Nine of every ten dollars Algeria gets for exports comes from natural gas and petroleum.

Long Name: Algeria has one of the longest names of any country in the world. The official name of the country is: Al-Jumhariyah al-Jaz'iriyah ad Dimuqratiyah wa ash-Sha'biyah. The name means: Democratic and Popular Republic of Algeria.

animals who once lived in the Sahara.

The Algerian cave paintings clearly show such animals as the hippopotamus and the elephant. These are animals that could not live in the Sahara today. The bones of such creatures have been found in parts of the Sahara. The cave paintings and the bones tell us of a time when the Sahara must have been a well-watered grassland. So the Tassili-n-Ajjer could well have been a plateau of rivers long ago.

We know from Bible history that by the time of Abraham, Isaac, and Jacob, Egypt was already a desert. This was about 4,000 years ago. We wonder what changed the Sahara to a desert. Will it someday become a land of rivers and grassy plains again? Such a change does not seem likely. Today the Sahara still seems to be growing.

The Coming of the Berber. When the Berbers came to Algeria, the Sahara was a desert. Again, no one knows for sure where the Berbers came from. Some believe they came from somewhere in the Middle East. Others believe they came across the Mediterranean Sea from Europe because some Berbers have blue eyes and blond hair.

The Berbers finally spread over most of the Sahara from Egypt to the Atlantic Ocean. Many Berbers lived in tents. They traveled across the desert hunting for food and water. They were nomads like their

over winding, steep trails to see the paintings. These cave paintings are amazing to the Tuareg. Visitors are also amazed. These paintings are as clear and colorful as if they had been painted recently. The dry, desert air has kept them beautiful. The paintings include pictures of people and

neighbors, the Arabs. Other Berbers settled in villages, especially those who lived near the Mediterranean Sea.

The Tuareg of southern Algeria and of the Sahel are a Berber people. Their language is similar to the language of other Berbers.

The Berbers have seldom known freedom from outside rulers. Algeria has been ruled by people from other lands for most of the last 3,000 years.

The first people after the Berbers to arrive in Algeria were the Phoenicians. You remember that they called the country the "Isles of the West." The Phoenicians came in ships from the coastlands of the countries we call Israel and Lebanon.

The Phoenicians were a trading people who sailed the Mediterranean Sea. The Phoenicians settled in trading cities along the coast. The Berbers who lived in the desert went on living much as they always had. They did not have much to do with the Phoenicians.

The next people to make Algeria and other parts of North Africa their home were the Romans. The Romans came to Africa from Italy. Northern Africa became a part of the huge Roman Empire. The Romans, too, settled along the coast. Life in the desert went on much as it always had. The Berbers continued to follow their desert customs and speak their own language.

Northern Algeria was a part of the Roman Empire for several hundred years. Finally the Romans could no longer hold many of their lands in Europe or in Africa. Italy and Northern Africa were invaded by tribes from the north called Vandals. The Vandals spent much of their time killing and destroying. They did not care for the beautiful buildings and cities the Romans had built. They destroyed many buildings and cities along the coast of Algeria and North Africa. The Vandals were very cruel. Today the name *vandal* has come to mean anyone who is cruel and destroys things.

Although the Berbers were ruled by different groups, they changed very little.

The Arabs Bring Changes. Around the year 640, new invaders called Arabs conquered Algeria. The Arabs came from Arabia, the land we studied in Unit 6. At first the Berbers fought the Arabs as they had fought all the other people who had tried to take their homeland. But the Arabs were more powerful. Slowly the Berbers accepted the Arabs. Berbers and Arabs began to marry each other. Many Berbers began to speak Arabic, the language of the Arabs. Slowly but surely, the Berbers became more and more like the Arabs. Most gave up their old religions and became Muslims. In some parts of Algeria today the people still speak Berber languages. But even these people are a mixture of Arabs and Berbers. In Algeria today it is hard to find any Berbers who are not mixed with Arabs.

The Phoenicians, Romans, and Vandals could not really conquer the Berbers of the desert. They did little to change the Berbers. Why then were the Arabs able to change the Berbers? We do not know all the reasons, of course. But the Arabs were also desert dwellers. They lived in the desert along with the Berbers. They did not stay only along the coast as did the Romans and others. The Arabs were in many ways more like the Berbers than any of the other invaders. The Arabs also came in larger numbers than most of the other invaders. Perhaps they worked harder to rule the Berbers. They tried to force people to accept their religion, Islam. Today many Berbers think of themselves as Arabs. Their religion is Islam.

Still More Invaders. In the early 1500s, the Spanish captured Algiers and other cities along the coast of Algeria. But only a few years later, invaders came from Turkey, from what was then called the Ottoman (ot′ ə mən) Empire.

The years which followed were years of much turmoil, especially along the Mediterannean coast. In 1830, the French captured Algiers. Between 1830 and 1914, the French slowly conquered and ruled all of what is now Algeria. Often the French took the best land for themselves. The Berbers and Arabs of Algeria were very unhappy with the French.

Between 1954 and 1961, the Algerians fought a bloody war with the French. Finally on July 3,1962, France gave Algeria its independence. Almost a million Frenchmen fled the country during and after the war.

Since 1962 Algeria has been a free country. This is one of the few times in its long history that outsiders have not ruled the country. The Algerians like to think of today as one of the few times their country has been at peace. But while Algeria no longer needs to fight the French or other outsiders, there are troubles within the country. The people of the desert are not always happy with the government of Algeria. The government would like these people to live in oases instead of wandering through the desert. Many of the Tuareg, especially, do not want to do this.

As in other countries of the world, there is much unhappiness in Algeria. Some say it is because the country is so poor that people fight for land and water and a better living.

But Christians know that more food, water, and better houses will not bring true peace to any country. There is much unhappiness and fighting in the richest countries. People keep wanting more and more.

The Bible tells us that the way of Christ brings true peace. Through faith in Christ, people find peace with God. Instead of selfishly fighting and killing, they learn to love even their enemies. They learn to be satisfied with God's blessing and

Timothy
6, 8

life's simple necessities. "But godliness with contentment is great gain. And having food and raiment let us be therewith content."

What Do You Say?

1. What do the cave paintings found in Algeria show about the climate of the Sahara long ago?

2. a. Beginning with the Phoenicians, list the main invaders of Algeria up to modern times.
   b. Which group brought the greatest changes to the Berbers?
   c. Why?

What Does the Bible Say?

1. Many who claim to be Christians have tried to conquer Algeria and rule it. The Muslims and the Berbers sometimes believe that Christians are enemies out to fight them. What does the Bible teach about fighting enemies? (See Matthew 5:44 and Romans 12:19-21.)

Christians in Algeria

No one knows when the first Christians came to northern Africa. The Bible tells us that Mary and Joseph fled to Egypt with the Baby Jesus. Egypt, of course, is part of northern Africa. Here Mary and Joseph lived for some time until the wicked King Herod had died.

We know also that the man who carried the cross of Christ was from Cyrene (sī rē′ nē). This was a city in the African country we call Libya (lib′ ē ə). We also read in the Book of Acts of Christians from Cyrene. The earliest Christians in Cyrene no doubt came from nearby Egypt. It is believed that the first Christians in Algeria came from Rome, in Italy.

History tells us very little about the earliest Christians in North Africa. We do learn about seven Christians who died for their faith on July 17, A.D. 180. They died in the city of Carthage. This city was in the country we call Tunisia.

By the year 200 there were strong Christian churches in Northern Africa. By 300 A.D. many churches were found in the lands we call Algeria and Morocco. Most of the Christians lived along the coast. The Gospel did not reach to many of the Berbers or Tuareg who lived in the mountains or desert.

Christians Suffer for Christ in Northern Africa. We know from writings handed down to us that many African Christians suffered for

Christ. The first time of great suffering was during the rule of wicked Roman kings or emperors. These rulers persecuted and even killed thousands of Christians. **Persecution** (pər si kyü′ shən) means anything harmful that is done to someone because of his beliefs. Early Christians in Africa were made fun of, put in jail, and sometimes fed to hungry wild animals. When a persecuted Christian dies for his faith, we say that he is a **martyr** (märt′ ər). The word *martyr* means "a witness." All faithful Christians witness for Christ even if they do not die for Him. But faithful Christians are willing to die for their faith in Christ if they need to do so.

Another great time of persecution for Christians in Africa came when the Muslim Arabs conquered the land. Many who said they were Christians became Muslims. They feared to suffer persecution.

Some African Berbers had been brought into the church with very little teaching. Many were Christians in name only. They were not true Christians at heart. These found it very easy to accept the new Muslim religion.

Most stories we have today of early Christian persecutions took place around the city of Carthage and the nearby lands called Numidia. Today this part of Africa is known as Tunisia. In a few places we can read of Christians who sufered in the part of Africa the Romans called Mauritania (môr ə tā′ nē ə). This was not the same as the modern country we call Mauritania. In Roman times, Mauritania was what we call Algeria and Morocco.

Two African Martyrs

Here is the story of two Christian women of northern Africa who suffered and died for Christ. The *Martyrs Mirror*, a book that tells about Christians who suffered for Christ, tells about these two Christian women of Africa.

Perpetua and Felicitas lived in the province of Mauritania (Algeria or Morocco) around the year 200 A.D. Exactly how long they had been Christians, we do not know. But people of their town knew them to be righteous, godly women.

The Roman Emperor Severus began a terrible persecution of Christians in the year 201. Both Perpetua and Felicitas were captured and put in prison. Both ladies had little babies. Felicitas' baby was just newborn. And both ladies were condemned to death, not because they had been wicked, but only because they were Christians.

The jailor cruelly teased Felicitas about dying and leaving her baby behind.

Felicitas, however, did not tremble or fear, but bravely replied, "Tomorrow I shall suffer as a Christian woman for the faith and the confession of Jesus Christ."

It was reported that Perpetua was given a vision that night of heaven. She saw many others who had died for their faith in Jesus. This vision helped her to be faithful in her suffering.

The next day, Perpetua and Felicitas were taken out of prison with at least three others. They were thrown to a group of wild animals to be torn to death.

The bodies of these two faithful women were then taken, probably by Christians, to Carthage for burial.

What Do You Say?

1. How do we know from the Bible that early Christians lived in Africa?

2. Name two Christian women who died for their faith in Northern Africa.

Using Globes and Maps

1. Using the map on page 376, draw a map of Algeria. Show the three main land regions on your map.

2. Draw and label a map of modern northern Africa. Write the names of countries and their capitals on your map. Include the countries that contain part of the Sahara and the Sahel.

3. Make a relief map of Algeria using modeling clay or papier-mâché. Color the desert light brown, the Tell olive green, and the High Plateaus dark brown. To find where to place the mountains, check relief maps in an

What Does the Bible Say?

1. Read Matthew 5:10-12. What promises did Jesus give to Christians who are persecuted for their faith in Him?

encyclopedia or a world atlas. Label land regions, major mountains such as the Atlas and the Tassili-n-Ajjer, and some large cities and towns.

New Words and Terms

Write a short definition for each of the following words. For names of people, tell who they are or where they live. For names of places, tell where they are located and something about them.

1. Algeria
2. Tell
3. High Plateaus
4. Saharan Atlas
5. Mediterranean climate
6. humidity
7. couscous
8. Tassili-n-Ajjer
9. Berbers
10. Phoenicians
11. Vandals
12. Ottoman Empire
13. martyr
14. persecution

Thinking Together

1. a. How large is Algeria from east to west? b. From north to south?

2. a. Name the three main land regions of Algeria. b. Where do the most Algerians live and why do they live there?

3. a. What is a Mediterranean climate? b. Name some places besides Algeria where this type of climate is found.

4. a. Name the main groups who invaded Algeria after the Berbers came. b. In what part of Algeria did most of these invaders live or rule? c. How was the rule of the Arabs different? d. How did the Arabs change the Berbers?

5. How do we know that many faithful Christians were once found in northern Africa?

For You to Do

1. Make a fact chart for Algeria listing the name of the country, the capital, the population, the main crops, and resources.

2. Write a short report on one or two of Algeria's natural resources such as petroleum, natural gas, or phosphate rock. See if you can discover ways these resources are used.

Africa South of the Sahara

What you will learn...
in unit eight

Over 500 years ago a sailor named Dias (dē′ əs) sailed from Portugal to Africa. His ship slowly followed the western coast of Africa. Finally it reached the southern tip of the continent. This was the first time anyone from Europe had sailed so far around Africa. Ten years later, another man from Portugal sailed around Africa and on to India, far to the east. These men were the first to learn the size and shape of Africa. They proved that people could sail around Africa to reach India and China.

Before the late 1400s, the people of Europe knew almost nothing about Africa south of the great Sahara. When they spoke of Africa, they meant northern Africa. You studied about northern Africa in Unit 7.

The discovery of southern Africa was almost like the discovery of a new continent. Southern Africa is so different from northern Africa that we will study it in a separate unit.

Most of northern Africa is a great desert, the Sahara. But south of the Sahara lie vast grasslands. Farther south are great forests. Still farther south are more grasslands and a southern desert. In one unit we can learn about only a few of the lands and peoples of this wonderful continent. We will first study the lands and resources of Africa. Later we will learn something about the people, their languages, and beliefs. Finally, we will study about the Congo or Zaire (zä ir′), one of the largest countries of Africa south of the Sahara.

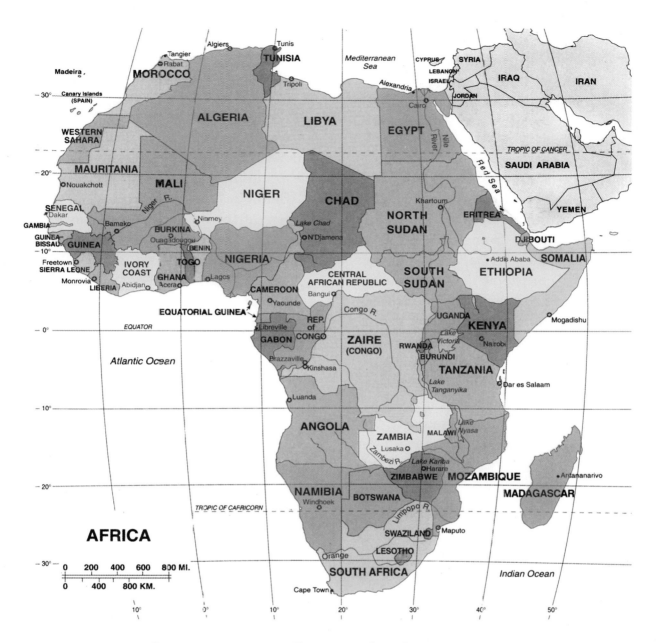

Map labels:

Madeira

Tangier
Algiers
Tunis
TUNISIA
Mediterranean Sea
CYPRUS **SYRIA**
LEBANON
IRAQ
IRAN
MOROCCO
Rabat
Tripoli
Alexandria
ISRAEL
JORDAN
Canary Islands (SPAIN)
−30°
Cairo
WESTERN SAHARA
ALGERIA
LIBYA
EGYPT
TROPIC OF CANCER
SAUDI ARABIA
MAURITANIA
−20°
Nouakchott
MALI
NIGER
CHAD
Khartoum
ERITREA
YEMEN
Niger R.
SENEGAL
Dakar
Niamey
Lake Chad
NORTH SUDAN
DJIBOUTI
GAMBIA
Bamako
BURKINA
N'Djamena
GUINEA-BISSAU
Ouagadougou
−10°
GUINEA
BENIN
NIGERIA
Addis Ababa
SOMALIA
Freetown
IVORY COAST
TOGO
CENTRAL AFRICAN REPUBLIC
SOUTH SUDAN
ETHIOPIA
SIERRA LEONE
GHANA
Lagos
Monrovia
Accra
CAMEROON
Bangui
LIBERIA
Abidjan
EQUATORIAL GUINEA
Yaounde
Congo R.
UGANDA
KENYA
Mogadishu
EQUATOR −0°
Libreville
REP. of CONGO
Lake Victoria
GABON
ZAIRE (CONGO)
RWANDA
Nairobi
Brazzaville
BURUNDI
Kinshasa
TANZANIA
Atlantic Ocean
Lake Tanganyika
Dar es Salaam
Luanda
−10°
ANGOLA
Lake Nyasa
ZAMBIA
MALAWI
Zambezi R.
Lusaka
MOZAMBIQUE
Lake Kariba
−20°
Harare
Antananarivo
ZIMBABWE
MADAGASCAR
NAMIBIA
BOTSWANA
TROPIC OF CAPRICORN
Windhoek
Limpopo R.
AFRICA
SWAZILAND
Maputo
Orange
LESOTHO
−30°
0 200 400 600 800 MI.
SOUTH AFRICA
Indian Ocean
0   400   800 KM.
Cape Town

10°   0°   10°   20°   30°   40°   50°

24. The Lands of Central and Southern Africa

Discovering Africa

By 1500, people from Europe had sailed along most of the coast of Africa. But people outside Africa still knew almost nothing about the con-tinent. No one knew what peoples lived in the interior of Africa. The interior of a continent is the part in the middle of the continent away from the ocean. No one in Europe

389

knew what great rivers or mountains might be found in the interior of Africa.

Mapmakers began to draw maps of Africa. They could draw Africa the right size and shape. Still they did not know what to put on the interior of the continent. Some mapmakers drew nothing inside Africa. They left the map blank. Some decorated the blank parts of Africa with drawings of animals or people. One poet named Jonathan Swift said this about some of these mapmakers:

Geographers, in Afric maps,
With savage pictures fill their gaps,
And o'er unhabitable downs
Place elephants for want of towns.

This poem was written over 200 years after the Portuguese first sailed around Africa. "Unhabitable downs" means plains where no one lives. One hundred years later, in the early 1800s, the rest of the world still had not filled in the map of Africa. Finally, between 1880 and 1900, explorers finished mapping the rivers and mountains of most of Africa.

Below is a picture of a map of eastern Africa found in a book over 130 years old. Did the mapmaker know for sure that his map was right?

Filling in the Map of Africa. During the middle of the 1800s, people from Europe and America began to visit the interior of Africa. Many of these people were Christian missionaries. Some of them tried to find out more about the rivers, mountains, and plains of Africa. Most of all they

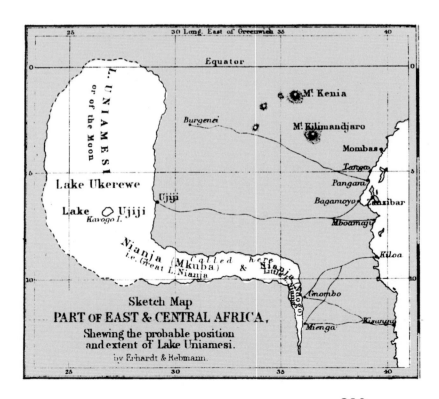

This map shows what is today Tanzania and Kenya. It was printed in 1863. This was before Livingstone explored the lake region of eastern Africa. Visitors in Africa heard about large lakes. Mapmakers drew their maps according to reports they heard. On a map of Africa, find Lake Victoria, Lake Tanganyika, and Lake Nyasa. Note how different they look from what is called Lake Uniamesi on the map. The mapmaker believed that all these lakes were one large lake.

were interested in telling the people who lived there about Jesus Christ.

The most famous explorer in Africa was an Englishman named David Livingstone. He was also a missionary. He believed that missionaries could do their work better if they had good maps of Africa. He spent the last 30 years of his life finding out about the interior of Africa. His work was a great help to other missionaries and travelers.

In Livingstone's time there were no roads or railroads across Africa as there are today. Livingstone spent much of his time trying to find rivers that missionaries and others could travel on. From 1841 to 1873 Livingstone spent most of his time in Africa. Follow some of his journeys on the map on this page. He began his travels at Port Elizabeth, now in the country of South Africa. He traveled north for over 1,000 miles (about 1,600 kilometers). He found the Zambezi (zam bē′ zē) River, which lies between Zambia and Zimbabwe (zim bäb′ wē). Livingstone then traveled west to Luanda (lü an′də) on the west coast of Africa. Luanda is now the capital of Angola (an gō′ lə).

Livingstone then returned to the Zambezi River and followed it to its **mouth.** The mouth of a river is the place it empties into a lake or ocean. The Zambezi empties into the Indian Ocean on the east coast of Africa. Find the mouth of the Zambezi on the map of Africa on page 389. The Zambezi meets the ocean in the country

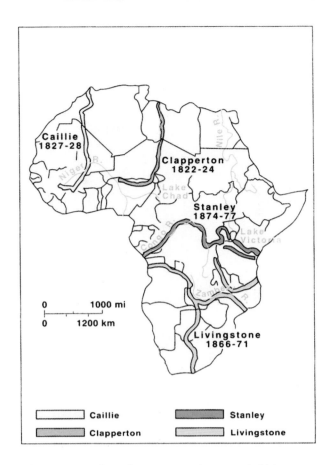

These were four famous explorers of Africa during the 1880s. Clapperton and Caillie were the first white men to cross the Sahara to the grasslands deep inside Africa. Livingstone and Stanley explored central and southern Africa. Which crossed Africa from east to west?

called Mozambique (mō′ zəm bēk′). Livingstone was the first European to travel all the way across Africa from the Atlantic to the Indian Ocean. Livingstone grew older and more tired. But he continued to explore. He spent the last years of his life exploring the lake country of eastern Africa. This is some of the highest and most beautiful land found in Africa. Huge, deep lakes fill valleys between forest-covered mountains.

In 1871 Livingstone disappeared. No one knew where to find

These beautiful grasslands and mountains are in northern Tanzania, East Africa. Some of these beautiful regions in Africa have been included in large parks called reserves. In these reserves the land and the wild animals are protected from man, their greatest enemy.

him. A man named Henry Stanley led a search party. After many weeks, they found Livingstone along the shore of Lake Tanganyika (tan′ gən yē′ kə). Find this lake on the map of Africa. It lies between the countries of Tanzania (tan′ zə nē′ ə) and Zaire (Congo). Lake Tanganyika is the longest lake in the world. It is 420 miles (680 kilometers) long. On the map find some other lakes in this part of Africa. Lake Nyasa (nī as′ ə) is also very long. It is 350 miles (570 kilometers) long. The mountains at the north end of Lake Nyasa are called the Livingstone Mountains. Can you guess why?

Livingstone continued exploring until his death in 1872. He had traveled north from Lake Tanganyika. He was trying to find the source, or beginning, of the Nile River. One morning one of his African helpers found him kneeling by his bed. He was dead. He may have been praying for the Africa he loved. His helpers carried his body west to the Atlantic Coast. It was sent home to England where he was buried near many other famous Englishmen.

We do not need to go many miles away as missionaries to pray as Livingstone did. We can pray for people in other lands at any time. When we learn about distant people and places, we can better know how to pray for them. This is one of the important reasons for Christian social studies. The Bible teaches us to pray not only for each other, but for all peoples. "I exhort therefore, that . . . supplications, prayers, intercessions, and giving of thanks, be made for all men." 1 Timothy 2:1

In Chapter 26 when we study Zaire (Congo), we will learn more about some of the lands that David Livingstone and Henry Stanley explored.

This is a view of Lake Tanganyika, one of the lakes discovered by David Livingstone. Lake Tanganyika is the world's longest freshwater lake. It is the second deepest lake in the world.

By 1900, the rivers, mountains, and lakes of Africa were placed correctly on maps. Names of many places and shapes of many countries have changed since 1900. But other than these changes, maps of Africa today look much as they did about 100 years ago.

What Do You Say?

1. a. When did people from Europe discover the southern part of Africa? b. About how long was it until the interior of Africa was mapped?

2. a. How did David Livingstone help fill in the map of Africa? b. Why did he want to explore Africa?

3. a. What might Livingstone have been doing for Africa at the time he died? b. Why do we think this?

What Does the Bible Say?

1. God is interested not only in what we do, but in why we do it. a. Read 1 Corinthians 10:31. What should be our reason for doing what we do? b. Livingstone explored much of southern Africa. Do you think his reason for exploring was to be famous or to glorify God?

2. Today, not many parts of the earth are left to explore. But there is something we can still explore or search. What is it? Read Acts 17:11.

High Africa South of the Sahara

In Unit 7 you studied about Low Africa. Much of northern and western Africa is called Low Africa. There the land is often about 1,000 feet (300 meters) above sea level. In this unit we will study the part of

Africa sometimes called High Africa.

Most of Africa south of the Sahara is High Africa. But High Africa is not as high as the western part of North or South America. There are no long and high mountain ranges such as the Rockies or the Andes.

In High Africa much of the land is hilly. In many places it is more than 3,000 feet (900 meters) above sea level. In High Africa the only land that is near sea level is found in narrow strips near the ocean. In some places hills or low mountains rise from the ocean's edge. In other places, just a few miles of lowland lie between the ocean and the hills.

Some people call Africa the plateau continent. You may remember that a plateau is a large area of land that is high above sea level. Plateaus are often fairly flat. Sometimes a plateau has rolling or hilly land.

The interior of Africa south of the Sahara is a vast plateau. Sometimes the plateau is hilly. In eastern and southern Africa, mountains rise high above the plateau in places.

Some of the flatter plateau regions of Africa are called plains. Many of the plains are very flat. Most of them are covered with grassland.

One famous plain in Africa is the Serengeti (ser′ ən get′ ē). The Serengeti Plain is part of the great African plateau in Kenya (ken′ yə) and Tanzania. Huge herds of giraffes, zebras, elephants, and gnus roam here. A gnu (nü) is a large, strange-looking antelope.

Another name for them is wildebeests. What might this tell you about them?

The Rivers of High Africa. The longest river in the world is the Nile River in Africa. This river flows for over 4,000 miles (6,500 kilometers) from its source. The source of the Nile lies deep inside High Africa. We often think of the Nile as a river of northern Africa or Low Africa. But for many miles it is a river of High Africa.

Almost all of the water in the Nile River comes from the rainy highlands in the heart of eastern Africa. The last 2,000 miles (3,200 kilometers) of its length, the Nile flows through desert.

Find the Nile River on the map of Africa. First find the place where the Nile meets the Mediterranean Sea. This is in Egypt in northeastern Africa. With your finger, follow the Nile south through Egypt and the Sudans. Continue to follow the Nile south toward the equator, Ethiopia, and Uganda. Now we are in the region where the Nile begins. This part of the Nile is in High Africa.

The Congo River. The Congo River flows mostly through the rainy country of Zaire (Congo). It is more than 2,700 miles (4,350 kilometers) long, which makes it the second longest river in Africa and the sixth longest river in the world. Only the Amazon in South America, carries more water than the Congo.

Find the Congo River on the

The Congo River is the largest river in Africa. This picture was taken in the country of Zaire (Congo) looking across the river toward Brazzaville, capital of the Republic of the Congo.

map of Africa. It meets the Atlantic Ocean on the west coast of Africa just south of the equator. With your finger, follow its course to the lakes of Zambia. You will find out more about this river when we study Zaire in Chapter 26.

The Niger River. Another great African river is the Niger (nī′ jər). This river gives its name to two countries through which it flows—Niger and Nigeria. The Niger River is the third longest river of Africa. It flows for 2,600 miles (4,200 kilometers) from its source to the ocean.

Find the Niger on the map of Africa on page 389. Notice the winding path it takes to reach the ocean.

Strangely enough, the Niger begins only a few hundred miles from the Atlantic Ocean. It begins in the country of Guinea (gin′ ē). The heavy rains in the mountains of Guinea provide plenty of water for the river.

The Niger does not flow immediately to the ocean. It flows north and then east through Mali, southwestern Niger, and northern Benin. Then it flows southward through Nigeria. At last it reaches the Atlantic Ocean.

The Niger carries more water than any other river in Africa except the Congo. The Niger is a special blessing of God to the people of western Africa. In Mali and Niger the

Victoria Falls is on the Zambezi River. The African name for this falls means "the smoke that thunders." Can you guess by looking at the picture how the falls earned this name?

river flows for hundreds of miles through very dry lands. At its northernmost point the Niger touches the Sahara. Millions of people depend on this great river. It brings them water to drink and to irrigate their crops.

The Zambezi River. The fourth longest river in Africa is far to the south. It is the Zambezi River discovered by Livingstone.

Find this river on the map of Africa. The source of the Zambezi is in Zambia. It is near the place where Zambia, Angola, and Zaire (Congo) meet. The river flows for a little way through Angola. Then it flows through western Zambia, then southward. For hundreds of miles the Zambezi forms the border between Zambia and Zimbabwe. Finally the Zambezi flows through Mozambique to the Indian Ocean. Altogether, the river flows for about 1,700 miles (2,700 kilometers). This is more than half the distance across the United States.

Two interesting sites on the Zambezi River are the famous Victoria Falls and Kariba (kə rē′ bə) Lake. Above Victoria Falls, the Zambezi is one mile wide. At the falls, it tumbles about 300 feet (90 meters) into a deep canyon. The mist and spray rise high above the canyon wall and can be seen for many miles. People who live near Victoria Falls call it the "Smoke That Thunders." What does this tell you about the falls?

The edge of Kariba Lake lies about 100 miles (160 kilometers) down the river from Victoria Falls. This is the largest man-made lake in the world. Kariba Lake backs up for over 175 miles (280 kilometers) behind Kariba Dam.

What Do You Say?

1. Why is much of Africa south of the Sahara called High Africa?

2. Why is Africa called "the plateau continent"?

3. Name the four longest rivers in Africa and tell the length of each one.

4. Name one unusual or interesting fact about each of Africa's four longest rivers.

What Does the Bible Say?

1. Only one of Africa's longest rivers is mentioned in the Bible. This is the Nile River. The Bible does not use the word Nile. What does it use? (See Genesis 41:1.)

2. The Niger River is a special blessing in the part of Africa through which it flows. Read Psalm 1:3 and Isaiah 32:2. What does the Bible say about the usefulness of rivers?

Climates in Africa

Africa is a warm continent. You can find out why by looking at the map of Africa on page 389. Find the **equator** on the map. The equator is an imaginary line around the earth halfway between the North Pole and the South Pole. In what part of Africa do you find the equator? Notice that Africa is divided about in half by the equator.

Find the dotted line across northern Africa. This is the Tropic of Cancer. Find the dotted line across the southernmost part of Africa. This is the Tropic of Capricorn (kap′ ri kȯrn′). The area between these two tropic lines is called the **tropics.**

You can see that most of Africa lies in the tropics. In the tropics the sun is almost directly overhead at noon throughout the year. The direct rays of the sun usually make the daytime temperature very warm or hot in the tropics.

But did you know that the very hottest parts of Africa are not in the tropics? The warmest weather is found in Low Africa, especially in the

Mount Kilimanjaro is the highest mountain in Africa. Elephants and many other wild animals roam the Serengeti Plain near this mountain on the border between Tanzania and Kenya.

Sahara. Although less than half of the Sahara is in the tropics, it is close enough that the sun's rays are very direct.

We find at least three reasons why the tropics in Africa are not as hot as we might expect. They are clouds, rain, and distance above sea level.

The sky in the desert is nearly always clear. The sun's warm rays heat up the bare ground. But tropical Africa south of the Sahara often has clouds. The clouds protect the earth from the sun's hot rays. This helps keep the African tropics cooler.

The climate near the equator in Africa is very rainy. In some places it rains almost every day. The rain also helps keep the temperature lower.

A third reason tropical Africa is somewhat cooler than the Sahara is the distance above sea level. You have learned that much of the interior of southern Africa is 3,000 or more feet (900 meters) above sea level. People have discovered that the higher you go above sea level, the cooler it is. This is true even at the equator.

Weather scientists tell us that the temperature is about three degrees cooler at 1,000 feet above sea level than at sea level. For each 1,000 feet higher, the temperature is about three more degrees cooler. If a place is 4,000 feet above sea level, it may be twelve degrees cooler than at sea level. (Using metric units, for every 1,000 meters higher, the temperature is about 5° C cooler.)

You remember that the hottest place in the world is in Libya. There the temperature has gone as high as 136° F (58° C). This place is in the Sahara not far above sea level.

In the interior of Africa near the equator, the temperature seldom goes above 90° F (32° C). Near the ocean along the equator, the temperature may rise to 100° F (38° C) or more.

Eastern Africa has highlands and some mountains. Here the weather is pleasantly cool all the time. Many people from Europe once settled in these highlands because of the pleasant weather.

Nairobi (nī rō′ bē), Kenya, is the largest city of the eastern highlands. It is just over 6,000 feet (1,800 meters) above sea level. In the daytime the temperature is often around 80° F (27° C). The temperature may go down to 40° F (4° C) at night.

Let us pretend that the temperature one afternoon is 80° F (27° C) in Nairobi. What temperature would you expect at sea level about 250 miles (400 kilometers) away? Remember to add three degrees Fahrenheit for every 1,000 feet down to sea level. (Or add 5° C for every 1,000 meters.)

Find Kenya on the map on page 389. You will discover that the equa-

tor runs through the middle of the country. Nairobi is less than 100 miles (160 kilometers) from the equator. Many people are surprised

This sign is along the road north of Nairobi, Kenya. How far above sea level is this sign located? What do you think the temperatures might be like at this place?

that the nights are so cool. Mount Kenya lies north of Nairobi and just south of the equator. The top of this mountain is covered with snow. About 200 miles (320 kilometers) farther south is Mount Kilimanjaro (kil′ ə mən jär′ ō). It is the highest mountain in Africa. Its peak is 19,340 feet (5,895 meters) above sea level. The top of this mountain is also covered with snow.

The picture above shows a grassland area of Africa during the rainy season. Grasses turn green and grow tall during the rainy season. Trees and bushes shoot forth green leaves. But brown is the main color of the grasslands during the dry season. The picture below shows that some of the trees have lost their leaves during the dry season.

Seasons in Africa. In much of the United States and Canada we have four seasons each year. Our seasons are summer, fall, winter, and spring. Tropical lands such as Africa do not have these four seasons. Even in the cooler highlands, the temperature changes little from one part of the year to another. Mount Kenya is snowcapped the year around. Only near the southern tip of Africa and in the Atlas Mountains of the far north is it cool enough to speak of winter as North Americans do. Nowhere is it

400

cold except on top of the highest mountains.

In tropical Africa no season is much cooler than another. The cool season, if there is one, may be only a few degrees cooler than the hot season. In the tropics the greatest drop in temperature takes place at night. Temperatures fall rapidly without the heat of the sun, especially in the thin air high above sea level. Night-time has been called the **"winter of the tropics."** Do you remember how cool the nights are in Nairobi? The daytime temperature is never that cold.

The Dry Season and the Wet Season. Many Africans speak of two seasons. These are the dry season and the wet season. Near the equator, the dry season may be very short. In some places there is no truly dry season. There may be a season with a little less rainfall.

Farther from the equator there is usually a longer dry season. Along the edges of deserts, the rainy season is very short. The rainy season is usually cooler than the dry season. Can you tell why? Remember what you just learned about clouds and temperature.

Where rain falls throughout the year, great forests grow. In the lands where there is a wet season and a dry season, scattered trees and grasses grow. Many of the trees in the grasslands lose their leaves in the dry season. New leaves grow out after the wet season begins. When do leaves fall from the trees in your area? Why? At what season do the new leaves grow?

The Rain Forest Climate. When many people think of Africa, they think of the great rain forests near the equator. Africa has much more desert, however, than rain forest. The continent also has more grassland than rain forest. Still Africa's great rain forest is hundreds of miles long and wide. About one-third of the country of Zaire (Congo) is covered with rain forest.

Just what is a **rain forest**? Really, any large forest in a rainy place can be called a rain forest. Rain forests near the equator are called **tropical rain forests.**

Tropical rain forests have many different kinds of trees. They grow very tall—some of them over 150 feet (45 meters) high. The tallest trees in the forest form a leafy cover. Shorter trees form another leafy cover. These leafy covers are called canopies. You may think of a canopy as something like an umbrella or roof. Two or more canopies may be found in a tropical rain forest.

In a tropical rain forest very little sunlight reaches the forest floor. Therefore, few plants grow there. Many people are surprised to learn that a person can easily walk through a rain forest. Usually one does not need to chop down trees and bushes to get through.

Many people call the tropical rain forests **jungles.** A jungle is a very thick growth of trees, bushes, and vines. Jungles are so thick that people must cut their way through. Jungles in tropical Africa can be found along riverbanks or in clearings in the forest. In these places sunlight can reach the ground. Therefore, many bushes and vines can grow. It is the tangle of low trees and bushes that makes a jungle a jungle.

Many visitors to Africa do not go deep into the rain forests. They see the jungle along the edges of the forest. They imagine that the whole forest must be a jungle. It is not correct to call a rain forest a jungle. Jungles are found only in places where much sunlight reaches the ground.

The Climates of Southern Africa. In the heart of Africa we find the rain forests. Find this area on the simple climate map below. Both north and south of the rain forests are vast stretches of grassland. The grasslands have a wet and a dry season. In Africa the grasslands are called **savannas** (sə van′ əz).

The farther we go from the equator, the longer the dry seasons become. Deserts are found about 1,200 miles (1,900 kilometers) north and south of the equator in Africa. The Sahara of northern Africa is very

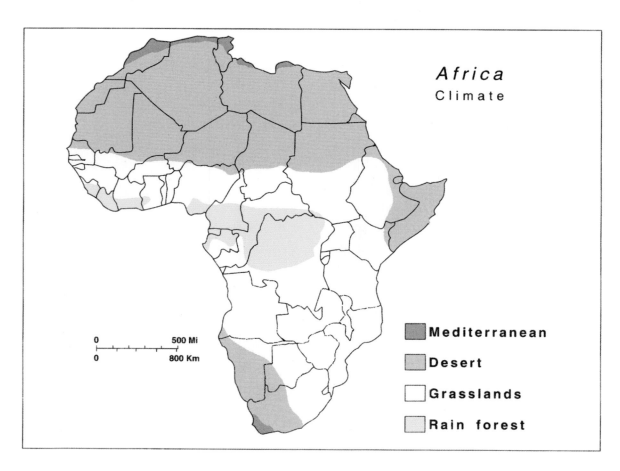

A type of antelope called impalas graze on the East African plain near Nairobi, the capital of Kenya.

large. The desert in southern Africa is much, much smaller. On the map of Africa find the country of Namibia. It is found along the southwestern coast of Africa. Much of this country is desert. Along the coast, the desert is called the Namib (nə mib′) Desert. The highlands east of the Namib are almost desert. A few grasses and bushes grow there. Eastern Namibia and western Botswana are in the Kalahari (kal′ ə här′ ē) Desert. This desert also reaches into the northern part of the country of South Africa.

This desert region is about as far south of the equator as the Sahara is north of the equator. The Namib, however, is much smaller than the Sahara. It is not quite as dry as the Sahara. Much of the Namib may have about 10 inches (25 centimeters) of rain each year.

Find the country of South Africa on the map of Africa. The far north and west are desert. Much of the east is grassland with scattered trees. The southern tip of the country has a Mediterranean climate like northern Algeria.

Namibia, Botswana, South Africa, and other countries of southern Africa are coolest in June, July, and August. The southern summer comes in December, January, and February. The seasons south of the equator are at opposite times of the year from those north of the equator. When North America has winter, southern Africa, southern South America, Australia, and Antarctica have summer. Spring in the southern half of the world comes in September, October, and November.

Do you remember the reason for this difference in the seasons south of the equator? When the noontime sun is highest in the sky, a place has summer. When the noontime sun is lowest in the sky, the place has winter. When the noontime sun is high north of the equator, it will be low south of the equator. The north will then be having summer while the south has winter.

In the lands near the equator, the noontime sun is always high overhead. These places have summerlike weather all year. The farther away from the equator you go either north or south, the cooler the winter season will be.

What Do You Say?

1. How does being in the tropics affect Africa's weather?

2. Give three reasons why parts of tropical Africa near the equator are cooler than some lands farther away from the equator.

3. What kind of seasons do many parts of Africa have instead of the four seasons of North America?

4. What is the "winter of the tropics"?

What Does the Bible Say?

1. In Bible lands there is a cool season called winter and a hot season called summer. Sometimes the people spoke of the seasons in a different way. They spoke of them as many Africans would. Read Ezra 10:9, 13 to find out about one of these seasons. What season was this? Bible lands also had a dry season. As in Africa, the dry season was hotter than the wet season.

2. What does Nahum 1:3 say about how the weather is controlled?

The Plants and Animals of Africa

What continent probably has more different kinds of plants and animals than any other? Yes, Africa. You have already read of the date palms and the camels of the great Sahara. Other animals of the Sahara include the gazelle (a deer), the jackal (a wild dog), the fennec (a foxlike animal), and the porcupine. Most of these animals are also found in other places besides Africa.

Some unusual animals and plants are found only in Africa. Other animals, such as the elephant and the camel, are found in Asia as well.

When we go to the zoo, our favorite section is likely to be the African section. Foreigners who visit Africa enjoy visiting the many wildlife and game parks.

Monkeys and apes can be found in most parts of Africa. Some monkeys are no larger than squirrels. The gorilla, the largest ape, grows about the same height as a person, five to six feet (150 to 180 centimeters). Some people think that apes are monkeys. But there are some important differences. Most kinds of monkeys have tails. Apes do not. Apes are usually larger and more intelligent than monkeys.

Some plants and animals were first found in Africa. We say they are **native** to Africa. This means they first lived or grew there. Some animals native to Africa are the giraffe, zebra, cheetah, hyena (hī ē′ nə), and baboon. The hippopotamus (hip′ ə pät′ ə məs) is also native to Africa. It is the third largest animal in the world. The aardvark (ärd′ värk′), another African animal, has a tongue about 18 inches (45 centimeters) long. It uses this long, sticky tongue to catch ants and termites for food. The name *aardvark* means "earth pig." The aardvark does have a long snout. But in no other way does it really look like a pig.

Africa also has many kinds

of plants and trees once found nowhere else in the world. Some of these are now grown in other parts of the world also.

Coffee trees were first found in Africa. Many people believe that Ethiopia is the home of the coffee tree. Much coffee is now grown in many other parts of the world. The kola tree is another African plant from which drinks come. Kola nuts are used to make cola soft drinks.

One of the most unusual African trees is the baobab (bau′ bab). It usually does not grow over 60 feet (18 meters) tall. But the huge trunk can be from 30 to 50 feet (9 to 15 meters) around. The baobab grows in hot, dry, grassy lands. The thick trunk stores much water. The tree is very useful. The fruit is called "monkey bread" and looks like one-foot-long (30 centimeters) lanterns hanging from long ropes. The fruit is used for food and for flavoring drinks. The leaves and bark are sometimes used for medicine. Paper, cloth, and rope can be made from the bark of the tree. The inside of the tree may be hollowed out to make a house. Baobabs are now grown in many warm parts of the world.

Another interesting plant of Africa is the welwitschia (wel wich′ ē ′). This plant is found in the desert of southwestern Africa. The plant grows two long, wide leaves. The desert winds tear these leaves into ribbonlike sections. The flowers grow up out of the center of the plant. The flowering stalk looks something like a cone on a pine tree. The welwitschia lives to be over 100 years old.

Resources God Gave Africa

God has blessed Africa with many natural resources. The part of Africa south of the Sahara has the most abundant natural resources. Africans have used some of these resources, but many more remain for the future.

Food Resources. Africa produces more of certain foods than any other part of the world. Africa leads the world in producing cocoa beans, cassava, cashews, cloves, oil palm kernels, vanilla beans, and yams. How many of these foods have you eaten? Cocoa beans are made into chocolate and cocoa which are used in drinks, candy, and other foods. Cassava is made into flour and used in making bread and other foods, especially in hot parts of the world. Our dessert food, tapioca, comes from cassava. Cashews are a delicious but expensive nut. Cloves and vanilla are used to add flavor to many foods. Palm kernels are used to make oil for cooking and oil for soaps. Palm oil is used more than any other vegetable oil except soybean oil. Yams are a starchy root something like sweet potatoes. Many people cook yams and eat them like sweet potatoes. Flour is also made from yams.

Mineral Resources. Some of Africa's most valuable resources are minerals found in the ground. More than half of Africa's income is from mineral sales. Three-fourths of the world's gold is mined in Africa. Almost all the world's diamonds are mined in Africa. The largest radium supply in the world is found in Zaire (Congo). Radium was once used to treat cancer. Now it is used mainly in making atomic weapons. Zaire (Congo) also mines nine-tenths of the world's cobalt. Like radium, cobalt is used in weapons and for treating certain kinds of cancer.

Other valuable minerals are also found in large amounts in Africa. You likely remember that Libya, Algeria, and Niger produce large amounts of petroleum and natural gas. Coal, lead, zinc, and silver are other valuable minerals mined in Africa.

Africa's most valuable natural resource is not gold, diamonds, or petroleum. It is water. We have learned before that water is the world's most important natural resource.

South of the Sahara, Africa has many rivers and lakes. If dams were built along the rivers, the Africans could use more of the water. Most of the rivers of Africa have many waterfalls. Water tumbles down mountainsides. Water falls from the plateaus to lower ground. Near the ocean, water falls from High Africa to the land near sea level. Hydroelectric (hī´ drō i lek´ trik) power plants could be built at many places to make electricity.

Hydroelectricity is electricity made by falling water. The power of the falling water turns giant engines called turbines. This makes electricity. Many people believe that more hydroelectricity could be made in Africa than in all the other continents put together.

Not all Africans, however, think like people in Europe and North America. In the European or American way of life, electricity is nice. But building power plants and keeping them running is different from the African way of life. Also, many waterfalls in Africa are in tropical rain forest areas where few people live. It would be very difficult to build the plants and to run electric lines through the rain forests to the larger cities. We must not think the Africans are lazy or foolish if they do not build power plants.

Gold and Diamonds—Useful? Most of the world's gold and diamonds are mined in Africa. These two products are some of the most valuable minerals on earth. When some people think of gold and diamonds, they think of jewelry. People use both to decorate themselves. We know that the Bible forbids people to decorate their bodies with such things. 1 Timothy 2:9 says, "That women adorn themselves in modest apparel, with shamefacedness and sobriety; not with broided hair, or gold, or pearls, or costly array."

The Bible also tells us that God "giveth us richly all things to enjoy."

1 Timothy 2:9

1 Timothy 6:17

Are there any ways to enjoy gold or diamonds in a right way? Yes, there are! Gold and diamonds are both very useful gifts from God. They can be used in many good ways.

For thousands of years people have used gold for money and coins. Gold is very scarce, and so it is very valuable. This helps make it useful as money. Even small amounts of gold are very valuable. For that reason, small gold coins are worth much money. People in the United States once used a gold coin worth ten dollars. This coin was about as big as a dime.

Now we do not use gold coins, but gold is still used for money. Countries exchange gold to pay for things. Much gold is stored in several places in the United States. It is used as money between countries.

Small amounts of gold mixed with other metals are also used for fillings in teeth. If you ever have a cavity and need it filled, ask your dentist. Maybe you have some gold in your mouth. Mixed with other metals, gold lasts a long time and does not easily wear away. This makes it good for tooth fillings.

Diamonds can be even more useful in everyday life than gold. Only a small part of the diamonds that are found are used in rings and other jewelry. A diamond is the hardest stone or mineral ever found in nature. These very hard diamonds can be used to cut very hard metals. They can cut, grind, or bore

holes very quickly. Diamonds are set in the end of drills and used for mining. Many record players have diamond needles. The needles pass over the grooves in the records. We then hear the sound. The diamond in a record needle never wears out. Needles must be replaced sometimes, however. Usually this is because some other part of the needle besides the diamond wears out. Diamonds are used to manufacture engines for automobiles, airplanes, and other machines with engines that use very hard metals.

As you can see, gold and diamonds have many good uses. Truly God created everything for a purpose. We must use wisely the blessings God has given.

What Do You Say?

1. Name at least three plants and three animals native to Africa.

2. Name seven foods that Africa produces more of than any other part of the world and tell how each one is used.

3. a. List four mineral resources that Africa leads in producing.
   b. How can gold and diamonds be useful?

What Does the Bible Say?

1. You have learned that gold may be useful in different ways. a. Read 1 Timothy 6:17. What is a danger to watch for even when gold or riches are used in a good way? b. Read verse 18. How should gold or wealth be used?

2. a. What does Ezekiel 16:17 say about who owns gold? (God is speaking.) b. What did the people make with the gold?

Using Globes and Maps

1. Using a large map in your text or in another book, draw an outline map of Africa. Trace on it the course of the four largest rivers of Africa and label them. Show also the name and course of the Orange River in South Africa. Can you see how the discovery of all these rivers helped open up the continent of Africa to travelers and missionaries?

2. From an encyclopedia map showing the plant and animal life of Africa, list all the animals and plants you find. Name as many of these plants and animals as you can that are native to Africa.

3. Use a scale of miles and measure the west coast of Africa on a map. Measure the distance all the way to the southern tip of the continent. About how far did early explorers like Dias have to sail to get to the southern tip of Africa?

New Words and Terms

Match the following words, terms, and places with the descriptions that follow the list. Each one will be used once.

a. interior	l. canopy
b. mouth	m. jungle
c. source	n. Namib Desert
d. High Africa	o. savannas
e. the plateau continent	p. native
	q. aardvark
f. Victoria Falls	r. baobab
g. Kariba Lake	s. welwitschia
h. tropics	t. yams
i. winter of the tropics	u. radium
	v. cobalt
j. rain forest	w. hydroelectricity
k. tropical rain forest	

1. These <u>four</u> terms have to do with the part of Africa where rainfall is the heaviest and the weather is always warm.

2. These <u>three</u> are plants or animals first found in Africa.

3. This word is used for grasslands.

4. These are all food or mineral resources of Africa (<u>three</u> items).

5. These <u>two</u> terms have to do with the beginning and end of a river.

6. These <u>two</u> places are found on the Zambezi River.

7. Something that has long lived or grown in a place is said to be _____ to that place.

8. This dry place is in southwest Africa.

9. These <u>two</u> terms speak of the distance above sea level in Africa.

10. The part of a continent away from the ocean is the _____ .

11. These <u>two</u> terms have to do with growth in the rain forest.

12. Electricity made by water power is called _____ .

Thinking Together

1. How was the discovery of Africa south of the Sahara much like discovering a new continent?

2. Why did mapmakers draw little or nothing on the interior of African maps for many years?

3. a. What great work did David Livingstone do for Africa? b. What was his reason for doing this?

4. a. How high above sea level is most of High Africa? b. Why is Africa sometimes called the plateau continent?

5. a. What are African plains usually like? b. Name some kinds of animals that often roam the plains of Africa.

6. Name the four longest rivers of Africa and tell how long each one is.

7. a. What is meant by the tropics? b. What kind of weather would you expect in the tropics? c. Why is the Sahara often hotter than places in tropical Africa much nearer the equator?

8. When people speak of seasons in Africa, what two seasons do they often mention?

9. Why is the wet season in Africa cooler than the dry season?

10. What is the weather like in tropical rain forests?

11. How are the seasons in southern Africa reversed or turned around from the seasons in North America?

12. Name some animals and plants that are native to Africa.

13. a. What are some important food

and mineral resources of Africa? b. What resource does High Africa have which it does not use as much as it might?

For You to Do

1. Find an encyclopedia article on each of the following African countries. From the part of the article on natural resources, agriculture, or minerals, name at least six natural resources found in each country. Find out about Nigeria, Zaire (Congo), Kenya, Ethiopia, Zimbabwe, and South Africa.

2. Begin a collection of pictures, articles from magazines and newspapers, stamps, and anything else you can find from Africa or about Africa. This may be a student project or a class project. Continue your collection until you finish studying this unit. Using what you have found, you may write a report, make a scrapbook, prepare a bulletin board, or make a display.

25. The Peoples of Africa

Who Is an African?

Suppose a visitor is coming to your school. Your teacher says he is an African. What would you expect? What color skin do you think he would have? How would you expect him to dress? How would he talk?

Most people would expect an African to be a black person. People might expect him to speak a different language. Perhaps he would even wear bright-colored clothing.

You and your friends might be in for a surprise when the African visits. He might be black. Far more than half of all Africans are. But again he might be blond-haired with light skin. He might have brown or yellowish skin. He probably speaks one or more African languages. He might speak good English. In many African countries, the government, traders, and many schools use English or French. In these countries dozens of African languages may be spoken. But many of the people can understand each other because they also speak English or French.

In this chapter, we will learn about the people who live in Africa south of the great Sahara. South of the Sahara more than nine of every ten Africans are black. This part of Africa is sometimes called Black Africa. When we think of Africans, we often think of people from this part of the continent.

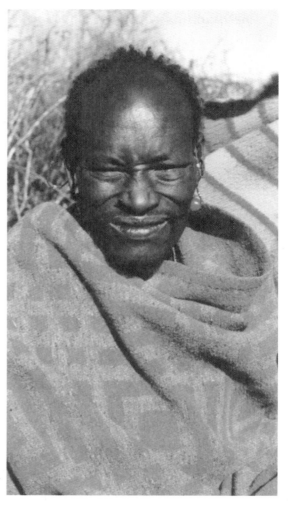

There are many black people in central and southern Africa. This man belongs to the Masai people of Kenya. The Watusi, who live not far away, are very tall. But the Pygmies of central Africa are the world's shortest people. A few Asians and white people live in parts of Africa south of the Sahara. All these came to Africa from other lands.

Tribes and Ethnic Groups. Look at a map of Africa. How many different countries do you see on the map south of the Sahara? How many different languages and groups of

412

people would you expect in this number of countries? In Europe and the Americas, most people in the same country are much alike. They may speak one or two languages. The people in any one country have customs which are much alike. Their beliefs may be much the same.

In most African countries, however, these things are not so. In any one country, different people may speak dozens of different languages. Their ways of life may be very different. They may even look very different from each other. These different people in the same country may have little to do with each other. They might not think of themselves as citizens of the same country. The village or the language group may be far more important than being part of a certain country.

No one knows for sure how many different groups of people there are in Africa south of the Sahara. Most of them are black, but they are very different from each other in many ways. Some scientists who study groups of people say there are over 800 different groups of people in Black Africa.

Many years ago these different groups of Africans were called tribes. A tribe perhaps included many families or even many villages of people. But each tribe shared the same language, the same beliefs, and the same ways of doing things. Many people today do not like to use the word "tribe." They believe that this word makes us think of poor people who live in grass huts. Not all "tribes" in Africa are like that.

Today scientists who study different groups of people use the term **ethnic group**. They use this instead of "tribe." The word *ethnic* comes from a word which means "the people." Many simply use the word *people* instead of tribe or ethnic group. So we speak of the Zulu (zü′lü) people who live in South Africa. The Yoruba (yòr′ ə bə) people live in Nigeria. The Ibo (ē′ bō) people also live in Nigeria.

Remember that over 800 ethnic groups live in Africa south of the Sahara. They live in about 40 different countries. We can study only a very few.

The Yoruba. One of the largest ethnic groups in Africa is the Yoruba of Nigeria. Some of them also live in the neighboring countries of Benin and Togo. About 17 million Yorubas live in these parts of western Africa. The Yoruba are not the only ethnic groups found in these countries. You can understand this when you learn that there are over 103 million people in Nigeria alone.

The Yoruba have their own language and ways of living. The Yoruba have long lived in towns and villages. They farm the land surrounding the towns. Today many of the Yoruba are city dwellers.

Did you know that many of the black slaves brought to America long ago were Yoruba people? Many black Americans can trace their family history back to the Yoruba.

Nigeria has most of the Yoruba.

413

But Nigeria is not really a Yoruba land. Nigeria has more than 250 other ethnic groups.

You can understand then how the Yoruba of Nigeria, Benin, and Togo feel like one great people. They think of themselves as Yoruba more than they think of themselves as Nigerians, Benins, or Togolese.

Today's African countries are divided in much the way Africa was divided many years ago when Europeans ruled. The British ruled what is now Nigeria. The French ruled in Togo and Benin. The Europeans were not careful to divide the land according to where certain ethnic groups lived.

One of the most difficult problems for African countries today is caused by having many ethnic groups. It is difficult for a country to have true **unity** unless its people have much in common. Unity means "feeling alike in many ways and working together." Many ethnic groups do not care to work together with other ethnic groups.

The Pygmies. One of the most interesting peoples of Black Africa are the Pygmies (pig′ mēz). Today most of them live in the rain forests

This map of Africa shows you where many of the ethnic groups live. A map like this can show only a few of the largest groups of Africans. In some cases two different ethnic groups live in the very same region.

414

near the heart of Africa.

Thousands of years ago Greek writers told of a race of very small people. The Greeks believed these small people lived far to the south in Africa. Artists even drew pictures of what these people were supposed to look like. The Greeks gave us the word *pygmy*. The word is used for any very short people.

Only 200 years ago many people did not believe the old stories of the Pygmies. They thought the Greeks made up the stories. Imagine the surprise of explorers in Africa about 200 years ago. They saw people who were indeed very short even when they were grown. The Pygmies reach a height of about four to four and a half feet (120 to 135 centimeters). This is the height of most fourth or fifth graders in North America.

Once the Pygmies lived in many parts of Africa south of the Sahara. Today only about 150,000 Pygmies are left. They live in the forests of about six central African countries. Many live in the Republic of Congo and Zaire (Congo).

The Pygmies do not call themselves Pygmies. They would not use a strange word from some other country. They call themselves Mbuti (əm bü′ tē). This is their word for "people."

Life Among the Mbuti

Most Pygmies live in small clearings in the forest. They stay in one place as long as they can find plenty of food. Later they move on to another place in the forest.

The Mbuti have an interesting way of building houses to live in. They find long, slender trees in the forest. They use trees that can be bent over. They cut down the trees. Sticking one end of the tree in the ground, they bend the top end over. Then they push the top end into the ground. After making a circle of such trees, they cover it all with leaves and branches. This makes a domed or igloo-shaped place in which to sleep. These houses also provide shelter when it rains.

The Mbuti live in groups of three or four large families. Everyone among the adults has a say in decisions. Everyone helps decide where to build houses or where to go hunting. At any time a person may leave one group of Mbuti and go to another. Men and women find wives and husbands from other family groups.

The months of May and June are very special for the Mbuti. This is the honey season. The Mbuti are especially fond of honey. Different tribes or family groups get together to hunt for fresh honey. Bee nests can be found in hollow trees throughout the forest. When an Mbuti family finds a honey tree, there is great rejoicing and celebration.

Other Peoples of Africa. Another interesting ethnic group of black Africans are the Watusi (wä tü′ sē). While the Pygmies are very short, the Watusi are very tall. Some of them are seven feet (210 centimeters) tall. The Watusi are usually very powerful in the countries where they live. Many Watusi live in Zaire (Congo) and in the small country of Burundi (bù rün′ dē). Pygmies also live in Burundi. The Pygmies were once servants of the Watusi.

There are about 40 ethnic groups in Kenya. The Kikuyu (ki kü′ yü) form the largest group. There are about two million Kikuyu in Kenya. They are some of the richest and most educated people in Kenya. Many live in cities or own large farms. Long ago the Kikuyu farmed and herded sheep and goats.

The Zulu form one of the largest ethnic groups of South Africa. These people were farmers and herders. When people from Europe came and took much of their land, they fought to keep it. They became known as warriors. They often lived in cone-shaped houses built in large circles. Today many live near the cities of South Africa.

What Do You Say?

1. What is a tribe or ethnic group?

2. How are some people in North America related to the Yoruba of Africa?

3. If you saw a group of adult African people together and one was a Pygmy, how could you tell which was the Pygmy?

4. What do the Pygmies call themselves?

5. In what part of the country do most of the Pygmies live?

6. Name two other ethnic groups in Africa besides the Yoruba and Pygmies and tell where each lives.

What Does the Bible Say?

1. When Christians learned about the many peoples of Africa, they began to help them find out about Christ. a. What does John 3:16 say about all the people of the world? b. What does Matthew 28:19, 20 tell the church to do for these people?

2. Some people have felt that certain ethnic groups are not as important in God's sight as others. What do Romans 10:12 and Acts 10:34, 35 say about this?

The Languages of Africa

In Canada and the United States one can travel for hundreds of miles in any direction and people speak the same language. Some people in our countries speak French, Spanish, or German. But these languages have many of the same words as English does.

Africa is very different. No one knows for sure how many languages are spoken in Africa. Scientists who study languages say there are 1,000 or more different languages. Scientists who study languages are called **linguists** (ling′ gwəsts). In northern Africa most people speak Arabic. Arabic is used all the way from the Red Sea to the Atlantic Ocean. Africa, south of the Sahara, is very different. Each ethnic group may speak a different language. Even neighbors a few miles apart may not understand each other.

Some of the languages of Africa are much alike, as are English, French, and German. Linguists list languages that are much alike into groups called **language families**. Languages in the same family have many words that are much alike. A few African languages are very different from any language used by people nearby. Linguists do not know which language families they are in.

Even the same language may be spoken in different ways. You have noticed that people in other parts of your country may speak English differently. Different ways of speaking the same language are called **dialects** (dī′ ə lekts′).

Only a few of Africa's languages have over a million people who speak them. Other languages are spoken by as few as several hundred people.

Missionaries and African Languages. Only about half of all African languages have an alphabet and can be written. Only two hundred years ago almost no Black African languages were written. Then missionaries came to Africa. One of the first things they wanted to do was to give the Bible to the people in their own languages. The missionaries were from Europe and chose to use our alphabet for writing the new languages. This makes learning African languages a little easier for us than learning a language such as Russian or Arabic.

For many of the languages of smaller African groups, only certain parts of the Bible have been written. In the box on page 420 are some Bible verses written in the five most-used Black African languages.

The Bantu Language Family. The largest family of languages in southern Africa is the Bantu (ban′ tü) family. The word *Bantu* in many of these languages means "people" or "men." The Bantu languages are spoken all the way from Nigeria on the west coast to Kenya on the east coast. Many languages in the country of South Africa are Bantu languages. There are about 300 different groups

African Languages South of the Sahara More Than 10 Million Speakers		
Language	**Speakers**	**Area**
Swahili	49 million	Kenya, Tanzania, Zaire (Congo), Uganda
Hausa	39 million	Nigeria, Niger, Cameroon
Yoruba	20 million	Nigeria, Benin
Amharic	20 million	Ethiopia
Igbo (Ibo)	17 million	Nigeria, Cameroon
Fula	13 million	Senegal, Guinea Bissau
Malagasy	12 million	Madagascar
Afrikaans	10 million	South Africa
Oromo	9 million	Western Ethiopia, Northern Kenya

of Bantu. Each group has its own language. While the Bantu languages are alike in many ways, they are also different from each other, much as English, German, and Spanish are different from each other.

Swahili. The most-used Bantu language is Swahili (swä hē′ lē). Many people in eastern Africa speak this language. Over forty million people speak Swahili. Many people who do not speak Swahili at home speak it in the marketplace. Swahili is the language of trade and business in much of eastern and southern Africa.

Swahili is the official language of Tanzania and Kenya. Find these countries on the map of Africa. An **official language** is the language that is used in the government and business of a country. Hundreds of other languages are spoken in eastern Africa, but most people can understand at least some Swahili. Most newspapers and books in eastern Africa are printed in Swahili.

Swahili is a fairly easy language to learn. It uses the same Roman alphabet as English. The sounds are not hard for us. On the next page is a chart showing some important Swahili words and sentences. Following each word is its pronunciation. Practice saying these words. Then you can greet each other in the most important African language south of the Sahara.

should put the clicks. Sometimes they use an unused letter like Q or X before the consonant to be pronounced with a click. Sometimes they use other marks like / or !.

Translators are people who take something written in one language and write it in another language. Bible translators around the world are working to put the Bible into many more languages.

This shows the Bible in one of the many languages of Black Africa. The entire Bible has been translated into dozens of African languages. Many more languages have New Testaments or books of the Bible.

The Click Languages. A most interesting language family in Africa is the click language family. It is also the smallest language family of Africa. Only about 100,000 people speak these languages. The Bushmen of southwestern Africa speak a click language. The Hottentots (hot′ ən täts′) of South Africa speak another click language. Several smaller groups in faraway Tanzania speak click languages.

In the click languages, the consonants are often pronounced with an unusual click sound. In some languages almost every word begins with a click. The click is made by a sucking action of the tongue.

Parts of the Bible have been written in different click languages. Translators had to decide on a way to show where speakers

The Bible in Africa's Languages

Here are some Bible verses in five of Africa's many languages and in English. After each African language you see the number of people who speak the language and the countries where the language is spoken. Find the various countries on the map of Africa in this unit.

Swahili—49 million speakers: Kenya, Tanzania, Zaire, Uganda, and other countries.

Mwanzo wa Injili ya Jesu Masihi, Mwana wa Mwenyiezi Mngu. Kama vile ilivyoandikwa katika chuo cha nabii Isaia: Mimi hapa, namtuma njumbe wangu mbele ya uso wako, Atakaeitengeza ndia yako.   Mark 1:1, 2

Hausa—39 million speakers: Nigeria, Niger, and neighboring countries.

Farkon Bisharar Yesu Almasihu, Dan Allah, ke nan: Yadda ya ke a rubuce a littafin Annabi Ishaya, cewa, Ga shi na aiko manzona ya riga ka gaba, Wanda zai shirya maka hanya.   Mark 1:1, 2

Yoruba—20 million speakers: Western Nigeria, Benin

Ibere Ihinrere Jesu Kristi, Omo Olorun. Bi a ti ko o ninu iwe woli Isaiah: Kiyesï, mo rán onse mi siwaju re, Eniti yio tún òna re se niwaju re.   Mark 1:1, 2

Igbo (Ibo)—17 million speakers: Eastern Nigeria

Nkembu Ökuómma nke Yisus Kreist, Opára nke Tšúku; Otúna Ödére na Ämónma, Le, Aziem ndé özim na ihũngi, nke ga dšikeren ūzóngi na ihũngi.   .   Mark 1:1, 2

Fula—13 million speakers: Nigeria, Cameroon

Pudduki linjila Yesu Almasihu, Biddo Allah; bana ko lati bindadum har annabo'en: Nda, me don nula nulado am jiha yeso ma, taskitanando lawol ma yeso ma.   Mark 1:1, 2

English

The beginning of the gospel of Jesus Christ, the Son of God; as it is written in the prophets, Behold, I send my messenger before thy face, which shall prepare thy way before thee.   Mark 1:1, 2

Missionaries and African Languages. Only two hundred years ago almost no African languages were written. Children had no books to read in their own languages. Most importantly, the Bible had not been translated into any African language.

Bibles or parts of the Bible are now printed in about 500 of Africa's languages. This is less than half of the languages found in Africa. The 500 or more languages that remain are spoken by small groups having only a few hundred to a thousand people.

All of this translation work has taken place in the last 200 years. Most of it has been done by Christian missionaries. The missionaries, more than anyone else, have been interested in helping Africans read. They have provided much literature for Africans. Without the missionaries, probably only a few of Africa's languages would be written today. In some African languages the only thing written is a portion of the New Testament. In many places, especially in the small villages, the only schools are those started by missionaries.

Many people have wondered what made so many missionaries work so hard to learn African languages. They wanted the people to be able to read the most important book of all, the Bible. The Bible commands the Christian church to spread the Good News about Jesus Christ. "Go ye therefore, and teach all nations, baptizing them in the name of the Father, and of the Son, and of the Holy Ghost: Teaching them to observe all things whatsoever I have commanded you." Christians can do this work much better when people can read the Bible in their own language.

Matthew
:19, 20

What Do You Say?

1. About how many different languages are spoken in Africa?

2. What is a language family?

3. a. How did missionaries help Africans learn to write their languages? b. Why did they want to do this?

4. In what parts of Africa are the Bantu languages spoken?

5. Why is Swahili such an important language in eastern Africa?

6. What is the most unusual thing about the click languages?

What Does the Bible Say?

1. Why are so many different languages spoken in Africa and the rest of the world? Find the answer in Genesis 11:9.

2. Read Ezekiel 3:5. How do other languages often sound to us?

This round house is in southern Africa. Notice the fence around the house with vines growing on it.

African Wisdom

It is hard to imagine what Africa was like before it had written languages. No one enjoyed the blessings of being able to read. There were no schools as we know them. This does not mean, however, that people were not intelligent before they had written languages. It does not mean that they did not learn anything. African children have long learned many useful things from their parents and the older people.

Because they had no writings, each village or group of people had those who remembered things and told them to the young. In many villages these people were called storytellers. These storytellers passed on the stories, sayings, and wisdom of the past. The storytellers took the place of family history books. If anyone wanted to find out who his great-grandfather was or who was related to whom, he could ask the storyteller.

Today, Africans still enjoy the stories and sayings of long ago. Even villagers who can read still enjoy these things. Some of this wisdom has been written down for people around the world to enjoy.

In many African countries, most of the people still cannot read. In countries such as Burkina Faso, Mali, Niger, and Somalia, only one of every ten people can read. In the large towns and cities more people usually know how to read. Out in the country very few can read. Usually more men can read than women.

Many Kinds of Stories

African storytellers tell many different kinds of stories. Some of them are about the history of their people. Other African stories are what we call **legends**. A legend is a story that comes to us from the past. It is passed from one person to another and is not usually written down. Many people believe legends. Parts of legends may be true. Other parts may not be true. They may have changed because they were passed from person to person many times. Some parts of legends may be **exaggeration.** Exaggeration is telling a story to make something in the story bigger or greater than what it really is.

Some African legends tell about famous men and women from the past. Other legends try to explain why things were created the way they are. Some legends tell about how the people believe the earth was created.

Perhaps the most helpful African stories are the **fables**. They are stories about animals. The animals talk. They often act like people, and so many of the stories are used to teach lessons to people. Some of the fables are like legends because they explain how things came to be. Christians have learned that many African fables teach lessons much like lessons from the Bible. Christian ministers and teachers use these stories to teach Bible truths. They may read a Scripture and then tell a story the people know to teach the same lesson.

Here are two African stories for you to enjoy. The first teaches some good lessons. Can you tell what they are? The second tries to explain why something is the way it is. What does it try to explain?

The Tortoise That Remembered

Once there was a fruit-bearing tree called the bojabi (bō job´ ē) tree, but none of the beasts knew its name. They did not know if the fruit could be eaten.

A famine came to the land and the beasts grew hungrier and hungrier. They wondered if the fruit of the tree they did not know the name of would be good to eat. They decided to inquire of a very wise creature named Mbama (əm bom´ ä) who lived about thirty miles away. They chose the rat to take a sample of the fruit to Mbama to discover its name and learn if it were good to eat.

The rat reached Mbama safely and learned the name of the fruit. It was very good to eat. On his way home he spent so much energy paddling his boat that he completely forgot the name of the tree. The beasts were very displeased and sent the porcupine to learn about the tree. The porcupine returned but forgot the name of the tree as he was entering the village. Next the antelope went, but as he was returning, a wave upset his boat, and he too forgot what he learned about the tree. Finally the tortoise said, "I will go to learn about the tree and its fruit." The other creatures laughed at him. How could a slow tortoise do better than the others! Finally they agreed that he could go.

The tortoise wisely consulted his mother before leaving. She carefully instructed him not to eat or drink on the way and keep his mind on his goal. The tortoise finally arrived at Mbama's and learned the name of the tree and that its fruit was indeed good to eat. On the way home the tortoise made up a song as he paddled along to help him remember the name of the tree. He sang:

Elephant! Eat the bojabi fruit!
Straight! Straight! Straight!
　Bojabi!
　Buffalo! Eat the bojabi fruit!
Straight! Straight! Straight!
　Bojabi!

The tortoise kept singing the song using the names of all the beasts of the forest he could think of. Waves turned his boat over, but he kept singing his message. The tortoise delivered his message, and all the creatures rejoiced that they could eat of the bojabi tree. The animals rushed to devour the fruit. The tortoise made sure to save plenty for his mother whose advice had brought him success.

The Leopard and the Dog

A long time ago all the animals of the forest agreed to have a great celebration. In making their plans, they discovered that they did not have a drum for the occasion. The leopard suggested that each animal give a piece of skin from his own body to make the drum. Each animal readily agreed. The dog was appointed to guard the pieces of skin until they were all collected. As the

bits of skin lay in the tropical sun, the smell became too much for the dog. He tasted one of the pieces and then ate it. He continued tasting pieces until he had eaten nearly all the skins.

The leopard came to look for the skins to make the drum. The leopard discovered what the dog had done. The leopard became angry and gave the dog a beating. Afterwards he chained the dog, making him a slave.

The leopard gathered all his children around him and made them promise to always hate the dog.

They promised to kill a dog whenever they saw one. The dog is still known as the leopard's slave, and they are still enemies.

The dog saw the babies of the leopard's daughter, the lioness. Cats look so much like baby lions that dogs imagine cats are the leopard's grandchildren. For this reason the dog is ever ready for a fight when he encounters the cat.

Proverbs From Africa

Another way Africans teach their children lessons is with proverbs. A **proverb** is a short, wise saying. Each proverb expresses an important lesson or a great truth.

Proverbs were used in Bible times to teach children. We have a whole book in the Bible called the Book of Proverbs. Many other proverbs can be found in the Bible. Here is what the Bible says about the reason for proverbs.

"The proverbs . . . to know wisdom and instruction; to perceive the words of understanding; to receive the instruction of wisdom, justice, and judgment, and equity; to give subtilty to the simple, to the young man knowledge and discretion."

Proverbs 1-4

Thousands of African proverbs teach children and adults lessons about how to live together. Many of these proverbs teach the same truths as Bible proverbs. Christian teachers in Africa enjoy African proverbs too. They especially enjoy those that teach the same lessons we find in the Bible.

One African proverb says, *The rain that falls on the master can fall on his slave too.* This teaches the same truth as the Bible. "He [God] maketh his sun to rise on the evil and on the good, and sendeth rain on the just and on the unjust."

Matthew 5:45b

Here are some other proverbs from various places in Africa, from the west coast to the east. What lessons do they teach? Can you find Bible verses that Christian teachers might use with many of these proverbs? Some of these lessons are given for you.

Someone who is greedy does not sleep at night nor go under the shade of a tree in the daytime. (A greedy person has no peace of mind.)

Might and strength cannot produce wealth. (Riches are a gift from heaven.)

425

The chimpanzee doesn't have a tail; he waited too long. (If there is something to do, do it right away.)

If money brings love into the house, it will carry it back when it leaves.

For wisdom's sake two people walk together.

A snake curled up eats nothing.

What Do You Say?

1. How did Africans pass their wisdom to their children before their languages were written?

2. Name and describe two kinds of stories told by Africans.

3. a. What is a proverb? b. For what purpose do Africans use proverbs?

4. Pick an African proverb given in this lesson and tell in your own words what you think it means. Use a proverb that does not have its meaning already given.

What Does the Bible Say?

1. Read Judges 9:8-15. This is a story much like the kind Africans use to teach their children. a. What is it that talks in this story? b. What lesson do you think this story might teach?

2. Read Proverbs 10 in your Bible. From this chapter list at least four short proverbs or wise sayings. What lesson do you think each one teaches?

The monkey ate with two hands, and fell from the tree.

African Religion

The first missionaries to Africa south of the Sahara found many different religions. Along the edges of the Sahara they found people who followed Islam. Islam is the religion of the Arabs. They also found this religion in places along the east coast.

Black Africans worshiped in many ways. Each ethnic group and sometimes each village had its own beliefs and gods. These religions used to be called tribal religions. Now they are usually called local traditional religions. Something that is **traditional** is something that has been done or believed for many years. Traditions are beliefs, customs, and ideas that have been passed on from parents to children for many years.

There are dozens of traditional religions in Africa. Each one is different. But in many ways these traditional religions are alike. All these religions teach that there is one supreme God. Usually the people do not worship this supreme God. African religions teach that people should seek help from other gods they believe are closer than the supreme God. The people also believe in many spirits. Many groups also worship the spirits of dead ancestors. Many groups worship the sun, rivers, mountains, and other things God created. People pray to or offer sacrifices to the gods and spirits. They do this hoping to gain good health, good crops, plentiful rain, and other things they need.

Many Africans believe that the

This fetish is from the country of Zaire in the heart of Africa. A fetish is an idol worshiped and honored by those who practice tribal religions. The worshipers hope the fetish will protect them or bring them good luck.

souls of their ancestors are reborn in other living things or even in objects. The Zulu people of South Africa refuse to kill certain kinds of snakes. They believe that the souls of their ancestors live in those snakes.

Many Africans use objects in their worship of the spirits. These objects are called fetishes. A **fetish** (fet′ ish) may be a stone or a piece of wood. Or it may be a beautifully carved statue. People believe that the fetish is the earthly home of some

427

god or spirit. Fetish worshipers believe the spirit in the fetish protects them from evil. They imagine that the fetish will bring them good luck. A fetish can also be an idol or the image of a god.

You may have heard of people who carry a rabbit's foot or a coin for good luck. Often these are hung on a chain around the neck. A rabbit's foot for good luck is a kind of fetish. Many people in North America also believe in fetishes.

This African witch doctor is from the country of Zimbabwe. The staff and the horn are symbols of the power he believes that he has.

Africans Ready to Accept Christianity. Many Christian missionaries in Africa have thought it would be hard for the Africans to become Christians. They thought about all the gods and fetishes the people would need to give up. In many communities men had many wives. The Bible teaches Christians to have only one wife.

Some of the missionaries had a surprise waiting for them. In some places, the people accepted Christianity very quickly. It seemed that something or someone must have prepared the people for Christian teaching.

One such group of people lived in the Central African Republic. This is a country in the heart of Africa. It lies between Zaire (Congo) and Chad. The Mbaka (əm bäk′ ə) people of the Central African Republic believed in a supreme God. They called Him *Koro.* This word is used for God in several Bantu languages.

The Mbaka used to tell a story that Koro, the Creator, sent a special message to their ancestors long ago. This message was that Koro had sent His Son into the world to do something wonderful for people. Later the forefathers turned away from Koro and forgot what it was that He did for them. Since that time the Mbaka have longed to know more about Koro and His Son. They believed that someday messengers would come to tell them more about Koro.

The Mbaka had some very interesting customs. They offered blood sacrifices. This reminded missionaries of the sacrifices in the Old Testament. Another most interesting custom was a kind of baptism. In many African religions, young people must pass certain tests or go through certain ceremonies. After these ceremonies, a young person is considered an adult member of the family or village. Among the Mbaka this ceremony was much like baptism. After an Mbaka young person

This is a church near Kinshasa in Zaire (Congo). Many churches and church schools are scattered across central and southern Africa. Some of them are little more than grass huts. This one is made of stone and has a metal roof.

was baptized, he had to pretend that he had been born anew. He was supposed to act like a young child. He did not talk or act like an older person for a few days.

Missionaries began to realize that long ago the Mbaka must have followed the true God. They forgot the truth and began to worship many gods and spirits. The missionaries realized that God had sent them to tell the people the truth about Koro. Many of the Mbaka people realized that the missionaries were indeed the messengers of Koro.

The Mbaka could easily understand that Jesus Christ was the promised Son of Koro. They understood and accepted baptism. The Bible says, "Ye must be born again." The Mbaka understood that this was

hn 3:7b

something like their custom of being born anew.

Not every group of people in Africa was so easy to win to Christ. Their beliefs were not as much like Christianity. But most of the African religions did teach something about the one true God. Christians have used this teaching to help the people understand that the Christian God is the one true God.

What Do You Say?

1. What do most traditional African

429

religions teach about God?

2. How do people who follow these religions try to find help for their problems?

3. What beliefs did the Mbaka people of the Central African Republic have that helped them to accept Christianity?

4. How has the African belief in one supreme God been helpful to missionaries?

What Does the Bible Say?

1. There is a story in the Bible about a people who believed in the true God. But they also worshiped many other gods. Read about them in Acts 17:22-25.
a. Who preached to them?
b. Whom did he say their unknown God was?

2. The Bible tells us about idols which are something like the fetishes you learned about in this lesson. Read Jeremiah 10:5. Name four things the Bible says an idol cannot do.

Using Globes and Maps

1. In an encyclopedia article on Africa, find maps showing where different peoples or ethnic groups live. You might also find maps that show where different languages are spoken. Often, the name of an ethnic group is also the name of a language. From the maps you find, make a list of at least ten peoples or languages found in Africa south of the Sahara. In what part of Africa is each found (eastern, western, central, southern)?

New Words and Terms

Here is a list of new words and terms you studied in this unit. Each term is followed by three choices. Choose the one that best describes the term.

1. tribe—a. one large family
b. people in the same country
c. a group with similar beliefs

and ways of doing things

2. linguist—a. a person who studies languages b. a person who studies geography c. a person who studies math

3. fable—a. a story that is true b. a story using animals and teaching a lesson c. a story about famous people of the past

4. proverb—a. a long story with a lesson b. a short, funny saying c. a short, wise saying

5. Swahili—a. a language spoken in northern Africa b. a language spoken in eastern Africa c. a click language

6. fetish—a. an object thought to bring good luck b. a foot doctor c. a witch doctor

7. click language—a. Swahili b. has special sounds made by the tongue c. official language of Nigeria

8. Kikuyu—A people who live in a. Kenya b. Nigeria c. Egypt

9. Pygmies—a. seven feet tall b. six feet tall c. four feet tall

10. dialect—a. a very different language b. one of several forms of the same language c. a click language

11. exaggeration—a. the truth b. bigger or greater than real c. not talking

12. traditional African religions— a. religions of many spirits and gods b. Islam c. an old Christian religion

13. The Mbaka believed in a supreme God and called Him a. Allah b. Guru c. Koro.

14. ethnic group—a. having different languages b. having the same language and customs c. one family

15. Mbuti—a. Pygmies b. Yoruba c. Zulu

16. official language—a. spoken by only a few b. spoken by everyone c. used in government and schools

17. legend—a. a story from the past b. a proverb c. a fable

18. language family—a. languages that are very different b. languages that are the same c. languages that are somewhat alike

Thinking Together

1. Nine of every ten Africans who live south of the Sahara are what kind of people?

2. Why do many people not like to speak of tribes when they speak of African peoples?

3. Why can we not speak of the Yoruba people as Nigerians only?

431

4. How do the Pygmies of the forest make their houses?

5. What great celebration do the Pygmies have in May and June?

6. About how many different languages are spoken in Africa?

7. Why is Swahili such an important language in eastern Africa?

8. Why have so many missionaries worked so hard to learn African languages?

9. What important work does the storyteller do in an African village?

10. a. What is a proverb? b. What is the purpose of a proverb?

11. Christians believe that the first people worshiped the one, true God. Later, many people began to forget God. What is it about African religions that shows us that their ancestors of long ago may have followed the true God?

For You to Do

1. Continue work on collecting information about Africa. This project is number two under **For You to Do** at the end of Chapter 24. By now, you should have decided what kind of display you want to make of Africa. If most of what you collected is pictures and flat items, you may want to make a bulletin board. If you have found some objects made in Africa, you might want to set up a table display.

2. In an encyclopedia, find five different countries of central or southern Africa. Find out what languages are spoken in each. If you can, find out what is the official language of each country.

26. Zaire (Congo)—Land of the Great River

Zaire (Congo), in the Heart of Africa

When some people think of Africa, they think of Zaire (zä ir′). Zaire lies near the center of Africa. Most of the country is far inland. Look at the map of Zaire below. Do you see the narrow strip of land on the left side of the map? This strip of land reaches out to the Atlantic Ocean. The Atlantic coastline of Zaire is only about 25 miles (40 kilometers) long. It is here that the great Congo River reaches the sea.

Zaire is the largest country in central Africa. The state of Texas would fit into Zaire three times! Zaire is about the same size as the

This village is among the hills of central Zaire. Much of this part of Zaire is grassland with forests here and there. Notice the round houses.

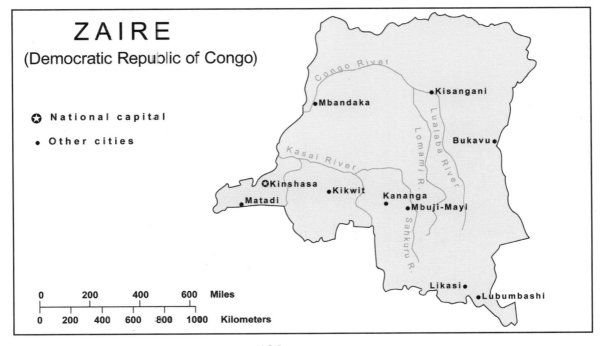

433

This beautiful waterfall is in the mountainous region of Zaire near the beginning of the Congo River.

has many rivers. We call the largest of these rivers the Congo, but in Zaire the people call it the Zaire. When your grandparents studied about Africa, Zaire was called the Belgian Congo. That is because the country once belonged to Belgium, a nation in Europe. A smaller country just west of Zaire is called the Republic of Congo. In 1997 a new ruler renamed Zaire the Democratic Republic of Congo.

A Trip Along the Mighty River. A trip along the mighty Congo River would tell you much about what the land of Zaire is like. Let us take an imaginary trip up this river. You draw near to the Congo River on an ocean freighter. Before you see land, you notice that the ocean water begins to look muddy. The muddy waters of the Congo reach out into the ocean more than 30 miles (48 kilometers). The Congo is seven miles (11 kilometers) wide at its mouth. The river's mouth lies between two

provinces of Ontario, Manitoba, and Saskatchewan put together. Among African countries, only Algeria is larger.

The name Zaire comes from an African word for "river." Indeed, Zaire

Dugout canoes are used by many people along the Zaire River. (This river is also known as the Congo.) Africans use such canoes to carry people and goods along the river and also from large boats to the shore.

Mangroves grow thick near the ocean in many warm parts of the world such as Zaire. Notice the roots of the trees in the picture. Such thick roots help hold dirt and sand. They also help keep ocean storms from washing away the land along the coast.

sandy points of land. They are called Banana Point and Sharks Point. No bananas grow at Banana Point.

Your ocean freighter travels inland for over 80 miles (130 kilometers) to the port of Matadi (mə täd′ ē). Along the way you see many islands in the river. Many creeks empty into the river. Along the shore you may notice thick clumps of mangrove trees. Mangrove trees must have their roots in water to grow. A person would need a strong ax or machete to chop his way through the thick growth of mangroves. Sand and soil wash among the mangrove roots. This slowly builds up rich soil. When enough soil builds up, the mangrove roots are no longer in water. The mangrove trees in the new soil die. In this way, mangroves help build up new land. They also help keep ocean water and storms from washing soil from the shore.

At Matadi, your ship must unload. To continue up the Congo, you must board a train to the capital city of Kinshasa (kin shäs′ ə). Between Kinshasa and Matadi, the Congo River falls over 800 feet (240 meters) from the highlands. You ride the train for over 200 miles (320 kilometers) to Kinshasa, and you bypass 30 rapids or low waterfalls.

At Kinshasa you can again board a ship. Many river steamers carry people and goods up and down the Congo.

You board a big three-decker steamer for the trip upriver. Two diesel engines pour out black smoke. Low, flat barges are tied to the ship. They carry extra cargo and people. One steamer with its barges may hold as many as a thousand people. The more well-to-do passengers stay in comfortable cabins on the third deck. The passengers below are crowded. Sometimes four to six passengers sleep in one small cabin.

You can travel for days on the river now. You travel northeast, deep into the heart of the greatest rain forest in Africa.

Life on the steamer is very different from anything you are used to. Each morning many of the passengers draw up water from the river for bathing and for washing clothes, pots, and pans. People called **vendors** sell food to the passengers. You might buy smoked fish, cassava, and various fruits and vegetables.

Each day you see men paddling out from the shore in long, narrow canoes called **pirogues** (pē rōgz′). These men have come from villages

This is a hydroelectric power plant near a large dam. Water falls through the large pipe near the top of the picture. The force of this falling water turns turbines that make electricity.

Interesting Facts About Zaire

Population: 46,498,539

Name: Zaire (means "river").

Congo: comes from **Kongo,** the name of an old African kingdom.

Size: More than three times larger than Texas.

People: More than 99 of every 100 are black.

Languages: More than 200 languages. French, a language from Europe, is the official language.

The River: The Congo River is the sixth longest river in the world. The Congo carries more water than any other river in the world except the Amazon.

The Rain Forest: Zaire has the world's second largest rain forest.

Chief Products: Corn, rice, cassava, cocoa, coffee, palm oil, cobalt, copper, gold, diamonds.

on the shore to trade with the people on the steamer. They also sell cassava and fish.

Your ship travels steadily on, day and night. It seems that the great rain forest will never end. Somewhere along the way, the river crosses the equator. It then curves to the east and slowly around to the south. The river again crosses the equator and heads southward. Near the equator is the city of Kisangani (kē´ sən gän´ ē). Again steamers must stop and unload. More rapids and waterfalls lie ahead. Above Kisangani is Stanley Falls. Do you remember the explorer for whom they are named?

Your ship is not traveling farther along the Congo. You could board another train to take you around Stanley Falls. Boats can travel further up the river until they reach more waterfalls.

Beyond Kisangani, the Congo River is called the Lualaba (lü´ ə läb´ ə). Livingstone discovered this river in his travels. He did not know that he had discovered a river that led to the Congo. He thought the river led to the Nile River.

If you were to continue up the Lualaba to its source, you would travel southward through grasslands with clumps of trees. You would be rising higher above sea level all the while until you are in highlands and mountains. You would reach several large lakes. Finally you would reach the source of the Congo River, high in the northern part of Zambia. There you would be some 6,000 feet (1,800 meters) above sea level.

Mangrove trees, grasslands, thick rain forests, more grasslands and trees, mountains, lakes, and waterfalls tell you a little about the African country of Zaire.

What Do You Say?

1. a. What is the meaning of the name *Zaire*? b. What was Zaire called before it was an independent country?

2. a. What do mangroves need in order to grow? b. How do mangroves help the coastline of Zaire?

3. Write a paragraph telling what it is like to ride a steamer up the Congo River.

4. Why cannot ocean ships sail to Zaire's capital, Kinshasa?

5. a. In what country does the Congo River have its source? b. How far is it above sea level?

What Does the Bible Say?

1. The Congo River is a great blessing from God to the people of Zaire. The Bible tells us some uses for rivers. Read Jeremiah 2:18 and 17:8 and find two important uses for rivers.

2. Read Ecclesiastes 1:7. What does the Bible say about where rivers like the Congo flow to?

Natural Resources in the Land of the Great River

As you might guess, water and rivers are the greatest resources found in Zaire. Today, railroads are found in parts of Zaire. But the railroads simply lead to rivers. Goods can be hauled much more cheaply on boats than on trains. Some roads and trails cross Zaire. But travel by river is usually faster. Zaire has about 7,200 miles (11,600 kilometers) of river that can be traveled by boat. The country has about 3,000 miles (4,900 kilometers) of railroad. The rivers are still the key to travel and trade in Zaire.

People who travel by river do not appreciate the many waterfalls in Zaire. The waterfalls stop steamers and boats. Goods must be unloaded and then reloaded on the other side of the falls.

But as we learned earlier, waterfalls can be useful. They can be used to make electricity. This hydroelectricity would be cheaper than petroleum, used to run the boats. Petroleum must be shipped in from the coast.

Zaire does not use many of its falls for hydroelectricity. Why not? Hydroelectric power plants are expensive to build. Once they are built, they provide inexpensive electricity.

This is a grove of cacao trees. Notice the long, rounded fruit hanging from the trunk of the tree. The fruit usually grows near the trunk of the tree rather than on the twigs like apples and peaches. The cacao tree grows well in Zaire and other hot, wet lands.

But someone must provide the money to build them. Sometimes the best falls for hydroelectricity are far from cities and other places that would use the electricity. Hundreds of miles of electric lines would need to be built. It is difficult to build power lines across rain forest and wide rivers. The area around the power lines would need to be kept free of trees and bushes. This is no easy task in the hot, wet rain forest.

438

Farming and Food Resources. Farming in Zaire still takes place mostly on small plots of land. After a few years the land is allowed to rest and become forest again. New land is cleared. This wise use of land has been followed for many hundreds of years.

In more recent times some farmers have tried clearing large tracts of land. This means cutting down much rain forest. But the farmers have found that after a few years the crops and heavy rains take much of the minerals and richness out of the soil. Then they must use expensive fertilizers to keep their crops growing well. Modern farming in the rain forest of Zaire has not turned out well. Outside of the rain forest, it is easier to farm large fields.

The main foods raised by Zairians are cassava, corn, and rice. Crops for sale include cotton, coffee, and tea.

The trees in the rain forest of Zaire are also important farming resources. Trees give the people of Zaire many things to use and sell. Tropical fruits such as bananas, coconuts, and mangoes grow in Zaire. Trees in Zaire also provide cocoa, palm oil, and rubber.

Cows, sheep, goats, and pigs are also found in Zaire. In many places, however, cattle cannot live because of the deadly tsetse (tset′ sē) fly. The fly carries a disease called

Beautiful palm oil trees grow near a stream. Like the cacao, these trees need plenty of water for growth. The palm kernels that are used to make palm oil grow near the top of the tree.

nagana (nə gän' ə), which affects cattle and horses. In people, the disease is called sleeping sickness. The fly bites an animal or a person that has the disease. Later, it bites another animal or person and passes the disease on. It seems that most animals native to Africa do not get nagana. Horses get the disease, for example. But zebras do not appear to get it.

In some places, spraying with **insecticides** has helped get rid of the tsetse flies. Insecticides are poisons that kill insects. They are too expensive to use all over Zaire. They can also be dangerous to other animals and to humans.

Mineral Resources. Zaire's most valuable mineral resource besides water is copper. In a recent year almost 600,000 tons (540,000 metric tons) of copper were mined in Zaire. The copper is used to make roofing, cooking pots, water pipes, gas lines, and electrical wires.

Diamonds are the next most valuable resource in Zaire. Zaire is the world's largest producer of industrial diamonds. Industrial diamonds are diamonds used for drills and saws in cutting hard metals.

Other valuable minerals found in Zaire include cobalt, gold, manganese, silver, tin, and zinc. Manganese is used in the making of steel. It helps to make steel one of the hardest metals.

The People of Zaire

Over 45 million people live in Zaire. More than 99 of every 100 are black Africans. The people belong to some 200 ethnic groups or tribes. The shortest people are the four-foot (120 centimeter) Pygmies of the forest. The tallest are the seven-foot (210 centimeter) Watusi farmers. But most of the people are about the height of North Americans.

Zairians speak dozens of different languages. Four main languages are used for trade. One of these languages is Swahili. In eastern Zaire many people speak Swahili as do their neighbors in Kenya and Tanzania. Another important language is Kikongo (ki kong' gō). It is used in western Zaire, especially along the Congo River. The official language of Zaire is French. Government leaders use French, and many study it in school. French was the language of the Belgians who once ruled Zaire. Although the people in Zaire speak different languages, if they learn French in school, they can meet and understand each other.

Life Among the People of Zaire (Congo).

About one out of three Zairians lives in cities and large towns. The rest live mostly in smaller villages. Not many people live in the open countryside between villages. Most people in the countryside live in houses made of mud bricks or dried mud and sticks. Most houses have thatch or grass roofs. People who are more wealthy live in houses with metal roofs. The wealthy in the cities live in modern houses much as Europeans and Americans do.

When the Belgians ruled, many of the people of Zaire began to wear clothing like Europeans or Americans. In 1960 Zaire became an independent country. The new rulers wanted the people to dress like Africans. Most Zairian men who have important jobs wear a special kind of clothing. They wear a suit without a collar and no shirt or necktie. Farmers and other workers wear long or short trousers and a shirt. Women wear long dresses made of colorful material. Women usually wear a cloth wrapped around their hair.

Tribal Religions in Zaire (Congo). About six of every ten Zairians follow traditional African religions. These people worship or honor spirits and false gods. They believe in the power of fetishes. When they are sick, many will go to witchdoctors. Witchdoctors use fetishes and magic. They pray to evil spirits. They also use herbs as remedies. But today more and more Zairians go to medical doctors and hospitals when they are sick. Many hospitals and smaller hospitals called clinics were started by Christian missionaries.

What Do You Say?

1. a. How is the Congo River a great natural resource of Zaire? b. What special use could be made of some of the waterfalls?

2. a. What size farms are most common in Zaire? b. Why?

3. Name three main food crops grown in Zaire.

4. a. List two main mineral resources found in Zaire besides water. b. What are some important uses of each?

5. a. Describe the houses of the poorer people who live in villages. b. What kind of houses do the rich have in the cities?

6. About what part of Zaire's people follow traditional African religions?

What Does the Bible Say?

1. Many Zairians are poor people. Read Proverbs 19:17. According to this verse, those who help the poor are actually doing what?

The History of Zaire (Congo)

The history of Zaire is much like the history of other African countries. Long ago, many tribes lived in the forests and grasslands. People

441

did not think of themselves as Zairians or even as Africans. The tribe was the most important government in each community. Many tribes were friendly toward one another. They traded with one another. But some tribes were enemies, and wars were fought. No one thought much about bringing all the tribes together into one country.

Pygmies were the first people known to live in what is now Zaire. They have lived there for thousands of years. About 2,000 years ago, other black Africans moved into this part of Africa. About 500 years ago, several powerful kingdoms ruled parts of the region. Each kingdom was made up of several tribes or ethnic groups. The largest kingdom was called the Kongo.

From this kingdom we get the name Congo.

The Coming of the European. In 1492 the first European explorer stopped at the mouth of the Congo River. Portugal was the first European country to trade with the Kongo kingdom. Roman Catholic missionaries came to teach their religion to the people. Many of the Kongo people became Catholics. Even the king of the Kongo kingdom became a Catholic.

Before long, the Portuguese began taking slaves from Africa to sell. They bought the slaves from traders in the Kongo kingdom. Many thousands of people from Zaire were taken as slaves. Most of them were sent to North or South America.

In 1876, Henry Stanley, the

This caravan of African slaves were chained together. The yokes sometimes tortured them to death.

442

You are looking at one of the main streets in Kinshasa, the capital of Zaire. The Congo River is on the right. Wide streets and skyscrapers were first built by the Belgians who once ruled Zaire.

explorer, crossed Zaire. He followed the Congo River from the eastern mountains to the Atlantic Ocean. Finally the interior of Africa and of Zaire could be mapped. Many more explorers, traders, slave traders, and missionaries traveled to the interior of Africa.

The Belgians Rule Zaire. The king of Belgium decided he wanted Zaire for his own. He hired Henry Stanley to set up a Belgian town along the Congo River. Many Belgians came to help rule the country for their king. Zaire became a colony belonging to King Leopold. A **colony** is a land that is settled and ruled by a distant country. At one time, nearly all the countries of Africa were colonies. They were ruled by different countries in Europe. England, France, and Belgium ruled the most colonies in Africa.

King Leopold of Belgium named his colony the Congo Free State. In 1908, the Belgian government took this colony away from Leopold. The Belgians renamed it the Belgian Congo.

The Belgians did much to help Zaire. They built many roads and railroads. They provided many jobs for the Africans. Christian missionaries took the Gospel to many peoples in the interior. Missionaries started most of the schools in Zaire. The first doctors were missionaries. The first clinics and hospitals were built by missionaries.

All was not well, however, in the Belgian Congo. The Belgians became very wealthy from the copper, gold, diamonds, and other resources of the Congo. They did not share this wealth with the Africans. They did not allow the Africans to have a part in the government of their country.

Independence Comes to Zaire. In 1960, the land we call Zaire became an **independent** country. Independence meant freedom from the rule of outsiders. No longer was this land a colony. Its people were free to form their own government and rule themselves. But in some ways they were not prepared to rule themselves.

After independence, the Belgian Congo became known as the Congo. Many tribes in the Congo did not trust the new government. Fighting started in many parts of the country. The southern part of the country was called Katanga (kə täng′ gə). The leaders of Katanga wanted it to become an independent country. The rulers of the Congo could not stop the fighting. They called in soldiers from the United Nations. Soldiers from many different countries came to help the Congo rulers. They wanted the Congo to remain one country.

In 1972 the Congo was renamed Zaire. The ruler of the country wanted the people to forget the past rule of the Europeans. He wanted them to think of themselves as Zairians and Africans. He renamed many towns and cities that had European names. The name of the capital city was changed from Leopoldville to Kinshasa. The ruler at that time was named Mobutu Sese Seko (mō bü′ tü sā sā′ sā′ kō). Mobutu encouraged his people to dress and act like Africans, not like Europeans. In 1997 the country's name became Congo again.

The Future of Zaire (Congo)

No one knows what may happen

This clinic was built by Mennonite missionaries in Zaire. It is for new mothers. Nearly all the hospitals, clinics, and schools in the country of Zaire were started by missionaries. This has been a great help to the people. Only in recent years have schools and hospitals been started by the government.

Missionaries started this elementary school in Zaire. The words on the blackboard are in French, the official language of Zaire. French is taught in most schools.

to the country of Zaire. Only God knows what the future will be. But we do know that this part of Africa will remain very important. For Zaire has more land and more people than most African countries south of the Sahara. We can expect Zaire to remain one of the most powerful countries of Africa.

Zaire has many important natural resources. It could become a wealthy country if it uses its resources wisely.

Historians, people who study history, tell us that Zaire's biggest problem is people. As long as fighting and hatred continue between ethnic groups, Zaire cannot become a strong country.

The people of Zaire need the Gospel of Jesus Christ. This is the greatest need of all the nations of the world. There are many false religions in Zaire. Many who say they are Christians mix Christian teachings with traditional African religions. Some who say they are Christians have become part of the wars and fightings.

Christians have translated the Bible into many of the languages of Zaire. This is giving more people an opportunity to understand the Gospel and follow Christ. We can pray for the people of Zaire that more would come to have the life and peace of Jesus.

What Do You Say?

1. How did the Portuguese mistreat the people of Zaire?

2. What are some things missionaries did to help the people of Zaire?

3. What does it mean for a country to become independent?

4. a. What would you say is the biggest problem in Zaire? b. What can be done about it?

What Does the Bible Say?

1. Treating people unkindly is called *oppression* in the Bible. Read Proverbs 14:31. a. What does the Bible say about the person who oppresses the poor? b. When a person honors God, how does he treat the poor?

2. Like many other countries, Zaire has problems with wars, fightings and hatred. a. What does Proverbs 10:12 say that hatred does to people? b. What is needed to overcome hatred, according to this verse?

Using Globes and Maps

1. Make an outline map of Zaire. Trace the main rivers in blue. On the map place the names of the larger cities and towns. Place a red star at the place where the capital is. You may use a map of Zaire in this unit for a guide, or you may use an encyclopedia or atlas map.

2. In an old encyclopedia, textbook, or other source, find a map of the Belgian Congo before independence. Your source must have been printed before 1960. Have your teacher or parent help you find the old map. Compare the old map with a map of Zaire today. List some changes in names of places since independence.

New Words and Terms

Define or tell something important about each person, place, or idea given below.

1. Zaire
2. Kinshasa
3. copper
4. Kikongo
5. colony
6. Mobutu
7. Belgian Congo
8. pirogue
9. Pygmies
10. Belgium
11. Matadi
12. insecticide
13. Watusi
14. French
16. independent

Thinking Together

1. a. How large is Zaire compared to the United States? b. How does it compare to Canada?

2. a. How is the Congo River a help to the people of Zaire? b. What makes travel on this river more difficult than on some rivers?

3. What kinds of land and plant life would you see on a trip up the Congo River from its mouth to its source?

4. How might many waterfalls in Zaire be put to good use?

5. How are certain trees important natural resources in Zaire? (Think of uses other than for wood.)

6. a. Name three languages spoken in Zaire. b. Why do you think it would be good to have an official language in a country like Zaire?

7. a. Who were the first people believed to have lived in Zaire? b. What was the name of the kingdom that has given us the name of the greatest river in Zaire?

8. a. How did Belgians help the people of Zaire? b. What did they do that was not good for the people? c. What did Christian missionaries do for the people?

9. Why do you think the name of the Congo and some of its cities were changed after the country became independent?

For You to Do

1. Finish collecting information

about Africa. Complete your bulletin board or display of items from Africa.

2. Make a wall map of Zaire, outlining its rivers in blue. Show Zaire's food, tree, and mineral resources with tiny pictures of the items placed at the proper place on the map. A natural resource map of Zaire in an encyclopedia will help you.

The Lands of the South

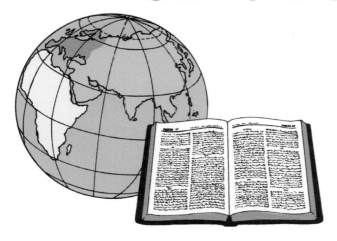

What you will learn ... in unit nine

In this unit we will study about the last lands of the world to be visited by explorers. These are lands far to the south of the equator.

About 2,000 years ago the Romans believed that a land or a continent lay far to the south. As explorers set out on their journeys, they found more than one southern land.

Almost 300 years after the discovery of southern Africa and America, explorers finally found a large land far south of Asia. At first they thought it was an island. When they found how large it was, they began to call it a continent. They named it Australia. Australia comes from a word which means "southern."

Explorers continued to sail south. Finally they discovered still another southern continent. They named it Antarctica.

In this unit we will learn more about Australia and Antarctica. We will also explore the islands of the Pacific Ocean south of the equator. These lands are so far from the Americas or Europe that we may forget them. But they are an important part of the world God created.

27. The Southern Lands and Climate

Lands "Down Under"

Look at a globe or a globe map of the Southern Hemisphere. If you look at the world with the South Pole in the center, what do you see? Did you realize that so much of the Southern Hemisphere is water? Most of the land in the world lies north of the equator. Parts of Africa and South America lie south of the equator. Most of the rest of the Southern Hemisphere is water except for the two continents of Australia and Antarctica.

Sometimes people call Australia "the land down under." They are used to looking at a globe from the north. Anything south of the equator is "underneath." How do you think a person who lives far south of the equator would look at a globe? He would most often look at it with his own country in view. He might look at it from the south. Then North America would be the land "down under"!

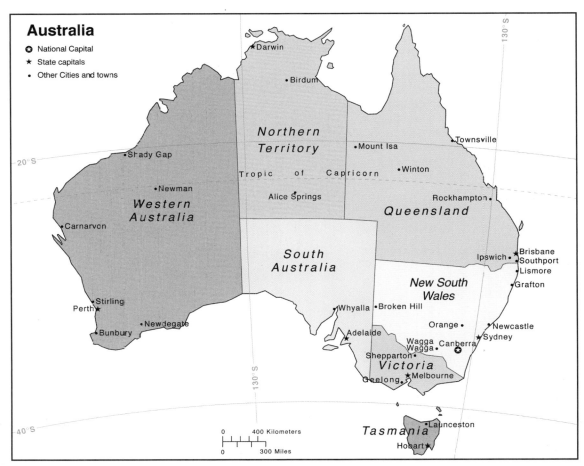

451

Australia and Antarctica lie far south of the Northern Hemisphere, where the most people live. They are on the opposite side of the earth. Did you ever hear anyone say that if you would dig straight down through the center of the earth, you would come out in China? This is not true at all. If you could dig through the center of the earth from the United States, you would come out in the Indian Ocean, near Australia.

Australia, the Island Continent

No one knows for sure who was the first explorer to see Australia. A Dutch sailor named Willem Janz (jäns) was probably the first person from Europe to see Australia. He probably saw northern Australia in 1606. He did not know that it was a continent. Another Dutch seaman named Abel Tasman sailed all the way around Australia, but did not see it! He landed on an island just south of Australia. He thought it was part of a great southern continent. Today this island is called Tasmania (taz mā′ nē ə). It is one of the states of Australia. Find Tasmania on the map of Australia.

Australia, a Big Land. It is surprising that Tasman sailed all the way around Australia without seeing it. How could he have missed a land so large? No one knows for sure. Australia stretches about 2,400 miles (3,900 kilometers) from east to west. From north to south it is almost 2,000 miles (3,200 kilometers).

Australia is nearly as large as the United States without Alaska. Some explorers called it an island. Because of its size, however, most people call it a continent today. Australia is the only continent that has only one country.

The first explorers to visit Australia did not have much good to say about it. They visited the northern and western coasts. They found great forests in the north and deserts in the west. In 1770, over 200 years ago, the British explorer James Cook explored the east coast of Australia. Here he found a well-watered land of hills and mountains. He liked what he saw. He claimed the land for Great Britain. He called it New

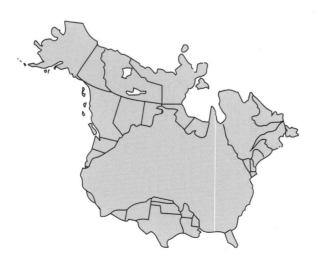

This illustration shows a map of Australia over a map of Canada and the United States. You can tell that Australia is about the same size as the United States. Canada, of course, is considerably larger than Australia. North to south, Australia would stretch from Hudson Bay in Canada to Florida in the United States.

Rich farmland is found in eastern Australia. Can you see the Great Dividing Range in the distance? This is one of the few parts of Australia with enough rainfall to do much farming. Farms or ranches such as this one are called "stations" in Australia.

South Wales. One of the states of Australia is still called New South Wales.

Australia—the Low Continent.

The mountains that James Cook saw were the only large mountains in Australia. These mountains run along the east coast of Australia. Cook found rich and beautiful lowlands along the east coast. But in the distance he could see the mountains. These mountains are not very wide or very high. They all lie 200 miles or less (320 kilometers) from the east coast. This range of mountains is sometimes called the Great Dividing Range. It divides the well-watered east coast from the drier interior of Australia.

The Great Dividing Range is not a large group of mountains like the Rocky Mountains in North America. It is not as wide as the Appalachian Mountain Range of eastern North America. And the mountains of the Great Dividing Range are not very high. The highest mountain in Australia is Mount Kosciusko (käz′ ē əs′ kō). This mountain is 7,310 feet (2,228 meters) high. Most of the mountains of the Great Dividing Range are much lower.

West of the Great Dividing Range, Australia is a very low continent. Much of the land is less than 1,000 feet (300 meters) above sea level. The average distance above sea level is lower in Australia than in any other continent.

The central part of Australia is a vast lowland. Much of the land is somewhat hilly, but it is not very high above sea level. These lowlands are called the Central Lowlands. The western half of Australia is called the Western Plateau. Most of it is 1,000 to 2,000 feet (300 to 600 meters) above sea level. Australia has several low mountain ranges, but few of them are over 5,000 feet (1,500 meters) above sea level.

Some of Australia's low western mountains rise from the almost flat desert floor. These mountains look more like giant rocks than like mountains. They are a brownish or reddish color. Almost no plants grow on them.

One of the most interesting sights in central Australia is called Ayers Rock. It is a huge rock, or maybe we could call it a small mountain. It rises suddenly from the desert floor. No other mountains are nearby. Ayers Rock is about 1½ miles long (2½ kilometers) and is 1,000 feet (300 meters) high. People fly out to the rock from the town of Alice Springs. This is the largest town in the central part of Australia. The photograph on page 455 shows you what this strange rock looks like. What color do you think it is? Tourists enjoy the colors of the rock. At different times of day, depending on the angle of the sunshine, the rock appears to be different colors. Usually it is a red or brownish-red color.

The walls of Ayers Rock have many small caves. The people who lived in Australia before the white man came did beautiful rock paintings on the walls of many of these caves. Some people enjoy climbing

This beautiful, fuzzy-leafed gum tree grows in the Australian desert. Another name for the gum tree is eucalyptus. Many kinds of gum trees grow in Australia, but most of them have bluish-green leaves. On page 462 you will read more about the eucalyptus tree.

Ayers Rock, but the climb is very dangerous. Some have fallen to their death. The government of Australia will not let anyone climb the rock without special permission.

Ayers Rock is very near the center of Australia. If a person would travel from the rock in any direction, he would need to go more than 1,000 miles (1,600 kilometers) to reach the ocean.

Lakes in the Desert! Australia has four large deserts. More than half of the country is either desert or nearly desert. The four deserts are almost like one large desert. But different parts of it have different names. In western and southern Australia, the desert reaches the ocean. Southwestern Australia and the northern part of the country have grasslands and trees.

Many people are surprised to learn of very large lakes in Australia's deserts. Yet these lakes usually do not contain much water. Most of the time the lakes are simply dry beds of clay or salt. Some of them are so hard that a truck can drive across them easily. Only after heavy rains do these lakes fill with water. Some of the lakes stay dry for years before a heavy rain falls.

The largest of these dry Australian lakes is called Lake Eyre (er). When there is water in it, it is shallow and salty. The lake is almost divided into two lakes. The northern part is largest and is 90 miles (145 kilometers) long and 40 miles (65

Ayers Rock in the heart of Australia. What people once lived in the caves in this rock? Can you see why the Australian government does not want people to climb the rock?

kilometers) wide. The southern part is about half as large.

The only lakes in Australia that contain water all the time are man-made lakes. These lakes are used for irrigation. Water from some of these lakes is allowed to flow into nearby rivers. This helps keep the rivers flowing during the dry season.

Rivers supply Australia with much of its valuable water resources. Can you guess what part of the country has the most rivers? If you guessed the eastern part, you are correct. All of Australia's longer rivers start somewhere in the Great Dividing Range. Shorter rivers flow from these mountains to the east coast. Longer rivers flow down the western side of the mountains. From there they flow to the Indian Ocean in the south. The longest river that

455

flows all the time is the Murray. This river is 1,609 miles (2,606 kilometers) long. The longest river in Australia is the Darling River. It comes from farther north and flows into the Murray. The Darling flows through dry country, and during the winter months it dries up. This is the dry season in central Australia. But in the south, the dry season is in the summer. Then, many southern rivers dry up. Water from the Darling River helps to keep the Murray flowing during the summer.

Northern Australia has a number of short rivers that flow into the Indian Ocean on the north. Heavy rains during the summer wet season cause these rivers to flood with water and rush to the sea. In the dry season some of them go dry. Western and central Australia have rivers too, but they are dry most of the time.

Australians can be glad that God has provided more water than what is found in their lakes and rivers. Too many of these go dry from time to time.

In parts of Australia, farmers depend on underground water. Much of this water is too salty for humans to drink, but cattle will drink it. In many places, cattle are watered altogether from underground supplies.

Most of eastern Australia has much water trapped underground. This water is under great pressure. Wells must be drilled. Australians call a well a **bore.** Bores drilled

where water is trapped under pressure do not need pumps. The water rushes to the surface and pours out on the ground.

A well which produces water without needing a pump is called an **artesian** (är tē′ zhən) **well.** Many artesian wells are found in eastern Australia. This area is called the Great Artesian Basin.

What Do You Say?

1. How did Australia get its name?

2. a. How large is Australia?
   b. Why do we call Australia the "island continent"?

3. In what way is Australia the lowest continent?

4. How are most of the lakes in Australia different from the lakes of North America?

5. Fill in the blanks:

   a. The word *Australia* comes from a word which means _____.

   b. The two continents entirely south of the equator are _____ and _____ .

   c. Another name for Australia is "the land _____ _____."

   d. The highest mountains in

Australia form the _____ _____ Range.

e. A famous rock in the heart of Australia is called _____ _____.

What Does the Bible Say?

1. The Bible lands are dry like much of Australia. People in both lands know what it is to have a short rainy season followed by a long dry season or drought. What does Job 24:19a say that drought does to moisture?

The Climate of Australia

Some of the first explorers in Australia believed it to be a wild, barren land. They found little water during the dry season. They found too much during the rainy season. They found a dark-skinned people who were not at all friendly to them. However, much of their problem with Australia had to do with the climate.

Explorers in eastern Australia had happier reports. Again these reports had much to do with the climate. The British explorer James Cook thought eastern Australia was a good place to live.

The best climate word to describe Australia is *dry*. This word does not describe all of Australia, of

Can you see why Australia is called the "dry continent"? Only the edges of the continent (dark green) have enough rainfall to grow crops without irrigation. Even in the wetter parts of Australia, droughts sometimes make problems for farmers.

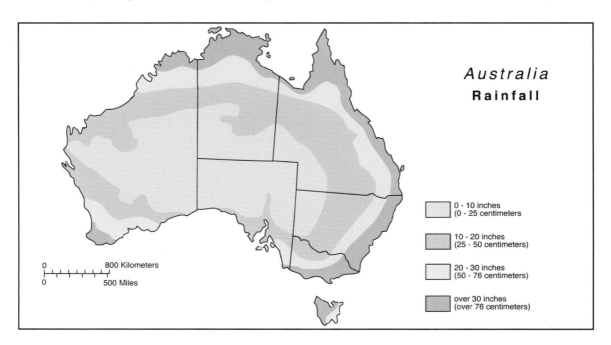

Australia
Rainfall

0 - 10 inches
(0 - 25 centimeters

10 - 20 inches
(25 - 50 centimeters)

20 - 30 inches
(50 - 76 centimeters)

over 30 inches
(over 76 centimeters)

0 ⊢⊢⊢⊢⊢⊢⊢⊢⊣ 800 Kilometers
0   500 Miles

course. But it does describe far more than half of the continent. Even where enough rain falls for crops usually there is a dry season. Almost all parts of Australia suffer droughts from time to time.

The desert areas of Australia receive less than 10 inches (25 centimeters) of rainfall each year. Some places receive only a few inches a year. But this is only on the average. A desert town may have a sudden rainstorm with many inches or centimeters of rainfall. They may then go a year or two until the next rain.

Most of Australia has a dry season and a wet season. In the north and northeast, the rain is especially heavy during the rainy season. Australians call this season "the Wet."

Geography and Climate in Australia. In Australia, we learn how geography affects climate. You learned earlier in this book that mountainous regions are often rainier than regions nearby. When warm ocean breezes blow inland and reach mountains, the moist air rises. As the air rises, it cools and clouds form. If the air cools enough, rain will fall.

Warm breezes from the Pacific Ocean blow toward the land along the east coast of Australia. The breezes soon reach the Great Dividing Range. Plenty of rain for crops falls along the coast and in the mountains. Some places along the northeastern coast receive over 100 inches (250 centimeters) of rainfall each year. More commonly along the east coast of Australia it may rain from 30 to 50 inches (75 to 125 centimeters).

You learned earlier that Australia is the lowest of all the continents. You would then expect much of it to be a dry continent. The west side of the Great Dividing Range is much drier than the east side. Much of western Australia is not very high above sea level. Breezes from the ocean cannot rise high enough to cool very much. Therefore, little rain falls. Cool ocean currents along the west coast and the southern coast also help keep the land drier. The air over cool ocean currents does not contain much moisture. Therefore, less rain falls, even if the air rises and cools.

In Australia the dry season of each year is a time of drought. Sometimes the dry season lasts longer than normal. In some years the rains are light in the wet season. It is then that Australians must be very saving with their water. We say that they are practicing water **conservation.** It seems that Australians must always be very careful in their use of water.

Another important word that describes Australia's climate is *sunny.* Of course, this is especially true in the desert where there are few clouds and where there is little rainfall. But even in the rainier parts of Australia, there are many sunny days.

Days and days of cool, cloudy, damp weather are unknown in Australia.

When rain falls in eastern Australia, it usually comes in short, heavy showers. The rest of the day is usually sunny and warm.

Another word that tells us about Australia's climate is *warm.* Look at the map of Australia on page 451. Find the Tropic of Capricorn on this map. The part of Australia north of the tropic is very close to the equator. The temperature is always warm or hot. The southernmost part of the continent of Australia is about as far from the equator as Virginia or southern Missouri in the United States. This means that it never gets as cold in Australia as it does in the northern United States and Canada.

In the coolest part of Australia, frost and snow are rare, even in winter. Only in the southern part of the Great Dividing Range does much snow fall. In June, July, and August snow falls high in the mountains. The lowlands nearby usually have rain.

Does it sound strange to you to hear of snow in July? You must remember that the Southern Hemisphere has winter while the Northern Hemisphere has summer. Southern Australians may play in the snow in July. During their Christmas vacation they may play outdoors or go to the ocean. If they want to escape the heat of December, they may go to the mountains.

So the words *dry, sunny,* and *warm* tell us much about the climate of Australia. Australians spend much time out-of-doors because of their climate. Their climate causes them to be more careful with water than many North Americans are. Frequent droughts help the people to appreciate the rains when they do come.

The Bible teaches all people to be thankful for the climate and weather that God sends. "[God] gave us rain from heaven, and fruitful seasons, filling our hearts with food and gladness." We should not wait for a drought to be thankful for all that God has done.

Acts 14:17b

What Do You Say?

1. Name three words that describe the climate in most of Australia.

2. a. What two seasons do many parts of Australia have as far as rainfall is concerned?   b. What do Australians call the season with the most rainfall?

3. Why is water conservation so important in Australia?

4. How should we feel about the climates God has given us?

What Does the Bible Say?

1. In this lesson, you learned about how geography can change the climate. Mountains and highlands often have more rainfall than lowlands. Read Job 24:8. What was true of the mountains described in this verse?

2. We know that water vapor from the ocean and winds are necessary to bring moisture to the land before it can rain. What does Psalm 135:7 say about water vapor and wind?

3. Read Ecclesiastes 1:6,7. a. What do these verses say about the winds? b. Where does some of the water go after it returns to the sea?

Natural Resources God Has Given Australia

Land and Water Resources. Most of Australia is a very dry land. Few people or animals can live in the driest parts of Australia. But this does not mean that there are few valuable natural resources in Australia.

Of course water is the most valuable natural resource in any part of the world. This is true for Australia as well. You have already learned about the great underground lakes and the artesian wells found in some of the dry parts of Australia. These wells provide water for sheep and cows. Often the water is too salty for people to drink.

The rains that fall on the Great Dividing Range provide water for crops and wells in eastern Australia. During the rainy season, heavy rains sometimes fall. Much of this rushes down the short rivers from the Great Dividing Range to the sea. This water is lost. But Australians have found a way to save some of this water.

This way of saving water that falls on the mountains is called the Snowy Mountains Scheme. The mountains in the southern part of the Great Dividing Range are called the Snowy Mountains. Many dams were built on the eastern side of the Snowy Mountains. But the water was needed more on the western side of the mountains. Great tunnels were built to carry water through the mountains to the Murray and Murrumbidgee (mər əm bij′ ē) Rivers. These rivers flow from the western side of the mountains. When these two rivers are about to go dry, water from dams in the mountains can help to keep them flowing.

Aqueducts (ak′ wə dəkts′) also carry some of this precious water to irrigate farmland west of the mountains. Aqueducts are ditches or channels which carry water from one place to another. Sometimes huge pipes are used for aqueducts. Water in these pipes does not evaporate as quickly as it would in the hot sunshine.

Many of the dams in the Snowy Mountain Scheme are also used to make hydroelectricity. Electric power plants at the dams change the power of falling water into electricity. Wires carry this electricity to the towns and cities of eastern Australia.

Mineral Resources in Australia. The first settlers in Australia soon learned of the vast desert that covered much of their country. They learned how dangerous it was to travel through this desert. Some people lost their lives trying to cross the desert. Many people thought these desert lands were of no value. Little did they know the great wealth that lay under the ground in many parts of Australia.

Australia produces more bauxite than any other country in the world. Bauxite is a soft rock from which most aluminum is made. Most of the world's opals are mined in Australia. Opals are jewel stones with beautiful rainbow colors.

Australia also mines large amounts of coal, copper, gold, iron, lead, nickel, silver, tin, and zinc. Petroleum is found under the shallow waters just off the southern coast. The richest deposits of uranium in the world are found in Australia. But other countries mine more uranium than Australia does.

Mining is often difficult and expensive in Australia because most of the valuable minerals such as uranium are found in desert areas. These places are usually far from where most of the people live. Roads or railroads must be built to these places. Towns must be built for the workers and their families. Still, Australia is becoming one of the most important mining countries in the world.

Farming in Australia. Farmers in Australia produce enough food for the whole country. They also sell or export much food and other farm products to other countries. Crops are grown on only five of every 100 acres (or hectares) of land. But over half the land can be used for grazing of sheep and cattle.

As you might guess, then, Australia's leading farm products are sheep, cattle, and products that come from these animals. Australia produces much wool, mutton (the meat of sheep), milk, and cheese.

Other important farm products from Australia are wheat, fruits, and sugarcane. Farmers raise sugarcane, bananas, and pineapples along the east coast in warm northern Australia. Crops such as apples and pears grow farther south. Southern Australia also produces oranges and grapes.

Some Plants and Trees of Australia

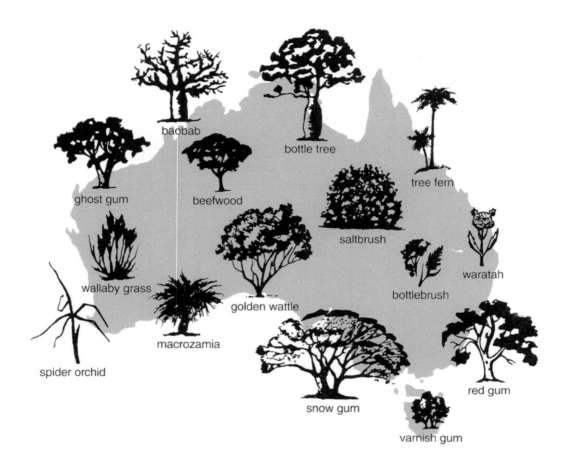

baobab

bottle tree

tree fern

ghost gum

beefwood

saltbrush

waratah

wallaby grass

bottlebrush

golden wattle

macrozamia

spider orchid

snow gum

red gum

varnish gum

Australia's Amazing Eucalyptus Trees

Nearly all of Australia's forests grow in the eastern highlands. Most of the trees that grow there are eucalyptus (yü′ kə lip′ təs) trees. There are about 600 kinds of eucalyptus trees in Australia. Some kinds of eucalyptus are used for making paper and furniture. Much eucalyptus wood is too hard for building houses and other buildings. Australians have planted forests of softwoods such as pine and fir to have more trees for lumber. The seeds came from other lands.

In Australia the eucalyptus is often called the gum tree. A sticky gum oozes out of the tree much like the pitch of pine trees in North

America. The eucalyptus is a valuable tree for things other than lumber. The sap is used to protect wood against boring insects of different kinds. The bark of some eucalyptuses is used to make **tannin.** This tannin is used in making medicines.

Have you ever sucked a eucalyptus cough drop? The strong smell and taste of these cough drops comes from eucalyptus leaves. This substance from the leaves of the eucalyptus helps soothe our throats and keep us from coughing.

Other countries have borrowed the eucalyptus tree from Australia. These trees grow well in the southern part of the United States, especially in California. In California they are planted near groves of orange trees as windbreaks. The eucalyptus trees grow very rapidly. In just a few years they become much taller than the orange trees and protect the tender orange trees from the wind. Eucalyptus leaves are long and feather-shaped. These gray-green leaves stay on the tree all year. Therefore, they are useful as protection against wind all year long.

Some Animals of Australia

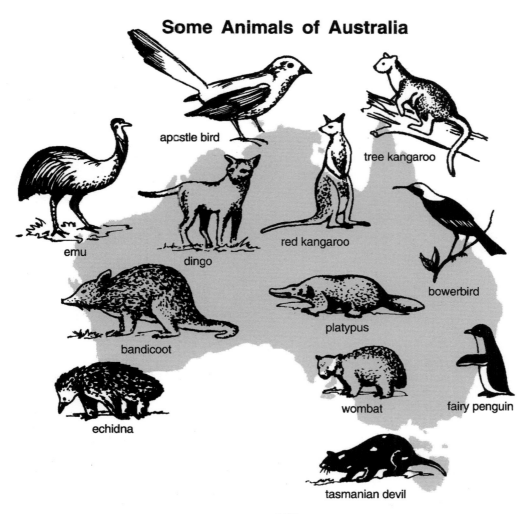

apostle bird

tree kangaroo

emu

dingo

red kangaroo

bowerbird

bandicoot

platypus

echidna

wombat

fairy penguin

tasmanian devil

Australia's most famous marsupial is the kangaroo. Australia has many different kinds of kangaroos. Some are as small as rabbits and some are taller than a grown man. Some kangaroos even live in trees, but most live on the ground. What is a baby kangaroo called?

Australia's Unusual Animals.

Australia has some of the most interesting animals in the world. The people who lived in Australia before the Europeans came had not tamed any of these animals. Today none of them are used as farm animals. All the horses, sheep, cows, pigs, chickens, and turkeys in Australia were brought there from other countries. Some native Australian animals can be used for meat. But most Australians would rather eat animals North Americans and Europeans are used to eating.

Most of Australia's land animals are **marsupials** (mär sü′ pë əlz). Marsupials are animals that carry their young in pouches on the underside of their bodies. The marsupials range in size from marsupial mice to large kangaroos. Look at the picture of the kangaroo, the most famous of the marsupials. Notice its front legs and feet. These can be used to fight enemies. God made the large hind legs for fast hopping. A large group of kangaroos is called a **mob**. A young kangaroo is called a **joey**.

Australia has about 45 different kinds of kangaroos. Some of them

The koala spends most of its time in eucalyptus trees where it eats the tender shoots. The koala is awake and feeds at night. The koala looks something like a child's teddy bear.

are only a foot (30 centimeters) tall. The largest of the kangaroos may reach nine feet tall (about three meters).

Another favorite marsupial is the koala (kō äl′ ə). Some people call the koala a bear, but it is not a bear. It is a marsupial which lives in trees. The koala eats only eucalyptus leaves and almost never drinks water. It gets its water from the leaves. The koala's name means "no water."

Perhaps the most unusual of Australia's animals is the platypus (plat′ i pəs). The platypus likes to swim in water. It has a bill that looks much like a duck's bill. It has webbed feet like a duck. It lays eggs. So, what is so unusual about this bird, you may ask? The platypus is not a bird at all! It has soft brown fur, not feathers. The platypus feeds its young with milk. No bird does that.

An unusual bird of Australia is the bowerbird (baủ′ ər bərd′). Like all birds, it has feathers and lays eggs. But its strange habits make it unusual. The male of some types of bowerbird builds a wigwam-shaped playhouse from twigs. It decorates its house with colorful feathers, pebbles, and other pretty things it can carry in its beak. It gathers moss and makes a pretty little lawn in front of its house. Then it hops and parades in its house until it attracts a female bowerbird. The female does not use the playhouse for a nest, but builds a simple nest in a tree for her eggs.

The wombat is also a marsupial and carries its young in a pouch. It has coarse brown fur and measures up to four feet long (a little more than a meter).

What Do You Say?

1. a. What water supply do the people in the dry central part of Australia depend on? b. Why can people not drink this water?

2. a. How do Australians get water from the eastern side of the Great Dividing Range to the western side? b. Why do they do this?

3. What do the following words mean? a. aqueduct b. tannin c. marsupial d. joey

4. In what ways are eucalyptus trees used?

What Does the Bible Say?

1. God has created many useful trees in different parts of the world. The eucalyptus tree is one of the most useful trees in Australia. The Bible tells many ways trees can be used. Read each Scripture below and list the use for trees found in each:

   a. Leviticus 19:23

   b. 1 Chronicles 22:4, 5

   c. Job 40:21

   d. Matthew 21:6-8

Other Lands of the Southern Ocean

The Lands Called Oceania. Australia is by far the largest land of the southern oceans. But millions of people live in other parts of these oceans, especially in the southern Pacific Ocean. Thousands of islands are scattered across the Pacific Ocean. Some of them are large islands, but most are very tiny. Hundreds of miles of water lie between most of the islands. Many people call the islands of the south Pacific, **Oceania** (ō′ shē an′ ē ə). The islands of Oceania lie just north and east of Australia. They reach far out across the Pacific toward North and South America. Japan, the Philippines, and Indonesia are Pacific Islands also. However, they usually are not considered part of Oceania. These islands are usually studied along with the continent of Asia.

Geographers divide the islands of Oceania into three groups. The island groups are called Melanesia, Micronesia, and Polynesia. The "nesia" part of each of these words means "islands."

The islands just north of Australia are called **Melanesia** (mel′ ə nē′ zhə). The word *Melanesia* means "black islands" or "dark islands." They are called this because many of the peoples of these islands have very dark skin. Some are as black as black Africans. It is believed that the Melanesians came from Asia or Africa thousands of years ago.

Most of the islands of Melanesia are very mountainous. Some of them are very large islands. The second largest island in the world is part of Melanesia. This island is called New Guinea (gin′ ē). Find it on the map of Oceania on page 467. New Guinea lies very near the equator. It is a hot, rainy land. However, some of its mountains are so high that they are snowcapped all year.

The second group of islands includes much smaller islands. They lie just north of Melanesia. These islands are called **Micronesia.** *Micronesia* means "tiny islands." Most of these islands are only a few miles long. A different, lighter-skinned people live in Micronesia.

The last group of islands is

466

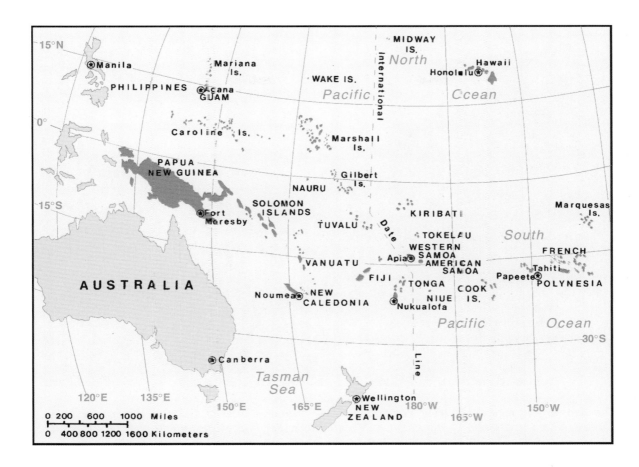

This map of Oceania shows the many islands that lie north and east of Australia. The map is able to show only a few of the larger islands. There are many thousands of islands too small to show on this map.

called **Polynesia.** *Polynesia* means "many islands." The largest island of Polynesia is New Zealand. It lies a few hundred miles or kilometers east of Australia. The other islands of Polynesia are scattered across the Pacific as far north as the famous islands of Hawaii (hə wä′ ē). Many of the people on the islands of Polynesia are of the Polynesian race. They are different from the peoples of Melanesia and Micronesia.

Different Kinds of Islands. Geographers also divide the islands of Oceania into two main kinds of islands. They speak of the high islands and the low islands.

The high islands are islands with hills and mountains. New Guinea is the highest of the high islands. New Zealand and Hawaii are also high islands. In places, steep mountains seem to rise right from the sea.

The second kind of islands are the low islands. These are low and almost flat islands. Most of them are smaller than the high islands. Most lie only a few feet or meters above

467

The two largest islands of New Zealand are the largest islands of Oceania except for New Guinea. The snow-covered mountain is Mount Cook, the highest mountain in New Zealand on South Island. The rolling pastureland below is on the less mountainous North Island. Visitors to New Zealand say it is one of the most beautiful lands in the world.

sea level.

Most of the low islands once lay just below the water. Millions of tiny sea animals lived on the rocks just below the surface of the ocean. When they died, they left behind their shells, called coral. Very slowly the coral shells piled up until some of them were above the water. This formed low islands.

Coral islands form a large circle in the ocean. The circular island is called an **atoll** (at′ ol). The area of shallow water inside the circle is called a **lagoon** (lə gün′). If you could look down on a coral island from the air, you would probably see coral around the edges of the island just below the surface of the water.

No one knows for sure how many islands are in Oceania. There are thousands of them. Many of them are little more than rocks rising out of the water. People live on only a few hundred of these islands. We say that the islands where people do not live are **uninhabited.**

If we could put all the islands of Oceania together, they would cover a smaller land area than the state of Alaska. This includes the islands of New Guinea and New Zealand. If we leave out New Guinea and New Zealand, all the other islands together would be no larger than the state of New Mexico.

Resources God Gave Oceania

Oceania is so much water and so little land. This means there is not much room for crops. Not many natural resources can be found on such small pieces of land. The larger islands and the mountainous islands usually have the most natural resources.

The people who live on the Pacific Islands have always had enough food and material to build their simple homes. However, not all the islands have natural resources to sell or export. The first white people who came to the islands were interested in gold and other minerals. The Polynesians, Melanesians, and Micronesians did not understand the white man's strange desire for such things. At that time, the islanders did not need them.

Mineral hunters in Oceania found some gold. They also found nickel, bauxite, and other minerals. Some of the islands had large

The hilly and mountainous Fiji Islands are among the larger islands of Oceania. The mountainous islands usually have more rainfall than the flatter islands. Do you know why?

deposits of phosphate rock. Phosphate is used as a fertilizer. Of course, miners could find only so much phosphate on small islands. Now most of the phosphate is used up.

Large islands such as New Guinea and New Zealand have valuable forests. Many of these have been cut for building and firewood.

Another interesting resource on some of the Pacific Islands is **guano** (gwän′ ō). Guano is the droppings or manure of sea birds. Thousands of birds roost on the islands. These droppings pile up on the rocks and bare ground. They make very valuable fertilizer. Some of the rocky islands of the Pacific are called guano islands. On many of them the guano soon ran out. It will take many years for guano to again pile

The photo above shows a quiet, peaceful Pacific Ocean. The first European to see this ocean saw a calm sea. He named the ocean the Pacific which means "peaceful." But the Pacific can be anything but peaceful as in the photo below. The islands of Oceania sometimes suffer from severe storms.

up in amounts worth taking for fertilizer.

The larger islands often have good soil for growing crops. Islands such as Hawaii and Fiji grow large crops of pineapples and sugarcane. Sugar is the main industry on Fiji. Find Hawaii and Fiji on the map of Oceania. The people of New Guinea raise much coffee and cocoa.

The Valuable Coconut Palm

What do you think of first when you think of the Pacific Islands? Many people think of the tall, beautiful coconut palms along the ocean.

The coconut palm tree grows easily on many of the islands of Oceania. It will grow in very sandy soil near the ocean where the water is salty. The coconut will grow where many other kinds of trees will not. Coconut palms are good for more than beauty, of course.

The coconut palm is most valuable for its nuts. One tree may bear as many as 100 nuts each year. It takes a whole year for a nut to ripen. Therefore, coconuts do best in places that are warm all year.

The nut of the coconut is surrounded by a smooth rind. Under the rind is a layer of loose fibers. Inside the fibers is the nut of the coconut. This seed is 8 to 12 inches (20 to 30 centimeters) long and 6 to 10 inches (15 to 25 centimeters) across. The nut has a very hard outer shell. The white of the nut must be peeled away from the inside of the shell. The coconut is hollow inside, but it is not empty. The hollow space contains a delicious liquid we call coconut milk. Coconut milk is especially valuable on islands where there is little good drinking water.

Coconut meat can be eaten raw. However, most of it is dried so that it can be easily shipped to faraway countries. Dried coconut meat is called **copra** (kō′ prə). Copra is the most valuable export of many of the Pacific Islands. It takes about 6,000 coconuts to make a ton of copra. At least how many trees would it take to produce 6,000 coconuts?

The most valuable copra is that which is dried in the sun. It keeps its white color. Some islands, however, have too much rainfall and dampness to dry coconut this way. In these lands, the meat is dried over fires built under shelters. This copra is dark-colored.

Copra has many important uses. It can be shredded into the coconut we use in cookies, candies, and other foods. Copra contains a very valuable oil used for cooking. Coconut oil can also be used to make magarines and soaps. Ask your parents if you can look at the ingredients listed on cereal boxes, store-bought candies, cookies, or crackers. How many of them do you find with coconut oil as an ingredient?

Pacific Islanders use coconuts in other ways we might not think of. The hard coconut shell can be scraped clean and used as a bowl. Half a coconut shell is about the size of a soup bowl. The fiber in the husk around the nut is called **coir** (kȯir). The islanders use coir to make mats, ropes, and brooms. Coir can also be used to make a coarse cloth. Coir was once used in padding car seats. Now most seats are padded with foam or other materials.

The trunk of the coconut palm is strong wood. It is valuable for building houses and other shelters. On some islands the coconut palms provide all the wood there is. The wood, husks, and coconut shells may all be used for firewood. The shells also make good charcoal.

The feathery leaves of the coconut palm may be used to make mats as well as walls and roofs of houses. The islanders also enjoy a delicious salad made from the tender shoots that grow near the top of coconut trees.

You can see that the coconut tree is as valuable to the people of Oceania as the date palm tree is to the people who live in the deserts of the Middle East. Almost every part of the tree is used. No matter where people live, God provides ways for them to find food, drink, clothing, and shelter. Truly He "giveth us richly all things to enjoy."

1 Timothy 6:17

What Do You Say?

1. Tell where the following places are found: a. Oceania b. Melanesia c. Micronesia d. Polynesia

2. What do each of the following words mean? a. atoll b. coral c. uninhabited d. guano e. copra f. coir

3. List as many uses as you can of the coconut palm for the people of Oceania.

What Does the Bible Say?

1. The Bible speaks of islands or isles. What does the Bible say about islands or the people who live on islands in each of the following passages?
   a. Isaiah 42:4
   b. Isaiah 42:12
   c. Psalm 97:1
   d. Revelation 16:20

2. In every land you have studied about in this book, you have learned of God's provisions for

food, water, and other things people need. We call these things natural resources. The Bible calls such things "blessings," and God's "mercy." Read Psalm 136:25, 26. a. What does God give? b. To whom? c. What should we do because of what He has given?

Chapter Twenty-Seven Review

Using Globes and Maps

1. From the maps in your text or other maps, draw a map of Australia. Draw dotted lines showing where all the states are. Name each state. Show the Darling and the Murray Rivers and Lake Eyre. Draw mountain peaks, something like this ⌃⌃⌃ ⌃⌃⌃⌃ to show the location of the Great Dividing Range.

2. On a globe or map of the Southern Hemisphere, use the scale of miles to find how far it is from Australia to the following places: Asia, California (North America), Peru (South America), the southern tip of Africa, Antarctica.

New Words and Terms

Fill in the blanks with some of the things you have learned in this chapter. Use the words and terms found in the list on page 474.

1. *Australia* comes from a word which means _____ .

2. The island just south of the continent of Australia is called _____ .

3. The explorer who liked what he saw on the east coast of Australia was named _____ _____ .

4. The mountains of eastern Australia are called the _____ _____ _____ .

5. _____ _____ is a huge rock found in central Australia.

6. Lake _____ is the largest lake in Australia. Most of the time it has no water in it.

7. A bore is the Australian word for a _____ .

8. Water from an _____ _____ is trapped under pressure. The water rushes to the surface without a pump to bring it up.

9. The longest river in Australia that flows throughout the year is called the _____ River.

10. The rainy season in Australia is often called _____ _____ .

11. _____ means being very saving with something such as water or other natural resources.

12. The system of dams and lakes which helps to conserve water in eastern Australia is called the _____ _____ _____ .

13. Most of the world's _____ are mined in Australia.

14. Australia's leading farm products come from _____ and _____ .

15. Australian animals that carry their young in pouches on the undersides of their bodies are called _____ .

16. A young kangaroo is called a _____ .

17. The _____ lives in trees and eats only eucalyptus leaves.

a. Murray
b. marsupials
c. cattle
d. well
e. Eyre
f. artesian well
g. southern
h. Great Dividing Range
i. Snowy Mountain Scheme
j. James Cook
k. joey
l. the Wet
m. sheep
n. Ayers Rock
o. koala
p. Tasmania
q. opals
r. conservation

Thinking Together

1. a. What does the name *Australia* mean? b. How is this a good name for the continent?

2. List at least two nicknames that have been used for Australia. Tell how each one describes the continent.

3. Why do geographers call Australia a continent instead of an island?

4. How high is the highest mountain in Australia?

5. How are the lakes in Australia different from most lakes in North America?

6. a. What are the rivers like in Australia? b. What does the climate of Australia have to do with these rivers?

7. What is the difference in the weather between the eastern side and the western side of the Great Dividing Range?

8. Name three climate words that describe most of the continent of Australia.

9. What are aqueducts, and how are they important in Australia?

10. a. List ten important mineral

resources found in Australia. b. Why is it difficult and expensive for Australians to mine these resources?

11. Name at least three uses of the eucalyptus tree.

12. Name four of Australia's famous animals and briefly describe each one.

For You to Do

1. Write to the embassy of Australia in Washington, D.C., and ask for literature and pictures of Australia. Your teacher can call the local public library to obtain the address. You may need to wait several weeks for an answer.

2. Write a report of at least 75 words on one of the following: kangaroos, koalas, exploration of Australia, the climate of Australia. Find at least one fact about the one you choose that is not found in your textbook. Use an encyclopedia or a book about Australia.

3. As a class project or a project to do at home, buy a coconut from a grocery store. Punch holes in the "eyes" at one end. Drain the coconut milk out and taste it. Now hold the coconut lengthwise. Get someone to help you. Using a very sharp knife, cut it in half. Now scrape out the coconut meat from both halves. The half without the eyes or any holes can be used for a bowl or dish as the Pacific Islanders do. Sand the shell to remove the loose fibers. If the shell does not sit evenly on a table, file off a flat place on the bottom until it does. The shell may be used for a dish.

This harbor is at Hobart, the capital of Tasmania. Who discovered the land of Tasmania? Today, Tasmania is one of the states of Australia. Many Australians take vacations to beautiful Tasmania. The summers are much cooler in Tasmania than in most of Australia.

28. History and Peoples of Australia and Oceania

The Aborigines. The first people to live in a place used to be called

These skyscrapers are in Sydney, Australia. Sydney is the oldest and largest city in Australia. Sydney was started as a colony for prisoners who were sent from Great Britain to Australia. Australia has a number of large cities along the coast, but few people live deep inside the dry continent.

aborigines (ab′ ə rij′ ə nēz). Today we might call them natives. Some people call the American Indians, Native Americans. The word *aborigines* has stuck as the name of the first people to live in Australia. When we speak of these Australians, we capitalize the word *Aborigines.* The word *aborigine* comes from two words which mean "from the beginning."

The Australian Aborigines did not live in Australia from the beginning of time, of course. No one knows how long they have lived there. But we believe they have been there for at least several thousand years.

Abel Tasman and other explorers

476

first visited Australia in the 1700s. Historians believe about 300,000 Aborigines lived in Australia at this time. After the white man came, many Aborigines were killed in battles with the whites. Others died of new diseases the white man brought to Australia. By the late 1800s only about 40,000 Aborigines were left in Australia. Today there are over 257,000 Aborigines. Many of these people are only part Aborigine. This means that one of their parents or grandparents was a white person.

Most Aborigines are dark-skinned people with dark brown hair. But others are lighter-skinned and have lighter-colored hair. Some people think the Aborigines are related to the African Negroes or blacks. But the Aborigines are quite different. For example, Aborigines usually have more hair and the men have bushier beards than African blacks have.

The Aborigines were once divided into about 500 tribes or groups. Each tribe had its own language. Today, not nearly so many languages are spoken. Most Aborigines can speak English, but many also speak their Aboriginal language. Some of the languages are almost gone. Only a few hundred people speak them now.

Life Among the Aborigines

Long ago the Aborigines hunted animals and gathered plants to eat. They never learned to raise vegetables or other crops in gardens or fields. They never tamed any

These high school students are from a church school in Papua New Guinea. About 98 of every 100 people in Papua New Guinea are Melanesians. They have dark skin and curly black hair. New Guinea is the largest island of Oceania and the second-largest island in the world.

animals except the wild dogs called dingos. It is believed that the Aborigines brought the dingos with them when they first came to Australia.

The Aborigines traveled from one place to another hunting food and water. They had no houses as we know them. At each place where they would stop, they would build shelters of branches and bark. The eucalyptus trees so common in Australia often shed their bark. The Aborigines would collect the bark for shelters and for building fires. The Aborigines used their shelters for protection from rain and from the cool nights. Many Aborigines slept out in the open, even when the nights were cool. Their bodies became used to the cool air and would stay warm even on cool nights.

The men among the Aborigines hunted large animals. The women captured smaller animals and collected plants to eat. The Aborigines hunted with spears, nets, traps, clubs, and **boomerangs** (bü′ mə rangz′). They made their tools of wood, stone, and animal bones.

Many of the first white settlers

The Boomerang

The boomerang was a special tool of the Aborigines. They used two kinds of boomerangs. The most famous is the returning boomerang. Returning boomerangs are curved sticks shaped something like a bird's wing or an airplane wing. The inside edge of the boomerang is thick, and the outside edge is thin. When a person throws this kind of boomerang properly, it returns to him. These boomerangs may travel up to 150 feet (45 meters) before they return. Many stores around the world sell wooden or plastic returning boomerangs. The Aborigines used returning boomerangs mainly for games. Children learned about throwing boomerangs with these toys. The returning boomerang is not very useful as a weapon to kill animals.

The most useful boomerang of the Aborigines was a kind which did not return. This boomerang could travel up to about 300 feet (90 meters). The Aborigines used non-returning boomerangs to kill animals such as kangaroos. A spinning boomerang had much more force for killing an animal than simply a thrown rock or stick.

The Aborigines used the boomerang for more than killing animals. They used it as a weapon in war to kill other people. Boomerangs were used as tools for cutting or scraping. They were used for trading with other tribes. Some boomerangs were painted with pretty designs to tell stories and legends. Boomerangs were even clapped together to accompany singing.

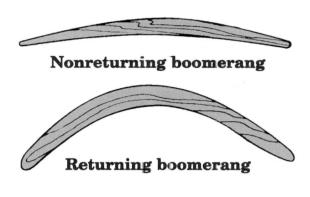

Nonreturning boomerang

Returning boomerang

Boomerangs were invented by the Australian Aborigines. They were invented not only to be used as toys, but to kill wild animals.

in Australia were very unkind to the Aborigines. They imagined that the Aborigines were not very intelligent. But the beautiful drawings and cave paintings done by the Aborigines show otherwise. Some of these paintings can be seen in the caves at Ayers Rock in the heart of Australia. Aborigines also wove beautiful baskets and mats. They carved statues from wood and stone.

The most important thing about the Aborigines is that they are humans made by God. For this reason they should be treated with kindness. The Bible says God "hath made of one blood all nations of men for to dwell on all the face of the earth."

ts 17:26a

The Aborigines were a very religious people. They believed in beings who had created the world, plants, animals, and people. According to their legends, a giant marsupial carved the hills, and a giant snake hollowed out the riverbeds.

The Aborigines also believed in

magic and the powers of dead ancestors. Some of them still hold to their ancient beliefs.

What Do You Say?

1. a. Who are the Australian Aborigines? b. What does the word *aborigine* mean?

2. a. About how many Aborigines are believed to have lived in Australia when it was first discovered by Europeans? b. About how many live in Australia today?

3. How did the Aborigines get food?

4. What did the Aborigines believe about the creation of the world?

What Does the Bible Say?

1. Read Jeremiah 10:2, 3. a. What warning does God give His people about the heathen and their customs? b. What does the Bible say about the sinful ways of the people?

479

2. The Australian Aborigines believed in magic and the power of evil spirits. The Bible calls this belief *sorcery*. Read about sorcery in Acts 13:6-10. a. What did the sorcerer (one who practices sorcery) do (verse 8)? b. What is a sorcerer like, according to verse 10?

Pacific Island Peoples

Melanesians. The first people to live in the islands just north of Australia were dark-skinned people. Some of them were black people who looked much like Africans. They were different from the dark Aborigines of Australia. The people are called Melanesians.

The Melanesians, like the Aborigines, spoke hundreds of different languages. Bible societies are still working on translating many of these languages. Then the people can have Bibles and other Christian literature in their own language.

The island of New Guinea is the largest land of Melanesia. On this island there are hundreds of tribes. The eastern half of the island is the country of Papua (pap´ yə wə) New Guinea. The western half of the island is part of the country of Indonesia. It is called West Irian (ir´ ē än´). Papua New Guinea alone has over 700 languages.

One of the most interesting languages of Papua New Guinea is called **Pidgin**. It is used in many

This village of grass houses is on the Fiji Islands. Such houses are cool in the hot climate of these islands. The islanders make good use of grasses and palm trees for building their houses.

places, especially along the coast. This language is a mixture of English and other languages. It is used for trading, but is also spoken by many people at home. A person who speaks English can soon learn Pidgin. Pidgin has many interesting ways of saying things. It often uses the word *bilong* which means "belong." For example, *grass bilong hed* means "hair." *Felo* is another important Pidgin word. It means "fellow" or "man" or "person" or "someone." It can also mean "thing" or "kind."

Here is a version of the Ten Commandments in the Pidgin of New Guinea. See how many words you can figure out:

I. Mi Master God bilong yu yu no ken mekin masalai end ol tambaran.

II. Yu no ken kolim nating nem bilong God.

III. Yu mast santiuim sande.

IV. Yu mast mekinggud long papamama bilong yu.

V. Yu no ken kilim man.

VI. Yu no ken brukim fashin bilong marit.

VII. Yu no ken stilim samting.

VIII. Yu no ken lai.

IX. Yu no ken duim meri bilong enaderfelo man.

X. Yu no laik stilim samting.

Did you understand what you read? You can soon understand that *papamama* means "father and mother." *Kilim*, of course, means "kill." In the sixth commandment, *brukim* means "break" and *marit* means "marriage." *Stilim* means steal and *samting* means "something." *Enaderfelo man* means "another fellow man."

The Micronesians. Just north of Melanesia lie the tiny islands of Micronesia. It is believed that people first came to these islands from Asia thousands of years ago. These people are a little lighter-skinned than the Melanesians. They are more like the people of southeastern Asia today.

Long ago these people must have sailed by canoe or boat from one island to another. We wonder how they did this when some of the islands lie hundreds of miles apart. The islanders were very wise in the ways of the sea. They learned to watch the sky to tell when storms were coming. They would not sail until the weather signs were good.

These people also learned to watch for signs of islands. One way they could guess where an island might be was to watch the way seabirds flew. These birds nested on islands. They could be followed to find another island.

Sometimes sailors could find an island by looking for clouds in the distance. Wherever a mountainous island rose from the sea, the air would rise as it passed over the mountain. This air would cool. The moisture in the warm air would condense. Clouds would form. From far away, sailors would see a group of clouds before they could see the island. If they sailed toward the clouds, they often found the island they were looking for.

The Polynesians. The Polynesians also came from Asia long ago. They moved farther away from the continent than any other people. Their islands lie widely scattered across the middle of the Pacific. The islands are much farther apart than the islands of Melanesia and Micronesia.

The Polynesians are a light-skinned people. They are also the tallest of all the Pacific Island people.

To explorers, the Polynesians were among the friendliest of the peoples of the Pacific. Early explorers admired the Polynesians and their simple way of life. They usually

This is a meeting place for Maoris in New Zealand. The Maoris were the first people to live in New Zealand. They are a Polynesian people as are the Hawaiians. The Maoris have lighter skin than some of the other peoples of Oceania.

had plenty to eat. They found in the coconut palm and other island plants all they needed for clothing, food, and shelter. Missionaries found the Polynesians very open to the Gospel of Christ.

But the explorers were not always kind to the Polynesians. Many wars were fought, and thousands of Polynesians were killed. On most of the islands, though, the majority of the people are still Polynesians. Only in New Zealand and Hawaii are less than half the people Polynesians today. New Zealand has well over three million people. Of these only about 180 thousand are Polynesians. The Polynesians of New Zealand are called Maori (maùr′ ē).

Life Among the Islanders. Life among the people of Oceania was simple before the Europeans and Americans came. The islanders raised or caught most of the food they needed. Sometimes trees and plants that grew wild provided them with much of what they needed. The sea provided them with fish to eat.

Islanders used long, swift canoes to sail from island to island. They also used these to go fishing. The Pacific Islanders invented the **outrigger boat**. These are boats or canoes with a large framework of lightweight wood that extends out from the boat on both sides. At the end of each framework, a pole is attached. This pole lies on top of the water and floats along in the same direction as the boat. These outrigger poles help

The outrigger canoe was invented by the people of the Pacific Islands.

keep the boat from turning over in rough waters.

Sometimes the islanders go fishing without boats. In some places the water is quiet enough for fish to come in close to the shore of an island. On some islands, the people wait until nightfall to fish. They wade out into the shallow waters near the island. Some of the people carry torches. The fish see the lights and swim toward them. Then other people throw nets into the water and catch the fish. On some islands the people have built stone traps out into the water. They lay stones close together in rows. The rows of stone reach out into the shallow water. Islanders then chase **schools**, or groups, of fish between these rows of rocks. The fish cannot escape to the side. The people capture many of them with nets and drag the nets to the beach.

As you read in the last chapter, the coconut is one of the most useful plants on many of the Pacific Islands. On islands where the soil is good enough, the people also farm other crops. Bananas and pineapples are excellent fruits raised on many of the islands. Bananas were brought to the islands from Asia. The pineapple came from the Americas after the

breadfruit

taro

pineapple

coconut

yam

white man came.

Many of the islands also abound in breadfruit trees. These trees were first grown on the Pacific Islands. They are now found in many other warm places in the world. The breadfruit tree is a tall tree with large leaves. The large, round breadfruit hang from the tree. Sometimes they are harvested by knocking them from the trees. You would not want to be standing under a breadfruit tree when the fruit falls. One breadfruit may weigh as much as five pounds (over two kilograms). The outside, or hull, of the fruit is rough and bumpy-looking. The fruit looks something like the balls that grow on sycamore trees, but breadfruit is much, much larger.

Breadfruit pulp is either white or yellowish in color. It feels and tastes something like bread. Breadfruit can be baked, boiled, or fried. Some people eat it much like potatoes. It makes a good substitute for potatoes in hot lands where potatoes do not keep well.

Another important vegetable native to the Pacific Islands is taro (tär′ ō). Taro grows best in rich, wet, or swampy soil. Taro leaves look much like the leaves of elephant ear plants. Taro plants have several thick underground stems. These stems are cooked and eaten much like breadfruit or potatoes.

Another crop grown in the Pacific Islands is yams. Like taro, yams are a starchy root vegetable. They look much like sweet potatoes. Their vines climb high into bushes and trees.

When the Europeans and Americans came, life began to change for many islanders. Today, many people on the Pacific Islands are trying to live more like Americans. They follow American or European customs of dress and living. Instead of eating the healthful foods native to the islands, more and more people are eating canned food shipped in from other countries.

What Do You Say?

1. a. What is the largest island of Melanesia? b. Name the country that covers the eastern half of this island. c. How many languages are spoken in this country?

2. When Pacific Islanders searched for new islands, what two things showed them they were nearing another island?

3. What do the Polynesians look like?

4. What kind of people were the Polynesians when explorers first came to their islands?

5. Name and describe at least three kinds of food raised in Polynesia.

What Does the Bible Say?

1. You learned in this section that the Pacific Islanders had much knowledge and skill. What does Daniel 1:17 say about where knowledge and skill come from?

2. According to Colossians 1:9, what is the most important kind of knowledge?

Beliefs of the Pacific Islanders

Long ago the peoples of Oceania worshiped many gods. They told many stories or myths about their gods and the creation of the earth. A few of the islanders still believe in these gods. Some other islanders no longer believe in the gods, but they still believe in magic and **witchcraft**. Witchcraft is the belief that certain people have magic powers and can get power from evil spirits. Someone who is believed to have these powers is called a witch. Someone who claims to cure diseases with magic or through spirits is called a **witch doctor**.

Some of the people of the Pacific Islands used to practice **cannibalism** (kan′ ə bə liz′ əm). Cannibalism is the sinful custom of eating human flesh. People who eat other people are called cannibals. Some of the islanders practiced cannibalism as a religious ceremony. They believed they would take on some of the good habits and other good things about the people they ate. Only on the island of New Guinea do any tribes still practice cannibalism. The governments of the countries on New Guinea are trying to stop this practice.

Some of the first Europeans to come to the Pacific Islands were missionaries. The Polynesians, especially, were quick to accept Christian teachings. Others accepted some Christian teachings, but wanted to keep following some of their old religious customs as well.

When the missionaries first came, many of the islanders wore little or no clothing. Some of the missionaries taught the people about **modesty**. Modesty is the opposite of display. One way the Bible teaches modesty is that it teaches us to cover our bodies with clothes. Because of this teaching, some of the people began to wear more clothing. Even today, on some of the islands, the people still dress more modestly than many Europeans or Americans do. The women wear long, full skirts. The men wear shirts and trousers. Of course, their clothing is often light in weight and color so they will be more comfortable in the hot climate of the islands.

Many other Pacific peoples do not practice modesty in clothing. They follow the immodest fashions and styles brought by Europeans and Americans.

485

The Bible for the Islanders. The first missionaries to the Pacific Islands soon found that they needed to prepare Bibles in the languages of the people. Among the Polynesians, for example, the languages were somewhat alike. Yet many languages had never been written down. The Melanesians and the Micronesians also had many languages. Languages were often different from one island to the next. On the larger islands, many different languages were spoken.

Earlier in this chapter, you learned that Papua New Guinea has about 700 languages. Papua New Guinea covers only about half of the island of New Guinea. Still other languages are spoken in the other part of New Guinea. Bible translators are still working to translate the Bible into many of these languages. Their goal is to translate the Bible into every language found in New Guinea. With so many languages, this is a huge task.

Here are some verses from the Bible in different languages. The first column is English. The middle column is one of the languages of New Guinea. The last column has the same verses in one of the Polynesian languages. Notice that translators have used the same alphabet that is used for English. This makes it easier for those who use our alphabet to learn other languages.

English	Toaripi	Samoan
The beginning of the gospel of Jesus Christ, the Son of God; As it is written in the prophets, Behold, I send my messenger before thy face, which shall prepare thy way before thee. (Mark 1:1, 2)	Iesusi Kerisito Valareve Atuteve ovorove omopa o meha. Peroveta Isaiave buka vo ukaiape mea o mofeare, Ofae eavaia Ara arave meu ave omopa vo itapai roi, Are ave otiharola pisosi roi.	Ole amataga o le tala lelei ia Jesu Keriso o le Alo o le Atua. E pei ona tusia i le au perofeta, Faauta, ou te auina atu la'u savali e muamua atu i ou luma, na te teuteua lou ala i ou luma.

Toaripi is a language spoken by about 15,000 people along the coast of Papua New Guinea. Samoan is a Polynesian language still spoken by about half the people of American Samoa and Western Samoa. Compare the words for Jesus Christ in these two languages. Notice how much shorter the Polynesian words are than those in the other language.

486

What Do You Say?

1. a. What did the Pacific Islanders worship? b. Name two sinful practices of many of these people.

2. What is the goal of the Bible translators on the island of New Guinea?

What Does the Bible Say?

1. Many people do not realize how many languages are spoken on the Pacific Islands, especially in New Guinea. Read Psalm 19:1-3. What is one way God speaks to the people of all languages?

2. God speaks to people in many ways. But it is very important for people to hear God's Word in their own language. Read Acts 2:8, 11. What did these people hear? Remember that this was a special miracle with languages. Today people of the world hear the Word of God in their own language if someone translates the Bible into their language.

Using Globes and Maps

1. In an encyclopedia, find a map of the Pacific Islands divided into the three parts: Melanesia, Micronesia, and Polynesia. Name at least five islands found in each group.

2. Many people believe that the Australian Aborigines came to Australia from southern Asia. On a map which shows both Australia and the southern tip of Asia, find the islands between. Name the islands you think would have been most likely the ones the Aborigines came to on their way to Australia.

New Words and Terms

Tell briefly where each place is or what each word or term means.

a. legend   b. Aborigines

c. dingos
d. boomerang
e. nonreturning
   boomerang
f. Melanesia
g. New Guinea
h. Papua New
   Guinea
i. Pidgin

j. Polynesians
k. outrigger
l. breadfruit
m. taro
n. yam
o. witchcraft
p. cannibalism
q. modesty
r. Samoan

Thinking Together

1. a. Who were the first people to live in Australia? b. How many may have lived there when the first white people came?

2. How many groups and languages of Aborigines were there?

3. a. How did the early Aborigines find their food? b. How did they prepare shelter from the rain and cold?

4. a. What special weapon and tool did the early Aborigines use? b. Which type was the more useful for hunting animals?

5. Name some things which show that the Australian Aborigines were very intelligent people.

6. What did the Aborigines believe about the creation?

7. a. What is Pidgin? b. How is it useful in Papua New Guinea?

8. How were the Micronesians and other Pacific Islanders wise in the ways of the sea?

9. What was the attitude of the early Polynesians toward missionaries?

10. What two islands in Polynesia no longer have a majority of Polynesian people living on them?

11. What important invention in the Pacific Islands helped the people get from one place to another?

12. How has life changed for the Pacific Islanders since Europeans and Americans came?

13. Name two evil practices of the early peoples of Oceania.

14. Why is it that more and more peoples of the Pacific are learning to read and write their languages?

For You to Do

1. Purchase or make a returning boomerang. Practice throwing it outdoors. Give a demonstration to your class of how it returns to the thrower.

2. Collect samples of foods from the Pacific Islands. You may have difficulty finding breadfruit in a grocery store. If you cannot find yams, sweet potatoes are very similar. Another fruit not mentioned in the text that the islanders raise is plantain. This looks like a green banana and can sometimes be found in larger grocery stores.

3. Make a miniature model of an outrigger from bamboo or popsicle sticks. Try to find pictures in encyclopedias and other books to use in planning your model.

29. The Frozen Continent, Antarctica

The Unknown Southern Continent

The story of the discovery of Antarctica is a story of excitement and danger. Some people lost their lives trying to learn about the lands around the South Pole.

Most of the early explorers of the southern seas were not trying to find a southern continent. Many were sailing farther south to find fish, seals, and whales. Storms blew some ships off their course and into the far southern ocean. Men from an American seal-hunting ship were the first people to set foot on the continent of Antarctica. This was in 1821. They did not know whether they had landed on an island or on a continent.

In 1841 a British explorer, James Ross, found a great **ice shelf** along the coast of Antarctica. An ice shelf is a great sheet of ice that reaches from the land out into the sea. He knew he had seen part of a continent. This part of Antarctica he

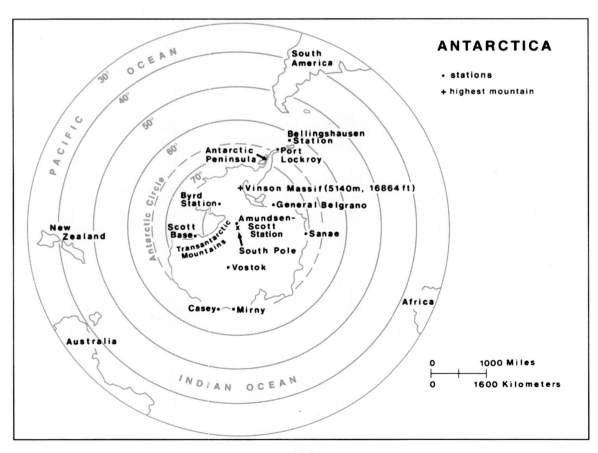

This iceberg is floating along the icy coast of Antarctica. Huge icebergs break off from the mainland and float in the cold Antarctic Ocean. Do you see the penguins on top of the iceberg?

named Victoria Land in honor of Queen Victoria of England.

The great ice shelf is named the Ross Ice Shelf. It is thick ice that never melts. It covers an area of water almost as large as the province of Alberta in Canada. At this place, explorers had to cross hundreds of miles (or kilometers) of ice to reach the continent of Antarctica.

After Ross explored along the coast in 1841, few people even tried to reach Antarctica again until the 1890s. The maps of those days showed only ocean around the South Pole. No one had sailed around the coast of the great continent to map it. The map on page 493 is a picture of a map printed in 1892. What does it tell about Antarctica?

Around 1908 people tried to reach the South Pole. Some tried and failed. Difficulties met them on every hand. To begin with, it is difficult for ships to reach the coast of Antarctica much of the year. Huge sheets of ice

Did you realize that Antarctica is nearly twice as big as Australia? On a map of the United States and Canada it covers much of the two countries. Why do so few people stay on this continent?

may form on the ocean as far as two hundred miles (320 kilometers) from the coast. Only in the southern summer is it easier to reach the coast. Even then ships may meet huge chunks of ice floating on the sea. The seas around Antarctica are the stormiest seas on earth. If ships do not have ice to battle, they may toss in stormy seas. The winds may blow at 100 miles (160 kilometers) per hour. Some people call the stormy sea around Antarctica the Antarctic Ocean. Most geographers, however, do not use this name. They consider the ocean around Antarctica to be part of the Atlantic, Pacific, and Indian Oceans.

Here is the story of two explorers who raced to reach the South Pole in 1911 and 1912. You will learn something of the dangers they faced.

The Race to the South Pole

In 1908 an explorer and his men had tried to reach the South Pole. They fought blizzards and illness. They came within 97 miles (157 kilometers) of the South Pole. The group could go no farther. They had to turn around.

Many people then became excited about reaching the South Pole. An Englishman named Robert Scott determined that he would be the first to reach the pole. He sailed to New Zealand where supplies were loaded onto his ship. While he was in New Zealand, he received word that an explorer from Norway was racing him to be the first to reach the South Pole.

The Norwegian explorer was Roald Amundsen (äm′ ən sən). He reached the coast of Antarctica and set out for the pole on October 19, 1911. Twelve days later, Scott and his four men set out for the pole.

Amundsen had practice exploring in the icy Arctic regions north of Norway. He went well prepared. He too set out with four companions. He and his men took 52 Eskimo dogs and enough food and other supplies to last for four months.

Scott used ponies to pull his sleds across the ice and snow. The hard work and the cold were too much for the ponies. They had to be shot. The explorers then pulled the sleds themselves. You can imagine that they quickly grew tired of this.

Amundsen's men and dogs quickly crossed the vast Ross Ice Shelf. Sometimes they traveled 30 miles (48 kilometers) a day. After crossing the ice shelf, they found themselves at the foot of a high mountain range. This range lay between them and the more level land near the pole.

Amundsen left a supply of food at the foot of the Transantarctic Mountains. He and his men spent two weeks making the difficult climb to cross the mountains. Once across the mountains, they shot all but 18 of the strongest dogs to provide food for the men and the rest of the dogs. On December 14, 1911, Amundsen and his men reached the South Pole

This is an old map of the South Pole region. It comes from a book that was printed in 1892. The map shows places where explorers had landed or visited along the coast of Antarctica. But no one then knew for sure that there was a continent around the South Pole or how it was shaped. The dotted line on the map encloses the area that was unexplored and unknown a hundred years ago.

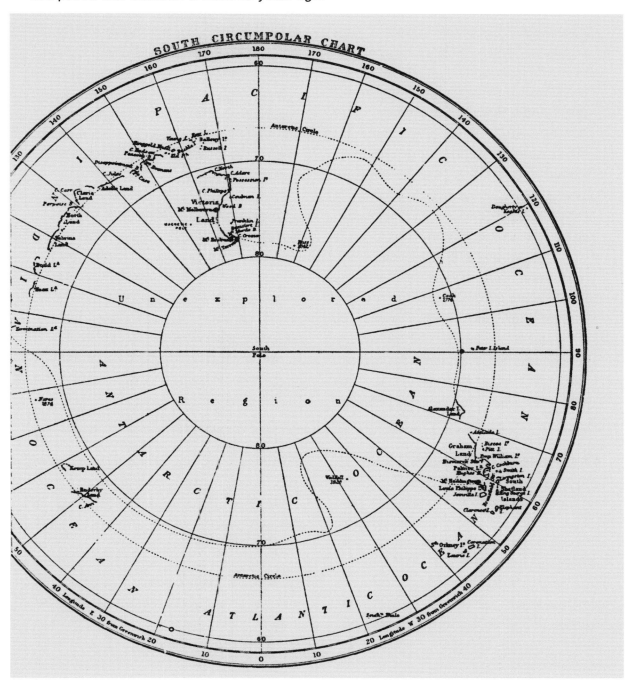

at last. They had arrived before Scott. They left behind a Norwegian flag, a tent, and a note for Scott. They had reached the South Pole in about seven weeks. The return trip took 38 days. Amundsen's party returned to the coast with twelve dogs and plenty of food.

Scott's party did not get along so well. They did not arrive at the pole until January 18, 1912, over a month after Amundsen. They found the things left by Amundsen. The bitterly disappointed men had spent 69 days to reach the pole. We know something of their disappointment because Scott kept a **log** of what they did each day. A log is a record or list of what someone does.

The weather on the return trip was very stormy. One of the party died after they returned to the Transantarctic Mountains. Another felt he could not go on. He walked away in a blizzard, never to return. The three remaining men struggled on. They began to lose hope of ever reaching one of the camps where they had food stored. Finally, they had to stop and wait for a nine-day blizzard to end. They never left their tent. Searchers found the tent and the three frozen men the next November.

The searchers found the tent only eleven miles from a place where Scott had left some supplies. They also found Scott's log that told the sad story. Scott's last words were these:

We shall stick it out to the end but we are getting weaker of course and the end cannot be far. It seems a pity, but I do not think I can write more — For God's sake look after our people.
R. Scott

It was 45 years before anyone else again tried to reach the South Pole by land. The airplane came into use during this time. A number of people flew over Antarctica and even landed at the South Pole.

Today the United States has a scientific station at the South Pole. It is named the Amundsen-Scott Station. Why is this a good name for the station?

What Antarctica Is Like. The short story about the men who first reached the South Pole tells you just a little about what Antarctica is like. The continent has earned many nicknames. It has been called *the white continent*. It is almost completely covered with ice and snow. Some people call Antarctica *the frozen continent*. This too is a good name. At no place in Antarctica does the temperature ever rise much above freezing. Even when the temperature rises above freezing in the summer, it does not do so long enough to melt much of the ice and snow.

Antarctica has also been called *the world's deep-freezer*. This name is certainly a good one as well. The coldest temperatures in the world are found in Antarctica. Deep inside the continent, the winter tem-

As Robert Scott and his men neared the South Pole, they found a black flag tied to a pole. By this they knew that the Norwegian explorers had already reached the South Pole. How disappointed Scott and his men were.

perature often drops to 100 degrees below zero (73° below zero Celsius). Along the coast the temperatures drop to less than 40 degrees below zero. The coldest temperature on earth was recorded in Antarctica at a Russian station. This temperature was 129 degrees below zero (89° below zero Celsius).

A tremendous amount of ice and snow always covers Antarctica. In some places the ice is two to three miles (three to five kilometers) thick. This ice is frozen fresh water. It has little salt in it like seawater. Scientists believe there is more fresh water in Antarctica than in all the rest of the world put together. It is frozen, however. Scientists believe

that if the great ice cap over Antarctica would melt, the level of the world's oceans would rise 100 feet (30 meters). This would flood dozens of great cities around the world. *Deep-freezer* is a good name for Antarctica.

Do you remember that Australia is the lowest continent? Antarctica is *the highest continent*. Some of its mountains reach over 20,000 feet (6,000 meters) above sea level. Even where there are no mountains, the ice cap is very thick. Much of Antarctica is over a mile above sea level. The area around the pole is buried under almost 9,000 feet of ice (2,700 meters)!

Antarctica could also be called *the lonely continent*. Turn a globe so that you are looking down on Antarctica. How many other lands can you see? The other southern continent, Australia, is over a thousand miles away (over 1,600 kilometers). Africa is still farther away. The nearest continent is South America. Antarctica has a long peninsula that reaches toward South America. But there are still six hundred miles of cold, stormy waters separating the two continents. It is very hard to reach the continent, even in the summer. In the long, dark winters, scientists who stay in Antarctica have contact with the outside world only by radio.

What Is the South Pole? Did you ever wonder what the South Pole (or the North Pole) is? Certainly no giant pole sticks up out of the snow to

495

tell an explorer that he has arrived, just as no line marks the equator. How did the explorers know they had found the South Pole?

The South Pole is the southern point of the earth farthest away from the equator. Explorers and scientists use compasses and other instruments to tell them when they have reached this point. Since explorers have found both poles, they have planted flags and other objects in the ice to show the spots. But these objects themselves are not the poles.

What Do You Say?

1. a. What were many of the early explorers near Antarctica looking for? b. Who were the first people to set foot on Antarctica? c. When?

2. a. Who was the first explorer to reach the South Pole? b. What happened to the other party trying to reach the Pole at the same time?

3. List four names that describe the continent of Antarctica and tell how each is a good description of the continent.

4. Exactly what is the South Pole?

What Does the Bible Say?

1. The ice and snow of the white continent may not be very useful to most people. But the snow can remind people of spiritual things. a. Read Job 9:30. What can snow be used for? b. Now read Isaiah 1:18. What should snow remind us of?

Antarctica—A Valuable Continent?

The Resources of the Frozen Continent. Many people think Antarctica is a continent with little value. It is covered with ice and snow. People cannot live there unless they have special shelters. They must bring their food with them or have it sent by ship or airplane. No trees or other large plants can grow on the icy continent. No large land animals live there.

The only plants that live in Antarctica are some mosses that grow during the short summers. The largest land animal is a little fly that could sit on the tip of your little finger.

Water is always a valuable

496

natural resource on any continent. Antarctica, of course, has more fresh water than all the other continents put together. People have dreamed of using the fresh water in the icebergs that break off the continent. Some have wondered if icebergs could be towed by ships to warmer lands where there is little fresh water. Such an effort presents many problems. One of them is finding ships strong enough to tow huge icebergs. Another problem is that such an iceberg would melt before a ship could tow it to dry places near the equator.

Most of the fresh water bound up in the great icepacks of Antarctica is not very useful for the rest of the world. To be sure, Antarctic explorers and scientists can melt some of it for drinking water, but most of it remains unused.

The snow and ice in Antarctica may be valuable in another way. So much ice and snow helps keep Antarctica cold. Scientists believe the weather in the Antarctic helps to control the weather in other parts of the world. Cold winds from the icy Antarctic help cool the southern parts of Australia, Africa, and South America. Without the cold of the Arctic and the Antarctic, the world would be a much hotter place.

We do not know all the value of the ice and cold in Antarctica. The Bible says it this way: "Hast thou entered into the treasures of the snow?" *Job 38:22a*

Scientists have found some mineral resources in Antarctica. Among them are coal, copper, and nickel. Scientists believe that petroleum may also be found in and near Antarctica. These are valuable resources, but they are hard to get to in Antarctica. The cost would be too great for people to try to take them to the faraway parts of the world that need them. Many valuable resources may lie buried under thousands of feet of ice in Antarctica, but we have no way of getting to them.

Antarctica does have some resources that have been used. Some of the sea animals that live around the frozen continent are very useful. Whales and seals are the most valuable. These animals store much fat, called blubber, under their skins. The blubber is cooked to obtain a valuable oil. Whale oil was once used for fuel. Today, it has many other uses. In some countries it is used in margarine, soap, and varnish. The oil of some kinds of whales may be used for lubricants. A **lubricant** (lü′ bri kənt) is an oily substance used to help machines and moving parts to run more smoothly. In some places the meat of the whale is used for food.

Penguins live along the coast of Antarctica. Notice the stubby wings that are quite useless for flying. God planned that penguins would be excellent swimmers, however. What do these birds find to eat in cold, barren Antarctica?

Antarctica's Most Interesting Animal

Do you remember how tiny the largest land animal in Antarctica is? You might not see the tiny insect unless you look hard for it. When most people think of Antarctica, they think of the bird called the penguin. The penguin is just one of the many birds that live on the ice around the edges of Antarctica.

Penguins are strange-looking birds. They are covered with white, short, thick feathers on the belly. They have black feathers on their backs. When penguins stand on ice or land, they stand upright with the white feathers showing. Instead of wings, penguins have feather-covered arms called flippers which they use for swimming. They are excellent swimmers.

Thick feathers and thick layers of fat help keep the penguins warm on the icy continent. There are many kinds of penguins. The smallest is only about one foot (30 centimeters) high. The largest may be four feet (120 centimeters) high and weigh around 100 pounds (45 kilograms).

Penguins spend much of their time in water. They eat fish. There are no plants to eat. Penguins lay their eggs and raise their young on land or ice. They make their nests in huge groups called **rookeries** (rük′ ə rēz). A rookery may contain as many as a million penguins!

One of the largest penguins is also one of the most interesting. This is the emperor penguin. Just before winter comes, the mother penguins

498

leave the water and lay their eggs on the ice. The emperor penguin lays just one egg per season. The father penguin does the job of hatching the egg. He rolls the egg onto his large feet and covers it with the lower part of his body.

The father penguin carries the egg around on his feet. He waddles into a large group of other father penguins carrying eggs on their feet. All these penguins huddle together to keep each other warm. Their eggs will take two months to hatch during the dark, cold winter. The father penguins do not eat during these two months.

When the chick hatches, its first food is a milk-like liquid that comes from the throat of the father penguin. Soon the mother penguins return to take care of the chicks. Then the males go back to the sea to get food for themselves and for the chicks.

The penguin parents gather their chicks together in large groups. The parents form a circle around their chicks to protect them and to keep them warm.

Penguins would be very interesting animals to watch at a zoo. But they do not make very good zoo animals. They easily catch diseases and die.

Penguins are not as useful as whales and seals. However scientists have studied them to learn more about living in cold climates. Scientists have attached instruments to penguins for a short time to try to find out how penguin body heat is controlled. Later they release the penguins to return to their rookeries.

More Birds of Antarctica. Antarctica has many other kinds of birds besides the penguin. All of them eat fish and other sea animals. They all live along the edges of the continent and especially on the long Antarctic Peninsula that reaches toward South America.

Another one of these birds is also very unusual, but not in the same way as the penguin. This bird is the arctic tern. It migrates over a longer distance than any other bird on earth. It is often called the migration champion of the world. **Migration** (mī grā′ shən) is the movement of animals from one place to another. Birds fly in order to migrate from one place to another.

Arctic terns raise their young along the northern seacoasts of North America and Greenland and on the northernmost islands of the Arctic Ocean. Near the end of August they and their young begin their flight south. Many stop off in South America, but others go all the way to Antarctica and nearby islands. They arrive about three months later and spend a few months near Antarctica. This is during the Antarctic summer when the sun shines almost all day. About March the terns start their flight back to northern North America. In June they arrive in the far north. The tern travels about 22,000 miles (35,000 kilometers) to fly to Antarctica and return.

This desire of the tern to migrate so far we call **instinct** (in′ stingt). Instinct is like a built-in computer or clock that tells terns and other birds how to behave. We say that instinct tells them when it is time to fly to far-off places. We know that God gave these birds their instinct. We do not always know why. Perhaps the tern needs a lot of daylight. It spends a large part of the year in places where the sun shines for most of the day.

What Do You Say?

1. a. How much fresh water is found in Antarctica? b. In what form is it found? c. What would happen if it all melted?

2. a. Name some valuable natural resources found in Antarctica. b. Why are they so difficult to reach?

3. a. What animal resources are found near the coast of Antarctica? b. What are they used for?

4. a. Why could penguins not live in the center of Antarctica, away from the ocean? b. How do emperor penguins hatch their eggs?

5. a. What is instinct? b. What does this instinct lead the arctic tern to do? c. Where does the tern get this instinct?

What Does the Bible Say?

1. Read Job 39:13-16, 26-30. a. What different birds are named? b. What are some of the interesting habits (or instincts) of these birds?

2. God has created many different and interesting animals all over the world. Many of them are very useful for people. Even the penguin has been used for food by some people. Read Genesis 1:28. How did God say people should relate to the birds and other animals?

Chapter Twenty-Nine Review

Using Globes and Maps

1. Using a globe or a map that cen-

500

ters on the South Pole, figure out how far it is across Antarctica. Use the scale of miles. Measure east to west and north to south. How much difference is there in your measurements?

2. Using a map or globe that has a scale of miles, measure the nearest distance from Antarctica to the southern tip of South America, Africa, and Australia. How far is Antarctica from where you live? How far is the South Pole from where you live?

New Words and Terms

Match each following term with its definition.

_____ 1. Antarctica
_____ 2. ice shelf
_____ 3. James Ross
_____ 4. Robert Scott
_____ 5. Roald Amundsen
_____ 6. South Pole
_____ 7. Transantarctic
_____ 8. log
_____ 9. lubricant
_____10. penguin
_____11. rookeries
_____12. migration
_____13. instinct
_____14. arctic tern

a. a record of what one does

b. nesting places for penguins

c. first man to the South Pole

d. second man to the South Pole

e. moving from place to place

f. a mountain range in Antarctica

g. discovered an ice shelf

h. the southernmost continent

i. thick ice reaching far out into the ocean

j. the southernmost spot on earth

k. makes parts run smoothly

l. something like a built-in computer or clock in birds and animals

m. a bird that may fly 22,000 miles (35,000 kilometers) per year

n. a fishing bird of Antarctica

Thinking Together

1. What did explorers discover as they sailed farther south than Australia?

2. a. What is an ice shelf? b. How large is the Ross Ice Shelf?

3. How did most maps show the area around the South Pole before the discovery of Antarctica?

4. a. Name some of the difficulties faced by the early explorers of

Antarctica. b. Why do you think exploration is not as difficult today?

5. a. What two men raced to be the first to reach the South Pole? b. Who was the first to reach the pole? c. In what ways was he better prepared for the trip?

6. a. What are at least three names that have been used to describe the continent of Antarctica? b. Why is Antarctica also known as the highest continent?

7. a. What is the South Pole? b. How did explorers know when they had reached it?

8. a. Name at least three natural resources found in Antarctica. b. Why are these resources not used more?

9. a. Where do nearly all the animals of Antarctica live? b. What kind of animals are they?

10. Where do penguins raise their young?

11. a. What is unusual about the arctic tern? b. How far does it fly in a year?

words on a sea animal or bird of Antarctica. Use at least two sources of information—one of them can be your textbook.

2. In an encyclopedia, find at least three facts about Antarctica that are not listed in your text.

3. You have now studied all seven continents. Which one would you most like to live on (other than the one you now live on)? Which one would you least like to live on? Why?

4. Find or make a map of the world naming the continents. On this map place a star at each place where you know of missionaries serving. You may need help from your parents, teacher, or minister to learn of those places. Why are Christian missionaries needed on every continent, including our own?

For You to Do

1. Write a report of at least 100

Glossary

In this glossary you will find many social studies words used in this book. These words appear in bold type in the book, like this—**bold**.

You can use the glossary as a dictionary to look up words you do not know. Only the meanings used in this book are given in the glossary. You may find other meanings for these words in a dictionary. After the meaning of each glossary word, the page number or numbers are given for the place where the word appears in the book.

The pronunciation key below shows you how to say the sounds of the words. Any consonant sound not in the following list is pronounced just as you say it.

Suppose you don't know how to say the word, "adobe." Find it in the glossary. You will see the pronunciation (ə dō′ bē). When you look in the pronunciation key, you learn that you are to say the ə like the a in alert. Look in the pronunciation key for ō. You say that like the o in flow. The ē is to be pronounced like the e in easy. You are to accent, or speak the strongest, the dō′ because of the accent mark.

Pronunciation Key

a	cat	ȯ	order
ā	bake	ȯi	oil
ä	father	u̇	put
â	care	ü	rule
au̇	out	ər	bird, herd, fur
e	pet	hw	which
ē	easy	ng	sing
ə	alert	th	thin
i	trip	th	these
ī	life	yü	use
o	cot	yu̇	furious
ō	flow	zh	measure

aborigines (ab′ ə rij′ ə nēz)—The first people to live in a place. *Page 476.*

active volcanoes—Volcanoes that still spew out lava or erupt. *Page 31.*

adobe (ə dō′ bē)—Sun-dried brick made from clay or soil. *Page 106.*

American Indians—The first people who lived in the Americas before Europeans came. *Page 89.*

ancestors (an′ ses′ tərz)—The people who lived before us. *Page 134.*

ancient times (ān′ chənt)—The

days of long ago, over 1,500 years ago. *Page 180.*

aqueducts (a′ kwə dəkts)—Ditches or channels that carry water. *Pages 305, 460.*

aquifer (ak′ wə fər)—An underground layer of rock or sand containing water. *Page 304.*

Arabic (ar′ ə bik)—The language of Arabia which has spread to many other places. *Page 318.*

archaeologists (är′ kē ol′ ə jəsts)—People who study things made and used by people long ago. *Page 91.*

artesian well (är tē′ zhən)—A well that water flows from, without need of a pump. *Pages 304, 456.*

atheist (ā′ thē ist)—A person who denies that there is a God. *Page 233.*

atmosphere (at′ mə sfir′)—The ocean of air that surrounds the earth. *Page 56.*

atoll (at′ ol)—Circular island, especially in the Pacific Ocean. *Page 468.*

axis (ak′ səs)—An imaginary rod around which a planet or other sphere turns. *Pages 13, 67.*

basin—A large area with all its streams draining into one river or lake. *Page 120.*

Bedouin (bed′ ə wən)—Arab wanderers or nomads. *Page 341.*

black earth belt—The richest farmland in Russia. *Page 208.*

black gold—A nickname for petroleum or oil. *Page 310.*

boomerangs (bü′ mə rangz′)—Curved sticks used for throwing, invented by the Australian Aborigines. *Page 478.*

bore—An Australian word for a well. *Page 456.*

boundaries (baun′ də rēz)—The borders or edges of countries. *Page 191.*

brigades (brig ādz′)—Groups of workers or soldiers. *Page 276.*

Buddhism (bü′ diz əm)—An Asian religion started by a man called Buddha. *Page 284.*

bulge of Africa—The western part of Africa farthest out in the Atlantic Ocean. *Page 350.*

"cake of the poor"—A nickname for dates. *Page 306.*

canal—A large ditch to carry water. *Page 110.*

cannibalism (kan′ ə bə liz′ əm)—The custom of eating human flesh. *Page 485.*

canopies—Leafy covers formed by trees in a rain forest. *Page 401.*

canyons—Steep-sided river valleys. *Page 88.*

caravans (kâr′ ə vanz′)—Groups of people traveling together using animals or vehicles. *Page 360.*

cash crop—A crop that is raised to sell for money to buy other things. *Page 327.*

cataracts (kat′ ə rakts′)—Low waterfalls scattered along a river. *Page 351.*

census (sen′ səs)—A counting of people in a country or part of a country. *Pages 261, 340.*

China's Sorrow—A name sometimes given to the Yellow River or Hwang He in China. *Page 257.*

chotts (shots)—Salty places in desert depressions. *Page 354.*

civilized (siv′ ə līzd′)—Having progressed in science, art, and inventions. *Page 265.*

climate (klī′ mət)—The weather over a long period of time. *Page 64.*

coal—A black- or brown-colored fuel that is hard like a rock. *Page 29.*

coastline—The place where land meets the ocean. *Page 26.*

coir (koir)—The fiber around the nut in a coconut. *Page 471.*

cold pole—The coldest region of Siberia in Russia. *Page 210.*

collective farm—A farm where families usually live separately and work together on the nearby land. *Page 225.*

colony—A land settled and ruled by a distant country. *Page 443.*

communes (kom′ yünz)—Farms where people live together and work in large groups. *Page 276.*

communists (käm′ yə nəsts)—People who believe that people should share their wealth equally with each other. *Page 219.*

condenses—Water drops form from the air around us. *Page 59.*

Confucianism (kən fyü′ shə niz′ əm)—An Asian religion started by a man named Confucius. *Page 284.*

conservation (kon′ sər vā′ shən)—Being careful and saving with natural resources. *Page 458.*

contour plowing (kon′ tür)—Plowing across rather than up and down hilly land. *Page 40.*

copra (kō′ prə)—Dried coconut meat. *Page 471.*

couscous (kūs′ küs)—A dish of steamed wheat eaten with meat, vegetables, and a sauce. *Page 366.*

Cradle of Civilization—A part of the Middle East where great nations of long ago began. *Page 294.*

crude oil—Petroleum as it comes from the ground. *Page 311.*

crust—The outer layer of the earth. *Page 25.*

Cyrillic alphabet (sə ril′ ik)—The alphabet used for most Slavic languages. *Page 198.*

czars (zärz)—A name for the rulers in Russia before the communists ruled. *Page 215.*

delta (del′ tə)—Land formed from sediment at the mouth of a river. *Page 39.*

depressions—Low places in the land. *Page 353.*

dialects (dī′ ə lekts′)—Different ways of speaking the same language. *Pages 247, 417.*

direction lines—Lines on a globe north and south or east and west. *Page 19.*

djellaba (jə lä′ bə)—A long, flowing garment worn by men in Egypt. *Page 329.*

dormant volcanoes (dȯr′ mənt)—Volcanoes that have not erupted for hundreds of years. *Page 31.*

droughts (drauts)—Times of dry weather. *Page 369.*

dunes—Mounds of windblown sand. *Page 305.*

Eastern Europe—The part of Europe including Poland, Romania, and Russia. *Page 190.*

Eastern Hemisphere—The half of the

earth including Europe, Asia, Africa, and Australia. *Page 85.*

emperor—A powerful ruler of a large country. *Page 268.*

equator (i quāt′ ər)—The line on a map halfway between the North Pole and the South Pole. *Pages 19, 118, 397.*

ergs—Great heaps or seas of sand. *Page 353.*

erosion (i rō′ zhən)—Soil being worn away or taken away by wind or water. *Page 37.*

ethnic group—A group of people who share the same language, beliefs, and customs. *Page 413.*

Eurasia (yù rā′ zhə)—Europe and Asia together. *Page 135.*

evaporates (i vap′ ə rāts′)—Water becomes vapor in the air around us. *Pages 58, 256.*

exaggeration (ig zaj′ ə rā′ shən)—Telling something bigger or greater than what it is. *Page 423.*

exports—Things one country sells to another country. *Page 123.*

extended families—Large families that include more relatives than father, mother, and children. *Page 229.*

extinct (ik stingt′)—Dead or no longer active. *Page 31.*

fables (fā′ bəlz)—Stories in which animals talk and teach a lesson. *Page 423.*

Far East—Lands in eastern Asia far to the east of Europe. *Page 250.*

faults—Cracks in the earth's crust. *Pages 33, 174.*

fellah (fel′ ə)—A farm worker in Egypt. *Page 326.*

fertilizer (fərt′ əl ī′ zər)—Anything added to soil to keep it rich. Page 36.

fetish (fet′ ish)—An object that is worshiped as the home of a spirit. *Page 427.*

fjords (fyórdz)—Little narrow arms of the sea reaching inland. *Page 147.*

fleet—A group of ships traveling together. *Page 152.*

flood plain—Part of a river valley that is sometimes flooded by the river. *Page 39.*

galvanized (gal′ və nīzd′)—Metal coated with zinc. *Page 360.*

geographers (jē og′ rə fərz)—People who study the earth and maps of the earth. *Page 135.*

geographical races (jē′ ə graf′ i kəl)—Races or groups of people from certain parts of the world. *Page 245.*

geography (jē og′ rə fē)—The study of the earth, its people, and its treasures. *Page 17.*

geologists (jē äl′ ə jəsts)—People who study the land and rocks. *Page 304.*

Germanic languages (jər′ man′ ik)—Languages that come from German. *Page 194.*

globe—A map that has been pasted or printed on a sphere. *Page 15.*

Golden Horde—A group of Mongols who once conquered Russia and Eastern Europe. *Page 214.*

gravity (grav′ ət ē)—A pull or force that holds us on the earth. *Page 10.*

groundwater—Water found many feet

under the earth. *Page 60.*

guano (gwän′ ō)—Manure of sea birds used for fertilizer. *Page 469.*

Gulf Stream—An ocean current that flows from the Gulf of Mexico past the east coast of the United States. *Page 51.*

heathen—People who worship false gods. *Page 158.*

hemisphere (hem′ ə sfir′)—One half of the earth. *Page 67.*

highlands—Hilly and mountainous places. *Page 26.*

holy—Clean, pure, or set apart for God. *Page 322.*

humidity (hyü mid′ ə: ē)—Water or moisture in the air. *Page 377.*

humus (hyü′ məs)—Soil formed from decayed plants and animals. *Page 35.*

hydroelectricity (hī′ drō i lek′ tris′ ət ē)—Electricity made by water power. *Pages 151, 407.*

hydroponics (hī′ drə pän′ iks)—Growing plants with no soil. *Page 338.*

ice shelf—A great sheet of ice reaching out into the sea. *Page 490.*

idolatry (ī dol′ ə trē)—The worship of false gods and their statues. *Page 321.*

idols—Statues of false gods. *Page 321.*

imports—Things one country buys from another. *Page 153.*

independent—Free from the rule of outsiders. *Page 443.*

insecticides (in sek′ tə sīdz′)—Poisonous sprays to kill insects. *Page 440.*

instinct (in′ stingt)—Something God has given animals to tell them how to behave. *Page 500.*

intensive farming—Raising as much as possible on a small amount of land. *Page 169.*

interior (in tir′ ē ər)—The part of a continent or country near the middle of the land. *Page 389.*

invention—Something new that people make from the natural resources God gives. *Page 269.*

Islam (is′ läm)—The Arab religion started by Mohammed. *Page 318.*

island continent—A continent, such as Australia, completely surrounded by water. *Page 21.*

isthmus (is′ məs)—A strip of land that joins two larger masses of land. *Page 21.*

joey (jō′ ē)—A young kangaroo. *Page 464.*

jungle—A very thick growth of trees, bushes, and vines. *Page 401.*

k'ang (jyang)—A raised bench or platform used for sitting or sleeping in China. *Page 278.*

lagoon (lə gün′)—An area of shallow water inside a circle of islands. *Page 468.*

landform—The shape of the land. *Page 87.*

language (lang′ gwij)—A way of speaking or writing that is different from other ways of speaking or writing. *Page 246.*

language families—Groups of languages that are somewhat alike. *Page 417.*

lava (läv′ ə)—Melted rock that pours out of the earth. *Page 31.*

legends (lej′ əndz) — Stories that come from long ago. Parts of legends may be true. *Page 422.*

linguists (ling′ gwəsts)—Scientists who study languages. *Page 417.*

living resources—Plants and animals God has given us to use. *Page 27.*

locks—Gates that allow boats to move from one water level to another. *Page 355.*

locust—A kind of grasshopper that ruins crops in many parts of the world. *Page 371.*

log—A record or list written down. *Page 494.*

lowlands—Low places near rivers, lakes, and oceans. *Page 26.*

lubricant (lü′ bri kənt)—An oily substance used to make moving parts run smoothly. *Page 497.*

machete (mə shet′ ē)—A knife with a long, heavy blade used for chopping weeds, corn, and bushes. *Page 107.*

maize (māz)—The grain also called corn or Indian corn. *Page 93.*

manganese (mang′ gə nēz)—A metal used in making steel from iron ore. *Page 206.*

manufacturing—Making things by machine. *Page 98.*

marchland of Europe—A nickname for the countries of Eastern Europe. *Page 197.*

marsupials (mär sü′ pē əlz)—Animals that carry their young in pouches. *Page 464.*

martyr (märt′ ər)—A person who dies for his beliefs. *Page 384.*

materialistic (mə tir′ ē ə lis′ tik)—Caring too much for money and the things it can buy. *Page 99.*

Melanesia (mel′ ə nē′ zhə)—The islands just north of Australia. *Page 466.*

mestizos (mes tē′ zōz)—People who are a mixture of two different peoples. *Page 106.*

Micronesia (mī′ krə nē′ zhə)— Small islands in the Pacific Ocean north of Melanesia. *Page 466.*

microscopic (mī′ krə skop′ ik)— Something so small we can only see it with a microscope. *Page 48.*

Middle East—The part of western Asia near Africa and Europe. *Page 292.*

migration (mī grā′ shən)—Movement of animals from one place to another. *Page 499.*

mineral (min′ ə rəl)—A useful substance found in rocks and soil. *Page 360.*

mineral resources—Stone and other nonliving things found on the earth. *Page 27.*

mob—A large group of kangaroos. *Page 464.*

modern times (mod′ ərn)—The present time or our own days. *Page 180.*

modesty—The opposite of display; keeping our bodies covered in public. *Pages 328, 485.*

Mongoloid (mong′ gə lóid′)—The Asian geographical race to which the Chinese belong. *Page 261.*

Mongols (män′ gōlz)—Tribes of long ago from deep inside Asia. *Page 214.*

monsoons (mon sünz′)—Winds that blow from one direction for a long time. *Page 244.*

mountain system—A large group of mountains spreading for hundreds of miles. *Page 241.*

mouth—The place a river empties into a lake or ocean. *Page 391.*

murky—Clouded and dirty. *Page 370.*

Muslims—Followers of Islam, the main religion of Arabia. *Page 322.*

native—Something or someone who first lived in a certain place. *Page 405.*

natural gas—A colorless, odorless gas found in the earth and used for fuel. *Page 29.*

natural resources (nach′ ə rəl)—Things on the earth that God has given us to use. *Page 27.*

New World—A name Europeans gave the Americas and the islands around them. *Page 85.*

nomads (nō′ madz)—People who wander from place to place. *Page 217.*

North Atlantic Drift—The warm waters of the Gulf Stream as it nears Europe. *Page 137.*

Northern Hemisphere—The half of the earth north of the equator. *Page 67.*

numeral—A sign or a picture that stands for a number. *Page 329.*

oasis (ō ā′ səs)—A place in a desert where there is enough water for plants and trees to grow. *Pages 96, 304.*

ocean currents—Streams of water that move or flow through the ocean. *Pages 51, 137.*

Oceania (ō′ shē an′ ē ə)—The islands of the South Pacific Ocean. *Page 466.*

official language—A language used by the government and businesses of a country. *Page 418.*

orbit—The path a planet or moon follows around the sun or a planet. *Page 11.*

outrigger boat—A boat with a light framework of wood extending out into the water. *Page 482.*

panicles (pan′ i kəlz)—The heads or tops of rice plants. *Page 280.*

parchment (parch′ mənt)—A kind of paper made from animal skins. *Page 269.*

pass—A low place between mountains or mountain peaks. *Page 125.*

pasta (päs′ tə)—A dough made of wheat flour and used to make such foods as macaroni and spaghetti. *Page 178.*

peasants (pez′ ənts)—A word used for poor farmers in Europe. *Page 216.*

permafrost (pər′ mə frȯst)— Ground that stays frozen all year. *Page 77.*

persecution (pər si kyü′ shən)— Anything harmful that is done to someone because of his belief. *Page 384.*

pesticides (pes′ tə sīdz′)—Poisons to kill insects. *Page 360.*

petroleum (pə trō′ lē əm)—A liquid fuel found in the earth. Petroleum is often called oil. *Page 29.*

phosphorus (fos′ fə rəs)—A valuable plant food found in phosphate rock. *Page 359.*

Pidgin (pij′ ən)—A mixture of English and other languages used in New Guinea. *Page 480.*

pirogues (pi rōgz′)—Long, narrow canoes. *Page 436.*

plains—Large areas of fairly flat land. *Pages 26, 86.*

plateau (pla tō′)—Highland (usually flat or hilly) between mountains. *Pages 101, 296.*

polar regions—Places near the North Pole or South Pole where the sun does not rise for at least a few days each year. *Page 66.*

pollution—Smoke and dirt in the air. *Page 151.*

Polynesia (pol′ i nē′ zhə)—Islands north and east of New Zealand. *Page 467.*

population (pop′ yə lā′ shən)—The number of people in a city or country. *Page 249.*

private farm—A farm owned by one farmer or family. *Page 276.*

prosperous—Having plenty of money and the things money can buy. *Page 98.*

proverb—A short, wise saying. *Page 425.*

race—A group of people who look somewhat alike in their skin color, hair color, size, and shape. *Page 245.*

rain forest—A place where much rainfall causes great forests to grow. *Pages 72, 122, 401.*

Romance languages—Languages that come from Latin. *Page 195.*

rookeries (rük′ ə rēz)—Large groups of nesting penguins. *Page 498.*

ruins—Very old buildings that have partly fallen down. *Page 179.*

safari (sə fär′ ē)—A trip to hunt or photograph wild animals. *Page 348.*

Sahel (sä hel′)—The region just south of the Sahara. *Page 367.*

savannas (sə van′ əz)—Grasslands in Africa. *Page 402.*

schools—Groups of fish. *Page 483.*

sea level—Place on land that is as low as the ocean. *Page 26.*

seasonal belts—Places between the Arctic Circle and the tropics. *Page 67.*

sediment (sed′ ə mənt)—Material a river drops as it slows down. *Page 39.*

serfs—Poor farmers or farm workers. *Page 215.*

shatter zone—Eastern European nations such as Hungary and Romania that have had many wars. *Page 197.*

ships of the desert—A nickname for camels. *Page 309.*

sirocco (sə räk′ ō)—A hot, dusty wind that blows frum the deserts of northern Africa. *Page 166.*

skerries (sker′ ēz)—Rocky islands off the coast of Norway. *Page 144.*

Slavic languages (släv′ ik)—A group of languages first spoken in eastern Europe. *Page 195.*

Slavs (slävz)—A people who come from Eastern Europe. *Page 195.*

slums—The poor parts of cities. *Page 109.*

snow line—The line, on the side of a high mountain, above which there is always snow. *Page 124.*

socialist (sōsh′ ə ləst)—One who believes that the government should own land and businesses. *Page 203.*

sod planting—Crops planted in dead grass or sod. *Page 40.*

soil—Ground, earth, or dirt. *Page 34.*

soil conservation (kon′ sər vā′ shən)—Different ways of trying to save the earth's soil. *Page 41.*

solar system—The sun and its planets. *Page 10.*

sombreros (som brär′ ōz)—Tall hats with wide brims worn in Mexico. *Page 107.*

source—The place where a river begins. *Page 355.*

soviet (sōv′ ē et′)—A Russian word meaning "a committee" or "a council." *Page 203.*

sphere (sfir)—Anything shaped like a ball. *Page 12.*

state farms—Farms where families live together in apartment buildings. They are paid wages for their work. *Page 225.*

strait—A narrow strip of water. *Page 21.*

strip farming—Planting crops in strips to help stop erosion. *Page 40.*

Sudan (sü dan′)—A country in Africa. The word means "black." *Page 368.*

tannin (tan′ ən)—A substance from the bark of a tree used to make medicine. *Page 463.*

Taoism (dau′ iz əm)—A Chinese religion of many gods. *Page 284.*

Tell—The hilly region along the sea in Algeria. *Page 376.*

terrace farming (ter′ əs)—Farming on hillsides by digging out flat places that look like steps for crops

to grow. *Page 170.*

thatch—A roof made of grasses. *Page 106.*

tide—The daily rising and falling of the ocean. *Page 49.*

tierra caliente (tē är′ ə kä yen′ tä)—Name for hot lowland region of Spanish America. *Page 104.*

tierra fría (tē är′ ə frē ə)—The coolest climate region in Latin America. *Page 104.*

tierra templada (tē är′ ə tem plä′ də)—Mild regions of Latin America. *Page 104.*

tone—How high or low the voice is when a word is spoken. *Page 263.*

traditional (trə dish′ ə nəl)—Something done or believed for many years. *Page 427.*

translate (trans lāt′)—To change from one language to another. *Page 198.*

translators—People who take something written in one language and write it in another. *Page 419.*

tropical rain forests—Large forests in the rainy regions near the equator. *Page 401.*

tropics (trop′ iks)—The places near the equator where the sun is directly overhead for at least part of the year. *Pages 66, 397.*

tundra (tən′ drə)—Land in cold regions where only grasses, flowers, and shrubs grow. *Page 77.*

turbans (tər′ bənz)—Cloths wrapped around the head. *Page 366.*

uninhabited (ən′ in hab′ ə təd)—Where people do not live. *Page 469.*

unity (yü′ nət ē)—Feeling alike in

many ways and working together. *Page 414.*

universe—The millions of stars and planets that God has created. *Page 10.*

vendors (ven′ dərz)—People who sell food or other items to buyers. *Page 436.*

volcano (vol kā′ nō)—A place (usually a mountain) where lava pours out. *Page 31.*

wadis (wäd′ ēz)—Places in the deserts of the Middle East where water can run. *Page 303.*

water cycle—The circle water makes from the ocean to the land and back again. *Page 61.*

waterfalls—Places where rivers drop from highlands to lowlands. *Page 351.*

weather—The conditions and the changes that take place in the atmosphere. *Page 57.*

Western Europe—Germany, Austria, Italy, and all European countries west of them. *Page 191.*

Western Hemisphere—The half of the world including North and South America. *Page 85.*

wind—Movement of the air or atmosphere. *Page 56.*

"winter of the tropics"—Nighttime, when it is coolest in lands near the equator. *Page 401.*

witchcraft—The belief that certain people have magic powers from evil spirits. *Page 485.*

witch doctor—Someone who claims to cure diseases through magic or spirits. *Page 485.*

Index

Use this index often to find what you want. It lists the people, places, things, and ideas in this book with their page numbers.

New South Wales, 453
New Testament, 324
New World, 85
New York, 71, 116, 120, 267
New Zealand, 70, 467, 469, 482, 492
nickel, 46, 469, 497
Niger, 365, 367, 395, 422
Niger River, 395
Nigeria, 395, 413, 417
Nile River, 72, 120, 296, 326, 355,
    356, 392, 394, 437
nitrate, 123
Noah, 247, 295
nomads, 155, 217, 341, 365
Norse, 158-160
North Africa, 381, 383
North America, 20, 52, 67, 85-112,
    116, 120, 125, 137, 208, 240, 248,
    250, 301, 307, 328, 352, 453, 463,
    499
North Atlantic Drift, 51, 137, 152,
    193
North Atlantic Ocean, 51
North Cape, 144
North Carolina, 137
North Dakota, 178
North European Plain, 140, 192
North Pacific Ocean, 52
North Pole, 19, 51, 67, 77, 86, 117,
    145, 241, 243, 397, 495
northern Africa, 323
Northern Hemisphere, 67, 68, 70,
    118, 145, 452
Northmen, 159
Norway, 51, 137, 139, 143-160, 166,
    191
Nova Scotia, 52
Nuevo Laredo, 101
number system, 329
numeral, 329
Numidia, 384

oases, 96, 304, 328, 340, 365
ocean, 18-22, 26, 44-53, 58
ocean current, 51, 137, 458
Oceania, 466-472, 482, 485
official language, 418, 440
Ohio, 89
oil wells, 303
Oklahoma, 166
Olaf I, 159
Old Testament, 322, 323
olives, 167
Oman, 334
Ontario, 52, 75, 98, 335, 375, 434
oranges, 461
orbit, 11
Oregon, 52, 211, 250
Oslo, 146
Ottoman Empire, 382
outrigger, 482
Pacific Islands, 482, 484, 485
Pacific Ocean, 18, 110, 127, 209,
    245, 250, 301, 450, 466-472
Pakistan, 250, 299
Palestine, 318
Pampa, 125
Panama, 110-112
Panama Canal, 110, 111
panicles, 280
Papua New Guinea, 480, 486
parchment, 269
Parícutin, 32
Paris, France, 193
pass, 125
pasta, 178
Patagonia, 125
peanuts, 65
pears, 461
peasants, 216
penguin, 498
Pennsylvania, 211
permafrost, 77

Scripture Index

This is a list of Bible passages used in this book. References given in italics are for Scriptures used in questions. References in regular type are for Scriptures quoted directly in the text.

Acknowledgements:

Artist—Daniel Zook
Cartographer—Deborah Sturm
Cover Designer—Elmore Byler
Designers—Miriam Shank, Sue Anderson, David Miller
Photo Researcher—Kevin Shank
Reviewers—John Coblentz, Fred Miller, Paul Reed, Ernest Witmer

Cover Photo Credits:

John M. Coffman—Grants Gazelles
Masai Village Elder. Huts made from cow dung and mud.
Visual's Unlimited/©Francis E. Caldwell—Indian Woman Spinning Llama Wool, Peru
Visual's Unlimited/©James Richardson—Victoria Falls

Photo Credits:

Adams, William, 392

American Bible Society, 130 (bottom), 270 (top and bottom)

American Museum of Natural History, courtesy of, 92 (bottom)

Andrew Baker Photography, 476 (bottom)

Bacon, Mike, © 1991, 69 (bottom)

Bacon, Nathan P., 27

Baxter, David A., 31

Baxter, Melva J., 331

Beach, Ellen, 261

Beachy, Ward, 40 (top), 124 (top)

Berry, Anna Lee, 182 (bottom)

Berry, Roger, 339

Carlton, Richard L., 297 (top), 326, 395, 403, 427, 434 (top and bottom)

Castelli, Agi, 140, 166, 170 (bottom)

CLP staff photo, 36 (bottom)

Crumm, Cheryl B., 298

Dalton, Anthony R., 364, 368 (top and bottom), 369, 370, 453, 476 (top), 480

Denham, Gail, 103 (top), 104 (bottom)

Dinodia Picture Agency, 241, 243,(bottom left and right), 286

Dittman, Joan, 282 (top and bottom), 283

Eastman, Don, 106 (top), 222, 229 (bottom),

Eberly, Willard, 167, 168, 172

Eric Sanford Photography, 139, 152

Fletcher, Thomas R., 69 (top)

Franklin Photo Service, 305, 329, 337, 338, 340

Galloway, Ewing, 32, 120, 151

Gammill, Bill, 398

Geographical Slides, Robert E. Cramer, 320, 365, 366 (left and right), 378, 438, 439, 468 (top),

Geological Survey of Canada, 76

Good, Kristin, 231

Gould, Suzanne, © 1991,

Hartzler, Lloyd, 94, 96 (bottom), 176, 183

Harvard University Art Museums, (Courtesy of), Arthur M. Sackler, Fogg Art Museum, 182 (top)

Hawaii Visitor's Bureau Photo, 26 (bottom)

iStockphoto.com, Robert Hackett, 435; Jim Pruitt, 99; David Raboin, 88 (bottom right)

Johnson, Bernice Q., 296 (top and bottom), 299 (bottom), 306 (top),316 (bottom), 317, 327, 353, 399, 428, 477

Keith, Bjorgne M., 226 (right), 229 (top)

Kidwell, W. L., © 1991, 209, 220, 230

Kirk, Darrell, © 1991, 256 (bottom left), 257, 284

Knudsen, Ellen S., 17, 72 (top and bottom)

Lambert, Harold M., 122 (top)

Maine Department of Commerce and Industry, 124 (bottom)

Martin, Judy, 266 (top)

Martin, Verna M., 106 (bottom)

May Reed Photography, 256 (top)

Miller, Paul S., 29, 36 (top), 38 (bottom), 96 (top), 103 (bottom), 104 (top), 105, 107 (top and bottom)

Mitchell, Rosemary, 249 (bottom), 278

Museum of the American Indians, courtesy of, 92 (top)

NASA 15

Ney, Bryan, 206 (top and bottom)

NOAA, EDS, 33 (bottom); 47

Organization of American States, 101

Panama Canal Commission, 110, 111 (top and bottom)

Paulman, Howard, 49

Phillips, Karen, 468 (bottom), 482

Photo Agora, David Kreider, 245 (left); Robert Maust, 244 (right), 299 (top), 318, 322, 357 (top), 393, 400 (bottom), 429, 433, 443, 444, 445; Blair Seitz, 244 (left)

Photos.com, 12, 16, 40 (bottom), 57, 59 (top and bottom), 69 (bottom), 77 (left and right), 88 (bottom right), 95 (top), 97 (top and bottom), 99, 108, 122 (top and bottom), 128, 179, 243, 249 (top), 250, 266, 280, 281, 285, 297 (bottom), 306 (bottom), 308 (top and bottom right), 318, 328, 352 (right and left), 396, 455, 464 (top and bottom), 465, 469, 498

Phototek, 95 (bottom)

Photri, 153, 156, 171, 177

Purcell, Carl, 304, 342

Reed, Ardella, 193, 356, 357 (bottom), 436

Remmen, Sharon, 316 (top), 412, 470 (bottom)

Rodale Press, Inc., 33 East Minor St., Emmaus, PA 18049, 36 (bottom)

Rydell, Claire, 245 (right)

Saint, Nate, 129, 130 (top)

Schultz, Lorraine 0., 295, 319, 351, 400 (top), 419, 422

Shank, Kevin D., 233, 234

Shaw, Kay, 454

Shelton, John S., 88 (top left and bottom left), 147 (top and bottom), 170 (top)

Tom Stack & Associates, Gary Milburn, 149; Tom Stack, 145, 148; Dave Watts, 491,

Trissel, Iva, 181

Tysseland, Elsie C., 157

Unicorn Stock Photos, Louie Bunde, 308 (bottom left); Kimberly Burnham, 226 (left); Greg Clark, 470 (top);

Dick Keen, 44; Ken Stevens, 197; Tom McCarthy, 46; Margo Moss, 355

USDA, 39 (top); Bill Cherry, 25 (bottom)

USDA Soil Conservation Service, 25 (top); Tim McCabe, 33 (top); 37; 38 (top); 39 (bottom); 97 (middle)

U. S. Department of the Interior, Bureau of Reclamation, 26 (top), 41,

Watson, Pat, 256 (bottom right), 277, 324, 325

West, Jim, 98 (top and bottom)

Wolas, Pierre, 52

Wray, Daniel E., 126